CENTRAL AMERICA
Anatomy of Conflict

Pergamon Titles of Related Interest

Bundy/Foreign Affairs AMERICA AND THE WORLD 1982
Bundy/Foreign Affairs AMERICA AND THE WORLD 1983
Delich SOCIAL CONDITIONS OF DEMOCRACY IN LATIN AMERICA
Foxley ECONOMIC STABILIZATION IN LATIN AMERICA
Harkavy GREAT POWER COMPETITION FOR OVERSEAS BASES
Jorge FOREIGN DEBT AND
LATIN AMERICAN ECONOMIC DEVELOPMENT
Kronenberg PLANNING U.S. SECURITY
Long THE POLITICAL ECONOMY OF EEC RELATIONS
WITH AFRICAN, CARIBBEAN AND PACIFIC STATES
Lozoya LATIN AMERICA AND
THE NEW INTERNATIONAL ECONOMIC ORDER
Mallmann CATASTROPHE OR NEW SOCIETY
Nogee SOVIET FOREIGN POLICY SINCE WORLD WAR II
Solis ECONOMIC POLICY REFORM IN MEXICO
Spanier CONGRESS, THE PRESIDENCY
AND AMERICAN FOREIGN POLICY
Wiseman PEACEKEEPING

Related Journal*

WORLD DEVELOPMENT

*Free specimen copies available upon request.

CENTRAL AMERICA
Anatomy of Conflict

Edited by
Robert S. Leiken

Published in cooperation with
Carnegie Endowment for International Peace

Pergamon Press
New York • Oxford • Toronto • Sydney • Paris • Frankfurt

Pergamon Press Offices:

U.S.A. Pergamon Press Inc., Maxwell House, Fairview Park, Elmsford, New York 10523, U.S.A.

U.K. Pergamon Press Ltd., Headington Hill Hall, Oxford OX3 0BW, England

CANADA Pergamon Press Canada Ltd., Suite 104, 150 Consumers Road, Willowdale, Ontario M2J 1P9, Canada

AUSTRALIA Pergamon Press (Aust.) Pty. Ltd., P.O. Box 544, Potts Point, NSW 2011, Australia

FRANCE Pergamon Press SARL, 24 rue des Ecoles, 75240 Paris, Cedex 05, France

FEDERAL REPUBLIC OF GERMANY Pergamon Press GmbH, Hammerweg 6, D-6242 Kronberg-Taunus, Federal Republic of Germany

Library of Congress Cataloging in Publication Data

Main entry under title:

Central America.

    "Published in cooperation with the Carnegie Endowment for International Peace."
    Includes index.
    1. Central America – Politics and government – 1979–
Addresses, essays, lectures.   2. Central America – Foreign
relations – United States – Addresses, essays, lectures.
3. United States – Foreign relations – Central America –
Addresses, essays, lectures.   I. Leiken, Robert S.,
1939–   . II. Carnegie Endowment for International
Peace.
F1439.5.C45 1984   327.730728   83-27440
ISBN 0-08-030950-X

NOTICE
In order to make this volume available as rapidly as
possible, the chapter notes have been reproduced in
the style as submitted by the authors. This method
will hopefully not distract the readers.

Printed in the United States of America

CONTENTS

ECONOMIC AND MILITARY REALITIES

THE POLICY PROCESS

PREFACE

This collection is a product of the collective dismay of Central American specialists. It is not a collective work. Each essay is an independent effort, and together they represent a cross section of American political opinion from conservative to radical. What the authors share, besides Central American expertise, is a recognition that if the region is small, it is not simple. Yet discussion of Central America in Washington regularly substitutes clichés and analogies for investigation and analysis. Policy has been predicated on unexamined premises and debate polarized in stereotyped positions. As if to correspond to its Central American subject matter, the national forum has come to resemble the "darkling plain" of Matthew Arnold "where ignorant armies clash by night."

When Central America entered crisis in the late 1970s, it became an object of intense attention in Washington. Thereupon like Southern Africa, the Soviet Union, China, and the Middle East, the region began to experience the swings of an increasingly partisanized U.S. foreign policy.

The Carter administration, unable to find a political solution to the Nicaraguan crisis, had to acquiesce to the Sandinistas' coming to power. When the Sandinistas embraced Havana and Moscow, the question "who lost Nicaragua" became a fresh embarrassment for President Carter and a boon for the Reagan election campaign.

Yet for the Reagan administration Central America has been even more burdensome. Repeated presidential initiatives have failed to win public backing for administration policy. The issue continues to provide ammunition for congressional critics and to be a source of discord between the administration and Western Europe and Latin America. It has generated severe tensions within the administration itself resulting in, but not resolved by, the removal of its chief Latin American policy maker, Thomas Enders, in May 1983.

At that time the threat of being charged with "losing Central America" diminished Democratic appetite for the issue. Yet as the president wooed Hispanic voters in key electoral states like Florida and Texas with the spectres of Fidel and "feet people," the Central American issue promised to be significant in the 1984 election campaign. The intractability of the Central American crisis, its sensitivity for certain sectors of the populace, and the controversial nature of administration policy lends the issue serious potential for polarizing the American public.

Dismay and alarm at this situation led the Carnegie Endowment for International Peace to assemble in the late spring and summer of 1983 a group of former government officials, diplomats, scholars and policy analysts familiar with Central America. Based on their recommendations and capitalizing on the timely offer of Pergamon Press of rapid production and dissemination, we decided in September 1983 to commission essays for a study to appear in time for the January 1984 renewal of the national debate on Central America. Our hope is to leave behind analogues and stereotypes and provide a fresh look at Central America and in its own concrete complexity so as to propose policy alternatives consistent with Central American realities and legitimate U.S. security interests.

The production of such a book in the space of three months obviously demanded intense and special efforts: essay topics had to be defined with precision; drafts submitted promptly; comments for each draft returned rapidly; manuscripts tracked accurately at each stage of the process; and fluid communication maintained among authors, editors, and publisher. Our challenge was to compress what is normally an 18-month process into 3 months.

Without word processors and electronic publishing, it would not have been possible to accomplish this. But technology proved double-edged. Manuscripts whizzed from final edit to typeset copy, but a massive word processor failure caused many manuscripts to vanish into electronic limbo. Nature also intervened. Messengers raced to and fro until they were grounded by two December ice storms. When water pipes burst in the frigid weather our publisher's New York facilities were disrupted and the entire book almost lost.

The real miracle of this book is the dedicated work performed by a dexterous and reliable staff of secretaries, word processor operators, fact checkers, style editors, and typesetters. In an atmosphere of pressing deadlines and barely controlled crises these people toiled from early morning into the night for weeks on end, straining family relations and sacrificing social life. Coordinating the entire operation for the Carnegie Endowment with skill, equanimity and grace under pressure has been Joseph Cirincione, our Assistant Editor. To him I owe, along with my enduring gratitude for his assistance, an embrace to a collaborator.

My secretary Lois Blackburn kept a steady organizational hand at the rudder whenever our small editorial bark foundered with excess velocity. Beth Carmichael, who came on board in midstream, proved to be a veritable life saver of efficiency and dedication—laboring nights and weekends on the word processor and on assorted editorial tasks. In the initial stages Barbara

Disckind worked far beyond the call of duty typing contracts, authors' letters and other start-up communications. Carnegie intern David Weiner's deft and gentle hand was everywhere — researching, style editing and performing a variety of "human services." Another Carnegie intern Laurie Derby and and Carol Evans worked wonders in style editing the essays.

I wish to thank Faye Rubenstein for her photographic research; Brian Burke, Laurie Derby, Lawrence Thomas and Kevin Grimms for fact-checking manuscripts; Scott Martin for copy editing; Linda Robinson for emergency style editing and Renee Key and Carol Goldberg for emergency keyboarding.

Nina Serafino deserves a special measure of gratitude for her assistance on two of the essays as does Bruce Cameron. Cynthia Arnson, Michael Clark, Gino Lofredo, Abe Lowenthal, Tom Martin, Richard McCall, and Oscar Menjivar made valuable comments on manuscripts. Among the many authors who did extra duty, Theodore Moran must be singled out. From Pergamon whose extraordinary organization, ultramodern technology and marvelous personnel turned December copy into a January book, we at Carnegie would like to thank Denise Hohl, Karen King, Kathi McCarty and Frank Margiotta and especially Kevin Maxwell who managed with extraordinary care each and every detail of the publishing process. At Carnegie the backing of Thomas Hughes, the assistance of Rosemary Gwynn and the understanding, patience and support of Michael O'Hare were indispensable.

Priscilla Labovitz kept Joe Cirincione sane and Drs. Chang and Marinakis helped to alleviate my "backache in the backyard."

A final thanks to my mother, Sam and Nancy, Susan and Rocky, who bore with me and without me while I absented myself from felicity for evenings, weekends, and holidays.

Robert S. Leiken
January 1, 1984
Washington, D.C.

OVERVIEW

Overview
CAN THE CYCLE BE BROKEN?

Robert S. Leiken

In the public debate Central America first figured only by analogy. In its earliest statements the administration presented the area's crisis as an East-West struggle whose "source" was elsewhere than the region itself. Administration critics replied that the struggle was North-South, not East-West, with indigenous rather than geopolitical roots. The critics saw Central America as a repetition of Vietnam; for the administration the cautionary example was Angola.

But events in the region as well as American politics urged that the Central American crisis be understood on its own terms. It became evident that the Soviet-Cuban hand was not absent from the region, and, as Americans became acquainted with the handiwork of the death squads, they gathered that conditions for revolution already existed without Moscow. In addition, domestic political realities dictated that reasonable proponents of both positions acknowledge some elements of truth in the other. Neither the administration nor the congressional opposition could impose its will on the other. Demands for a bipartisan consensus arose from various quarters and for various motives (see essays in this volume by Barry Rubin and I.M. Destler).

But consensus around the wrong policy is useless, and even harmful. And sound policy begins with an accurate appreciation of Central American reality.

CENTRAL AMERICAN REALITIES

The first necessary and longest step toward understanding Central America is the one that leaves behind the United States and Western Europe. One travels to Central America through time as well as space. The region is not just poor, but "underdeveloped." A short step from the Central American

3

capitals, and one encounters the middle ages, with its wooden plows and draft animals and seasonal rhythms. Medievalism casts a long shadow on the Central American present.

Nonetheless in the past two decades, the region has known rapid economic growth, new political ideologies and the revolution in telecommunications. The Central American *campesino* lives at once in the middle ages and in the "global village." The contradiction between the old and the new is one of the central components of the Central American crisis.

While a Central American "Marshall Plan" is sorely needed, Central America does not provide the ready preconditions that Western Europe provided for the original Marshall Plan's aid and trade programs. Those were modern economies with a developed working class, an entrepreneurial spirit, which needed only to be reconstructed and to "recover." But recovery for Central America would signify a return not to prosperity and modernity, but to poverty and backwardness. While their prospects are "far from hopeless"—as Richard Feinberg and Robert Pastor stress—no Central American economic miracles are on the horizon. Moreover, as the Alliance for Progress experience has shown, outside aid can spur economic growth without necessarily translating either into development or stability. As Feinberg and Pastor indicate, Central America must rebuild after a crisis comparatively more devastating than World War II was for Western Europe. Moreover, unlike Europe, Central America must renegotiate its international economic position in order to achieve balanced and sustained growth and must contend with social classes whose privileges and power are threatened by economic growth. Central America must not only rebuild, it must build anew; it must restructure patterns of power if it is to emerge from the shadow of its medieval and colonial past. (Also see the essay by Walter LaFeber.)

The revival of the Central American common market is prerequisite to Central American economic recovery and development. Yet here another shadow of the colonial and feudal past intrudes. One such legacy peculiar to Central America is what historian Ralph Woodward has called "a nation divided."[1] In the sixteenth century the isthmus was organized as part of New Spain in the "Captaincy General of Guatemala." However political unity was beset by rivalries among the individual *conquistadores*. Each conquest justified a new government, giving rise to governmental rivalries, later institionalized by the Spanish colonial "intendancy" system. In this way the Spanish colonial system helped both to create and to reinforce local factional rivalries.

These centrifugal tendencies rapidly became linked to international imperialist rivalries. Already by the sixteenth century, the French, the Dutch, and later the English were competing for hegemony with the Spanish. In the nineteenth century, aided by the British and the Americans, Central America became independent from Spain. However, efforts to create a united Central

American nation foundered on internal factionalism and outside interference. Colonial divisions were crystallized into nations. These divisions were intensified by factional fighting. While the factions were often called "liberal" or "conservative," they resembled Western European political parties only in name. They were more reminiscent of the retinues of a feudal warrior or *caudillo*.

Factional or inter-party rivalries transcended frontiers. Central American states customarily harbored exiles from rival states and habitually meddled in the internal affairs of their neighbors. These phenomena were the negative expression of Central American unity as a "nation divided."

Outside powers, now mainly England and the United States, took advantage of these factional disputes. Frequently one of the feuding factions would invite a major colonial power's assistance. Warlordism, or *caudillismo*, under the banner of "conservative" or "liberal" political parties, thus became a perpetual obstacle to both national unity and Central American federation as well as an open invitation to foreign intervention.

As Richard Millett notes, the establishment of Central American armies was a step forward in the struggle for national unity and against outside intervention. But the armies themselves became new arenas for factional and personal struggles. Armed power was displaced from the "political parties" to the national army, establishing the army as the arbiter of national politics. To this day the *coup*, and not the elections, remains the traditional means for transferring power in Central America.

Central American armies cast a shadow from the past over Central American political life. The tradition of cross-border rivalries linked to international sponsors also persists. The difference is that now the superpower rivalry has superceded that between England and the United States.

In the twentieth century, the United States has enjoyed nearly unchallenged hegemony in the region and has monopolized foreign intervention. The road to hegemony and intervention was nearly always smoothed by illusions of establishing "democracy," "free elections" and a "non-partisan army." But the residue for Central America usually has been dictatorship.

President Reagan has frequently reminded us that Central America is no further from Texas than is Washington. Indeed Central America is often treated as if it were an outlying voting district pining away for "free elections." On behalf of "free elections" in the 1920s the United States created a "non-partisan," "professional" army in Nicaragua (the National Guard) and led it into battle against Sandino's guerrillas — providing not only equipment and training, but also Marines as officers as well as roads, medical care, and the inevitable electoral apparati. After discontent at home and casualties in Managua forced the Marines to abandon their "democratic project," General Somoza, our hand-picked head of the National Guard, shoved aside (via the traditional Central American military coup) elected government, democracy, and all other Western paraphernalia, and established his forty-year dictatorship. Nonetheless, in Franklin D. Roosevelt's famous phrase, he was *"our* son of a bitch."[2] Future generations of Nicaraguans would draw the conclusion that American electoral parochialism and innocence abroad was simply a cover for American hegemonism.

If American innocence and Washington-made democracy has its disingenuous and imperial side, the Central Americans had the studied habit of "obeying" (in form) but not "complying" (in substance). "Se obedece pero no se cumple" was the Spanish motto for this deep-seated cultural resistance to outside dictates. Just as they had formally "freed" the slaves in accordance with Spanish and clerical dictates while converting them into peons, Central American rulers learned to hold "elections" and to observe the forms of democracy while the military retained its stranglehold. Christopher Dickey shows how the multiple and systematic cover-ups for the assassination of U.S. religious workers and labor advisors is but one example of the quagmire in which American reformist illusions sink in Central America.

THE CENTRAL AMERICAN CRISIS

Central America entered the modern era against a social, economic and historical backdrop similar to many Third World countries. But unlike most of the rest of the Third World, Central America has remained under the tutelage of a major power, and unlike many other Latin American countries, Central America's politics generally have not emerged from medieval shadows. After 150 years of formal independence, the Central American economies remain largely export economies, mainly dependent on two or three export crops. Although what was exported was hardly vital to its metropolitan importers — the coffee, sugar, and fruit to top off a rich meal — the export economy formed the social and political structure of the exporting countries. However, Central America has seen appreciable economic growth in the past two decades. Many countries, such as El Salvador and Guatemala, have achieved a higher level of modernization than many of their Third World counterparts. However, under the social and political conditions prevailing in Central America, economic growth has not been a force for stability as it was in Western Europe in the late 1940s, but for the opposite. Although the medieval landscape of Central America acquired some of the appurtenances of the twentieth century and the old landlords and a small new rural bourgeoisie prospered, the producers themselves suffered a dramatic deterioration in their living standards.

As landless peasants poured into the suburban shantytowns, trebling urban populations since the 1960s, the Central American countryside began to invade cities, such as San Salvador, where the wealthy sought sanctuary in armored cars and behind guarded, electrified walls. When regional economic growth slowed to a standstill in the late 1970s, a major crisis was unfolding.

The previous status quo in Central America rested on a relatively immobile socioeconomic structure, authoritarian governments monopolizing armed power, the allegiance of the Catholic church, an economic dependence on the United States, and, in the last instance, U.S. intervention. All of these pillars have cracked in the last several years; some have crumbled altogether.

From 1950 to 1980 the countries of Central America passed through profound changes. There was now a middle class, an urban working class, rural landless laborers, and masses of impoverished peasants. Moreover, the shock of earthquake and massive relief efforts caused a profound impact on social awareness at the local level. Church and other socially-concerned sectors were mobilized in relief efforts.[3]

The centuries-old Central American alliance between sword and church has ruptured. The new activism in the Central American church reflects the emergence of a national middle class rooted in the industrial and service sectors and, cosmopolitanized by international financial institutions, university education, and exposure to Western media. The church has been deeply permeated by new social forces and ideas, but Central American armies have resisted similar modernizing currents of military reform movements.

Officers and oligarchs also resisted pressure for agrarian reform which built in Nicaragua, Guatemala, El Salvador, and Honduras during the 1960s. Agrarian reform was one of the demands common to the economic and political reform movements that emerged nearly simultaneously in each of these countries in the early 1970s. The reform movements suffered similar fates. In 1972 the Salvadoran electoral coalition led by Napoleón Duarte and Guillermo Ungo was deprived of victory by fraud and military *coup*. The populist reform movement led by young military officers that came to power in Honduras in the same year had been dispersed by 1975. In Guatemala the reform coalition led by General Efrain Ríos Montt was robbed of victory by an electoral fraud in 1974.

Thus economic, social and ideological transformations were not followed by adjustments in the political apparatus, or by the kind of democratic revolutions that took place in the West during the late eighteenth and nineteenth centuries after similar socioeconomic changes. Instead, democratic political channels were blocked. Agrarian reform was stymied or paralyzed. Labor unions encompass only a small minority of the working population, and "labor is relatively unable to defend its interests in an organized way in most of Central America."[4] Instead in El Salvador, Guatemala and Nicaragua, left-led popular organization and guerrilla movements, often with powerful Soviet and Cuban influence, have incorporated and directed popular discontent. For 20 years, the Sandinistas had been calling for an armed struggle against Somoza. The Central American crisis helped make their tactics viable. The Sandinista victory in Nicaragua was bound to have a ripple effect throughout the region, with its interwoven histories and shared conditions.

SOVIET PRESENCE

The crisis of the American-backed Central American status quo offered Moscow an unexpected opportunity to bedevil its superpower rival — but one to be managed discreetly. As Morris Rothenberg points out, Moscow had consigned Central America to the U.S. sphere of influence by "geographic fatalism." When this region, like other "backyards" of the world, was belatedly swept into the vortex of national revolution beginning with the 1979 Sandinista insurrection, Soviet interest quickened. Revolutions in the U.S. "backyard" will inevitably target U.S. hegemony and find favor with its enemies. Yet, precisely because it is in the American zone of influence, Moscow's capacity to project power is clearly limited. These opportunities and limitations form the parameters within which Soviet policy must operate.

In those Central American countries where the United States has been the backer and the perceived beneficiary of the *ancien régime*, anti-Americanism has all too naturally translated to pro-Sovietism. Nowhere has this been more true than in Nicaragua, where the United States created and backed Somoza's National Guard for four decades. This factor helps explain the pro-Soviet bias of many Sandinista *comandantes*. The Nicaraguan government sought from the outset a special relationship with the Soviet bloc. Soviet generals paid a secret visit to Managua a month after the Sandinistas took power.[5] Subsequently a major Soviet and Cuban military security and intelligence role emerged during the Carter administration.

Just as Moscow did not create the Central American crisis, President Reagan did not create the Soviet problem in Central America. The latter is the residue of history, not of the policies of any particular administration. But Reagan administration policies certainly fufilled the prophecies and vindicated the proclivities of the more dogmatic Sandinistas. (See the essay by Arturo Cruz Sequeira.)

Moscow's chief strategic asset in Central America is the United States' long backing of reactionary oligarchies and the legacy of anti-Yankeeism. Moscow's second greatest asset is Cuba. Castro's alignment with the Soviet Union in the late 1960s, largely due to erroneous American policies, has yielded rich military, political and ideological dividends for its superpower patron. Moscow's influence in Latin America can now appear in the form of the Cuban David struggling against the American Goliath.

This alliance does not signify that there are no interesting differences in approach between Moscow and Havana. Some go on to argue that because

Cuban national interests differ from those of the Soviet Union the former is independent of the latter. However, Czeckoslovak and Mongolian interests also differ from those of Moscow. But those leaderships have pursued Moscow's goals. Especially since 1970, objective ties of economic, political and military dependence and a major Soviet security and intelligent presence on the island have severely limited Cuban automony. Nonetheless, Havana appears to retain a certain margin of independence and may be seeking to expand it.[6]

There is some evidence that the Cubans have been interested in promoting a social democratic tendency in the Caribbean, via former Jamaican Prime Minister Michael Manley and previously via Grenada's late Maurice Bishop. Havana may even be serious when it speaks of a "social democratic stage" in the Central American revolution. These political overtures may be efforts to gain space vis-à-vis Moscow, although such overtures are not necessarily antithetical to Moscow. But one can speak with far more certainty of independent, even anti-Soviet, trends in the Central American left. (See the essay, "The Salvadoran Left," by Robert S. Leiken.)

While the complexity of the Soviet relations with the region's left suggests that an array of policy instruments other than force are available to the United States, it does not mean that the Soviet problem can be whinked away with economic and trade concessions. The Soviet-Nicaraguan relationship illustrates the depth and difficulty of the problem. This relationship has evolved under a curious paradox. Soviet "penetration" of Nicaragua has been promoted more eagerly by the Sandinista leadership than by Moscow. Managua has eagerly embraced Soviet foreign policy positions from Afghanistan, Poland and Kampuchea to strategic and intermediate nuclear force negotiations.[7]

Sandinista Nicaragua quickly began to sport the Soviet bloc division of labor familiar in some African and Asian countries. The East Germans specialized in communications, security and intelligence, the Cubans in party and military affairs, the Bulgarians in economic planning, the Russians in security, and so forth.

Since the early 1970s, Soviet strategy has been to downgrade economic ties with the Third World, in favor of footholds in the political, military, intelligence, and security spheres. While evidence is typically partisan and partial, according to diplomats, former Sandinista leaders, defectors from the security apparatus, and many observers, a similar process is underway in Nicaragua.[8] In addition, there are pronounced pro-Soviet proclivities within the Sandinista leadership. (See the essay by Arturo Cruz Sequeira.)

Managua's efforts have gone largely unrequited. Moscow has not attempted to alleviate Nicaragua's grave balance of payments crisis, offering only long term development aid, arms, and re-exported American grain. While the Sandinistas first covertly then overtly sought Soviet MiGs to counterbalance Honduran air superiority, to this date Moscow has not delivered. Moscow has even avoided acknowledging Daniel Ortega's call for fighter air-crafts, and has carefully utilized intermediaries insofar as possible to deliver arms to Nicaragua. These have included not only Bulgaria, East Germany and Cuba, but non-bloc countries like Algeria and Libya.[9] The Soviets were "unusually restrained" when U.S. vessels exercising off Nicaragua queried Soviet ships en route to Nicaragua in the summer of 1982. Moscow clearly shied away from a confrontation with the U.S. in the Western hemisphere.[10]

The "global correlation of forces" which Soviet publicists found quite favorable during the 1970s, shifted against Moscow during the first year of the Sandinista government.[11] Resistance to the occupations of Afghanistan and Kampuchea; the challenge of Solidarity; the economic difficulties of Cuba and Vietnam; political friction with Third World allies such as Ethiopia and Angola; the movement of significant non-aligned countries like India, Iraq, and Algeria away from Moscow; the NATO resolve to deploy the Pershing and Cruise missiles and the American rejection of SALT II all darkened Moscow's international panorama. Domestically, the U.S.S.R. had been plagued by economic stagnation and poor harvests, a recurring succession crisis, problems of morale and materiel in the armed forces, and rising tensions among its national minorities. As a result, the Soviet worldwide offensive, with Cuba as its spearhead, came to a pause, if not a halt, in 1980-81.[12]

Another motive for Soviet caution may have been the Reagan administration's evident disposition to use force to shore up the American sphere of influence. In addition, Moscow's early enthusiasm apparently was dimmed by the repeated mistakes of the Central American revolutionaries: the failure of the "final offensive" in El Salvador, and the Sandinistas' economic, political and diplomatic errors.

The short-term Soviet danger — widely exaggerated by the Reagan administration — has receded. But the real Soviet danger in Central America is not short-term. According to Rothenberg there were 675 Costa Ricans studying in the U.S.S.R and Eastern Europe in 1981. Costa Rica has been the exception in Central America, enjoying years of sustained economic growth and pluralist political stability. It has a peaceful pro-Soviet communist party and only an embryonic armed revolutionary movement. Yet, Costa Rica is also edging toward social and economic crisis. American overreaction to the short term Soviet threat could sow seeds to be harvested in the next generation or the next decade. Long-range Soviet efforts in the region, the legacy of anti-Yankeeism, the current Soviet presence in Nicaragua, and the ongoing nature of the Central American crisis lead to the conclusion that the Soviet problem in Central America is long-term and historical. (See the essay by Morris Rothenberg.)

The widening cycle of U.S. military exercises, the multiplication of U.S. advisors in Honduras, the establishment there of U.S. training bases for Honduran, Salvadoran and Guatemalan troops, expanding U.S. military aid to El Salvador, the quickening activity in U.S. bases in Panama and the American-inspired revival of CONDECA (Central American Defense Council) have resurrected the familiar shadow of U.S. interventionism and the ingrained Latin reaction to it. (See the essay by Richard Millett.) To many Latins the precipitous Sandinista military build-up, if not their misplaced confidence in their "natural allies" in Moscow, now appears prudent. As Joseph Cirincione and Leslie Hunter clarify, the current Nicaraguan buildup is fundamentally defensive, and the Nicaraguan army poses no immediate threat to its neighbors.

Therein arises another curious contradiction. As the Soviet-Cuban threat recedes, and the threat to Nicaragua mounts, the clamor about the Soviet menace from Washington and from Central America grows louder, not softer. The Soviet-Cuban connection and Sandinista militarism and intransigence frighten its Central American neighbors — but for different reasons and in different degrees. The oligarchs fear the Sandinista revolution spells the end of their rule. The democrats are concerned that Sandinista authoritarianism jeopardizes prospects for democratic change by polarizing the region. Many in Honduras and Costa Rica (not to mention Panama and Venezuela) who made major sacrifices in the anti-Somoza resistance feel betrayed by subsequent developments in Managua. Even the guerrillas of neighboring countries, especially El Salvador, worry that the Sandinistas' persecution of their former allies jeopardizes their own necessary alliances with non-Marxists.

In Central America there is both a fear of Sandinista exported revolution as well as fear of revolution itself. Sandinista vaunts of "making war all over Central America," vows of "five or nothing" (meaning all of Central America revolutionary or none), their apparent support of terrorism in Costa Rica and Honduras, and their invectives against their neighbors have done nothing to clarify the distinction between exported revolution and genuine national revolutionary struggle. At the same time current U.S. administration policy seems intent on stoking the fears of both the Sandinistas and their neighbors.

TWO FALSE PATHS

In the view of Arturo Cruz Sequeira, the Sandinistas' attempted "direct transition to socialism" has been an economic and political failure. While the policies of the Reagan administration and the prejudices of the Nicaraguan private sector have surely aggravated Nicaragua's economic problems, defenders of the regime acknowledge that Sandinista economic policies have contributed to the country's balance of payments crisis, mounting unemployment, widening scarcity of consumer goods, and a price squeeze on the peasantry. It has been argued that the failure to preserve the revolutionary alliance with the middle class and small producers, as well as sectarian political and cultural policies, has polarized the country, led to disinvestment, falling productivity and wages, labor discontent, and an agrarian crisis.[13]

From the standpoints of the development of the "productive forces" and of "mass participation," the Nicaraguan revolution seems to contradict its own rhetoric. Nor has it provided the "pluralistic, democratic, non-aligned model" that the revolutionary leadership promised the Nicaraguan people and their international supporters. That leadership has earned a reputation for post-revolutionary conspicuous consumption and corruption.

But perhaps the most serious indictment of the Sandinista National Directorate is its polarization of the Nicaraguan people. As so often happens in Central America, this polarization has been encouraged and utilized by outside powers. There is now reason to fear that the poor judgement of the Sandinista leadership may return Nicaragua's "beautiful revolution" to the medieval factionalism and civil wars which characterized the pre-Somoza period. Still, some observers believe that the pragmatism demonstrated by the Sandinistas before the revolution may be reawakening under pressure. To what extent recent concessions are a result of pragmatic readjustment or another effort to seduce international opinion will be demonstrated by events.

The credibility gap in Sandinista rhetoric is surpassed by the distance between image and reality in "reformist," "democratic" Honduras. In 1980 and again in 1981 the Honduran people voted for civilian government, peace, and an end to corruption. They have been disappointed. Defense Minister General Gustavo Álvarez gradually has accumulated real power in the country. He has had himself elected leader of powerful civic organizations while "patriotic" Hondurans rush to name buildings and streets after him. He presides over the oligarchical group called APROH (the Association for Honduras). This group has gained control of the National University, teachers' colleges and associations, and has intimidated and bribed trade and peasant union officials. It has succeeded in dividing both traditional political parties. Democratic elements from all the political parties fear APROH will become the springboard for a *Somocista*-style Álvarez dynasty.

Álvarez has also created a special forces command for internal security, and a "National Security Council," dominated by the real decisionmaking power in Honduras — the military. On several occasions Álvarez himself has flouted the Honduran constitution as when he agreed, without congressional approval, to establish American training bases for Salvadoran troops in Honduras. Álvarez closely cooperates with the Nicaraguan *contras* and is widely believed to enlist them for kidnapping and torture inside Honduras. The defense minister's ascendency is associated with a widening American political and military role in the country, not unreminiscent of the U.S. presence in Nicaragua in the early 1920s. Again, behind a language of "democracy," etc., America could be creating a military dynasty.

Honduran leaders seem to have democracy on their lips, but war on their minds. If the democracy of Honduras is America's standard, U.S. avowed support for democratization will appear to Central Americans as one more example of U.S. hypocrisy masking U.S. hegemonism. In Honduras democracy seems to have become a geopolitical concept. Now "democracy made in Washington" is providing ideological cover for a regional military pact against Nicaragua.

Four years into the Sandinista revolution, it is increasingly evident that neither the Nicaraguan nor the Honduran model is capable of meeting the region's needs. These needs are five-fold. Central America must return to the path of development, on which it was proceeding in the years of the Central American Common Market. Second, this path cannot repeat the polarizing and impoverishing development of the 1960s and 1970s. There must be development with equity. Third, for economic growth to occur, Central America needs a democratic form of government which permits the dynamic and productive social forces to participate fully in political life. That means a place for the middle class in Nicaragua, for the workers and peasants in El Salvador or Guatemala. Central American democracy may not — probably cannot — resemble Western democracy. Yet democracy need not necessarily rest on a multi-party system, as long as all sectors of society are represented (although this has not been the case in Nicaragua). As in El Salvador, or in Somoza's Nicaragua, elections alone can make a mockery of democracy. In Central America, those who own land govern it. If what counts is substance, not mere form, then democracy must be coupled with land reform.

Fourth, if Central America is to attain development, equity, and democracy, it cannot be a neo-colony or an arena of a superpower confrontation. Fifth, Central America's most pressing need is peace. War between Honduras and El Salvador rang the death knell for the Central American Common Market in 1969. A war between Honduras and Nicaragua would postpone Central America's development agenda indefinitely.

Central America is at an impasse. The models of pseudo-democratic reform and dogmatic, sectarian revolution are not meeting the needs of the region. They have led not to development, independence, and peace, but to economic dislocation, superpower clientage, and militarization. Honduras and Nicaragua presented as alternatives, sometimes appear rather as mirror images: Honduras of reform with repression, inequality and dependence; Nicaragua of revolution with repression, scarcity and dependence. Is there a third option?

AN HISTORICAL COMPROMISE

A genuine alternative must involve an historical compromise among the region's dynamic social forces and the displacement from power of the oligarchy.

The Salvadoran landed and financial elite, the main obstacle to Salvadoran development, continues to block land reform and the reallocation of resources. It siphons off the wealth of the country and external aid into American and Swiss bank accounts. The Salvadoran feudal rule via the system of *patronato* and *colonato* must be terminated if Salvador is to achieve development, equity and democracy.

The productive middle class does have an essential role to play thoughout Central America. National capital in association with foreign investment and aid is an engine of growth and innovation. The technical and administrative expertise of the middle class is indispensable. But Central America cannot harbor the oligarchical capitalism of El Salvador which pays below-subsistence wages, harasses labor and peasant unions and is intolerant of political debate. If a broad spectrum of the left is not permitted to play a major role in countries like El Salvador, there will be no stability, necessary reforms will not be implemented, and economic growth will be unequal and politically destabilizing.

If the challenge for El Salvador is to have growth with distribution, Nicaragua's challenge is to have redistribution with growth. Nicaragua needs growth to consolidate its distributive gains. Both of these tasks can only be accomplished through public and private sector collaboration. These two sectors can only play their roles if they are working together and in some equilibrium. In the interest of both, mutual concessions are necessary. In the case of Nicaragua and El Salvador, negotiations are a necessary first step.

BREAKING THE CYCLE

The United States has three basic policy options in Central America. It can seek, primarily through force, to revive American hegemony in the region, to achieve what Viron Vaky has called "an isthmus restored." It can unilaterally withdraw from the region. Or it can seek to promote and support a regional settlement.

A policy which seeks to fortify American hegemony would incur disproportionate costs in the short term while aggravating the problem in the medium — and long — term. Theodore Moran has sought to calculate concretely the economic and human costs of a deepening U.S. military involvement in El Salvador. He has also provided some estimates of American casualties in a direct U.S intervention in Nicaragua. The figures are admonitory. Moreover, there is no calculation of how long the resistance would last, where it would spread, where else the United States would then have to intervene, and whether such intervention would lead to new rounds of anti-American upheavals in the future. Other essays — especially that of Viron Vaky — stress the collateral costs to U.S. domestic consensus, to U.S.-Latin America relations, with our European alliances, and around the world. Morris Rothenberg suggests the benefits accruing to Moscow from a fresh example of imperialism.

Walter LaFeber believes that each round of U.S. intervention has cost far more in treasure, in lives, in time, and internal consensus than the last. He affirms that such policies not only have failed to stabilize Central America, but the reaction against them has been on a wider and more global scale.

According to its proponents, an increased U.S. military involvement in the region would be accompanied by its counterpart — the "economic shield."[14] This too, as LaFeber suggests, is nothing new, and in the past the "economic shield" has inevitably served the "military shield" — with security considerations prevailing and economic development and reform secondary.

Viron Vaky argues that the securty priority has never been more predominant than today. Reagan administration economic programs — such as the Caribbean Basin Initiative (CBI), while potentially constructive — have been security motivated.

Can an American administration provide new "shields," achieve — in the late Salvadoran Archbishop Romero's ironic phrase — "reform with repression"? (See the essay by Christopher Dickey.) American efforts to rein in the abuses of the Salvadoran military and the death squads do not bode well for such a policy.

Among the richest ironies of the March 1982 Salvadoran election, intended to legitimate a centrist, reformist regime, was the emergence of Roberto d'Aubuisson's ultra-right ARENA as a power sharer, and General José Guillermo García as the protector of the reform process.

With the eclipse of the Christian Democrats, General García replaced Napoleón Duarte as the American point man in El Salvador. García, realizing that continued U.S. assistance depended on preserving a modicum of the reforms, resisted the counter-reform efforts of the oligarchy, led by Roberto d'Aubuisson. Within the army García relied on a handful of cronies from his own and allied factions. García's policies and his cronies' military passiveness were major factors prompting Colonel Ochoa's rebellion in January 1983. Ochoa's rebellion fell narrowly short of an intramural armed conflict. For this he was "disciplined" with a coveted post in Washington. By the fall, García had been removed from command, his successor, the American embassy's favorite, General Vides Casanova, had been stripped of power, and Ochoa's faction was in the driver's seat. The outcome of the whole episode was that America's main allies, in a policy of repression with reform, Napoleón Duarte, and Generals García and Vides Casanova were reduced first to impotence and then to irrelevance.

A rhetoric of reform has been accompanied by the resumption and expansion of the death squads. Meanwhile, the war is farther from a conclusion than ever. By December, the administration was again striving to recapture the initiative, get Duarte elected and the death squads to hybernate. The cycle seems endless. Millett's and Dickey's observations about the resistance of the Central American military establishment to American pressures and blandishment have been amply underscored. The historical record warrants deep skepticism about U.S efforts to "manage" reforms in Central America.

"Reform with repression," the "two shields" policy, is unworkable and costly. It is unworkable because American will — at best of short-term duration when it comes to foreign involvement, especially in Central America — cannot reform the Salvadoran military. Reform with repression will continue to put the United States in thrall to the Salvadoran right which will "obey" but not "comply." Pursuing the chimera of reform with repression the United States will continue to produce larger and more deeply anti-American and pro-Soviet revolutionary movements.

Cirincione and Hunter indicate that the effort to restore U.S. hegemony in the region will ineluctably involve direct U.S. military intervention. Despite increases of U.S. military aid, a wider role for U.S. military advisers, and a vastly expanded training program for Salvadoran soldiers, the Salvadoran army is further from defeating the guerrillas. The administration has sometimes argued that this failure is because the "source" of guerrilla success is Nicaragua. While there is considerable reason to question that assertion, Cirincione makes clear that, short of direct massive U.S. military involvement, the Sandinista "cancer" cannot be extirpated. Combining the Guatemalan, Honduran and Salvadoran armies will not do the job. As Richard Millett points out, even to get these armies to collaborate continues to be extremely difficult. Guatemala's recent retreat from CONDECA illustrates the problem. Even should that obstacle be overcome somehow, Cirincione notes, how ill-suited these armies are for invasion. According to Millett, at best CONDECA would serve only as symbolic and political cover for U.S. troops, something like the role of the organization of Eastern Caribbean States in the Grenada invasion.

Cirincione, Hunter and Moran suggest that the most likely result of U.S. intervention would be a long, enervating, and costly guerrilla war. But, in the very unlikely event that such an operation proves successful and short, what would "success" signify? At best America would be perpetuating the cycle of U.S. intervention, popular resistance, and revolution. This cycle will not be broken by a policy of "reform with repression." We have seen too often how well the Central American elites have learned to resist reform while appearing to embrace it.

"Reform with repression" is also unworkable and costly at home. I.M. Destler suggests that a policy of restoring the isthmus will sharply divide the

American public. With the right clamoring for the scalp of those who have almost "lost Central America," and the left organizing against the war, the United States could experience the worst of the McCarthy and Vietnam periods combined.

According to Leonel Gomez, if the Central American conflict widens, we can expect more "feet people," waves of immigrants fleeing war, misery, revolution and death squads. He fears that some expatriot "feet people" residing in the United States may collaborate with the Central American revolutionary groups in terrorist reprisals in the United States. Then we might be confronting bombs not left in the lavatories of public buildings at night but in the subways at midday.

In reaction to this grim scenario there are those who advocate a diametrically opposed policy approach. Declare Central America not to be a "vital interest" and withdraw. (See the essay by I.M. Destler.)

Cirincione and Hunter show that the national security danger, though exaggerated, is not a figment of the American right's imagination. Cuba is already a valuable asset in the context of a NATO/Warsaw Pact conventional war. A capacity to preposition armor, planes, and troops on the Central American isthmus significantly supplements Cuba's modest air and sea lift capability. The United States has legitimate security interests in the Caribbean basin and Panama Canal region. But a distinction must be made between legitimate national security concerns and hostility to social movements opposed to the Central American status quo and determined to exercise foreign policy independence.

Some draw this line between the domestic and the external and with the chalk of "Finlandization." The Sandinista leadership could do as it pleased domestically, while coerced to pursue a Finlandized foreign policy "sensitive to the interests of the neighboring superpowers."[15] While the Sandinistas might harbor pro-Soviet convictions and even erect a tropical totalitarianism, as long as this were kept to Nicaragua, it would not warrant U.S. armed hostility.

Although Finlandization is an attractive option, it is vulnerable to objections from opposite sides of the political spectrum. It is a form, albeit mild, of what might be called "backyardism." Should proximity to a superpower obligate nations to forfeit pieces of their sovereignty? Finlandization is only acceptable if redefined to signify the pursuit of foreign policy independence. But then the term "Finlandization" could be exchanged for "Mexicanization," insofar as our Mexican neighbor has for decades pursued a foreign policy quite independent of that of the United States.

However, there is another objection to "Finlandization." What guarantee is there that a Sandinista leadership, which sees its fate tied historically to that of the Soviet Union, will honor agreements to de-Sovietize foreign and military policy once U.S. attention is no longer riveted on the area? While there is much to recommend a policy which lays stress on the West's economic strengths, such a policy might founder on the anti-Americanism and pro-Sovietism of the Sandinista leadership.

That might be a risk worth taking. But in Central America co-existence among different political and social orientations have been the rare exception. Finlandization could lead to the Balkanization of Central America. Given Central America's history and proclivities as a nation divided, it may not stay antagonistically divided for long. The danger is that Finlandization would lead to regional war. By putting the lid back on the boiling pot, Finlandization could simply return us to our original dilemma: restoration of American hegemony or Sovietization?

However, a formal Nicaraguan guarantee of genuine non-alignment should be welcomed and could be a useful step forward, especially if as part of a process leading to an historical compromise.

RECIPROCAL AND REGIONAL NEGOTIATIONS

Administration spokepersons have argued that there is "symmetry" between the situations in El Salvador and Nicaragua. They assert that symmetry legitimizes covert aid to Nicaraguan insurgents, and "free elections" as a solution for both countries.[16] The Achilles' heel of the administration's polemic is that symmetry can justify power-sharing negotiations as well.

In fact, the cases of El Salvador and Nicaragua are not symmetrical, though they are analagous. Both countries are polarized, but they are polarized in different ways. In El Salvador the polarization is vertical — poor versus rich. In Nicaragua it is horizontal, with pro- and anti-Sandinista workers, businessmen, peasants, and clergy. In both countries there is a civilian, as well as an armed, opposition. In Nicaragua only a part of the civilian opposition has been banned, but the rest of it is harassed systematically. There is an opposition press, but it has been heavily censored. Civil liberties (such as freedom of speech, assembly, unionization, etc.) have been curtailed on the grounds of war emergency. In El Salvador the civilian opposition is in exile, there is no daily opposition press, and civil liberties are severely circumscribed. Human rights abuses exist in both countries, but, except for the Indians on the Nicaraguan Atlantic coast, they are on an incomparably larger and bloodier scale in El Salvador.

The Nicaraguan insurgent movements are of recent vintage, and they have held territory only in the south. There are more armed insurgents in Nicaragua, but they have less logistical support among the population. Both movements are linked to foreign supporters, but in the case of Nicaragua the support has been far more critical (with the important exception of Eden Pastora's movement in the south). Nonetheless, internal contradictions are responsible for the existence of large bodies of combatants willing to fight against the regimes. As Richard Millett points out, the base of even the U.S. trained and equipped FDN, the most dependent of all the insurgent movements, is made up of "peasants and shopkeepers" with grievances against the government. (See the essay by Richard Millett.)

Both countries are aligned in varying degrees with one of the superpowers. Many would characterize the American embassy and military advisers in El Salvador as "neo-colonial." As already seen the Soviet bloc presence in Nicaragua has become a major one.

The sources of legitimacy of the two regimes, formally at least, are quite different. The Salvadoran government derives its legitimacy from the 1982 elections. However, many informed observers question their validity as a test of popular will for a variety of reasons. (See essays by Dickey, Farer and Leiken.) Many contend that the source of power in El Salvador remains what it had been—the armed forces. The Nicaraguan government derives its power from the Sandinista revolution. Still, many observers argue that the Sandinistas had no ideological and political mandate when they came to power; that most Nicaraguans were unaware of, and would not have supported, the Sandinista ideological, political and economic program. They would argue that with the rupturing of the original coalition that brought the Sandinistas to power, and with the Sandinistas' monopolization of the military resources of the country, real power once again lies with the military. However, most would concede that the Sandinistas are closer to the original source of legitimacy, the revolution, than the Salvador regime is to any popular mandate.

These similarities and differences call for solutions which are similar but not "symmetrical." In the case of El Salvador, as Thomas Farer argues, there needs to be a power-sharing arrangement, a transitional governmental mechanism in which the left would be incorporated and the guerrilla army integrated. However, no stable and viable economic and political system will emerge in El Salvador that does not constrict the oligarchy. A negotiated settlement would remove from power this grouping responsible for death squads and for the landlord system.

In Nicaragua the aim of negotiations should be to broaden the government and the political life of Nicaragua. This task does not require the displacement of a social class or political elite. That was achieved by the revolution which brought down Somoza and his cohorts. Negotiations in Nicaragua would seek to bring about the reconciliation of the revolutionary alliance. They need not be explicitly power-sharing negotiations, but they should involve negotiations among peers seeking consensus—not concession decreed from on high. Negotiations would also bring about the reintegration of the armed opposition, and of former national guardsmen—those who have not committed crimes — into Nicaraguan civil society. (It must be added that if the Sandinista leadership does not choose to reach a consensus with the opposition — the church, the press, the dissident unions and political parties, the Indians — it may well find itself eventually obligated to accept power-sharing.)

Negotiations in both countries are not only individually necessary, they are linked. For example, as Tom Farer asserts, negotiations in El Salvador would help put "political and psychological pressures on Nicaragua . . . to negotiate a specific program for opening its politics. . . . " Furthermore by lowering the danger of external aggression, negotiations in El Salvador would make it easier for the Sandinistas to broaden their political system. To the extent that the United States showed itself prepared to accept accommodation in the region, moderate elements in Nicaragua would be strengthened. By the same token, negotiations in Nicaragua would lessen the fears of Salvadoran moderates about negotiations in their own country by demonstrating that a left-led government can accommodate other political forces. Similarly, negotiations in Nicaragua would reduce Salvadoran fears about Nicaraguan interference in their internal affairs.

THE BENEFITS OF NEGOTIATIONS

Nicaragua suffers from a grievous international commercial and financial deficit. This deficit is a result not only of deteriorating international terms of trade, but from the shrinking volume of Nicaraguan exports due to falling productivity. Among the main causes of this situation are the distrust of domestic and foreign investors, the insurgents' attacks on the economy, an inefficient state sector, and the emigration of hundreds of administrators and technicians. Negotiations in Nicaragua could alleviate all these problems. By restoring business confidence, returning inefficient nationalized companies to their owners and encouraging the return of middle class administrators and technocrats, negotiations would lead to increased productivity, thus reducing the shortage of consumer goods and improving Nicaragua's export picture. This recovery would narrow the balance of payments gap, reverse the trend of falling wages and rising unemployment in the urban sector, and of falling prices in the countryside. By reducing Nicaragua's external debt, the country would become more independent. These measures would not be inconsistent with "socialist principles" as the Sandinistas could recognize in reviewing the experience of the Soviet New Economic Policy in the 1920s, or that of the Hungarians and the Chinese more recently.

Negotiations with the Indians could bring peace to the war-torn Atlantic coast. By collaterally negotiating an end to the war with the *contras,* or stripping them of any legitimate reason to fight, the Sandinistas could help rebuild

CENTRAL AMERICA

ERRATUM

The last line on page 121 is missing.
It should read.......

"the FPL, resulting in the violent and obscure deaths of its two top leaders."

473-8800

the national unity essential to confront the economic crisis that Nicaragua and all Central America faces.

Nicaragua must have economic development to realize the redistributive gains of the revolution. The government has revamped and popularized medical services, building clinics in hitherto unattended slums and villages. Yet for lack of foreign exchange these clinics are frequently without medicine. There has been a massive literacy campaign, yet higher and secondary education is in crisis because of constant "mobilization," the polarization of the student body, the loss of teachers.

Nicaraguans will have to choose between two futures: a repetition of the cycle of civil war which characterized Nicaraguan history until Somoza, or mutual concessions for the sake of national unity and progress.

The case for negotiations in El Salvador is made by Tom Farer. There can be no growth and development in El Salvador until the war is ended. El Salvador has the potential to become the industrial heartland of Central America.

By lowering tensions in Nicaragua and El Salvador, negotiations in Nicaragua and El Salvador would create conditions for the re-emergence of the populist-reformist trend within the Honduran military. These officers would ally with now latent but numerous liberal and progressive elements in Honduran society. Honduras would be able to realize the promises of its elections. The United States could withdraw militarily from Honduras, and convert its military aid into economic assistance.

Peace inside Nicaragua and El Salvador could restore conditions for economic growth in Costa Rica by reassuring its panic-stricken bourgeoisie. Although Costa Rica is often cited as a bastion of democracy, growth and stability, that country has been moving toward the brink of social upheaval over the last few years. Land redistribution may now be a necessity, and recently spontaneous urban demonstrations have erupted.

The conflict in Guatemala will not be resolved by negotiations. However, negotiations elsewhere would have the effect of quarantining Guatemala's internal conflict. The greater danger of it becoming regionalized or becoming part of a regional war would thus be removed.

Most important of all, political negotiations would clear the way for reviving the Central American Common Market. The economies of Central America are highly vulnerable to external forces. Only by cooperating and utilizing their potential interdependence can they reduce this vulnerability and achieve self-sustaining growth. The tiny markets of individual Central American countries can only sustain the earliest stages of industrialization.

Economies of scale and specialization would be necessary and feasible in the context of a revived Common Market. Nicaragua, with its vast expanse of rich soil, is the natural grainery of Central America; El Salvador, with its abundant and skilled working class is a fitting manufacturing complement to Nicaragua. As Feinberg and Pastor emphasize, during the Common Market years a good measure of growth, industrialization, and specialization was achieved. The market permitted labor mobility throughout Central America helping to offset individual weaknesses.

Central Americans must solve the problems of Central America. They cannot be resolved either by the United States or the Soviet Union. Honduras and El Salvador are demonstrating today what the Alliance for Progress demonstrated in the 1960s: U.S. assistance cannot be the decisive factor for Central American development. Nicaragua has demonstrated the futility of depending on the Soviet bloc for development. In the wake of a political settlement, foreign economic assistance and tariff concessions can play a significant complementary role.

THE NEGOTIATING VEHICLE

Just as Central Americans, and not the superpowers, must resolve their own crisis, their regional neighbors are the best qualified to be the intermediaries. The numerous and varied regional efforts at mediating and negotiating have crystallized in the Contadora group (Columbia, Mexico, Panama, and Venezuela). They have received vigorous support from the UN Security Council.

Contadora moved by fits and starts through 1983. Only recently has it been acknowledged that for Contadora to succeed it cannot shelve the question of internal negotiations. Until now, the Mexicans have blocked discussion of negotiations in Nicaragua, and the United States has done the same vis-à-vis El Salvador. Some rapprochement between the Mexican and U.S. position is necessary if Contadora is to makes its indispensable contribution to a regional settlement.

Relations with Mexico are becoming—strategically as well as economically—the cornerstone of U.S. Latin American policy. Between the two countries there are unresolved historical issues but also abundant and profound mutual interests. The United States must work together with Mexico in Central America.[17]

The Sandinista leadership is now aware that it cannot survive by relying on Soviet bloc political, military, and economic backing. Sandinista domestic and foreign policies and U.S. hostility have reduced Nicaragua's broad regional orbit of support basically to Mexico. Thus, Mexico is in a unique position. Nicaragua depends on Mexican oil and needs Mexican political support. Without Mexico its last vestiges of support inside the Socialist International could crumble. But Mexico will take no initiative with the Sandinistas if this is to lead to a restoration of U.S. hegemony in the region. The Mexicans believe that such a situation would be inherently unstable, dangerous and inimical to their national interests. Only if the United States could accept a compromise in the region, beginning with El Salvador, would Mexico be likely to help out with Nicaragua.

Reciprocal negotiations in Nicaragua and El Salvador are the most secure foundations for durable, regional arms control negotiations. But proposals for limiting arms flows, prohibiting foreign bases and advisers, etc., should not however, be rejected out of hand until internal negotiations have been completed. As Viron Vaky states, such agreements can be a confidence-building first step towards pacification of Central America.

Nicaragua has recently shown some willingness to negotiate seriously Contadora's agenda requiring a ban on foreign troops, facilities, military bases, and advisers, the elimination of arms traffic, and of armed interference in neighboring states. They now profess to accept Contadora's principle of "free access of the various political currents to the electoral process." Lately it has been Honduras and El Salvador which have been applying what some Latin diplomats are calling "obstructionist tactics." These diplomats believe that it is the United States which has been encouraging Honduran and Salvadoran intransigence. Their feet are said to grow cold at any prospect of the withdrawal of U.S. advisers, equipment, facilities, and bases.[18]

The biggest incentive for negotiations in Nicaragua is not the use of force against the Nicaraguan regime from bases in Honduras, but the promise of negotiations in El Salvador. That carrot will be far more effective, far safer and more humane, and far less costly, than the stick of intervention.

It now appears quite possible that Havana could support this historical compromise. Since the failed "final offensive" in El Salvador, the Cubans have been urging FMLN groups to negotiate with the government. They have taken the extraordinary step of inviting one of the Nicaraguan insurgent groups (Eden Pastora's ARDE) to Havana to discuss the prospects of a negotiated settlement. For the past two years Cuban officials have been saying privately and publicly that a radical revolutionary solution is presently ruled out in Central America, and what is necessary is a "social democratic" solution. Cuban support for negotiations in Nicaragua as well as in El Salvador, and Cuban analyses of the region suggest that their conception of a "social democratic stage" in Central America is not inconsistent with an "historical compromise." Cuba does not appear to represent the main obstacle to such a settlement.

U.S. REALITIES (INTERNATIONAL AND DOMESTIC)

Is Central America's historical compromise also viable for the United States?

The road to a U.S. consensus on Central American policy could be cleared by an historical compromise. However, as stated at the outset, a policy can win a consensus without being sound. How does a compromise square with U.S. interests in Central America?

Several authors in this volume, particularly Cirincione, Hunter and Leiken, state that U.S. security interests in Central America are jeopardized by strategic alignment with the Soviet Union, but not by leftist power (or power-sharing) as such. History has shown that there is no obligatory relationship between a socialist internal regime and pro-Soviet external policies. Socialists, even expressly Marxist-Leninist regimes, exhibit a variety of attitudes toward Soviet expansionism — from adamant resistance, as in the case of Yugoslavia and China, to collaboration and clientism, as in the case of Bulgaria and Vietnam. Third World revolutionary movements exhibit a similarly wide spectrum. To construct a successful anti-Soviet policy, U.S. policymakers must distinguish between Soviet expansionism and Third World revolution, Sovietism and Socialism.[19]

One must examine specifically the regime or movement in question to determine if its brand of socialism (or of capitalism for that matter) is strategically aligned with the Soviet Union. Leiken argues that the widely unappreciated policy differences between the Sandinistas and the Salvadoran guerrillas illustrate this distinction.

The pro-Soviet bias of much of the Sandinista leadership (and of some of the Salvadoran left) is in good measure the consequence of a bad history. Unless we wish to produce in our own backyard a seething replica of Eastern Europe and Afghanistan, U.S. policy must seek to accommodate this reality. From the point of view of short-term U.S. security interests, the United States can and should coexist peaceably with Sandinista Nicaragua.

The current unfavorable swing in the "global correlation of forces" and in the regional balance has diminished the short-term threat of Soviet-Cuban penetration in Central America. The Reagan administration has exaggerated this short-term threat, at the expense of forging a common policy with Latin America. As to the more serious long-term Soviet danger, the disposition of Latin Americans to resist Soviet inroads will be profoundly influenced by the United States capacity to accept genuine non-alignment, to accept a third option between American and Soviet hegemony.

Viron Vaky has pointed to some of the weaknesses in the argument that U.S. "credibility" rests on the maintenance of U.S. hegemony in Central America. If the U.S. does not act to prevent Soviet penetration in its own "backyard," what signal will be sent to U.S. allies elsewhere?

The triumph of the Sandinistas in the American "backyard" in 1979 was greeted by many as a new height in the cresting movement for Third World national independence. But since the Soviet invasion of Afghanistan later that year, "backyardism" has become an increasingly powerful countertrend in world history. Moscow has fortified its bloody occupation of Afghanistan, and helped to impose martial law in Poland. The United States has organized a "secret war" against the Nicaraguan regime and has invaded Grenada.

Yuri Andropov, in an interview in *Der Spiegel* (April 1983) specifically compared U.S. interests in Nicaragua to Moscow's in Afghanistan, "our corner of the world."

Andropov, as have other Soviet officials on other occasions, was suggesting a trade-off involving mutual respect for "corners of the world." (The Tass version of this interview suppressed the phrase "our corner of the world." That flagrant acknowledgement of the sphere of influence orientation of Soviet policy was presumably in embarrassing contradiction with its avowed support for national self-determination.) Similarly, geographical proximity allows Americans to regard Central America as their "backyard."

Backyardism condemns those countries located in the vicinity of a superpower to limited sovereignty. The peoples of Afghanistan and Eastern Europe, of Mexico and Central America and the Caribbean, are not the only actual or potential victims of such an arrangement.

Backyards tend to expand. For Hitler "national security" could only be assured by world domination. Many suspect this is also true for Moscow today. The logic of backyardism ultimately jeopardizes national self-determination and non-alignment everywhere. That kind of superpower security will lead to global insecurity.

CONCLUSIONS

I.M. Destler, in his study of the search for the "elusive consensus" in Washington D.C., concludes that "getting in deeper [in Central America] will not bring us together" at home. According to a recent ongoing study of opinion polls, there is a profound ambivalence in domestic attitudes towards Central America.[20] Most Americans agree with the president that Soviet activities in the region represent a threat to American national security. But pluralities or majorities oppose nearly all of the Reagan administration countermeasures, including covert action, joint military exercises in Honduras, military equipment sales in El Salvador, and a U.S. naval blockagde. Americans fear the "loss of Central America," but they also oppose direct U.S. intervention to "save it."

Grenada has not rescued American policymakers from this dilemma. While according to public opinion polls, the president himself gained personally from the invasion (his approval rating was restored to its "honeymoon level"), even after his persuasive televised defense of the Grenada action, pluralities of Americans have "no confidence" in Reagan's "handling of crises in foreign policy" and believe that he is "trying to do too much with his armed forces overseas."[21] After the speech more Americans than ever before (60%) opposed policies designed to help overthrow the government in Nicaragua.

This ambivalence in public attitudes, combined with congressional opposition and resistance within the administration itself, has paralyzed administration policy. (See the I.M. Destler and Barry Rubin essays.) Administration hardliners would prefer stronger measures, but public attitudes, and the contemplated costs of such measures obligate them, in Viron Vaky's phrase, to go "round the mulberry bush," condemned to a netherworld of half-measures.

The U.S. public will be satisfied with a policy that opposes Soviet expansionism, but only if it is non-interventionist. The way out of this dilemma could be the linkage of Salvadoran and Nicaraguan negotiations.

It is obvious that it would be far easier to sell Salvadoran negotiations in Washington with the Sandinistas negotiating in Nicaragua. It is difficult to imagine Washington approving negotiations in Salvador without some major internal concessions on the part of the Sandinista government. But it would also be far easier to get liberal support for U.S.-backed negotiations in Nicaragua if these were linked to conservative support for negotiations in El Salvador.

As the guerrillas expand their "zones of control" and as the Salvadoran armed forces continue to prove ineffective despite bigger and quicker fixes of U.S. aid and training, U.S. policymakers will approach a crossroads: negotiations or direct intervention. U.S. military intervention would only regionalize war, making it ever more costly. U.S. intervention will not lay the basis for peace and stability in the region, it will not even guarantee ultimate victory. At best it will only perpetuate and deepen the tortured cycle of Central American history and of U.S.-Central American relations. Breaking that cycle requires U.S. acceptance of negotiations in El Salvador.

Support for negotiations in El Salvador is our most effective and least costly bargaining chip with Nicaragua, and it would clear the way to cooperation with Mexico. With Mexican support, and given Nicaragua's economic and military problems, there would be sufficient leverage to move Nicaragua into serious and sincere negotiations with its opposition. U.S. support for negotiations in El Salvador would enable Contadora to realize its objective of promoting a democratization of the region. Only such a democratization, but on Central American not U.S. terms, could avoid the Balkanization of Central America. Moreover, negotiations in El Salvador and Nicaragua are the only way to deal with the problem of the reintegration of the *contras* and the "feet people." Democratization rather than Balkanization is the best guarantee for realizing Contadora's agenda for regional accords with respect to arms flows, military advisers and bases.

The negotiating route is the only one that leads toward the political stability required for a successful "Marshall Plan." Reconstruction can begin only when the war ends. "Reform with repression," Marshall Plan with war, a policy of "two shields," are condemned to plugging holes in a crumbling dike — the regionalization of what we now do in El Salvador. The American people no longer have the luxury of supporting an aid program that cannot promise results.

After a political settlement, productive social forces in Central America could take the initiative. This would make it more likely that U.S. aid money would be invested constructively and not end up in exile bank accounts. It is the only way U.S. aid programs could help to break the cycle.

But continued and deeper U.S. involvement will perpetuate the cycle, divide the United States, divide Central America, increase instability, and provide long-range opportunities for the Soviet Union — a struggle of hegemonies regionally and globally, a widening cycle of destruction, dependence, dictatorship, rebellion and war.

As Viron Vaky and Howard Wiarda stress, something has been wrong not only with our policies but with our thinking. We have been guilty of an "ethnocentric," "parochial" approach. We can exchange arrogance for humility by doing the region the honor of seeing it in its own time and place. Central America is not Vietnam or Angola. Its crisis cannot be understood by analogy or through modish clichés. To develop an effective policy and win a consensus for it we need to take a fresh look at Central America. This could be a start toward breaking the cycle.

NOTES

1. Woodward, Ralph Lee, Jr., *Central America: A Nation Divided* (New York: Oxford University Press, 1976)
2. Though it is commonly associated with Somoza, Roosevelt's epithet was originally aimed at Rafael Trujillo, the military ruler of the Dominican Republic from 1930 to 1961.
3. Reynolds, Clark, "Fissures in the Volcano? Central American Economic Prospects," in *Latin America and World Economy: A Changing International Order*, vol. 2, ed. Joseph Grunwald (Beverly Hills: Sage, 1981), p. 209.
4. William R. Cline and Enrique Delgado, eds., "Economic Integration in Central America" [study sponsored jointly by the Brookings Institution and the secretariat of Economic Integration of Central America (SEICA)] (Washington, D.C.: Brookings Institution, 1978), p. 189.
5. Miguel Bolanos Hunter, a Sandinista defector who had worked in the internal security apparatus, claims that within weeks of the Sandinista victory he was sent to the airport in Managua to transport five Soviet generals. (Seib, Gerald and Walter Mossberg, "Arming a Region: Central America Grows Even More Militarized as Superpowers Vie," *Wall Street Journal*, August 17, 1983, p. 1.

6. For an extended discussion of Soviet-Cuban-Caribbean relations see Robert S. Leiken, *Soviet Strategy in Latin America*, The Washington Papers, No. 93, (New York: Praeger, 1982), chapters 5 and 6.

7. By going to such lengths to please Moscow (and to vex Washington) the Sandinistas sometimes have embarrassed the Soviets and themselves. Thus, apparently, without ever having been asked by Moscow, Defense Minister Humberto Ortega told a *New York Times* reporter (Oct. 4, 1983) that Nicaraguan national security justified his seriously examining a proposal for installing Russian SS-20s in Nicaraguan territory. After the Soviet ambassador appeared on American television to deny that Moscow had made such a proposal, Head of State Daniel Ortega at length categorically denied that Nicaragua had ever entertained the notion.

8. On Soviet-bloc penetration of the Nicaraguan internal security military and political aparatuses, see the transcript of the "Face-to-Face Dinner Discussion" with Eden Pastora Gomez, Commander of the Democratic Revolutionary Alliance (ARDE) *contra* forces at the Carnegie Endowment for International Peace, Nov. 14, 1983, and Don Oberdorfer and Joanne Omang, "Nicaraguan Bares Plan to Discredit Foes," *Washington Post*, June 1983, p. A1. Unpublished paper by Peter Clement, "The Soviets in Nicaragua: Cultivating a New Client," prepared for the annual Conference of the American Association for the Advancement of Slavic Studies, Oct. 21-25, 1983. Richard Halloran, "U.S. Reports Sharp Rise in Arms Aid to Nicaragua," *New York Times* Aug. 2, 1983.

9. Unpublished paper by Peter Clement, "The Soviets in Nicaragua: Cultivating a New Client," prepared for the Annual Conference of the American Association or the Advancement of Slavic Studies, Oct. 21-25, 1983, p. 11.

10. Doder, Dusko, "Moscow Criticizes U.S. for Following Vessel Headed for Nicaragua," *Washington Post*, August 12, 1983, p. A1.

11. See Robert S. Leiken, *Soviet Strategy in Latin America*, pp. 11-14, for a discussion of the offensive undertaken by the Soviets in the favorable circumstances of the 1970s' "global correlation of forces."

12. See the essay by Seweryn Bialer, "The Harsh Decade: Soviet Policies in the 1980s," *Foreign Affairs* (Summer 1981), pp. 999-1020.

13. For a cogent presentation of this argument see the forthcoming essay by Arturo Cruz Sequeira, "Nicaragua: A Revolution in Crisis," *SAIS Review*, Winter 1984.

14. The concepts of economic and military shield were originally introduced in May 1983 by Senator Henry Jackson while proposing to the Senate the establishment of a bi-partisan commission to "help build the necessary consensus on a long-term, comprehensive policy" for Central America. (*Congressional Record*, Vol. 129, No. 65, May 12, 1983). These terms have subsequently been adopted and frequently employed by administration spokesmen, incuding George Schultz, Jeane Kirkpatrick, and Henry Kissinger.

15. Jakobson, Max, "Substance and Appearance in Finland," *Foreign Affairs* (Summer 1980). Jakobson has eloquently conveyed what "Finlandization" entails for a nation: "The Finns deny themselves the luxury of making emotionally satisfying gestures. . . ." Finland tends to play down its foreign policy differences with the Soviet Union.

16. This version of the "symmetry" concept is developed in the following sources: Phillip Taubman, "Are U.S. Covert Activities Best Policy on Nicaragua?" *New York Times*, June 15, 1983, p. A22. "Elliot Abrams, "El Salvador: A Matter of Principle," *Los Angeles Times*, March 22, 1983 p. II-5; Jeane Kirkpatrick, "UN 'Mugging' Fails," *New York Times*, March 31, 1983, p. A20; Bernard Weinraub, "Reagan's Policy in Central America," *New York Times*, January 25, 1983, p. A1; "Pros, Cons, and Contras," *Time*, June 16, 1983, pp. 16-18.

17. For a more comprehensive discussion of this subject see Robert S. Leiken, "Bitter Wine," *The New Republic*, February 7, 1981, pp. 15-18.

18. See the "Consolidated Twenty-One Point Declaration" of the Fourth Joint Meeting between the Contadora group and the Central American foreign ministers, September 10, 1983; also see Stephen Kinzer, "Honduras Said to Snag Latin Peace Bid," *New York Times*, December 15, 1983. p. A3; and Loren Jenkins, "Peace in Central America Remains Elusive for Contadora Group," *Washington Post*, December 25, 1983, p. A20.
19. For further elaboration of these ideas see Robert S. Leiken, "Eastern Winds in Latin America," *Foreign Policy*, No. 42 (Spring 1981), pp. 94-113; and Leiken, *Soviet Strategy in Latin America*.
20. These conclusions are drawn from the work in progress on public attitudes towards Central America by George Moffett, Senior Associate at the Carnegie Endowment for International Peace.
21. Citations are taken from an unpublished study of Gallup, Roper, CBS, ABC and other polls, George Moffett, *ibid.*

LEGACIES AND CONTEXTS

1
"OBEDEZCO PERO NO CUMPLO"
["I obey but I do not comply"]

Christopher Dickey

I. INTRODUCTION

After a couple of years serving in El Salvador, the political officers at the United States embassy start tending toward the mystical and the imponderable as they try to explain where Washington's policies have gone astray; how despite its best intentions the United States is stumbling ever deeper into the quagmire.

One chief of the political section used to talk about the endless personal connections, friendships and animosities in Central American elites that influenced the course of events in those countries in ways no North American could ever hope, truly, to comprehend. He finally left El Salvador and retired from the foreign service. His successor, a long-time Latin Americanist, was more theoretical in his approach to the quagmire mystery. He would hold his pen in the air, then simply drop it. In the Spanish language, he would explain, you do not say that you dropped the pen, you say the pen dropped itself. At the linguistic core of the society, even on the simplest question, responsibility was avoided. Another more junior officer liked to go on about the world-view of Indian villagers and the kind of map they would draw of their universe, their *pueblo* always at the center.

Experience had taught the political analysts to identify, at least for themselves, those cultural blind spots that seem inevitably to subvert the best-laid plans of Washington and its embassies in Latin America; those traditions anyone who lives in the area or studies it is likely to view as commonplace, but which the North American public and often its policymakers seem rarely to take into account.

In Central America Washington has discovered — since the Reagan administration grandly drew the line against Communism in El Salvador and irrevocably committed American prestige, once again, to "building democracy" in the region — it has been working in an environment where words are often expected to substitute for realities and where institutions, laws, consititutions are most often little more than facades. In this contradictory world the military guarantors of democracy that Washington depends upon may in fact be democracy's greatest opponents. Elections may undermine lasting pluralism rather than build it. Reforms may work against the interest of those they were intended to benefit and the courts may even serve to guarantee the perpetuation of institutionalized murder.

These problems spring from the most obvious and dangerous of those many political and cultural traditions of which Washington seems so unaware. They spring from the region's traditional response to what it sees as foreign dictates and ideals: accepting them on the surface but ignoring their substance. It is a pattern that goes back to the conquest, the days of the *criollos* and *peninsulares*, and that now blights virtually every assumption Washington makes about what is happening in Central America.

For 300 years the colonial administrators of Spain's New World empire were accustomed to receive their orders from the king with obsequious ceremony. The members of the *audiencia* kissed the royal seal. The parchment was held above the forehead as a sign of obeisance. Yet virtually from the time of the conquests that ceremony was, in effect, a masquerade. The colonists often believed, with reason, that the crown did not understand their needs nor the society they were creating. The orders of the king in many cases were regarded as unwise, impractical and potentially destructive.

The most persistent problem, as it happened, was with royal edicts seeking some reprieve for the Indians from the legendary severity of their new conquerors. Only fifty years after Columbus's first voyage Carlos V enacted the *Nuevas Leyes* forbidding enslavement of the Indians, assuring that they would not be forced to perform personal services, regulating their working conditions and guaranteeing reasonable wages. Promulgated at the instigation of reformist priests, these laws were enlightened, remarkably progressive, laudably humane and never seriously enforced. Those who did seek to press the King's will on the issue risked disaster. When the viceroy of Peru complied with the *Nuevas Leyes* in 1546 and freed the Indians, the colonists rose up against him. The revolt was suppressed only after the viceroy had been killed and his successor had redistributed the Indian serfs among the colonists. But the crown, hardly daunted, continued fostering laws designed to promote its authority and noteworthy for their good intentions. By 1635 there were more than 400,000 edicts in effect.[1]

Early on, the colonial administrators had arrived at a formulation to deal with the impossibility, as they saw it, of actually enforcing such decrees. After the kissing of the seal, the elevation of the parchment and the reading of the law they might respond to the king with the phrase, "Obedezco pero no cumplo." I obey but do not comply.[2] This is, to say the least, an odd notion to anyone steeped in Anglo-Saxon legal and political traditions. After all, how does one obey an order without carrying it out? Washington is learning. As Latin Americans consider the potentially disastrous effects of North America's myriad blind spots, they deal with them the way they have always dealt with the misconceptions of those who would try to dominate them. Let the *yanqui* see what he wants to see. Then do what you want to do.

After nearly five hundred years, the phrase "obedezco pero no cumplo" still captures quite precisely the traditional Latin way of resolving the discrepancy between progressive ideals, which are accepted in principle, and the almost feudal social and economic realities of the region.

As French author Jacques Lambert noted two decades ago in *Latin America: Social Structure and Political Institutions*, institutionalized contradictions between lofty goals and grim realities did not end with the empire in 1821. They intensified, becoming more ingrained than ever. "During the revolutionary period liberty, equality, fraternity were ideals cherished by the very people who owned slaves or serfs and took advantage of independence to acquire more of them." This was, of course, a paradox not unknown to the United States at the time. But it tended to lose its importance in Europe and North America as they continued their rapid, sometimes violent social and economic development in the 19th century. Latin America, however, kept pace only politically and mainly on paper. "Latin America never lagged when it came to guarantees of individual freedom, declarations of economic and social rights, affirmation of the principle of universal suffrage," Lambert wrote. "The contradiction between, on the one hand, institutions and ideologies of the most developed societies, and, on the other hand, a partly archaic social structure that no one tries to change, produces a proliferation of reforms, laws, and regulations as well as systematic efforts to evade the law and rob the reforms of their substance. The process is cumulative. Reforms are enacted with an ease and frequency proportional to their relative futility; political life is active and agitated in proportion to its lack of effectiveness. Latin America suffers as much from the complexity of politics as from its sterility."[3]

Even the Soviet Union, in its dealings with Cuba, has stumbled over the problem of form without substance. During the 1960s, Fidel Castro often frustrated his friends in Moscow by paying lip service to their Marxist orthodoxy while pursuing his own quite distinct revolutionary goals. Many western European nations have become disillusioned with the course of the Sandinista revolution in Nicaragua because they had more or less taken the Sandinistas at their word when they promised to foster a pluralistic democratic society based on relatively conventional European and North American norms. Not surprisingly, given the upheaval that normally follows any revolution and considering the countless economic, ideological and political forces unleashed in Managua, the Sandinistas made much show of obeying the desires of the West in this regard while ultimately demonstrating little interest in complying with them.

But it is the United States, with its everlasting tendency to think the world was created in its own Anglo-Saxon image, that most often has been fooled and most often has fooled itself in dealing with the region. Throughout this century declarations of good intentions by Latin American dictators on both the right and, to a lesser extent, the left, have been accepted and extolled by Washington when nothing about the governments that made them suggested they had any substance. The result, almost without exception, has been to deepen sometimes potentially grave misunderstandings.

Nowhere is this more obvious than in the Reagan administration's pursuit of that hoary policy, attempted on and off by various presidents throughout this century, of "building democracy" by backing up right-wing military establishments. Nowhere is it more dangerous than in El Salvador.

II

On the stairway nearest the chief executive's office in the Casa Presidencial of San Salvador there hangs a large portrait of nineteenth century Salvadoran hero Gen. Manuel José Arce in his full dress Napoleonic uniform. He holds a slip of paper on which is written the legend, "The Army shall live as long as the Republic shall live." It might as easily and truthfully say, at least as far as the nation's soldiers are concerned, that the republic is the army and the army is the republic.

Given such a conception of the state, virtually any civilian institution — a legislature, a constitution, a civilian president — is likely to serve as window dressing for a government that is founded on force rather than laws. Democracy at best is an exercise. Certainly it is not coincidental that the only long-term conventional democracy in Latin America is in the one nation, Costa Rica, that has abolished its army. Yet U.S. policymakers continue to believe, and it is not clear why, that armies can be built or trained in Latin America which will guarantee democratic development rather than subvert it.

The "establishment of nonpartisan constabularies in the Caribbean states" has been "one of the chief objectives" of U.S. policy at least since the 1920s.[4] But as fast as the United States has "professionalized" an army, it has been converted to political ends. The most conspicuous example was Nicaragua's *Guardia Nacional*. Through the almost 20 years it occupied Nicaragua, the United States attempted to depoliticize its armed forces, first through training, then by building a new force, the Guardia Nacional, from the ground up. But even as Secretary of State Henry Stimson was warning Nicaraguan President José Maria Moncada in 1929 that Nicaragua's future was riding on "the establishment of an absolutely nonpartisan, nonpolitical Guardia which will devote its entire attention to the preservation of peace, law and order," Moncada was using it to round up his political enemies in the Conservative party.[5] By the time the U.S. Marines finally pulled out of Nicaragua in 1932, the force they had intended to be politically neutral served as the power base on which Guardia Commander Anastasio Somoza García constructed a family dictatorship lasting more than 43 years.

The idea that the most powerful institution in the country should *not* be politicized simply had no place in Nicaraguan tradition, just as, today, it has no place in the view of the Salvadoran officer corps. When Salvadoran officers say they are not involved and do not want to be involved with political parties, they are not removing themselves from the political arena, they are placing themselves squarely above it. The Salvadoran military may directly name a civilian president, as happened in April 1982, but no civilian president has the power to make even relatively minor changes in the military command structure.

Thus, for more than four years, ever since the October 1979 coup began the latest phase of El Salvador's relentlessly grim history, civilian politicians have said they were in a "process of control" over the army and security forces when in fact the reverse was true.

The young officers who had ousted Gen. Carlos Humberto Romero in 1979 were always strong on written ideals. They published a lengthy statement of principles the day of the coup in which they promised reforms and called for the establishment of truly democratic insitutions. Many civilian politicians were brought into the newly formed government, including even members of the Communist Party, and the military took only two of the five seats on the five-man "revolutionary" junta. But as promising as all this might have seemed, when the civilians and some of the more radical young officers tried to gain effective veto power over the more traditionalist Defense Minister José Guillermo García, he and the commanders he had appointed forced the civilians out. Ten weeks after the new government was formed, the three civilians on the junta and every civilian in the cabinet resigned. García, of course, remained.

Then the Christian Democrats joined the government on the basis of a sweeping agreement that this time the military would abide by the promises of the coup. It was during this period — after the security forces slaughtered several leftist protesters occupying Christian Democratic headquarters, after a death squad probably connected with the security forces murdered one of the party's most charismatic leaders, as members of government farming cooperatives were being killed in wholesale lots and the national university was shut down — that Christian Democratic leader José Napoleón Duarte talked the most about the "process of control."[6]

San Salvador Archbishop Oscar Romero, before he was assassinated in March of that year, described the Salvadoran reality much more accurately with one of those classic, anomalous-sounding Latin phrases: "Reform with repression."[7]

After considerable prodding from the United States, in March 1980 the military finally did decree what were supposed to be sweeping reforms. But the only ones ever put into effect were aimed at the only group of civilians, the oligarchy, that had ever been able to share or subvert the military's domination of the country. None were meant to, nor did, touch the army's own power. Those that might have affected the holdings of some officers were never enforced.[8]

And the repression? The U.S. press, prompted by the U.S. embassy, tended to explain it in circular terms. The murderers "of the extreme right" were simply political neanderthals. They killed all those people, presumably, just because they were there or because for some reason they were intent on destroying "the center." Certainly, they were out to stop the reforms.

In the complex netherworld of El Salvador's clandestine political violence all of the above may be true. Some murders were completely incomprehensible and much of the slaughter did grow out of vendettas so involved and so obscure that no one but the killers and, perhaps, the victims could be expected to decipher them. But a great deal of the murder in El Salvador was and is committed because the Salvadoran officer corps believes that on the most basic level, it works.

It is vital to remember this. The overall policy of repression, far from being the work of madmen who fail to understand the reality of their country, is carried out with cold calculation by officers who feel certain that Washington has no conception of where its demands are likely to lead. As they see it they are dealing with a logic — a reality, if you will — that Washington refuses to acknowledge. The human rights demands of Carter, of Reagan, of Congress are not enforced for much the same reason the *Nuevas Leyes* were not enforced four centuries ago: because to do so would very likely bring the whole structure of government crashing down. If Carlos V wanted gold, finally, he had to let the colonists get it by the means they chose otherwise they would simply go home, leaving him with no gold and no colony. If Washington wants to stop communism, it has found itself obliged to let the Salvadorans do the job as they, not as it, sees fit. To do otherwise, it would have to be ready to accept revolutionary change in the region. That, Washington has made clear, it will not do. The result, the Salvadoran military realizes, is de facto acceptance of the means it chooses to employ.

Ironically, but in line with the classic pattern, Washington has multiplied its demands on El Salvador in proportion to their ineffectiveness. Every time the United States sets goals and they are ignored, then changes the definition of its goals to make it seem, for reasons of domestic political consumption, that they were obeyed, the gap between what it says it wants and what it gets grows wider. Disobedience—or, rather, non-compliance—is endorsed.

Again, consider the way Washington read the events of 1980 in El Salvador. It emphasized the efficacy of reforms that did not work and attempted to disavow or deny the effectiveness of repression which did.

The immediate goal of the Salvadoran army and security forces—and of the United States—in 1980 was to prevent a takeover by the leftist-led guerrillas and their allied political organizations.[9] At this point in the Salvadoran conflict the latter were much more important than the former. The military resources of the rebels were extremely limited and their greatest strength, by far, lay not in force of arms but in their "mass organizations" made up of labor unions, student and peasant organizations that could be mobilized by the thousands in El Salvador's major cities and could shut down the country through strikes. The immediate goal of anyone interested in stopping the advances of the left had to be the elimination of the guerrillas' urban bases. This the government did. U.S. officials argued then and now that the land reform initiated in March 1980 played a major role in undercutting the guerrillas' popular support. They note that the same organizations that were able to march hundreds of thousands of people through San Salvador's streets on January 22, 1980, could not mount a successful general strike by August of the same year, and showed virtually no major support by the time they staged their abortive "final offensive" in January 1981.

But if the reforms did in fact undermine popular support for the guerrillas, and this is far from certain, they would have had their greatest impact in the countryside—whereas today the rebels are stronger than ever in the countryside.

The great setback for the guerrillas in 1980 came not in their rural strongholds but in the cities, not as a result of the reforms but precisely because of the ruthless repression that killed almost 10,000 people in a year, among them many key members of the rebel organizations.[10]

Washington repeatedly condemned the abuses as both morally wrong and politically counterproductive. U.S. Ambassador Robert White and his successors in the U.S. mission argued that right-wing death squads and the military's semi-clandestine slaughter ultimately benefitted the rebels; that people forced to choose sides by such violent tactics might be likely to choose the left; that on the international front the human rights issue was the most powerful weapon in the guerrilla arsenal. Yet this rather abstract reasoning, particularly at that point in the war, was difficult for many officers to understand. They did not see people flocking to the rebel banner as a result of the repression. Quite the contrary, they saw the rebel movement in the city dying. Literally.

As for the human rights "weapon" in the hands of the guerrillas, many officers probably underestimated its impact abroad in 1980 and 1981. But the certification process initiated by the U.S. Congress in 1982 to demand improvements on that front served after two or three instances to allay rather than aggravate the concerns of the most extreme officers. The certifications made it increasingly clear that the Reagan administration was not going to choose human rights over the fight against communism. The certification in the summer of 1983 drew little or no attention from the North American press and public, and by the fall the military could consider that whatever might have been lost on the human rights front was more than balanced by the elimination of the rebels' urban base. The high command wrote pages and pages of rules promoting the observance of human rights, so many pages that one must wonder what the semiliterate Salvadoran infantryman was expected to do with them. But the conviction remained among many officers that repression was not only useful, it was necessary, and that lip-service to human rights was all that the U.S. really demanded.

Events in the fall of 1983 suggest just how seriously Washington had been fooled, or had fooled itself about the Salvadoran army's response to its demands for improvements in human rights and improved "command and control." There had been embarrassments and anomalies all along. One example was the conduct of U.S.-trained batallions in the field. The commander of the first to enter combat, a generally capable officer of moderate politics by Salvadoran standards, was referred to around the embassy as "Thumbs-Behind-the-Back" Monterrosa because of recurrent reports about his units slaughtering civilians.[11] But throughout 1982 and early 1983 the U.S. State Department was at least able to argue that "abuses" by the security forces were decreasing and the "death squads" disappearing. The embassy's regular reports known as "grim grams" cited statistics based on local press accounts and noted, accurately, a general reduction of tension in the capital. U.S. policy was working, U.S. officials said. Its demands on the Salvadorans were understood and were being complied with, they said.

In retrospect it is now apparent that the decline in urban slaughter came about less because of improved command and control than because the left had basically abandoned the capital after January 1981. With few suspects there were fewer killings. Murder in the countryside, meanwhile, was less frequently reported in the local papers and thus did not show up in the "grim gram" statistics. As soon as the left's efforts to renew operations and organizing in the capital became evident in mid-1983, the death squads and the "abuses" began to rise once again. The "process of control" over the armed forces, at least insofar as the slaughter of suspected rebel sympathizers was concerned, proved once again to be a paper promise.

Compounding the political problems raised by the revival of the death squads in the cities, from Washington's viewpoint, was the military dilemma provoked by the Salvadoran army's seeming inability to mount effective campaigns against any force capable of shooting back. At weekly background briefings in the U.S. embassy during 1982 and 1983, top U.S. advisers talked to the press about the ineptness of many Salvadoran commanders, especially those who had proved unable or unwilling to adopt the kind of search and destroy tactics the Pentagon recommended.

The advisers blamed the cliquishness of the Salvadoran officer corps for much of the problem. Men who had known each other since they were in their teens, who were bound by tradition, by *compadrazco*, in some instances by marriage, tended to cover for each others' abuses or incompetence in any case, and all the more so when the charges were coming from foreigners considered ignorant of Salvadoran realities. As this deeply imbedded cronyism proved virtually impossible for Washington to overcome there was increasing talk in early 1983 about what then-U.S. Ambassador Deane Hinton called "generational change": training virtually an entire new officer corps from the ground up. Salvadoran ninety-day wonders would not only emerge from their training at Fort Benning, Georgia, as better soldiers, they would be transformed overnight, as it were, from Latin American soldiers into North American soldiers.

Not surprisingly, the Salvadorans are remaining Salvadorans. The U.S.-trained second lieutenants and cadets are carefully watched by their superiors to make sure they conform to the traditions of the Salvadoran, not the United States army.

Meanwhile the most extreme right-wing clique of officers in the army has not only proved impervious to Washington's dictates, it has prospered and become ever more influential. This group, conspicuous for its fascist ideology and peculiarly tight-knit personal relationships, is dominated by Col. Nicolás Carranza and represented most publicly by Constituent Assembly President ex-Major Roberto d'Aubuisson.

Three years ago that group appeared to have been squeezed out of any significant role in the army or the nation's politics. Its senior commanders had been removed from positions of authority by then-Defense Minister García after their ties to the death squads had become embarassingly public and their ultra-rightist ideology made them too intractable to control.[12]

Since former Guardia Nacional Commander Gen. Carlos Eugenio Vides Casanova took over the defense ministry in April 1983, however, those officers have reemerged with more conspicuous power than they ever had before. A key element in their resurgence has been their adoption of Washington's language even as they ignore its principles. They have embraced the ideal of "professionalism," the latest Pentagon buzzword for a "nonpartisan constabulary." Senior U.S. advisers repeatedly have cited them as examples they wish the rest of the Salvadoran officer corps would follow. Yet these golden boys have a persistent way of becoming grave embarrassments;

the very model of a modern lieutenant colonel proves either murderous or mutinous or both.

One of the most conspicuous examples is Lt. Col. Jorge Adalberto Cruz, commander of Morazán province. He was among those officers arrested with d'Aubuisson while plotting a coup against the Christian Democratic junta in May 1980. Papers seized with this group suggested links to the death squads and to the assassination a few weeks earlier of San Salvador's archbishop. Shipped off to the Chilean police academy for two years, Cruz is now back in El Salvador commanding the front-line garrison in San Francisco Gotera. In August 1983 he openly denounced El Salvador's political parties, said flatly that his country is not ready for U.S.-style democracy, and named several other commanders in the region as incompetent. As of December 1983, he was still in command in Gotera.[13]

Lt. Col. Mario Denis Morán was head of the Guardia Nacional intelligence unit in December 1980 when four North American churchwomen were killed by members of that security force. When two U.S. labor advisors and the head of the Salvadoran agrarian reform agency were gunned down in the Sheraton Hotel a few weeks later, Morán was there. Although no conclusive evidence has implicated him in the crime, and he reportedly "passed" a lie-detector test, it is suggestive, certainly, that his personal bodyguard and that of his second-in-command have confessed to being the trigger men. After that, Morán spent two years attached to various Salvadoran embassies in South America before Vides Casanova brought him back to command the garrison at Zacatecoluca—the same town, as it happens, where the alleged killers of the nuns are being tried.

The path to professional redemption for these officers was opened up by one of their old classmates, Lt. Col. Sigifredo Ochoa. As acting head of the notorious Treasury Police in the days immediately following the October coup, Ochoa had been implicated in the politically sensitive murder of a sacristan in one of San Salvador's working-class barrios.[14] He was shipped off to diplomatic exile almost immediately. Then on his return to El Salvador he was given command of the rugged, poor, remote and guerrilla-infested province of Cabañas. In less than a year he had "pacified" his territory and established himself not only as the dominant military force, but the political leader of the province. U.S. Military Group Commander Col. John Waghelstein repeatedly lauded him as the most effective departmental commander in the Salvadoran army. But in January 1983, García, apparently irritated with Ochoa's increasing notoriety, and certainly aware of his close personal connections with d'Aubuisson and the ultra-rightists, ordered Ochoa to give up his command once again and accept de facto exile in Uruguay.

Ochoa's reported response was short and simple as he initiated a six-day mutiny that effectively ended García's authority and eventually led to García's removal, throwing the Salvadoran military into the renewed, relentless series

of intrigues that increasingly crippled it through the course of the
year.

"Obedezco," said Ochoa, "pero no cumplo."[15]

III

Once the pivotal power in the country had proved able to substitute words
for deeds on the basic question of command and control, reform and repression, such institutions as the courts and such events as elections can hardly
be expected to bring substantial change. At best they add a little superficial
complexity to the show of obeisance, a bit of nuance to the reality of non-
compliance with Washington's expressed wishes. At worst they may undermine everything Washington says it is trying to do in Central America.

The most dramatic test case of North American will versus Salvadoran
stonewalling has centered on the murder of United States citizens, the investigation of the crimes and the prosecution, or as it were, the non-
prosecution of the killers.

Washington has retreated from virtually every demand it has made on
the Salvadoran government regarding these cases. After four churchwomen
were killed on December 2, 1980, the Carter administration suspended all
economic and military aid to the country. But the economic assistance was
renewed after a few days, and after the guerrillas' offensive six weeks later
military aid was not only renewed but greatly increased by the new Reagan
administration.

During the first four months of the Reagan administration, the Salvadoran
armed forces made only the most grudging movement on the cases under
constant pressure from U.S. chargé d'affaires Frederic Chapin. According
to U.S. diplomats serving in El Salvador at the time, Col. Vides Casanova
was particularly obstructive until late in the investigation.[16]

When five enlisted members of the Salvadoran Guardia Nacional were
finally detained in the late spring of 1981, senior officials at the U.S embassy made it clear that they did not believe there was sufficient evidence
to pursue the question of who higher up in the military might have ordered
the murders. Off the record, they said frankly they had no interest in following
up the question of a cover-up. Then, when it became apparent in the spring
of 1983 that Vides Casanova would become the new Salvadoran defense
minister, the U.S. embassy in El Salvador began the arduous job of
rehabilitating his reputation, claiming that he had provided vital help all along
the way.[17]

Washington did try to make some headway against higher Salvadoran officials allegedly involved with another case: the murder of the two U.S. labor advisers and the head of the Salvadoran agrarian reform institute just a month after the killing of the nuns. Not only were senior members of the Guardia Nacional such as then-Major Mario Denis Morán and Lt. Isidro Lopez Sibrian apparently involved, but wealthy right-wing businessmen were implicated as well. Despite what the embassy felt was an open and shut case, however, charges proved impossible to sustain in El Salvador's courts against anyone but the two trigger-men—enlisted men who confessed.

It was frustration with this case in October 1982 that led then-Ambassador Hinton to denounce what he called El Salvador's "mafia." In effect he was making the strongest accusations against members of the Salvadoran military since the Reagan administration took office. But then the White House, through press leaks, appeared to disavow Hinton's address. From that point on, although Hinton continued for a while to believe that some means of working through the courts might be found, no movement was made in the prosecution of the case.

By the time Hinton's replacement, U.S. Ambassador Thomas Pickering and President Alvaro Magaña began trying to curtail the resurgence of the death squads in the fall of 1983, they had given up any intention of using the country's courts as a vehicle for the operation.[18]

The most right-wing elements of the military were mounting a direct challenge to Magaña's authority and, by inference, to that of the United States. They used death squads and the threat of death squad killings as a tool in this showdown, first menacing American reporters, then moving against labor leaders who were heavily backed by the U.S. embassy.[19] Magaña and the embassy sought ways of striking back, but the court system was considered, by this point, worse than useless. Magaña, according to one source close to him, believed that any attempt at a showdown in the courts would end up undermining his own tenuous authority over the armed forces, since every previous attempt to move through legal channels in prosecuting those linked to the death squads has resulted in failure.[20]

In order to bypass the courts, the embassy and the presidency began leaking information about several middle-level army officers believed involved with the death squads. But at the same time care was taken not to cast the net too widely. U.S. officials in San Salvador and Washington were concerned that the pattern of complicity with the ultra-right and death squads inside the armed forces touched precisely those officers on whom they depended to fight the war.[21]

The Salvadoran military had been reluctant but finally willing to enforce Washington's demands in the cases of a few enlisted men if that was what it took to demonstrate the necessary pro forma obeisance. But if compliance of a higher degree was demanded, Washington and El Salvador's president had to resort to complex Machiavellian strategems in order to win even short-term gains against the most radical element of the government, even though that government was almost entirely dependent on Washington's aid for its survival.

In the meantime, the political centerpiece of Washington's policy toward El Salvador, "free elections," became more and more obviously untenable.

The Reagan administration had dramatically elevated the already high level of double-think on this question after the much publicized polling of March 1982. There was nothing new about elections in El Salvador. The same General Romero ousted as a "dicatator" in the October 1979 coup had been duly elected in at least superficial accordance with the country's laws only two years before. Most of El Salvador's rulers in this century have participated in similar exercises. But the difference this time around was that they were supposed to be fair. Decisions would be left up to the electorate, the government would have the consent of the governed as well as the international legitimacy needed to start resolving the nation's problems. In early 1982 the Reagan administration in Washington went so far as to say, several times, that elections were *the* political solution for El Salvador, even if Ambassador Hinton, on the ground, found it difficult to make such a patently naive assessment.[22]

The elections of March 1982 sold a misleading image of democratic development in El Salvador to the people of the United States and Europe. But worse, that image was based on a bill of goods that was sold to the war-weary Salvadorans themselves.

The Salvadoran left, which suffered a tremendous, if brief, propaganda defeat on election day 1982 has attempted to rationalize the events of that day by emphasizing the "coercion" that compelled people to turn out in massive lines all over the nation to cast their ballots. The left has also done much arithmetical analysis of the time it would take each person to vote, the number of polling places, and so on, in an effort to lop a couple of hundred thousand off the voter turnout officially estimated at over 1 million people (a phenomenal figure in a nation whose total population is less than 5 million). But such Jesuitical arguments are not altogether convincing to those reporters who spent election day traveling around the country and saw many people braving the very direct threat of live gunfire at the hands of the guerrillas in order to vote.

No, it was apparent at the time that the incentive for many if not most people, was hope rather than fear. And that hope was encouraged through a cynical publicity campaign directly funded by Washington.

According to U.S. embassy documents, the U.S. Agency for International Development put $240,000 into the Salvadoran Central Election's Council's efforts to convince the Salvadoran people that their vote was "the solution." By the estimate of Jorge Bustamante, president of the council at the time, that represented 60% of the funds spent on its get-out-the-vote initiatives. U.S. officials in San Salvador said another $200,000 was provided by the Reagan administration to bring in the international observers who watched the polling and endorsed the result.

"Our role," said Bustamante at the election council, "was to get two things: free elections and massive elections."

With the Marxist-led rebels and their more moderate political allies boycotting the polls and calling for the rest of the nation to follow suit, the question of how many people would vote was portrayed as a kind of referendum on the guerrillas regardless of who the voters ultimately chose on the ballot.

"In order to get the people to vote," Bustamante said in one interview, "we were not telling them lies, [but] maybe we were naive." He pointed to a wall full of advertisements: a picture of a fist, a photo of a forlorn little girl, a shroud covered corpse, a windshield riddled with bullets. "This is the first part of the campaign. Violence. What can you do to end the violence? Elections might be a way to end the violence. . . . It did not come out that way, but it's not my fault."

Later stages in the campaign included the production of a sophisticated, full-color comic book inserted in newspapers a few days before the vote. The leader of the guerrillas vaguely resembled a sinister brown-skinned version of the Hulk.

And what did all that effort buy? A short-term propaganda victory over the left, and long-term disillusionment. As a bus driver in San Salvador suggested, people voted for peace and all they got was a constituent assembly full of "gunslingers." Even from Washington's viewpoint, the big winner at the polls was altogether the wrong man.

Unfortunately for the optimists, however, the wrong people got elected. Convinced, at least publicly, that the reforms had been a tremendous success, many U.S. officials believed the Christian Democratic regime that implemented them would win handily. Instead, the several parties to the right of the Christian Democrats, lead by d'Aubuisson's Nationalistic Republican Alliance, joined forces to command the majority of seats in the newly elected constituent assembly. In order to keep d'Aubuisson from being appointed acting president of the nation, which the clearly articulated democratic rules of the assembly would have permitted, the embassy and the High Command it backed at that time under General García stepped in to dicatate the choice of president: Magaña, who was not a member of a party but had close ties with top military leaders dating back to their days at high school; Magaña, for whom not a single vote was cast at the polls, was named president by the armed forces and the U.S. embassy. The assembly merely ratified the decision.

With the non-election of Magaña, Washington in effect publicly endorsed the old discrepancy between high-flown ideals and pragmatic realities. It became complicit in evading its own goals.

As the Spring 1984 date for the direct election of the president approached, Magaña and the U.S. embassy saw the gap between what they had said they wanted for El Salvador and the pragmatic demands of sustaining the regime widen into an abyss. The fascist right wing of the officer corps was maneuvering itself into a position to veto the outcome of the elections should Duarte somehow win them, and if d'Aubuisson should take the prize this time in direct elections there would be no way to deprive him of it without totally discrediting the democratic facade Wahington had labored so long to build.

As of December 1983 many of the same Salvadoran moderates who had previously advocated elections were looking for ways to postpone them lest they tear the country apart.

The erratic course of U.S. policy in El Salvador has led it to a point where it no longer appears to expect – and perhaps does not even hope – that its substantive demands will be complied with. It has increasingly endorsed the facade of democracy and democratic institutions and is now attempting to work behind the false front to achieve much more limited goals than it originally thought possible: as in its attempts to curb the death squads, for instance. It has adopted the pragmatism of its clients. But as Washington increasingly accepts the discrepancy between ideals and realities, in effect endorsing those who obey its edicts without carrying them out, it confronts an ever more complex and frustrating situation.

The tendency of the Salvadoran military has become not only not to comply, but not even to obey, and the Central American situation as a result is rapidly careening out of control. For several years Guatemala has made great show of ignoring Washington's wishes altogether. Even in Honduras the pretenses of democracy are slipping away as the chief of the armed forces increasingly overshadows the elected president.

Having stumbled insensibly into the quagmire by failing to discern the difference between words and deeds on the part of its clients, Washington may soon confront a situation – if indeed it does not already – in which its clients are not only not obedient to its policies, but in fact are in command of them.

NOTES

1. This general reading of colonial history is to be found in Herring, Hubert, *A History of Latin America from the Beginning to the Present,* Knopf, New York, 1969, pp. 154-156, and in Lambert, Jacques, *Latin America: Social Structure and Political Institutions,* University of California Press, Berkeley, 1967, pp. 114-121.
2. Another translation is "I obey but do not carry out." Every historian seems to find a different way of translating this anomalous phrase. Herring uses "I obey but do not enforce." Another variant is "I obey but do not execute," the connotations of which are perhaps excessively suggestive in the context of this paper.

3. *Op. cit.,* Lambert, pp. 123-124.
4. Millett, Richard, *Guardians of the Dynasty,* Orbis, Maryknoll N.Y., 1977 p. 41.
5. *Ibid.,* pp. 112-113.
6. This was a theme reiterated in several press conferences which I attended by then-Junta member José Napoleón Duarte and also in interviews with him and other Christian Democratic officials during the course of 1980.
7. See Archbishop Oscar A. Romero's letter to President Jimmy Carter, February 17, 1980, and Dickey, C., "U.S. Warned on Assisting El Salvador," *The Washington Post,* February 19, 1980, p. A1.
8. Dickey, C., "El Salvador's Dilemma: Hopes Raised by Land Reform Program Undermined by Political Violence," *The Washington Post,* March 14, 1980, p. A1 for an early discussion of this problem. For a more recent one, see Dickey, C., "Dreams of Agrarian Reform Seem to be Dying in El Salvador," *The Washington Post,* October 3, 1983, p. A12.
9. Interviews with James Cheek, acting chargé d'affaires of the U.S. embassy in San Salvador during week of Feburary 17-24, 1980, and with U.S. Ambassador Robert White in June-July 1980. Also see Dickey, C., "Centrists Feel a Squeeze in El Salvador," *The Washington Post,* February 27, 1980 p. A1.
10. Americas Watch Committee and the American Civil Liberties Union, *Report on Human Rights in El Salvador,* Janury 26th, 1982, Vintage, New York, 1982, p. xxvi. The damage done to the rebel organizations has been recognized by several rebel leaders in the last year, including Joaquín Villalobos in his October 1982 interview with Marta Harnecker, available in Managua as a "Punto Final" monograph.
11. The officials were talking, specifically, about Lt. Col. Domingo Monterrosa, whose troops were responsible for the infamous Mozote massacre of December 1981 and for the more recent killing of about 20 peasants at the village of San Nicolás.
12. The Christian Democrats made up a specific list of about 20 names of officers they wanted removed, and with the exception of García's own key crony who headed the Treasury Police, they were.
13. H.D.P., "Duel in the Jungle," *Rolling Stone,* No. 407, October 27, 1983, p. 72.
14. Interviews with senior Salvadoran military officers, October 1983.
15. This remark is noted in the files of both the U.S. embassy and the "José Simeon Cañas" University of Central America in San Salvador.
16. Interviews with William Hallman, former chief of the political section at the U.S. embassy in San Salvador and with other officials who served in the embassy during the spring of 1981. Frederic Chapin, who was chargé d'affaires for four months, told the assembled diplomatic corps in his farewell remarks that there were times he felt more as if he were running a police station than a U.S. embassy because of his frustrations investigating the killings of U.S. citizens.
17. Massing, Michael, "About-Face on El Salvador," *The Columbia Journalism Review,* Vol. 22, No. 4, pp. 42-49.
18. Dickey, C., "Behind El Salvador's Death Squads," *The New Republic,* Vol. 189, No. 26, December 26, 1983.
19. *Ibid.*
20. Notes from interviews with senior Salvadoran government officials, October 1983.
21. *Op. cit.,* Dickey, *The New Republic.*
22. Dickey, C., "U.S. Envoy Expresses Doubts," *The Washington Post,* January 31, 1982, p. A1.

2
THE BURDENS OF THE PAST

Walter LaFeber

In 1906 senior military officials asked President Theodore Roosevelt for a special favor. They wondered whether he might give U.S. diplomats and naval commanders on the spot sufficient authority to stop Central American revolts and permanently stabilize the area. The request reached the desk of Assistant Secretary of State Alvey A. Adee. A wise, experienced man, Adee had served as the department's permanent bureacracy for a quarter century. "How could we do this," he jotted on the request, "without actually acquiring all these little countries?" The proposal promptly died.[1]

Not since pre-Civil War days, when pro-slave filibusterers actually controlled Nicaragua for a short time, have Washington officials seriously considered "acquiring" Central America. The revolts that plagued Roosevelt's advisers have meanwhile matured into revolutions. Nearly 80 years after the Rough Rider publicly vowed to act as "an international police power" to halt the "chronic wrongdoing" of the Caribbean-Central American regimes,[2] the United States has still not found the magic formula that can transform its unquestioned power in the area into equitable economic development, military security, and political stability. The failure has not been due to lack of effort. Contrary to the conventional wisdom sometimes heard in Washington, the problem cannot be blamed on North American neglect of Central America. The United States landed troops in the region some 20 times between 1898 and 1920 alone. During the 1920s it learned in the Dominican Republic, and particularly in Nicaragua, how to train native national guards and place them under pro-U.S. officers to replace the increasingly unpopular marines and to maintain the peace. After World War II, these forces received regular military aid, as well as training, at North American bases. During the 1950s, the Central Intelligence Agency worked closely with U.S.-trained Guatemalan officers who had gone into exile to oppose the reformist governments. In 1954, these officers acted as a surrogate U.S. force to overthrow

49

the Guatemalan government and then instituted a brutal military regime. As revolutionary bands spread in the region during the 1960s, the Kennedy and Johnson administrations trained Central American officers in sophisticated civic action and counterinsurgency techniques. During the 1970s, President Richard Nixon accepted the advice of Governor Nelson Rockefeller, one of the most knowledgeable North Americans about the regions to the south, and stressed increased arms aid while vowing to work with any de facto government. In reality, Nixon's policy meant working with the military regimes that either ran or dominated every Central American nation except Costa Rica. After its 1948 civil war, the Costa Ricans disbanded their army and depended on highly efficient police forces to maintain order. With a long democratic tradition, a viable middle class, a relatively equitable economic system and a more homogeneous population, Costa Rica is the exception to the generalizations that apply to Guatemala, Honduras, El Salvador, and Nicaragua.

This long relationship with the Central American military has ironically accelerated revolutionary activity in Central America since 1960 and steadily radicalized the revolutionary movements themselves. Central American militaries have not been able to exterminate these movements, regardless of the amount of North American help. Even Guatemala, which since the 1950s has been operated by a staunchly independent army with a strong, almost exclusive, allegiance to its own institution, has been able neither to stop revolution nor, most recently, to conceal growing divisions in its own ranks. Nicaragua's National Guard, despite massive U.S. help, nearly disintegrated during the crisis caused by the 1972 earthquake. As the forces of dictator Anastasio Somoza joined in looting or rushed home to be with families, only U.S. troops quickly flown in from the Panama Canal Zone managed to maintain a semblance of order — and Somoza's authority. Seven years later the guard proved to be no match for the less well-armed troops of the Sandinista revolution. In the early 1980s a similar story is being played out in El Salvador where, despite massive U.S. aid, army morale and reenlistments are dangerously low. In Honduras, corruption and an incompetent officer corps have prevented the U.S.-trained and equipped army from becoming any match for the Sandinista military.

Throughout the twentieth century, economic development programs have often been the companion of military aid as the United States, Sisyphus-like, tried to stabilize Central America. Economic policies, like military approaches, have gone through various incarnations. The Truman and Eisenhower administrations stressed trade and private investment. This view began to change in the late 1950s with the surprising success of Fidel Castro in Cuba and a sharp downturn in Latin American economies. President John F. Kennedy responded with a massive government and private sector program in the Alliance for Progress. When (as described below) the Alliance failed, the Nixon administration returned to the traditional emphasis upon the private sector. The real stress in Nixon's policy was on military security, not economic development, and that emphasis continued into the 1980s. Ronald Reagan's Caribbean Basin Initiative (CBI) and his advisers' discussions about a "Marshall Plan for Central America" have amounted to little as yet. The CBI's proposed $350 million hardly begins to replace the billions of dollars that have fled the region's war-torn economies since the 1970s. The Marshall Plan idea requires, but does not create, political stability and responsible governments to handle funds, much as Western European governments and bureacrats handled the original Plan's monies in the late 1940s. The necessary stability, economic infrastructure, responsible governments, and efficient bureaucracies do not exist in Central America outside of Costa Rica. Consequently, U.S. development plans have consistently failed to create either stability or more equitable societies. President Eisenhower once complained to his Cabinet, "We put a coin in the tin cup and yet we know the tin cup is still going to be there tomorrow."[3]

As the United States has failed to provide stability through military or economic tactics, so it has been unable to discover a workable political approach. This inability can be traced to a failure to comprehend the political realities of Central America. Since at least Woodrow Wilson's presidency, for example, the United States has repeatedly tried to encourage stability by sponsoring elections. Other than Costa Rica, however, no Central American country has a tradition of fair and open elections. In some countries, such as Nicaragua between 1912 and 1927, Guatemala during the 1954 to 1963 years, or El Salvador in 1982, heavy-handed U.S. involvement in the election process has actually helped de-legitimate what was supposed to be a legitimizing act. "Elections" in Central American politics bear even less resemblance to the North American process than, say, Yankee football resembles Latin American *fútbol*. The United States has tried to use elections to stabilize and legitimate regimes, but has instead only illustrated the Central American joke that the ballot box is *La Urna Magica* — the Magic Box that produces any desired result. They can be no more democratic and open than the societies in which they occur.

The history of the last century reveals that U.S. military intervention, economic aid, and elections have not been able to stablize and more equitably develop Central America. U.S. policies might have given some hope in the simpler pre-1920 years, but when applied in areas where mass revolutionary movements exist, the policies have worsened, not improved, the crises.

Five brief case studies provide evidence to support these generalizations. The first addresses the initial U.S. military intervention in Honduras that largely established the course of the Central American nation during the 20th century. The second describes the North American occupation of Nicaragua between 1912 and 1933. This involvement marked a major transition in U.S.

relations with the region: it created the belief that a Washington-built indigenous military force could replace the Marines. After the bitter experience in Nicaragua during the 1920s, U.S. officials have never again tried to maintain political stability by militarily occupying a Central American nation. The third case study examines the overthrow of an elected Guatemalan government in 1954 by a U.S.-trained force. For the first time, North Americans used military power to stop an attempt by an elected government to carry out a program of indigenous economic and political liberalization. The fourth case examines the Alliance for Progress, not only for its better-known economic objectives, but for the military aid program that necessarily became an ever more important part of the Alliance. The final section analyzes post-1960 developments in El Salvador, where the United States has become mired down in fighting revolution. The Salvadoran experience vividly demonstrates that without major political change, economic aid programs helped cause, not prevent, revolution. Two general conclusions can then be drawn from these case studies.

U.S. INTERVENTION IN HONDURAS

Honduras occupies a highly strategic position, with borders on three of the other four Central American countries and an Atlantic coastline easily accessible from the United States. Its history also links it to the United States. North Americans controlled the major export industry (bananas), the transportation network, and the government soon after their first major investments in the 1890s. Honduras, along with El Salvador, has also become most dependent on U.S. military aid. The two forms of dependency, economic and military, are not unrelated.

U.S. forces periodically landed in Honduras during the late 19th century to quell local revolts and protect North American interests, but the first significant intervention occurred in 1911-1912. The occasion was the rise to power of Miguel Dávila, who, apparently not understanding the rules, began to associate with anti-U.S. politicians in the region and also with wealthy U.S. financiers, including J. P. Morgan, who contemplated assuming the government's debt. The banana kings, led by a U.S. investor, Sam Zemmurray, disliked both Dávila's anti-American friends and the prospect of Morgan's involvement. Zemmurray helped organize an expedition in New Orleans that tried to overthrow the Dávila regime. The U.S. Navy intervened to stop the fighting, and the U.S. consul then named an acting president. Dávila's power collapsed, Zemmurray's was firmly entrenched, and from behind the facade of the Honduras government, North American investors again controlled the economic and political systems.

U.S. military forces helped produce a success story, judging at least from the raw figures. Between 1913 and 1929, Honduran exports leaped from $3 million ($2 million in bananas), to $25 million (including $21 million worth of bananas). Forty million dollars of North American investment controlled the economy. This capital, however, failed to immunize Honduras against political revolts, and the United States had to dispatch troops six more times before 1925. During the 1930s and 1940s, authoritarian rulers managed to stabilize the nation. But in the early 1950s, pressure again built up. Labor unions demanded better wages and conditions from the banana companies. A successful strike ushered in a period of liberal reform between 1957 and 1963, just as the Alliance for Progress got underway.

Washington's policies in Honduras during those decades after 1912 might be viewed as strong evidence for the good results that can be produced by U.S. military and economic intervention. Such a view, however, confuses a unique past with a highly complex present. That past, unlike the present, was not haunted by mass revolutionary movements, precedents of a successful anti-U.S. insurgency, hemispheric economic models that served as an alternative to North American capitalism, and global villagers, who through modern technology, could act as a chorus — and sometimes as direct participants — in the drama. These complications began to appear in the 1950s as the Honduran liberals found themselves at cross purposes with the foreign investors and the army. Liberals were bolstered but private investment discouraged by new labor laws, social security measures, corporate taxes, and promises of land reform. That discouragement proved costly, for the basic economy remained the system of the 1920s. Two U.S. companies controlled fully half the country's exports and owned the key railroads which, in any case, had been built not for local use but to ship bananas to ports. The army had its own concerns, especially with the civil guard which the liberal president, Ramón Villeda Morales, had created for his personal protection. In 1963, the military turned on the guard and, in a brief struggle, wiped it out. An army strongman replaced Villeda Morales. Reform stopped. U.S. investment returned and Honduran dependence on the United States tightened.[4]

Such dependence, however, now created dangers. As industry, and especially agriculture, became capital intensive, unemployment rose. The benefits of new foreign investments, such as the purchase of the two largest financial institutions by New York banks, too seldom reached the grass roots. More than half the children were malnourished, 88% of the homes did not have clean piped water, 49 years was the average adult life expectancy, and the country's poverty ranked next to Haiti's as the worst in the hemisphere.[5] The U.S.-equipped army maintained order and controlled the country despite the election of a civilian president in 1981. Civilians had little political power; the 1957 Constitution had placed the military forces directly under the chief of the armed forces, not the president.[6] As revolutions accelerated in nearby Nicaragua, El Salvador, and Guatemala during the late 1970s, the United States pumped increasing amounts of military aid into Honduras, including 54 military advisers who in 1981 began teaching rural counterinsurgency tactics to friendly armies in the region.

Such tactics were now required in the Honduran countryside itself. In the fall of 1981, a left-wing guerrilla group declared that the shooting of two U.S. military advisers and the bombing of the Honduran Congress marked the beginnings of an "armed struggle against Yankee imperialism."[7] The U.S. military presence grew as the Reagan administration stepped up the anti-Sandinista war along the Honduran-Nicaraguan border. But this presence found its major Central American base to be shaky. Corruption and inefficiency were so rampant that, despite a quarter century of help, the Honduran army remained dependent on the United States. A U.S. Army colonel remarked in early 1982 that the force "would have to commandeer every school bus in the country" simply in order to mobilize.[8] A Salvadoran guerrilla leader declared that his forces purchased the rifles they needed in Honduras: "For arms and drugs, Honduras is the most important market in Central America."[9]

The 1911-1912 intervention had placed an elite faction in power that cooperated with, and made Honduras totally dependent on, the United States. By the late 1960s, that dependency had so unbalanced the nation's development that the army became the main instrument for stability. By the 1980s, as U.S. dependence on Honduran bases grew, that instrument, like the economy, grew increasingly brittle. If the United States continues to depend on Honduras as its key strategic base in Central America, it depends on a country whose primary assets are its coastline and borders. Its weaknesses are its terrible poverty, skewed economic development, powerless civilian government, and highly corruptible army. In other words, the core of Washington's closest Central American ally is hollow.

THE MARINES IN NICARAGUA

At the same time that U.S. power removed the uncooperative Dávila in Honduras, Nicaraguan President José Santos Zelaya had long been fighting against the growing Yankee presence in the region. Nicaragua's first major 20th century nationalist figure (and revered by the Sandinistas in the 1980s), Zelaya had tightly controlled the nation's affairs and was especially vigorous in preventing foreigners, including resident North Americans, from cutting into Nicaraguan concessions. He meanwhile interfered in other Central American nations' affairs in an effort to enhance his personal power and create a broad anti-U.S. front. In 1909, an anti-Zelaya group in Bluefields triggered an uprising with the full support of the U.S. consul. The revolt centered on the Atlantic coast where North American interests were concentrated. Zelaya caught two U.S. soldiers of fortune laying dynamite to blow up one of his troop boats and promptly executed both.

He carried out the executions despite strong protests from Secretary of State Philander C. Knox. A noted banker and corporate lawyer, Knox had his own plans for using U.S. investment to stabilize Latin America. He seized upon Zelaya's action to dispatch U.S. Marines, depose the Nicaraguan ruler, and establish Adolfo Díaz, a former clerk in a U.S. firm in Bluefields, as president. Knox next negotiated deals with the pliant Díaz that placed Nicaraguan finances and transportation in the hands of New York City banks. Customs houses fell under the control of a U.S. agent.

Knox and President William Howard Taft believed they had discovered the formula of how to stabilize Central America while profiting North American investors. As Knox explained in early 1912:

> In Central America the administration seeks to substitute dollars for bullets by arranging, through American bankers, loans for the rehabilitation of the finances of Nicaragua and Honduras. The conventions with those countries . . . will take the customs houses out of politics. . . . By this policy we shall help the people of these rich countries to enjoy prosperity instead of almost incessant revolution and devastation. We shall do noble work. [10]

Unhappily for Knox's plan, angry Nicaraguans accused Díaz of auctioning off his country. The president appealed for protection, and Taft landed 2,600 marines to quell the rebellion. A top State Department official, Francis Huntington-Wilson, advanced a domino theory to justify smashing the revolt before it could spread to Cuba, Panama, or Mexico.[11] In reality, of course, the policy did nothing to improve conditions in neighboring nations. More to the point, the intervention did not end the unrest in Nicaragua itself. The marines had to remain for the next thirteen years to maintain peace and oversee elections. Fresh agreements meanwhile gave the bankers the remainder of the Nicaraguan railway system and granted the United States the right to build naval bases and a future isthmian canal in the country. The marines thus acted as a shield while the U.S.-directed development of Nicaragua accelerated. In the political arena the troops ensured tranquillity while the Conservative Party ensured its power by fixing presidential elections. The troops finally left in August 1925. In the words of one North American critic, "Peace reigned in Nicaragua for three weeks, four days, and thirteen hours. . . . "[12]

The Liberal Party rapidly tried to gain power in the only way possible, by force of arms. That attempt occurred, however, as the region still felt the aftershocks of the Mexican Revolution, an upheaval the United States had tried to control with several military interventions and constant political pressure. As a result of Washington's efforts, Mexico had become a center of anti-Yankeeism. When the Mexicans moved to support the Nicaraguan Liberals, President Calvin Coolidge and his top State Department advisers immediately branded the Mexicans the Bolsheviks of the hemisphere. Coolidge then ordered the marines to return to Managua. A State Department explanation entitled "Bolshevik Aims and Policies in Mexico and Latin America" was closely examined and then labeled "drivel" by *The Baltimore Sun*, a judgment historians continue to hold valid.[13]

The charges of "Bolshevism" now assumed an interesting meaning. They did not indicate that a Soviet base was about to appear in Central America; such a possibility was so remote that it was hardly imagined. Coolidge instead worried that the Mexican revolution challenged both the network of U.S. investments in the region and the military interventions that for several decades had protected those holdings and maintained stability. His charge of Bolshevik influence merely provided a convenient, well-understood rationale for Washington's interference. The U.S. troops had returned in 1927 to protect a Nicaraguan regime that had become so addicted to North American dollars and soldiers that it no longer could function independently.[14]

The U.S. forces who reentered Nicaragua in 1927 encountered ominous signs. The War Department's policies and the financial investments had created not stability and closer ties between North Americans and Nicaraguans, but a nationalism easily exploited by a new type of revolutionary. The revolutionary leader was Augusto César Sandino. His support arose especially from the peasants who had long been exploited by the urban elites. His cause was to drive the United States out of his country.[15] Washington officials supervised an election in 1927 that blocked Mexican influence, but they had little success against Sandino's forces. Demands meanwhile grew in Congress that U.S. troops (whose numbers had grown from 1,200 in 1927 to 5,400 a year later in an effort to combat Sandino's guerrilla-like tactics) be brought home. The second intervention was becoming too costly politically and economically.[16] In 1932 President Herbert Hoover announced the troops would come home in early 1933. He left behind, however, a native national guard, trained by the United States and designed to act as a politically neutral referee in mediating future crisis.

The Washington-appointed commander of the guard, Anastasio Somoza, seized the power but scorned the neutrality. After U.S. troops left, Sandino laid down his arms and opened negotiations with the Nicaraguan government. Somoza murdered him and his top aides in cold blood. Two years later in 1936, Somoza used the guard's power to vault himself into the presidency. The U.S. Department of State refused to help the civilian government on the interesting grounds that North Americans should not interfere in Nicaragua's internal affairs.[17]

The United States left behind a stable, if dismaying situation. Overwhelming numbers of the population had so few schools, health facilities, or political rights (except to pay taxes regularly) that Sandino's anti-Yankeeism had thrived. The United States nevertheless believed it had resolved the problem by giving Somoza power. The guard commander established a dictatorship, and worked closely with U.S. investors and diplomats while bringing much of the most profitable industry and productive land under the control of his family and fellow national guard officers. By 1949 a State Department intelligence report noted that Nicaraguans endured "repression, widespread illiteracy, intimidation, and poverty."[18] A two-decade-long U.S. attempt to forestall Zelaya's Nicaragua terminated in Somoza's Nicaragua.

THE GUATEMALAN EXPERIENCE

Honduras and Nicaragua were Washington's closest allies in the region, but Guatemala had been the dominant Central American power since colonial days. It was also a weather vane; Guatemalans tended to experience problems that only later afflicted the people of smaller nations. So it was in 1944 when a revolt overthrew a long-time dictator and, the following year, brought to power Juan José Arevalo. Formerly an exiled university professor, Arevalo typified in many ways the small new middle class that led the revolt. He advocated a reform program that was laudable for its intention to shake up the oligarchy and help the long-suffering Indian population, but that proved to be short on understanding how to bring about such fundamental reforms, especially without suffering unwanted advice from Washington. Arevalo won the presidency in the freest and least corrupt vote in the nation's history and embarked on his reform program. By 1948 Washington officials did not share Arevalo's priorities; their attention was riveted on the Soviet Union. The U.S. Department of State worried that "economic development," not the Cold War, had become "the dominant force behind policies and actions" in Latin America.[19] A State Department intelligence report warned that Guatemala was one of five Latin American nations in which significant steps had been taken to make the government — not the private sector — responsible for a "phenomenal growth of social and economic legislation designed to protect labor, distribute land more widely, [and] improve sanitition . . . and . . . education."[20]

After 1951, Arevalo's constitutionally-elected successor, Jacobo Arbenz, focused on land reform. Arbenz thus entered into a final showdown with the United States. Approximately 2% of the population owned 70% of the land. That figure was dramatized by the dependence of at least 60% of the population on land for the barest means of survival.[21] Arbenz concluded that his program's success required expropriating property from the nation's largest landowner, the United Fruit Comapny of Boston (UFCO). He claimed 234,000 acres which, Arbenz argued, the company had refused to cultivate. UFCO fought back. It turned down Arbenz's offer of $1.2 million compensation (calculated from UFCO's own tax forms) as outrageously low. At stake, however, was more than property. Arbenz was establishing a model for other nations to follow as he used state power to expropriate private property and carry out broad reforms. UFCO, moreover, directly controlled 40,000 Guatemalan laborers and hundreds of square miles of company land; its fleet was the country's shipping. Its railroads, telegraphs, and port facilities were the nation's transporation and communication systems.[22] Arbenz aimed at bringing key sectors of Guatemala's economy under Guatemalan control. By early 1954, his plan was working. As 1,500,000 acres of private holdings and 700,000 acres of government territory were redistributed in 1953-1954, the production of both export crops and staple foods increased. Many peasants, including Indians who comprised a majority of the population, owned land for the first time and joined unions to make their voices heard politically.[23]

By late 1953, Communist Party leaders had become dominant in important union movements, but no U.S. official claimed that the three most important institutions — the presidency, army, and Church — were threatened by communist control. In early 1954, the pivotal issue was not the possibility of a Soviet base, but rather an issue that resembled the problem of the 1920s when the Coolidge administration targeted Mexican influence: Whether a nation could set a successful example by determining its own economic and social policy, then force U.S. corporations, which had dominated the country for decades, to pay for much of that policy. At stake was economic dependence and political defiance, not military security. The security issue moved to the center of the controversy only in May 1954 when, after the Eisenhower administration tried to isolate the Arbenz government in the hemisphere and began to train Guatemalan exiles for an invasion, the Guatemala City officials received a shipment of arms from the Soviet bloc. The following month the CIA-directed exiles overthrew the Arbenz government and installed military rule.

The army regime proved to be so disastrous that the leader of the 1954 invasion was murdered three years later by his own military colleagues. In 1961, several military officers, trained by the United States, turned into revolutionary leaders and tried to overthrow the government. That attempt failed, but it triggered a chain reaction. The revolutionary movement grew in the 1960s, split into several factions, and by 1967, pushed Guatemala to the top of the State Department list of Latin American nations threatened by insurgency.

One aspect of this rapid, bloody slide deserves emphasis; the deterioration occurred even though Washington officials pumped more money into

Guatemala between 1954 and 1970 than into any other Central American country. Several dozen U.S. military advisers tried to help a fiercely independent Guatemalan Army. Civilian casualty figures mounted. Torture and brutality escalated. Finally in 1968, two U.S. advisers and the U.S. ambassador to Guatemala, John Gordon Mein, were murdered by the revolutionaries. The first privately-controlled right-wing terrorist groups also appeared.[24]

As the United States injected more money into Guatemala after 1954, the economic and political systems became worse. The root problems were not an insufficient amount of U.S. military aid or economic help. The problems were Guatemalan officers whose allegiance was to their own military institution and the oligarchs, instead of to the nation and the people, and a U.S. policy that overthrew an elected government which was carrying out a program of reform. The post-1954 regimes stopped the reforms, returned much of the expropriated land to UFCO, endured a deteriorating export economy, and dealt with the resulting unrest with force. With few interruptions, the Guatemalan revolutionary movements continued into the 1980s.

THE ALLIANCE FOR PROGRESS

Despite the lesson supposedly taught Latin American reformers in 1954, despite 60 years of direct and indirect U.S control, and despite millions of dollars in U.S. military aid and training, the Cuban dictatorship of Fulgencio Batista fell to Fidel Castro's revolutionaries in 1959. Castro's victory was the gravest of the afflictions suffered by U.S. officials and their Latin American friends in the late 1950s. Declining economies and restless military officers also caused problems, particularly in El Salvador, Guatemala, and Honduras. To remedy these ills, and especially to prevent future Castros from seizing power, President John F. Kennedy announced the Alliance for Progress in March 1961.

The ten-year plan aimed to channel $100 billion into Latin American development in return for reforms (especially tax and land reform, carried out by the recipient governments. The United States pledged approximately $20 billion, with the remainder to come from the Latin Americans themselves. The Alliance aimed at an annual real per capita growth rate of 2.5%, or about 5.5% given the rate of the region's population increase. But the actual target was Castro. Kennedy accused the Republicans of losing Cuba, vowed not to lose another nation to communism on his watch, and determined to disprove Nikita Khrushchev's boast that the Monroe Doctrine was dead. The President planned to use the Alliance to develop stable economies and growing middle classes that would be resistant to Castro-type revolutions. Military security and economic growth would develop hand-in-hand.[25] And so they did, but not in the fashion hoped for by Kennedy.

Funds channeled through governmental institutions, including the new Inter-American Development Bank, were accompanied by increasing amounts of private capital. Investors were especially attracted by the Central American Common Market (CACM) that began to unite the five small, severely limited markets in a larger regional marketplace after 1962. The book value of U.S. private investment in the region rose, particularly in banking and small manufacturing.[26] On their face, growth rates in Central America were impressive during the 1960s: the per capita increase of gross national product for the decade was 32.6% for Costa Rica, 25.8% for El Salvador, 21.2% for Guatemala, 11.7% for Honduras, and a remarkable 34% for Somoza's Nicaragua.[27]

These figures seemed impressive but it turned out that the most important development of the decade was the appearance of significant revolutionary guerrilla bands in Guatemala, El Salvador, and Nicaragua. One crucial reason for their appearance related directly to the gross national product figures. Neither the U.S. nor Central American officials could transform those growth figures into more equitable societies and political stability. As early as 1964, the Central Intelligence Agency warned President Lyndon Johnson that "the hazards of governing may be increasing rather than lessening" because by promising too much, the Alliance had become a target: the Latin American "public blames governments for most evils and failures, while both governments and peoples look abroad for convenient scapegoats."[28] By the end of the 1960s, the Alliance was nearly moribund. It had been victimized by Johnson's preoccupation with Vietnam, growing congressional antipathy to foreign aid and determination to protect U.S. private interests in Latin America regardless of long-term consequences for the Alliance, and the refusal of the Central American oligarchs and military officers to reform their societies while the dollars poured in.

The last two points are of special importance. Congress tied amendments to Alliance funding that forbade the use of monies to purchase land for redistribution. That reform had become the most important for the peasants in El Salvador, Guatemala, and Nicaragua. Congress also tied aid to purchases in the expensive North American market. With the Hickenlooper amendment of 1962, the legislature aimed to stop aid to any nation that expropriated U.S. property without quick compensation. The amendment made impossible the redistribution of large amounts of property in poorer countries unless they plunged into debt to pay for the redistribution.[29] The oligarchs meanwhile siphoned off Alliance funds to relieve their own tax obligations. They also bought up additional areas for producing export crops, thus driving peasants off the land and forcing many to depend increasingly on more expensive imported food for survival. In many areas, malnutrition ironically rose with the amounts of food exports. Of each $100 per capita increase in Latin American income during the 1960s, only $2 reached the poorest 20% of the population.[30] Even the gains that the Alliance did produce only led the region to tie itself dangerously to foreign lenders. In 1958, Latin America's debt service was $1 billion, or 10.5% of its export earnings; a decade later it was $2 billion and 16% of export earnings.[31]

Central American development followed these trends, and its military also exemplified changes occurring throughout the southern hemisphere. Kennedy and Johnson accompanied Alliance development funds with a large military assistance program that nearly doubled the arms-related aid that entered four Central American nations during the 1960s.[32] New programs also appeared. Washington officials touted civic action projects in which the military worked with civilians in grass roots economic programs. These projects, however, allowed army officers to expand their personal power (and wealth), militarize former civilian sectors of the economy, and establish police networks that could suppress peasants.

The military used its growing power not to encourage democratic processes but for two other purposes. The first was to strengthen itself as an institution until in Honduras, Guatemala, and El Salvador the military became the most efficient instrument for governing the country. The officers' first allegiance, however, turned out to be to their own institution and the oligarchs, not the country. The second purpose was to prevent reform groups, which Kennedy had hoped to strengthen, from gaining power, particularly when those groups threatened the highly profitable prerogatives of the military-oligarchic complex. In Guatemala and Honduras, for example, the military aborted elections that might have brought reformers, not revolutionaries, to power.[33] Military influence also grew in Nicaragua, but it did so along with the power of the Somoza family which proved to be skilled in enriching itself from Alliance funds. As insurgent movements emerged in the late 1960s, the United States counted increasingly on the U.S.-trained and equipped Central American armies to maintain stability, if not always peace. Although the Nixon administration and Congress cut back military grants to South America after 1968, the program remained stable for Central American recipients through the early 1970s. Arms sales meanwhile rose steadily. In terms of annual percentage change, Central America spent twice as much on military expenses in 1973-1978 as it had between 1968 and 1973.[34] But there was little political payoff; instability spread throughout the area.

Nicaragua and Costa Rica proved to be instructive comparative case studies. Nicaragua's growth rate spiraled upward, but the figures hid a growing concentration of wealth that only frustrated the middle class. Mechanization in agriculture and industry drove unemployment higher, especially as illiteracy prevented a majority of Nicaraguans from qualifying for certain jobs. Somoza and his friends in the national guard funneled Alliance funds into businesses they controlled. Meanwhile, only 2% of the rural population had potable water by the late 1960s, and only 28% of Managua's residents had access to sewage services. Land and tax reforms were nonexistent.[35] Out of the Managua *barrios* and other urban slums, many of whose inhabitants had been forced off their land in the 1960s, came the mass support that helped the Sandinistas overthrow Somoza in 1979.

In Costa Rica, however, the high growth rate during the 1960s did not create vast new slums nor could the growth benefit a nonexistent institutionalized military. Because of the more open, democratic system and the greater equality in property holding, the middle and lower classes gained a share of the national income they found acceptable. Even the land concentration that occurred was somewhat modified as the government opened new areas during the 1960s and began a land reform program in the 1970s.[36]

The Alliance worked better in Costa Rica because the political structures redistributed some of the growing wealth, and because no military force was present to quarantine a small elite from reforms and open political processes. In the other Central American nations, economic reforms did not exist; these countries lacked a supporting political structure that was either open (as in Costa Rica) or dedicated to radical change (as in Cuba).

U.S officials thus confronted stark alternatives. They certainly wanted no more Castros. Yet they were also reluctant to rein in Central American military officers who seemed the best bet to provide short-term stability. The United States thus had to choose between a military-oligarch group that offered misleading growth rates and stability at the point of a gun, and radical political changes that might bring about more equitable, but also less dependent societies. In the 1960s, North Americans chose the former. In the 1970s and 1980s, they were confronted by the latter.

THE ROOTS OF THE WAR IN EL SALVADOR

During the 1960s, Washington policymakers viewed El Salvador much as they did Nicaragua; that is, as one of the Alliance's success stories. One analysis even had the Salvadoran growth rate peaking at an astounding 12% in 1965. The number of small manufacturing industries rose until the country possessed the largest number of such firms among the five nations. It prided itself on being known as the "Ruhr of Central America." U.S. direct investment helped fuel the boom; it rose from $31 million in 1960 to $76 million in 1971. Half of all foreign investment that entered El Salvador after 1900 appeared in the Alliance decade.[37]

Nevertheless, by the late 1970s a revolution had grown until it threatened the existence of the Salvadoran government. The paradox was not new. It had been explained to U.S. State Department officials as early as 1949. Salvador's export-dependent economy was necessarily unstable, the U.S.

Ambassador, Albert F. Nufer, reported. "This, together with the fact that the bulk of the population exists on a bare subsistence level, [provided] fertile soil for the seeds of communism."[38] Later that same year, another U.S. official warned that the Salvadoran oligarchs (the so-called Fourteen Families that had dominated the country since the 19th century) were so jealous of their prerogatives and power that "new American capital certainly would not receive a warm welcome." The small amount of existing U.S. capital could meanwhile be endangered by the "excessive nationalism."[39] The oligarchs had looked skeptically on foreigners, even those on whom they depended for markets. When the Fourteen Families welcomed Alliance and private monies, it was on their clear understanding that control would remain in their hands, and that President Kennedy's demand for reforms would be given no more than lip service—if that. Thus U.S. funds merely reinforced earlier trends. The mass of Salvadorans were fastened even more closely to: a dependent export economy; an increasingly mechanized productive system that drove up unemployment; a land policy where officials seized plots from peasants in order to produce more export crops; and a condition in which the majority of the population had neither work, land, nor sufficient food.[40] By the 1970s, after the exploding growth rates of the Alliance, El Salvador was one of the world's five most undernourished nations. Functional illiteracy among peasants approached 95%. The population increased at a high 3.2% per year, but that was not the central problem. Salvadoran agricultural production actually kept pace with the population rise. The problem was that the agricultural system profited very few and starved many. During the Alliance decade after 1961, the number of landless Salvadoran families more than tripled.[41]

In 1960, the Christian Democratic Party (PDC) was formed to offer an alternative to the military-controlled PRUD party. Finding a base in the growing urban areas, the PDC doubtlessly won the 1972 presidential election for its candidate, José Napoleón Duarte, but the military openly interfered to reverse the results. It dispatched Duarte to exile in Venezuela. The army thus continued the rule it had assumed in 1932 when, challenged by an uprising of poorly-led peasant groups, the Fourteen Families worked with the military to exterminate as many as 30,000 Salvadorans. The country's politics did not recover until the 1960s. The 1972 action by the military, and the imposition in the 1977 election of another harsh army regime, destroyed any hopes of a budding democracy that had been sown in the Alliance years. Between 1946 and 1979, the United States publicly associated itself fully with these army rulers. It trained 2000 Salvadoran officers and maintained in San Salvador an unusually large staff of U.S. advisers for such a small country.[42]

During the early 1970s, revolutionary groups appeared, most notably the People's Revolutionary Army and the Popular Liberation Forces. These organizations could not agree on common tactics or objectives (other than to overthrow the military-oligarch regime). By late 1980, their power had nevertheless grown until they believed a "final offensive" could be mounted. President Jimmy Carter had cut off military aid to the Salvadoran government because of widely publicized human rights violations. Now he urgently reversed course to help a more moderate junta that had seized power in 1979. The Salvadoran Army repulsed the revolutionary offensive just as Ronald Reagan assumed the presidency. The losers melted back into the mountains to rebuild their forces. At this decisive moment Reagan disregarded possible political solutions and decided to push for total military victory. By 1983, however, the rebuilt and better coordinated revolutionary groups could again threaten the government. The junta, for which Washington officials had great hopes, had fragmented and given way to a U.S.-sponsored election in 1982. That balloting gave power in the new Consituent Assembly to right-wing military and civilian groups.

Using words that echoed those noted above of 30 years before, Assistant Secretary of State Viron P. Vaky explained the dilemma in 1979: "The export-oriented economy," Vaky warned, "is characterized by a highly skewed distribution of income, wealth, and land."[43] In the intervening years, the Alliance for Progress had reinforced the inequities and introduced U.S. capital and military advisers in historically large numbers. By the early 1980s, the United States had become the only major supporter for a Salvadoran regime that could not halt the slaughter, feed its people, or reform itself.

HISTORY LESSONS

Two broad conclusions can be drawn from these case studies. The first is that each time the United States has attempted to intervene militarily in Central America after 1920 it has, in the long run, worsened the situation it meant to correct. Intervention in Honduras achieved short-term North American objectives in 1911-1912 because no revolution, not even a reformist group, existed. The major dilemma at the time was to decide which group of U.S. entrepreneurs was to control the country. After the 1920s, the environment sharply changed. Despite occupying Nicaragua for much of the 1912-1933 era, the United States could not defeat the guerrillas led by Augusto Sandino. The North Americans returned home, leaving behind the Somoza dictatorship. Results were similar in the aftermath of the U.S. interventions in Guatemala during 1954 and El Salvador during the 1970s and early 1980s. Right-wing military governments unwilling to carry out fundamental reforms produced radical revolutions.

In each instance of a significant U.S. military intervention in Central America after 1925, the effect has been to polarize the country involved and drive the groups espousing fundamental reforms farther to the left. The importance of this effect can hardly be overemphasized. U.S. policy has produced the opposite of its intended result. The U.S. and Organization of American States intervention in the Dominican Republic during the spring of 1965 is no exception to this rule, for, in the apt phrase of Professor Robert W. Tucker, "There was no prospect of a guerrilla movement emerging phoenix-like from defeat" in the Dominican Republic because "there had never been a guerrilla movement to defeat."[44] That judgment cannot apply to the U.S military interventions in Central America, whether they were direct (as in opposing Sandino during the late 1920s) or more indirect (as in Guatemala and El Salvador after 1954 or in aiding the Nicaraguan counterrevolutions after 1981).

Some North Americans, most importantly John Kennedy, perceived the conditions in Central America that produced radical guerrilla movements. The United States attempted to change those conditions with the Alliance for Progress. Instead it worsened the inequality. By the early 1970s the revolutionary movements had grown into significant threats in Guatemala, Nicaragua, and El Salvador. Thus appears the second conclusion warranted by a study of the recent past: no major U.S. aid plan can sufficiently improve economic conditions and deal with the structural political problems until governments attain power that have no interest in maintaining the status quo. That conclusion rules out those traditional civilian elites and their military cohorts who have long worked with the United States in helping to bring about the present crisis.

This conclusion leaves several alternatives for U.S officials who search Central America for groups that can fundamentally restructure the region's politics and provide more equitable and peaceful societies: the revolutionary movements themselves, or coalition governments of revolutionary and more moderate factions that are put into place and supported by regional powers. There is a third alternative for pacifying the region: a U.S. policy that uses massive military intervention to destroy the revolutionary groups, conducts supposedly democratic elections, and pours millions of dollars into economic development. The history of the past half-century proves that the third has already proven to be a futile when not disastrous alternative.

NOTES

1. Challener, R.D., *Admirals, Generals and American Foreign Policy*, Princeton University Press, Princeton, 1973, p. 167.
2. The classic Roosevelt statement on Caribbean-Central American policy, from which the quoted words are drawn, is the so-called Roosevelt Corollary to the Monroe Doctrine, issued in his 1904 annual message to Congress. It is in U.S. Government, *House Documents* (4780), 58th Congress, 3d. Session, pp. 41-42.

3. "Minutes of the Cabinet Meeting, July 3, 1953," *Cabinet Meetings of President Eisenhower*, Dwight D. Eisenhower Library, Abilene, Kansas.

4. Morris, J.A., and Ropp, S.C., "Corporatism and Dependent Development: A Honduran Case Study," *Latin American Research Review*, Vol. 12, No. 2, 1977, pp. 32-33; Blutstein, H.I., et al., *Area Handbook for Honduras*, Government Printing Office, Washington, 1971, pp. 107-110, 137, 158-159.

5. Durham, W.H., *Scarcity and Survival in Central America*, Stanford University Press, Stanford, 1979, p.7; Catholic Institute for International Relations, *Honduras: Anatomy of a Disaster*, Catholic Institute, London, 1975, pp. 3-5; Molina Chocano, G., "Dependencia y cambio social en la sociedad hondureña," *Estudios Sociales Centroamericanos*, Vol. 1, Enero-Abril 1972, pp. 14-17, 21-22.

6. Johnson, J.J., *The Military and Society in Latin America*, Stanford University Press, Stanford, 1964, pp. 162-163; Blutstein, *Area Handbook for Honduras*, pp. 110-111, 187.

7. Associated Press report, *The New York Times*, Sept. 25, 1981, p. A7. Some Hondurans believe Honduran military leaders trumped up the so-called "guerrilla movement" to justify internal repression.

8. Wright, M., "U.S. War Materiel Stars in Honduras," *The New York Times*, Feb. 10, 1983, p. A3.

9. Bonner, R., "Salvador City is Shaken by Surprise Rebel Raid," *The New York Times*, July 1, 1981, p. A2.

10. Langley, L.D., *The Banana Wars; An Inner History of American Empire, 1900-1933*, University of Kentucky, Lexington, 1983, pp. 55-66 has the quote and a good analysis.

11. Challener, *op. cit.*, pp. 302-305.

12. Langley, op. cit., p. 184.

13. Kornbluh, P.R., "Coolidge's Latin Folly," *The New York Times*, April 27, 1983, p. A19.

14. Wood, B., *The Making of the Good Neighbor Policy*, Norton, New York, 1961, pp. 14-15.

15. Buell, R.L., "Reconstruction in Nicaragua," *Foreign Policy Association Information Service*, Vol. 6, Nov. 12, 1930, pp. 339-345.

16. Millett, R., *Guardians of the Dynasty*, Orbis Books, New York, 1977, pp. 116-120.

17. Sacasa, Chamorro, Díaz to Hull, Nov. 30, 1936, U.S. Department of State, *Foreign Relations of the United States*, Government Printing Office, Washington 1954, Vol. 5, pp. 844-846.

18. "Political Developments and Trends in the Other American Republics in the Twentieth Century," Office of Intelligence Research Report No. 4780, Oct. 1, 1949, pp. 2-3, Record Group 59, National Archives, Washington.

19. Memorandum by the Secretary of State to Diplomatic Representatives in the American Republics, March 19, 1948, U.S. Department of State, *Foreign Relations of the United States*, Government Printing Office, Washington 1974, Vol. 9, pp. 11-16.

20. "Political Developments and Trends in the Other American Republics in the Twentieth Century," p. 3.

21. Stuart, G.H. and Tigner, J.L., *Latin America and the United States*, Prentice-Hall, Englewood Cliffs, N.J., 1975, pp. 519-520.

22. Schneider, R.M., *Communism in Guatemala, 1944-1954*, Praeger, New York, 1958, pp. 48-49.

23. Pearson, N.J., "Guatemala: The Peasant Union Movement, 1944-1954," *Latin American Peasant Movements*, Landsberger, H.A., ed. (Cornell University Press, Ithaca, 1969), pp. 326-327, 344; Giniger, H., "Guatemala is a Battleground," *The New York Times Magazine*, March 16, 1969, p. 17.

24. Booth, J.A., "A Guatemalan Nightmare; Levels of Political Violence, 1966-1972," *Journal of Interamerican Studies and World Affairs*, Vol. 22, May 1980, pp. 196-197; Plant, R., *Guatemala, Unnatural Disaster*, Latin American Bureau, London, 1978, pp. 19-20, 22; Stuart and Tigner, *op. cit.*, pp. 525-526.

25. *Public Papers of the Presidents/John F. Kennedy,1961*, Government Printing Office, Washington 1962, p. 175; Schlesinger, A.M. Jr., *A Thousand Days: John F. Kennedy in the White House*, Houghton Mifflin, Boston, 1965, pp. 185-205, 790.

26. Wionczek, M.S., "U.S. Investment and the Development of Middle America," *Studies in Comparative International Development*, Vol. 5, 1969-1970, pp. 4-5; Wionczek, M., "Latin American Integration and U.S. Economic Policies," *International Organization in the Western Hemisphere*, Gregg, R.W., ed. (Syracuse University Press, Syracuse, 1968), pp. 129-130.

27. U.S. Senate, Committee on Foreign Relations, *Interamerican Development Bank Fund for Special Operations, June 4, 1971*, Government Printing Office, Washington 1971, pp. 55-56.

28. Central Intelligence Agency, "Survey of Latin America, April 1, 1964," *NSC Country File, Latin America*, Container No. 1, Lyndon B. Johnson Library, Austin, Texas.

29. Green, D., "Paternalism and Profits: The Ideology of U.S. Aid to Latin America, 1943-1971," *Historical Papers,*, 1972 edition, J. Atherton, ed. (Canadian Historical Association, Ottawa, 1973), p. 351.

30. Commission on U.S.-Latin American Relations, *The United States and Latin America: Next Steps. A Special Report*. [No place of publication], 1976, p.22.

31. Sloan, J.W., "Three Views of Latin America: President Nixon, Governor Rockefeller, and the Latin American Consensus of Viña del Mar," *Orbis*, Vol. 14, Winter 1971, pp. 935-936, 948.

32. Baines, J.M., "U.S. Military Assistance to Latin America: An Assessment," *Journal of Interamerican Studies and World Affairs*, Vol. 14, Nov. 1972, p. 481.

33. Lieuwen E., "The Latin American Military," *Survey of the Alliance for Progress* (U.S. Senate Committee on Foreign Relations, Government Printing Office, Washington, 1969), pp. 95-98, 115.

34. Dominguez, J.I., "U.S. and Its Regional Security Interests," *Daedalus*, Vol. 109, Fall 1980, p. 126.

35. Ryan, J.M., *et al., Area Handbook for Nicaragua*, Government Printing Office, Washington, 1970, pp. 208-210, 214, 284, 295-297, 308.

36. Booth, J.A., "Toward Explaining Regional Crisis in Central America: The Socioeconomic and Political Roots of Rebellion," Paper for 44th International Congress of Americanists, Manchester, England, September 1982, p. 13. [In author's possession.]

37. Arnson, C., *El Salvador: A Revolution Confronts the United States*, Institute for Policy Studies, Washington, 1982, p. 20; Stuart and Tigner, *op. cit.,* pp. 530-531.

38. Albert F. Nufer to Robert A. Lovett, Nov. 17, 1948, 711.00/11-1748, Record Group 59, National Archives, Washington.

39. George P. Shaw to Dean Acheson, Dec. 10, 1949, 711/00/12-1049 A-EP, Record Group 59, National Archives, Washington.

40. Durham, p. 54; Karush, G. E., "Plantations, Population and Poverty," *Studies in Comparative International Development*, Vol. 13, Fall 1978, p. 69.

41. Karush, pp. 62-63; Durham, pp. 30-35; West, R. C., and Augelli, J.P., *Middle America: Its Lands and Peoples*, Prentice-Hall, Englewood Cliffs, N.J., 1976, pp. 407, 410; Bonner, R., "The Agony of El Salvador," *The New York Times Magazine*, Feb. 22, 1981, pp. 26ff.

42. Petras, J., "White Paper on the White Paper," *The Nation*, March 28, 1981, p. 371.

43. U.S. House of Representatives, Committee on Foreign Affairs, *Central America at the Crossroads. Hearings*, Government Printing Office, Washington, 1979, p. 5.

44. Tucker, R.W., "Their Wars, Our Choices," *The New Republic*, Oct. 24, 1983, p. 29.

3
PRAETORIANS OR PATRIOTS?
The Central American Military

Richard Millett

The Central American militaries have contributed significantly to the region's violence, and their current political power complicates efforts to end the crisis. They are plagued by conflicting and often contradictory trends, a situation which consistently frustrates the efforts of external forces, domestic elites and even their own officers to control the power which they possess. The armies are a bulwark against communism but, at the same time, their corruption and abuses of human rights provide invaluable propaganda and recruits for the radical left. Deeply rooted in regional history and tradition, the military is also one of the most modern institutions in each nation. Highly dependent on external support, it is also strongly nationalist and even xenophobic.

THE HERITAGE OF CENTRAL AMERICA'S ARMED FORCES

The regular military institutions of Guatemala, El Salvador and Honduras have all been shaped by Spanish colonialism; their domestic political, social and economic environments; and the impact of foreign contacts, notably those with the United States.

Although actual military forces were rather weak in Spanish Central America, one enduring colonial concept has been that of the military as a special, privileged class, exempt from the jurisdiction of the rest of society. This was embodied in the Spanish *fuero militar*, the exemption of members of the armed forces from the jurisdiction of civil courts and their elevation to the status of privileged class. In the words of historian Lyle McAlister the military was:

a class apart and so regarded itself. The possession of special privileges enhanced its sense of uniqueness and superiority, and at the same time rendered it virtually immune from civil authority. Unfortunately, power and privilege were not accompanied by a commensurate sense of responsibility. A large proportion of officers and men regarded military service as an opportunity for the advancement of personal interests rather than as a civil obligation.[1]

The colonial emphasis on class also helped create the immense gap between officers and enlisted men which still characterizes Central American armed forces. The gap between the military and civilians was even wider; those abused by military personnel had little opportunity for redress. The lower classes, especially Indians, suffered most. Soldiers frequently seized what they wanted from Indian communities without compensation.[2] Military corruption also has roots in the 18th century. Many officers habitually used their positions to engage in contraband trade, a further example of the abuses of the *fuero militar*.[3]

The military's ability to abuse its power grew after independence due to a patron-client relationship between officers and enlisted men. Troops gave their loyalty not to elected officials nor even to the nation itself, but to their immediate commander. This system even operated within the officer corps, where officers addressed superiors as *mi general* or *mi coronel* (my general or my colonel). Local commanders' absolute control over pay, discipline and promotion reinforced this pattern, enabling officers who revolted against the central authority to count on the support of their troops. Thus, in order to win military allegiance governments had to negotiate with individual officers. Leading officers, frequently from prominent families, were little more than the armed partisans of the party in power. The real struggle was between elite sectors who viewed the coup (or *golpe*) as the normal means of transferring power. As Professor John J. Johnson observed, "Liberty, equality and fraternity gave way to infantry, cavalry and artillery," and "the rule of force became more meaningful than the rule of law."[4]

This endemic conflict facilitated foreign intervention and exploitation and hampered development, although changes were sought in the last third of the 19th century. Military academies were established in 1868 in El Salvador and in 1873 in Guatemala.[5] Similar efforts in Nicaragua in the 1890s and in Honduras at the start of the 20th century *failed*, but nonetheless indicated a desire for greater military professionalism. These initial efforts leaned heavily on the services of foreign instructors, usually Chilean or German; since then, dependence on external training and support has caused tension.

Previously little more than an extension of semi-feudal elite factions or traditional political parties, the 20th century military began to develop a separate identity as it became more professionalized. Officers rose to power because of their ability to manipulate politics within the military rather than because they came from prominent families. Graduates of the new military academies increasingly resented the power of amateur generals. The advent of new technology—notably the machine gun and later the airplane—also made the career of a military officer increasingly a full-time profession. Political elites continued to have to negotiate with the military as a separate force, for losing its support meant loss of power and could even place life and property at risk.

The military did not become an opponent of the ruling class, but rather a vital ally of that class. The military's allegiance had to be assured through financial support, co-optation into the elite by marriage or other means and expansion of its role in politics. The officers themselves now decided assignments and promotions and selected the army's commander and military cabinet members. Civilians could influence these decisions but no longer had the final say. External forces, especially the U.S., sought to influence the emerging military institutions, adding to their power but further complicating the political equation. In the 20th century, the U.S. tried to create a rural constabulary in Panama and to improve the professional level of Nicaragua's armed forces. In the 1920s, Secretary of State Charles Evans Hughes promoted arms limitations and military reorganization in the region. A 1923 conference of Central American states in Washington adopted a Treaty of Arms Limitation and considered establishing non-partisan constabularies trained by American instructors. A leading State Department official noted that:

> The old armies were or seemed to be one of the principal causes of disorder and financial disorganization. They consumed most of the government's revenue, chiefly in graft, and they gave nothing but oppression and disorder in return. We thought that a disciplined force, trained by Americans, would do away with the petty local oppression that was responsible for much of the disorder that occurred and would be an important step toward better financial administration and economic progress generally.[6]

Washington also feared that the weakness and corruption of existing armies might make those nations susceptible to other foreign influences. During World War I, U.S. efforts focused on eliminating German influences. In the 1920s, especially during the tenure of Secretary of State Frank Kellogg, the Mexican government was imagined to be the source of "Bolshevik influences."

Only in Nicaragua were U.S. efforts to reshape the military effective before World War II. Armed factions were forced to disband and the *Guardia Nacional* was created and initially officered and equipped by U.S. Marines.[7]

One unforeseen result of this was that enemies of the Nicaraguan regime became, ipso facto, enemies of the United States. The United States was thus drawn into five-and-one-half years of inconclusive guerrilla warfare against the forces of General Augusto César Sandino. This conflict later came back to haunt Washington policymakers.

Elsewhere U.S. influence grew slowly. During World War II many Central American officers received American training, either in their own nations or in the United States. The Lend-Lease programs considerably upgraded the equipment of regional militaries, especially the air forces. Exposure to North American ideas and training increased discontent among many junior officers and contributed to the overthrow of long-lasting dictatorships in Guatemala and El Salvador in 1944. As Guatemala's new rulers moved to the left, Washington became increasingly concerned over possible communist influence and rushed military supplies to neighboring countries. These arms were used by the CIA in 1954 to help topple the Guatemalan government. Shortly thereafter, the U.S. signed mutual assistance pacts with most Central American nations and large military training missions. In 1961 the United States ambassador to El Salvador noted that the advisory group in that nation had grown so large that "there were more men in the Air Force Mission than El Salvador had either pilots or planes."[8]

Fidel Castro's rise to power and the expanding guerrilla conflicts, notably in Guatemala and Nicaragua, led to further U.S. involvement in the 1960s. The Kennedy administration promoted military reforms and civic action programs, but in later years the emphasis was increasingly on internal stability and counterinsurgency.

Though direct United States aid and training diminished steadily during the 1970s, both Central Americans and North American policymakers continued to believe that the United States could easily dictate the actions of Central America's armed forces. In reality, the military establishments were becoming less dependent on the United States and more responsive to the institutional interests of the officer corps. The 1969 Honduras-El Salvador War left both nations' military leaders feeling let down by the United States. As the 1970s progressed, Central American nations sought other markets for military equipment. Honduras acquired combat aircraft from Israel, while El Salvador began to buy supplies from a wide variety of nations. Congress prohibited U.S. training of Central American police forces but the impact of the United States continued to be important. Partly due to American influence, many officers became militant anti-communists. Civic action programs, prevailing counterinsurgency doctrines and the structure for regional military cooperation also reflected U.S. influence. Many officers had received at least part of their training in U.S. schools, and most uniforms were modeled on North American styles. Both the traditional right and the radical left cultivated the belief that the United States exercised significant influence over the military. That belief also endured in Washington, creating more problems than benefits in the 1980s.

EL SALVADOR

Today the most crucial and difficult U.S. military relationship is with El Salvador. It has generated strong criticism of American policies at home and abroad, and few successes within El Salvador.

El Salvador's armed forces have expanded rapidly in recent years. In 1976 total military personnel numbered approximately 8,000, over half of which were assigned to the security forces (National Guard, National Police and Treasury Police). Only about 200 were assigned to the Air Force. By 1983 the Army had expanded to 22,000, the Air Force to 2,350 and the security forces to 9,500.[9] The budget had grown from $50 million in 1978 to $139 million in 1982, plus an additional $82 million in United States military assistance.[10]

The National Guard is a 3,500-man rural constabulary, created in the 1920s on the model of the Spanish *Guardia Civil*. The National Police, the only urban police force, has nearly 4,000 members; the Treasury Police, a body formally charged with controlling customs, borders, alcohol production and related tax matters, has nearly 2,000 individuals. These "security forces" are currently all under the control of the Ministry of Defense and are largely commanded by army officer graduates of the military academy. These forces, notably the National Guard and the Treasury Police, have been the principal perpetrators of indiscriminate violence against dissidents. They have been used by the traditional rural elite against peasant organizations, agrarian reform and potential "trouble-makers." The Treasury Police also maintains an extensive network of rural informers. These security forces do much of the "dirty work" of maintaining control and eliminating "subversives" leaving the Army free to concentrate on national defense, national politics and self-enrichment. Before 1980 the Army suppressed only extreme dissent, for example, after the fraudulent elections of 1972 and 1977.

The one-man military rule of pre-1944 El Salvador has given way to a trend towards corporate control by the armed forces, signaled in the 1950s by the rise to power of military academy graduates.[11] While generally united in their determination to control the country, they are divided by ideology, personal loyalties and, most importantly, graduating classes from the *Escuela Militar*. Each year well over a hundred cadets are admitted to this institution, but just 10% graduate *four years later*. Brutal discipline, at times verging on sadism, weeds out those lacking strength, determination and ambition. The school admits boys of 15-18 and graduates hardened men, bound by lifelong loyalty to their classmates. Each class, known as a *tanda*, strives to protect and advance its members' fortunes. Success for one member means success for all and failure for any weakens the entire group. Hence they protect the less competent, more blatantly dishonest among them, viewing those outside the *tanda* system as unfit to judge the officer corps.

To advance their ambitions, *tandas* form alliances with other *tandas*, though rarely with the class one year ahead of them in *Escuela Militar* (which had brutalized them during their plebe year), nor with the class a year behind (which they had brutalized). Under this system, loyalty becomes incestuous, and group advancement, rather than defense of the national interest, becomes the ultimate goal.[12] Officers in the security forces are bound to officers in the army through these *tanda* bonds, a tie which makes it virtually impossible to discipline an officer for crimes against civilians. In 1982 El Salvador's Defense Minister admitted to two United States Senators that "there is no formal system of punishment for abuses by members of the Salvadoran armed forces."[13]

For this reason, the United States probably had less influence over El Salvador's military than over that of any other Central American nation. This *tanda* system made the military resistant to foreign influences. By law, Salvadoran army officers had to attend their own service schools, including the Command and Staff College. Given the post-1969 cutoff of arms sales and training of police forces it was not that difficult for El Salvador to respond to Carter administration human rights pressures in 1977 by abrogating the military assistance agreement.

During the 1970s, increased social pressures and the growing strength of the left made a major outbreak of domestic violence increasingly likely. The military's control was weakened by corruption and growing factionalism. The Sandinista victory in Nicaragua further encouraged the left and increased the military's fears and internal divisions.

When junior officers ousted General Carlos Humberto Romero's weak and corrupt administration, the Carter administration leaped at the chance to improve contacts with the military. A small amount of training funds (IM-ET) and authorization for $5.7 million in foreign military sales (FMS) were hurriedly included in a supplement to the fiscal year (FY) 1980 budget. Throughout 1980, however, civil conflict mounted and the military drifted back into the control of traditional senior officers. Human rights abuses escalated steadily, culminating in charges of military involvement in the December murder of four American churchwomen and two American agricultural advisers. Shortly thereafter, Colonel Adolfo Majano, leader of the "reformist" element within the armed forces, was dropped from the ruling junta. U.S. hopes for a moderate civil-military coalition were rapidly falling apart.

U.S.-Salvadoran military relations dramatically changed in January 1981. Military assistance, suspended following the December murders, was hurriedly reinstated when guerrilla forces launched a major offensive. In addition, emergency appropriations, ultimately totaling $25 million, were added to provide equipment and supplies for the Army. This was the first direct grant program for military hardware appropriated for Central America in several years. Even greater changes followed President Reagan's inauguration later that month.

The Carter administration's objectives were to persuade the army to curb human rights abuses, make basic reforms and ultimately permit civilian rule. The internal realities of Salvadoran military politics and the instransigent nature of the armed right confounded these efforts. The Reagan administration's priority was defeating the guerrillas. Restoring domestic order required creating a more effective military. Military assistance was raised to $82 million for FY 1982, and scores of U.S. military advisers were dispatched to El Salvador on missions lasting from a few weeks to a full year. This policy assumed that defeating the guerrillas was the Salvadoran military's top priority too, and it would increase military professionalism, which would decrease human rights abuses and enhance the armed forces' public image. All of these assumptions proved mistaken because, as those dealing directly with the Salvadoran military soon realized, the armed forces had their own agenda. Their top priority was *protecting* the military institutions from radical guerrillas, civilian politicians and foreign reformers. Next was promoting one's own *tanda* and excluding from the system those who had not passed through the *Escuela Militar*. Political ideology was low priority except for those officers linked to the extreme right such as former Major Roberto d'Aubuisson.

Under such circumstances, U.S. involvement with the military produced endless frustrations. It proved impossible to convict officers for human rights abuses, including those involving U.S. citizens. The war with the guerrillas was stagnating; economics and political costs rose steadily. To fill the expanding army's need for company-level officers, the United States began training Salvadoran noncommissioned officers in Panama. But the Salvadoran military refused to give graduates of this program regular commissions, keeping their status inferior to the *Escuela Militar* graduates'. U.S.-trained enlisted men often performed reasonably well, but a combination of high casualties and low reenlistment rates meant that the majority were out of the military a year after they were trained.[14]

The January 1983 conflict between Defense Minister José Guillermo García and Colonel Sigifredo Ochoa disrupted the military command, paralyzed the war effort and resulted in the removal of the Defense Minister and the Colonel's departure for Washington. Part of this conflict stemmed from differences over strategy, with Ochoa and his supporters advocating a more sophisticated approach to counterinsurgency, emphasizing aggressive small unit actions and patrolling combined with political pacification. Traditional military rivalries, however, were at the heart of the conflict, with General García striving to maintain his supporters in key positions, despite their incompetence.

By late 1983, in part due to the change in Defense Ministers, the Salvadoran Army showed some signs of improved command and combat capability, although it was still insufficient to subdue the guerrillas. Widely publicized area offensives had limited results, casualties remained high and human rights abuses were again increasing. The military's low morale and the rural population's apathy were chronic problems. $136 million in military assistance for FY 1983 had done little to transform El Salvador's army into an efficient, modern force and there was little reason to think that the $86.3 million initially requested for FY 1984 would be any more effective. Despite three years of intensive U.S. efforts, the military still abuses its own citizenry, and responded more to its internal power struggles than to the civil conflict. U.S. officials feared that forcing the military to change might cause its collapse. But the military's failure to change increased the risk of a U.S. withdrawal. Disaster awaits for both the Salvadoran Armed Forces and the U.S. in Central America unless the officer corps is persuaded that its survival demands basic changes — including: removing incompetent officers, disciplining those involved in human rights abuses, abandoning some degree of power and privilege and, in all probability, supporting a political rather than a military solution to the current conflict.

GUATEMALA

U.S.-Guatemalan military relations over the past five years have been at least as frustrating (although considerably less publicized and less extensive) as those with El Salvador's military. Two military coups in less than a year and a half have intensified U.S.-Guatemala problems. Like its neighbor in El Salvador, the Guatemalan officer corps is a proud, largely self-trained body but there are also important differences.

Long considered the strongest and most professional military force in Central America, Guatemala's Army today numbers approximately 22,000, and is steadily growing.[15] Security forces and other paramilitary groups are both smaller and less significant in Guatemala than in El Salvador.

The Guatemalan officer corps today is a contradictory mixture of nationalists and opportunists, professionals and partisans, reformers and upholders of the status quo. It is dominated by graduates of the *Escuela Politécnica*, Guatemala's military academy, but non-graduates can rise within the officer corps. Graduating class loyalties are less binding than in El Salvador.[16] Though the military has dominated politics for the past half-century, it has permitted civilians to occupy the top government positions.

It has, however, placed strict limits on their actual power.

Politécnica

Graduates played a major role in the 1944 revolution which overthrew long-time dictator General Jorge Ubico and inaugurated basic reforms. President Jacobo Arbenz, overthrown by the 1954 CIA-sponsored coup, was a *Politécnica* graduate, as was the man who replaced him. Though most officers opposed drift to the left, they resented more heavy-handed U.S. involvement in the fall of Arbenz and the U.S. ambassador's dominant role in installing a successor regime.[17] U.S. use of Guatemalan territory to train Cuban exiles for the 1961 Bay of Pigs invasion of Cuba further aroused nationalist sentiments, leading some young officers to leave the military and form guerrilla groups in the early 1960s.[18] Later in the decade, other Guatemalan officers turned on these insurgents. In the 1970s, yet others sought to apply the Peruvian military reform model to their nation while others converted their rank into personal gain.

U.S. problems with Guatemala's military have worsened since 1976. That year's presidential election was won, amid widespread charges of fraud, by General Romeo Lucas García, who was known chiefly for his unimaginative hard line and his blood ties to one of Guatemala's richest families. President Lucas, like his Salvadoran counterpart, responded to Carter administration protests over mounting human rights abuses by abrogating the military assistance pact with the United States.

On May 29, 1978 Government troops massacred a group of protesting Indians at the town of Panzos, signaling a new wave of government-supported, right-wing terrorism. Victims included two leaders of the democratic left, Alberto Fuentes Mohra and Manuel Colón Argueta, and scores of moderate politicians, labor leaders, university officials, students and journalists. The left responded with selective assassinations of government officials; more important, the guerrillas steadily gained strength in rural areas.

Conditions deteriorated further in 1980. Especially in rural areas, army units, the police and right-wing death squads were increasingly charged with atrocities. In September Guatemala's civilian vice-president resigned and fled the nation to avoid being killed by the president's supporters.

The army and far-right groups such as the National Liberation Movement (MLN) were forging an alliance. The right's private armed units took on the fight against "subversive elements," as did the *comisionados militares*, civilian recruiting and intelligence agents of the army in rural areas. The extreme right also told the military that the Carter administration wanted to install a Marxist regime in Guatemala, citing as evidence both its human rights campaign and its acceptance of the Sandinista victory in Nicaragua. Finally, the right played on the military's growing economic stake in the status quo which included one of the nation's largest banks, a cement factory and individual officers' huge land holdings for cattle and timber production.[19]

Carter administration efforts to break this alliance were ineffective, if not counterproductive. When the United States tried to change ambassadors in 1980, the Guatemalan government refused to accept the nominated successor. Ronald Reagan's victory was celebrated by the right and the military as signaling an end to human rights pressures and a resumption of badly needed military assistance.

But the anticipated rapprochement between the United States and the Lucas García regime did not occur in 1981. The Reagan administration's low-key human rights efforts proved no more effective than the Carter administration's public ones. Political murders averaged 250-300 per month in 1981, three times the level of 1980.[20] Meanwhile, the insurgency spread and the economy began to deteriorate rapidly. The military took greater casualties, found its resources spread ever thinner and began to experience severe equipment problems. All of this produced growing dissent within the military, especially among junior officers. One lieutenant colonel observed in late 1981:

> The government has no strategy to deal with the guerrillas. It has used the tactic of disorganizing society, labeling any vocal leaderships as subversive [and] attempted to use brute force against a political problem. The guerrillas would not be a serious military problem if not for the corruption, inability to govern, exploitation and violence that provides the guerrillas recruits and legitimacy.[21]

It was not surprising that junior officers installed a new regime after the incumbent rigged elections in March 1982. The Reagan administration welcomed the change and offered assistance to the new government headed by General Efrain Ríos Montt.

The 1982 coup reflected a consensus among junior officers that internal corruption and international isolation not only hampered the fight against the insurgents, but jeopardized the army's very survival. The junior officers were, however, divided over the solution. As a compromise, they installed a three-member junta of Ríos Montt, General Horacio Maldonado Schaad and Colonel Francisco Luis Gordillo. But considerable power was retained by an advisory council of junior officers because most feared a plot by the extreme right and wanted to keep civilian politicians on the sidelines, at least for the moment. Elections were projected, but there was no agreement on the date. There was considerable support for social and economic reforms, but wide disagreement as to their exact nature.

Under the new regime, murders of civilian intellectuals, politicians and labor leaders dramatically declined. A few officers who had committed crimes under the previous government were retired, or placed in inactive status; some individuals even fled into exile, but no officers or other high officials were actually tried or imprisoned. Guatemala's new rulers feared that prosecution might further divide the officer corps, weakening the army in its fight against the guerrillas. Ríos Montt issued verbal and written orders for officers to respect civilian rights, abstain from partisan politics and end corrupt practices, but did not enforce them. The officers hoped for external support, notably from the United States, from Israel and others, but feared being linked with U.S. interests. Ríos Montt claimed that he could obtain major funds from evangelical church groups, but received only small amounts of private and U.S. government aid.

The new regime did successfully combat some rural insurgency. Following an unsuccessful amnesty program, the military embarked on a pacification program combining heavy and often indiscriminate use of force with rural resettlement. It organized, often with considerable coercion, local civilian defense forces (CDF) and provided food and work for rural inhabitants, usually Indians, who came under government control.[22] Known as *"fusiles y frijoles"* (rifles and beans), this program decimated the guerrillas' rural support network (along with much of the rural population). By 1983, it had significantly reduced insurgent-controlled areas and the level of combat. But the tactics used roused opposition abroad, especially in the U.S. Congress, which blocked most economic and military assistance. A small amount of training (IMET) funds was provided in FY83 and $10 million in FMS credits were included in the FY84 budget.[23] But Guatemala could not afford to take advantage of U.S.-authorized military sales, and Ríos Montt's requests for small arms and for equipment for an engineer batallion remained unfulfilled.

In June 1982, Ríos Montt forced his two fellow junta members to resign and installed himself as president. But his evangelical religious fervor antagonized the dominant Roman Catholic church; his erratic style offended broad elements of society; his reform proposals, including one for agrarian reform, upset the established oligarchy; and his ties with the junior officers were resented by senior commanders. By mid-1983, even many of Ríos Montt's original supporters were losing their enthusiasm for his regime. His independence in foreign policy had created growing problems with the United States and, as opposition to him mounted, Washington feared he was more a source of instability than of stability. Reports of direct U.S. involvement in the August 1983 coup which finally toppled his regime seem exaggerated, but the Reagan administration did nothing to discourage such action. Defense Minister General Oscar Humberto Mejía Victores justified his leading the coup by the need to "preserve and fortify the unity of the Army and maintain the principle of hierarchy and command".[24] While many officers were not happy to see Mejía Victores take power, the coup encountered only limited resistance.

The new president was a career military officer with a reputation as a hard-liner. Mejía Victores had earlier gained notoriety in a sharp verbal clash with

U.S. Congressman Clarence Long. But once in power he pledged to hold prompt elections and gave strong support to U.S. policy. He cooperated with Honduras and El Salvador in dealing with the Contadora Group and took a leading role in reviving the Central American Defense Council (CONDECA). Internally, he dissolved the Council of State, which under Ríos Montt had provided some limited Indian participation in the government, and quickly discarded all plans for agrarian reform. By Fall 1983 both guerrilla activities and internal repression were apparently again on the rise.

The Reagan administration at first sought aid for President Mejía Victores, but without success in the U.S. Congress. Relations cooled further in November 1983 after Indians working under an U.S. AID contract were killed. The Guatemalan government failed to take action against those responsible and the Reagan administration suspended efforts to increase assistance. Meanwhile, guerrilla activities increased as government efforts to pacify the countryside suffered from lack of funds, lack of direction, rising human rights violations and continued dissension within the officer corps. The new president's control over the military seems limited and his hold on power tenuous. Another coup is possible, but so are elections for a constituent assembly. Increased guerrilla activity seems likely, but the chances that the insurgents will seize power in the next two or three years are still remote. The key to Guatemala's future remains the army, yet the army remains divided. The Reagan administration wants to support a strong, tough military which can defeat the guerrillas, but does not want a return to the conditions of 1981 and 1982 with the accompanying slaughter of noncombatants and murders of moderate politicians. There are military elements which share these goals, but no effective means has been found to support them without strengthening the hard-liners at the same time. Guatemala offers more frustration than hope for U.S. policies, primarily because they cannot influence that nation's dominant institution, the army.

HONDURAS

The Honduran military differs from its Guatemalan and Salvadoran counterparts, but it shares the region's heritage and its current conflicts. As the most developed institution in the region's least developed nation, it will play a key part in Honduras' future. Long neglected, it is now the focus of intense U.S. involvement, a development which offers major risks as well as opportunities.

The Honduran security forces (FUSEP) play a smaller role than they do in either El Salvador or Guatemala. Honduras lacks powerful private right-wing armies but it does have the strongest, most independent air force in Central America and a small but growing navy. Army strength is over 13,500 and increasing and an additional 1,200 men serve in the air force.[25]

The composition of the Honduran officer corps differs from its counterparts. Both the army and the air force run military academies, but some officers receive their education abroad and others are promoted from the ranks. When the United States trained a group of noncommissioned officers for Honduras as company grade officers for the expanding army, the graduates were commissioned immediately by the army commander, a sharp contrast to the Salvadoran approach. Honduran officers often come from rural areas and from families of lower social class standing. They are less likely than their Guatemalan counterparts to come from career military families.

The Honduran military, lacking the Guatemalan and Salvadoran history of ruthlessness in combating insurgencies, is less isolated and alienated from the civil population. Nothing in Honduran history compares with the 1932 peasant massacre in El Salvador or the Guatemalan counterinsurgency actions of the late 1960s and early 1980s. In addition, while the Honduran military openly ruled the nation from 1963 through 1981, it always allowed civilian politicians some power and never served as an instrument for eliminating political rivals. The military also lacks extremely close ties to the rural oligarchy; in the 1970s they actually implemented limited agrarian reforms.

There has been considerable corruption, brutality and crime against dissenters and peasant and labor groups. But on occasion, members of the military, including officers, have been disciplined for such action. Imprisonment is exceptional, but nevertheless sets a precedent.

The differences in the Honduran military reflect the different social structure and national history. By Central American standards, Honduras is large, very poor and underdeveloped and somewhat isolated. Since independence it has been the victim of its neighbors' ambitions and fears, suffering more invasions than any other Latin American nation, the last by El Salvador in 1969. Honduran society and especially the military hold an attitude of rational paranoia and assume that neighboring nations holding strongly divergent ideologies will support Honduran insurgents. And Hondurans who express sympathy for an opposed ideology held by a neighboring nation are suspected of conspiring to subvert the government. The military believes that Guatemala did this in the 1950s and that Nicaragua is doing this today. Their recourse has been to seek foreign support against foreign enemies. The British helped counter William Walker in the 19th century, and the United States opposed Nicaraguan efforts to dominate in the early 20th century.

This history and national psychology have given the Honduran military a genuine national defense mission with some popular support. When El Salvador attacked in 1969, thousands of peasants rushed to defend the nation, a fact which may have influenced the military's later decision to support agrarian reform. But facing a history of credible external threats can lead to equating all dissent with subversion and relying more on force than on diplomacy for protection. The Honduran military still views El Salvador as no less a long-range threat than Nicaragua. Salvadoran refugees are barely tolerated and important territorial disputes with El Salvador still exist.

Strong U.S. ties with the Honduran military date back to the 1930s. The Honduran military helped support the 1954 CIA-backed Guatemalan invasion, the 1961 Bay of Pigs operation and the 1965 intervention in the Dominican Republic. Involvement increased greatly in 1980 after the Sandinista victory in Nicaragua and the spread of civil conflict in El Salvador. Military assistance for FY80 was under $4 million, but approached $9 million in FY81, and exceeded $31 million in FY82.[26] The number of U.S. military advisers in Honduras also expanded steadily, reaching 300 at one point in 1983. Ten helicopters were loaned to Honduras, U.S. Army engineers began improving roads and airports and a U.S.-operated radar station was set up.

There were numerous reasons for this increased involvement. The United States hoped to use the Honduran military to interdict supplies destined for Salvadoran insurgents and to prevent them from establishing bases along the Honduran border. In addition, it was assumed that a strengthened military would deter a resurgence of Honduran guerrillas, and that military aid would symbolize U.S. support for Honduras. But as time passed, stability in Honduras was increasingly subordinated to the desire to use Honduras as a base for the U.S. confrontation with Nicaragua.

Honduran motives for accepting U.S. military involvement are less clear. The Honduran military believes that the civil conflict in El Salvador and the Sandinista regime in Nicaragua threaten Honduran national security. The U.S. buildup of El Salvador's armed forces produced pressures within the Honduran military for substantial external assistance. The military also found evidence linking domestic terrorists with El Salvador's guerrillas and Nicaragua's government. Some support was obtained from Argentina and Israel (the Israeli Defense Minister even visited Tegucigalpa), but the Honduran military felt that only the U.S. could provide minimum security requirements. But past U.S. support had been neither constant nor reliable. To insure that it would be this time, some Hondurans felt they must support virtually any U.S. regional project, adopt an extremely hard line in dealing with the Sandinistas, support Nicaraguan counterrevolutionaries and even let the U.S. train Salvadoran troops in Honduras. The latter was particularly objectionable, but was accepted as necessary. All of this risked escalating internal conflicts, straining civil-military relations, reducing Honduran international prestige by giving it the image of a U.S. client state, and could ultimately lead to war with Nicaragua.

The alignment has resulted in a series of large-scale, joint maneuvers with U.S. forces and a large, semi-permanent U.S. military presence in the country. Military assistance and economic aid have also increased steadily, with the latter reaching $37.3 million in FY83 and $41 million requested for FY84.[27]

For Honduras, the risks in this arrangement include increasing guerrilla activity linked to Nicaragua and military repression within Honduras. A war with Nicaragua could bring down both the civilian and military leadership. A change of U.S. administrations could leave Honduras with no effective external support against hostile neighbors. Recognition of these risks has produced some nervousness and dissent within the military and more discontent among civilian politicians, but the civilians have limited capacity to alter the situation because the Honduran Constitution leaves effective control of the military in military hands. Basic decisions are made by the commander of the armed forces and the superior council of the armed forces, a body of senior officers chosen by the officer corps. The commander can be removed by a two-thirds vote of the Congress but in reality, the armed forces commander is much more capable of removing the president than vice versa.

For the United States, the risk is that its policies are militarizing Honduras, undermining its fragile democracy and increasing internal conflict. The attempt to promote stability could actually create instability. This policy also risks a regional war and exacerbates disputes within the United States over the entire region.

THE *CONTRAS*

The most controversial and potentially most dangerous of all the U.S. involvements with Central American armed forces is that with the counter-revolutionary bodies fighting Nicaragua's Sandinista government. The *contras*, as they are known, are a disparate amalgamation of forces unified only by opposition to Nicaragua's current rulers. U.S. activities to date may have been more effective in producing strong domestic and world criticism of its Central American policies than in weakening the Sandinistas' grip on power.

Evaluating the *contras* and their U.S. links is difficult, given the covert nature of their relations, largely handled by the CIA. There is little agreement even as to the composition and nature of *contra* forces. For the Sandinistas and their supporters they are all *somocistas* (supporters of ex-dictator Somoza) or traitors, while the Reagan administration portrays them as democratic "freedom fighters." In addition, they are divided into several feuding groups, operating out of two different nations and espousing different programs.

By far, the largest and most closely linked to the United States is the Nicaraguan Democratic Force (FDN), headquartered in Miami and operating out of bases along the Honduran-Nicaraguan border. Its armed strength is variously estimated at from 5,000 to 10,000 men. Its leaders are conservative civilians, many of whom opposed Somoza during his last years in power.

But the majority of FDN's military general staff and many of the field officers are ex-officers of Somoza's national guard. An undetermined part of the rank and file consists of ex-enlisted guardsmen. Thus, the FDN is called *somocista*, and is accused of being composed of individuals guilty of genocide during the 1978-79 civil conflict and determined to restore the old order in Nicaragua. The FDN denies the charge and discounts its ties to the defunct national guard.

The truth, as usual, lies somewhere between the accusations and the denials. One of the seven directors is Brigadier General Enrique Bermudez Varela, a career guard officer; but he spent the last several years of that career in diplomatic exile in Washington and Japan. He was viewed by Somoza as too popular with the troops and not sufficiently committed to the Somoza family. Furthermore, he had independent contacts with U.S. military personnel dating from his command of the Nicaraguan contingent in the 1965 U.S.-led intervention in the Dominican Republic. Bermudez had no connection with the atrocities of the regime's last years in power. As a result, he was chosen by U.S. military and intelligence planners to head a reorganized guard in a government succeeding Somoza. A few other FDN officers have similar records. Others, especially enlisted men, were last-minute additions to the guard; had they been offered any chance to return after the revolution, most would have done so, providing they did not risk imprisonment. But no offer was made and they became permanent exiles whose only real hope of returning to home and family was to overthrow the new regime. They have few ties to Honduras, and the Hondurans, in turn, do not know what to do with them. Honduras preferred that they be supported and kept busy by anti-Sandinistas (and later, by the CIA) than that they wander around Honduras, seeking jobs, land or plunder.

Many ex-guard officers felt betrayed by Somoza, and few have any desire to return that family to power. In that sense, they are not *somocistas*. But most are very conservative, have little loyalty to democracy and are linked by training and history to the guard, a force almost universally hated in Nicaragua. Some want revenge against the Sandinistas; others simply want to return home; few qualify as ideologically inspired freedom fighters.

Many of the FDN's rank-and-file are peasants, small landowners or shopkeepers who are unhappy with the Sandinistas for religious or ideological reasons. Many are Miskito Indians, reacting to Sandinista actions which disrupted their traditional patterns of living, destroyed their homes and transformed them into bitter refugees. The political leaders include anti-Somoza businessmen such as Adolfo Calero, who originally gave some support to the revolution. The FDN has not, however, overcome the taint of the ex-guardsmen's participation.

Another force, Democratic Revolutionary Action (ARDE), operates out of Costa Rica. Like the FDN, it is an amalgam of Miskito Indians, civilian politicians and veterans of Nicaragua's 1978-79 civil war. But ARDE's veterans are ex-Sandinistas, not ex-guardsmen, and are led by former Sandinista hero Eden Pastora, who claims to be the true defender of Sandinista ideals. He has resisted close ties with the Reagan administration and the CIA and has warned against U.S. military intervention in Nicaragua. In contrast, some of the FDN's leadership has stated that it would welcome U.S. military involvement against the Sandinistas. At one time Pastora was the most popular military figure in Nicaragua; he believes he is still popular, but some observers believe that the Sandinista's portrayal of him as a traitor aligned with the CIA and the ex-Somoza guard has reduced his support.

ARDE forces, much smaller than those of the FDN, are estimated at 2,500 to 4,000, of which less than 2,000 are regular combatants. They are chronically short of funds and equipment, and receive much less cooperation and tolerance from Costa Rican authorities than the FDN enjoys from Honduras. At one point, ARDE was forced to suspend military operations, but revived their operation with funds from a variety of sources (reportedly including Israeli, Columbian, Panamanian, Venezuelan and South American and European groups).

While it has greater political credibility than other guerrilla groups, ARDE is weak and divided. It has occupied some territory along the vulnerable southern border of Nicaragua, but seems unable to push far inland. Its spectacular air assaults have garnered considerable publicity but little military advantage. Internal disputes, notably between Pastora and ARDE's chief political spokesman, former Junta member Alfonso Robelo, also plague ARDE's efforts and one small faction has left ARDE and launched its own guerrilla force.

Another guerrilla force opposed to the Sandinistas is Fernando (*El Negro*) Charmorro's Nicaraguan Armed Revolutionary Forces (FARN). Having neither ex-guard support nor many ex-Sandinistas, it is small (a few hundred at the most) and it is of minor importance. While the *contras* have made little progress in toppling the Nicaraguan government, their presence in Honduras and apparent links with the Honduran armed forces and the United States have sharply escalated tensions between Nicaragua and Honduras. These tensions will continue unless *contra* activities decline, something the FDN is unlikely to accept. Much of the Honduran military would also resist such a decline, believing that the *contra* forces help defend Honduras and insure U.S. support.

ARDE has become a major political issue in Costa Rica. The Costa Rican government of President Luis Alberto Monge, officially neutral, has limited ARDE's action. But it has not closed down ARDE operations along the Nicaraguan border. Current levels of *contra* activity clearly present a serious problem, but the prospects for the future are much graver. Current efforts, it seems, will not topple the Sandinistas. Cuba appears to be promoting negotiations between Pastora and the Nicaraguan government, though its motives are unclear. The Cubans may hope that an accommodation with Pastora will ease the pressure on the Sandinistas and weaken the counter-revolution. They may even be acting for the Sandinistas, who for political reasons cannot make overtures. Or, they may simply be trying to further divide ARDE and the FDN whose efforts to form a common front have failed.[28] In any case, the *contras* are under increasing pressure to make major gains in 1984. Many of their troops, especially in the FDN, were recruited with the expectation that the total operation would be over within a year, and their enthusiasm and reliability will likely decrease. Should President Reagan not be reelected, they will face a major crisis. Their only hope of success seems to lie in a regional war, a development which would be disastrous for Honduras without U.S. support.

These divisions may explain U.S. efforts to persuade the *contras* to offer the Sandinistas a truce in return for basic democratic reforms and negotiations. The major U.S. reason, however, may be to undermine the Sandinistas' offers of peace and amnesty to guerrillas who abandon the struggle. At any rate, the Sandinistas rejected any possibility of direct negotiations with their armed opponents.

Some accommodation might ultimately be reached between much of ARDE and the Sandinista leadership allowing ARDE some political participation in Nicaragua and the return of ARDE combatants. Such negotiations would be long and arduous and require foreign intermediaries.

The Miskito Indians may have the best prospects for a political settlement with the Sandinistas. Indeed, the Nicaraguan government itself has recently made some gestures in this direction. The Miskitos and their Suma allies located on the isolated, thinly-populated Atlantic Coast offer no major threat to the central government. But their bitterness and deep distrust based on past events and their ties to the FDN and ARDE complicate any formal arrangement.

Negotiations with the FDN are the least likely. The Sandinistas might be able to deal with the FDN political leadership and many of the rank-and-file but are extremely unlikely to negotiate with the ex-guard element which dominates the military commands. The ex-guards know this and therefore seek a military victory, even if it requires outside intervention.

Many *contras* will not accept a political settlement, even if some *contras* eventually negotiate, or more possible, if the United States ends its support. Some of their leaders might settle in Miami, but thousands would likely stay in Honduras, with weapons and training, but without funds or jobs or any real hopes of going home. They could create significant problems for Honduras and for the entire region and there is no evidence of serious planning for this eventuality.

THE REGIONAL MILITARY SITUATION: CURRENT STATUS AND FUTURE PROSPECTS

In 1984, Central America's armed forces will face key decisions on the fate of their institutions; in El Salvador and Guatemala, they must decide about relations with civilian political parties, holding elections, conducting the war and possibly negotiating. The Honduran military's key decisions concern their links with the United States and the Nicaraguan *contras*. The *contras* need some successes against the Sandinistas and improved relations among themselves.

Major decisions also must be made about linking armed forces and about ties to the United States. Central American armed forces consult frequently, and officers from different nations often attend common meetings. The various nations' forces have shared classes at the U.S. Army School of the Americas, the Inter-American Air Force Academy in Panama and service schools in the United States.

In 1963, with strong U.S. urging, a Central American Defense Council (CONDECA) was established to promote regional military cooperation and training. Joint exercises were held in 1965 between Honduras, Guatemala, El Salvador and Nicaragua with significant U.S. support.[29] Neither Costa Rica nor Panama joined CONDECA, giving it a decided right-wing cast. The absence of a common, credible threat kept the organization from developing beyond the embryonic stage, and its permanent staff became a rest or exile tour for officers assigned to it. CONDECA agreed on such matters as standardizing insignias, but proved impotent in serious matters such as the 1969 Honduran-Salvadoran war. After that conflict, Honduras suspended its CONDECA participation. Guatemalan interest also declined as other members became less supportive of its claims to Belize. The Sandinista victory completed CONDECA's decline until 1983.

The Reagan administration had long been interested in forging a new Central American alliance which would exclude Nicaragua. The first effort was political, to create a Central American democratic community, but it failed. As the Nicaraguan and Honduran confrontation escalated, interest grew in reviving CONDECA to oppose Nicaragua. At an August 1983 meeting of Central American military commanders with the new Commander-in-Chief of the U.S. Southern Command, General Paul Gorman, CONDECA's reactivation was formally suggested, probably by Honduran General Gustavo

Alvarez. Guatemalan Defense Minister General Oscar Mejía Victores seized power on his return from this meeting, provoking speculation of U.S. participation in the fall of Ríos Montt. In September he invited his Salvadoran and Honduran counterparts to a meeting in Guatemala where CONDECA was formally resurrected. Panama's military commander joined them and indicated that his nation would take an active role in CONDECA. Nicaragua was excluded and Costa Rica's Defense Minister canceled his planned participation without explanation. General Gorman attended with the official status of observer.[30]

The motives for CONDECA's revival and the U.S. role in it are not obvious; there is evidently a division among CONDECA's members as to whether that organization should serve an offensive, defensive, or primarily psychological role in the confrontation with the Sandinistas. CONDECA might demonstrate strength and unity among its members, or willingness to use military force against Nicaragua, or support of U.S. policy. Some CONDECA members may also hope for increased military aid to the region; Guatemala and, perhaps, Panama have special interest as they lack the large U.S. bilateral programs operating in Honduras and El Salvador. There is also speculation that Honduras and/or Guatemala might eventually use CONDECA as a cover for intervening in El Salvador to prevent a guerrilla victory.

The United States may view CONDECA as capable of offensive actions against Nicaragua, but all of its members' armed forces suffer from severe logistical and communications deficiencies and would have difficulty operating more than a few miles inside Nicaraguan territory. Most of Panama's armed forces are militarized police, virtually useless in offensive operations, and El Salvador's army is already overextended in its fight against domestic guerrillas. Guatemala's initial interest in CONDECA has declined rapidly, leaving CONDECA with little more than the Honduran Army. CONDECA might call for U.S. armed intervention against Nicaragua but the legitimacy of its request would be questioned.

What is clear is that the reactivation of CONDECA's highlights the growing militarization of Central America and increases the possibility of regional conflict. The danger is further increased by Nicaraguan military support for guerrillas in El Salvador and Honduras and by the close ties between the Honduran military and the Nicaraguan *contras*. The Honduran and Nicaraguan militaries funnel U.S. and Soviet supplies to guerrilla forces; this superpower involvement raises the stakes of regional conflict yet higher. It is in this context that the United States must evaluate the Honduran government's suggestion to the Kissinger Commission of adopting "a Special Bilateral Treaty of Mutual Defense" which would be "similar to the United States agreement with South Korea" and would provide for the "establishment of mixed air and naval bases."[31]

U.S. support has now become vital for the institutional survival of Central America's armed forces. The Sandinistas' destruction of the *Guardia Nacional* exemplifies the fate of forces which lose that support. To maintain U.S. assistance, Central American governments increasingly back U.S. policy, especially toward Nicaragua. This escalates tension with Nicaragua, giving even greater credibility to the "Nicaraguan threat." This, in turn, persuades much of the military leadership that it should forge ever closer ties with the United States to lessen the chance that a change in Washington's policies will leave them isolated and vulnerable. Requests for greatly increased military assistance, the revival of CONDECA, and the Honduran treaty proposal all exemplify this pattern.

These relationships pose major dangers for the United States, tying it closer to military solutions. It focuses world attention on military aspects of U.S. policy, perceived as supporting the military in internal political disputes, undermining civilian political sectors, especially in Honduras, and abandoning a U.S. commitment to democratic practices. Efforts to curb human rights abuses are fatally compromised by such actions as the veto of requirements that military assistance to El Salvador be conditioned on human rights improvements. Offhand remarks suggesting that some death-squad killings might actually be attributable to the left absolve the governments and the military leadership from responsibility for ending such activities. All this reduces actual and potential U.S. influence over the armed forces, creating instead the impression that Washington's policy is so dependent on the Central American military that those forces will be supported regardless of what policies they pursue or fail to pursue.

For the Central Americans, these policies increase the risk of regional war and decrease pressure on the military to engage in or even allow serious negotiations. They set the stage for prolonged and increasingly destructive civil conflicts, a scenario likely to erode U.S. support for the Central American military. They may lead ultimately to major reductions in or even termination of military assistance, leaving Central America's armed forces angry, frustrated and vulnerable.

No policy toward Central America can ignore the central role played by the region's armed forces. But a successful policy cannot give *sole* priority to the military. National security is a legitimate concern in Central America, and dismissing or minimizing this concern will only reduce U.S. influence. Nonetheless, security depends on the popular perception that the military serves national rather than class interests, that it defends rather than abuses individual rights. For much of their history, regional armed forces have put parochial concerns above national interest. They have been praetorians far more than patriots. Previous U.S. efforts have failed to alter these patterns. In Nicaragua, the U.S. eliminated the old inefficient and corrupt military system and created in its place the *Guardia* which turned out to be efficiently brutal and corrupt. U.S. involvement in Guatemala in the 1950s and early 1960s helped precipitate the political polarization and insurgency which have plagued that nation ever since. Nearly four years' work with El Salvador's military has given it greater firepower, but no discernible sense of civic resonsibility or accountability. Continuing these policies only insures repeated failures.

The future of Central America's armed forces depends upon their ability to evolve from repressive praetorianism into an institution which defends the interest and security of the entire nation. U.S. policy needs to help the armed forces realize that supporting the status quo will only lead to their own destruction. They must also realize that insurgency is more a political than a military problem, and that it can be better resolved by eliminating the causes of injustice than by eliminating the dissenters. A better-educated officer corps and carefully tailored external aid can help change existing patterns. Such change will be slow and perilous, but the alternatives — for both Central America and the United States — offer only more repression, conflict and very possibly a regional war.

NOTES

1. Lyle McAlister, *The* Fuero Militar *in New Spain*, Gainesville: University of Florida Press, 1957, p. 15.
2. Christon I. Archer, *The Army in Bourbon Mexico*, Albuquerque: University of New Mexico Press, 1977, p. 257.
3. *Ibid.*, p. 219.
4. John J. Johnson, *The Military and Society in Latin America*, Stanford: Stanford University Press, 1964, p. 37.
5. Gabriel Aguilera Peralta, *La interración militar en centroamerica*, n.p.: INCEP, n.d., p. 14.
6. Letter from Dr. Dana G. Munro to Richard Millett, Feburary 14, 1965. For details on the 1923 Conference see Thomas Leonard, *United States Policy and Arms Limitations in Central America: The Washington Conference of 1923*, Los Angeles, California State University at Los Angeles, 1982.
7. For details on this see Richard Millett, *Guardians of the Dynasty*, Maryknoll, N.Y.: Orbis Books, 1977.
8. *Washington Post*, March 15, 1980, p. A1.
9. International Institute for Strategic Studies, *The Military Balance, 1983-1984*, London: International Institute for Strategic Studies, 1983, p. 110.
10. *Ibid.*, p. 127. *El Salvador Military and Economic Reprogramming*, Hearing before a Subcommittee of the Committee on Appropriations, U.S. Senate, 98th Congress, 1st Session, March 22, 1983, p. 76.
11. Robert V. Elam, "Appeal to Arms: The Army and Politics in El Salvador, 1931-1964," unpublished Ph.D. dissertation, University of New Mexico, 1968, pp. 176-77.
12. Carolyn Forche and Leonel Gomez, "The Military's Web of Corruption," *The Nation*, October 23, 1982, p. 391.
13. *El Salvador: The United States in the Midst of a Maelstorm. A Report to the Committee on Foreign Relations and the Committee on Appropriations, U.S. Senate*, 97th Congress, 2nd Session, 1982, p. 6.

14. *Foreign Assistance and Related Program Appropriations for 1984,* Hearings before a Subcommittee of the Committee on Appropriations, House of Representatives, 98th Congress, 1st Session, March 1983, pp. 326-27.
15. Institute for Strategic Studies, *op. cit.,* pp. 110-11.
16. This is due in part to the fact that the *Politécnica*, while extremely rigorous, usually manages to graduate up to half of those who enter.
17. For details of this operation see Richard H. Immerman, *The CIA in Guatemala*, Austin: University of Texas Press, 1982, and Stephen Schlesinger and Stephen Kinser, *Bitter Fruit*, Garden City, N.Y.: Doubleday, 1981.
18. Richard N. Adams, *Crucifixion by Power*, Austin: University of Texas Press, 1970, p. 261.
19. Thomas P. Anderson, *Politics in Central America*, New York: Praeger, 1982, pp. 52-52. Gabriel Aguilera Peralta, "The Militarization of the Guatemalan State," *Guatemala in Rebellion*, Johnathan L. Fried *et. al.*, eds. New York: Grove Press, 1983, p. 118.
20. *U.S. Policy Towards Guatemala*, Hearing before a Subcommittee of the Committee on Foreign Affairs, House of Representatives, 98th Congress, 1st Session, March 1983, p. 37.
21. *Ibid.*, pp. 43-44.
22. *Ibid.*, pp. 56-59.
23. *Foreign Assistance and Related Programs for FY1984*, p. 72.
24. *Central American Report* (Guatemala), 10, August 12, 1983, p. 241.
25. Institute for Strategic Studies, p. 111. The Air Force operates a squadron of *Super Mystère* B2 fighters and hopes to acquire U.S. F5Es in the near future.
26. *Foreign Assistance and Related Programs for FY1984*, p. 73.
27. *Ibid.*
28. *La Nación Internacional*, San José, Costa Rica, May 27-June 6, 1983, p. 6.
29. Don L. Etchison, *The United States and Militaries in Central America*, New York: Praeger, 1975, pp. 64-65.
30. *La Nación Internacional.* October 6-12, 1983, p. 7.
31. Government of the Republic of Honduras, *Executive Summary: Document Presented to the Bi-Partisan Commission of the Government of the United States for Central America*, October 14, 1983, p. 14.

SOCIALISM AND SOVIETISM

4
THE ORIGINS OF
SANDINISTA FOREIGN POLICY

Arturo Cruz Sequeira

When the Sandinistas overthrew Somoza in July 1979, they had the choice of splitting the broad coalition that had brought them to power and advancing directly to "socialism"; or else maintaining that alliance and building a new model based on a mixed economy, political pluralism and non-alignment. But, in effect, the choice had already been made.

For years before victory, members of the National Directorate of the Sandinista National Liberation Front (FSLN) debated the necessity of a coalition with the middle class. Before victory was achieved via this alliance, there was consensus in the Directorate over the socialist objective. But power itself has created new tensions, as the more pragmatic *comandantes* have begun to question the feasibility of a direct transition to socialism, and whether socialism itself necessarily entails alignment with the Soviet bloc.

THE APPROACH OF THE "MODERATES"

The "moderate" advisors of the Sandinista Front took a somewhat different position in the debate than did those inside the Sandinista Party. They favored a "third option" based on the belief that neither the Cuban model nor that of Costa Rica was applicable in the case of Nicaragua. In terms of domestic policy, their goal was a welfare state which would include a private sector. They maintained that foreign policy could not simply be the expression of ideological preference. A realistic assessment of Nicaraguan

I would like to express my sincere gratitude to Laurie Derby, William Hellert, Bruce Cameron, and Donald Castillo for the valuable comments and assistance they provided me in the course of writing this essay.

95

constraints was primary, demanding a concern with the means of achieving their political objectives, as opposed to an exclusive concern with the objectives themselves. The moderate advisors thus recommended a foreign policy based on three broad considerations: the constraints imposed by the geopolitics of Nicaragua; its fragile, dependent economy; and the revolutionary crisis in Central America.

While the advocates of this position shared the nationalism impelling the revolution, they insisted on finding a modus vivendi with the United States. Nicaragua's eventual walk down a socialist path would have to accommodate the geopolitical constraint of existence within the American sphere of influence.

The moderate advisors felt that the structural nature of Nicaragua's economic dependence, the immediate problem of acquiring external funds for economic reconstruction, and the difficulty in making a direct transition to socialism under these conditions were considerations every bit as important as ideological imperatives they shared with the Sandinista *comandantes*. According to the moderates, the revolutionary ideology of the new state in no way altered the objective characteristics of the Nicaraguan economy. It remained open, with a small internal market producing primary commodities and agricultural goods, and dependent on subsidized petroleum imports. The external sector (exports and imports) accounted for approximately 35% of the national product. Nicaragua's dependency was further exacerbated by the country's post-war needs. Large capital inflows were necessary to compensate for the sharp drop in domestic savings. The moderates, thus, were concerned with crafting a foreign policy in line with these needs; one that was sensitive, though not subject, to the principal aid donors, the United States, Western Europe, and the regional powers.

The moderates believed that a direct transition to socialism under these political and economic conditions would be premature and quixotic. They stressed that Nicaragua's financial dependence on western aid sources, the state of economic disarray, and the petit bourgeois nature of the society (the preponderance of small farmers and businessmen) created unfavorable conditions for a rapid transition. Excessive and empty socialist rhetoric during the first years of the revolution would alienate the private sector, impeding the class cooperation necessary for economic reconstruction. It was important to avoid alienating the conservative small land-holders, who were vital for development purposes.[1] Given these economic realities, the moderates recommended patience. They hoped that tactical concessions to the private sector and the middle class would endure, developing a hybrid revolutionary model in the process.

Equally important, the moderates felt that the Sandinista Front had an obligation to the left in El Salvador and Guatemala, regional powers such as Mexico and Venezuela, and neighboring Costa Rica and Panama. This would lead to political caution and avoidance of unnecessarily strong links with the Soviet Union. The FSLN's behavior would affect the credibility of other Central American revolutionaries. If Managua radicalized the revolution, neighboring states would not accept the Salvadoran left's claims to moderation. To many, Nicaragua represented the possibility for a non-aligned "third option," in which Marxists and non-Marxists alike could enter into a strategic alliance. This hybrid model would be both novel and eclectic, encompassing, among others, the Christian and leftist elements involved in the struggle for social change in Nicaragua.

The moderates asserted that the Nicaraguan political system should evolve into a democracy, however imperfect, implying a formal pluralist system consistent with the Front's own stated goal of a broad class alliance. This partial, ill-defined democracy would help prevent international isolation and future recrimination from the West. From this standpoint, diplomacy would have to adjust to the dynamics of geography and the weakness of the country's material base. If the third option were to materialize in Nicaragua, it would not merely be a product of Sandinista will. It would be a product of the tension between what the *comandantes* desired—in actuality something resembling the Cuban model—and what was possible given these objective constraints. In the final analysis, a third option was possible only if the National Directorate's immediate tactical concessions to the non-Marxist groups would envolve into strategic concessions.

In their eagerness to persuade the Sandinista Front leaders to accept a third option, the moderate advisors argued that the Cuban experience could not be transferred to Nicaragua. They felt that changes in the global power structure had created by 1979 a much more tolerant and open context for the establishment of revolutionary regimes than when Cuba was consolidating its socialist polity in the early 1960s. When Castro had come to power in 1959, Cuba had one of two options: to remain linked to the United States, or to become part of the socialist camp. At that time, the United States exercised world economic primacy, and its leadership within the Atlantic alliance was unquestioned. The influence of regional powers in the Caribbean was negligible. In this, context, U.S. policy forced Cuba to turn to the Soviet bloc for economic assistance. However, the existence both of a liberal administration in Washington willing to be flexible with the Sandinistas (in contrast to the Cuban policies of previous administrations) and of progressive governments in Europe enabled the Sandinistas to choose from a varied consortium of potential donors. For the first time, room for a third option existed.

The moderates admitted that the Carter administration had sought reformist, not revolutionary change in Nicaragua. However, President Carter exhibited goodwill and flexibility towards the new regime. The United States at that time felt that if it accommodated Third World revolutionary regimes, these, in turn, would accommodate U.S. interests. The moderates claimed that such goodwill was evidenced by the $75 million loan (a supplement to FY1980) opposed in Congress by a conservative minority which succeeded only temporarily in delaying legislative action. By postponing the loan, this group hoped that Managua would finally display its "true colors." (This strategy almost succeeded, for Nicaragua's position on Afghanistan, the PLO and the Soviet Union in general disappointed many congressmen, who, in spite of the administration's active lobbying in favor of the loan, ended up voting against it.)

Further assistance from the Carter Administration included support through multilateral lending institutions such as the World Bank, the Inter-American Development Bank, and assistance in the restructuring of Nicaragua's external debt. During the first eighteen months of the revolution, Nicaragua received $117.6 million in soft loans and $20.3 million in transfer payments from the United States. The U.S. also participated actively in the $189.1 million commitment from the Inter-American Development Bank and $102.7 million from the World Bank. Between July 19, 1979 and February 11, 1982, Nicaragua received $1,552.7 million in loans, credit extensions, and transfers, mostly from Western sources. This represented almost 75% of the Nicaraguan gross national product of 1980.[2]

The Carter administration, the moderate advisers argued, recognized that the victory of the revolution was a fait accompli, and did little more than attempt to encourage the FSLN to move towards an "imperfect democracy." In the view of Carter's ambassador to Managua, this included limited participation by competitive political parties under FSLN direction, and the ensured survival of the private sector. Even under the later, less sympathetic Carter policy, the U.S. was willing to coexist with a socialist Nicaragua, providing that the leadership in Managua was aware of its geopolitical responsibility within the U.S. sphere of influence. At worst, a policy of "Finlandization" would be acceptable to the United States.[3] This would entail de-emphasizing foreign policy differences with the United States while maintaining a certain ideological distance. Such a policy would be designed to avert antagonism from either the United States or the Soviet Union, a necessity for any small, neutral state heavily dependent on foreign trade.

The moderates also looked towards the opportunity offered by the rise of Mexico and Venezuela as regional powers, now hoping to wield influence in Latin America. Most of the European countries were willing to make a long-term effort to accommodate the revolution and assist Nicaragua in maintaining a position independent of the United States. The moderates dared to question what the Soviet Union could offer Nicaragua apart from military assistance. They further doubted the possibility of a Soviet commitment to Nicaragua paralleling that to Cuba. In essence, the moderates recommended a pragmatic foreign policy that would leave ideology aside and concentrate on the gradual achievement of the revolution's objectives.

Considering the geopolitical imperatives, the economic incentives and regional conditions, why did the National Directorate of the FSLN insist from the beginning on a pro-Soviet foreign policy? Why did they select a policy that went so far as to preclude establishing relations with the socialist People's Republic of China while maintaining relations with Somoza's ally, Taiwan? From the outset, the FSLN had identified with the Soviet agenda, from the problem of Kampuchea, to the deployment of missiles in Europe. Yet, the political parties representing the petit bourgeoisie and middle class insisted in the Council of State on establishing diplomatic relations with China. These same parties also insisted on condemning Soviet intervention in Afghanistan and supported the demands of the Solidarity movement in Poland.[4] Equally important, why did the moderate advisers ultimately fail in their central objective, the "education" of the FSLN leadership? An understanding of the origins of the Sandinista Front ideology — hence the world view of those who would become leaders of the party, state, and armed forces — is a prerequisite to understanding current Nicaraguan foreign policy.

THE ORIGINS OF SANDINISTA FRONT IDEOLOGY

One of the most interesting, if little known, phenomenon of the first phase of the Somoza regime was its break with the conservative-liberal power bloc in the 1940s and the fact that Somoza offered the working class a populist alternative. Both the trade unions and the only leftist party, the pro-Moscow Nicaraguan Socialist Party (PSN), lent their support to the consolidation of the first Somoza regime. In return, inspired by the Peronist movement in Argentina, they were rewarded with a labor code and the country's first social security plan.

Over the years, the Somozas managed to depoliticize Nicaraguan society, turning political life into a family monopoly. The intellectuals of the time settled for "educating" the dictator, concerning themselves solely with intellectual matters and leaving the management of all political affairs entirely to Somoza. With the exception of certain landed families like the Charmorros, the Nicaraguan bourgeoisie was never a "ruling class." There was virtually no correlation between political power and economic power in Nicaraguan society. The bourgeoisie was left to its sole interest, increasing its wealth, first through banking and cotton production and, later in the 1960s through Central American economic integration.

Nicaragua experienced enormous economic expansion in the 1950s and 1960s. According to the United Nations Economic Commission for Latin America (ECLA), the Nicaraguan economy had the highest rates of real growth in Latin America during this twenty-year span. The export structure of the country was diversified into five principal export commodities including sugar, cotton, coffee, beef, and fishing; the manufacturing sector jumped from 10% of the GNP in 1960, to 23% in 1970. Yet despite this growth, civil society as such under Somoza rule was nonexistent, political discourse in the country was sterile, and all social classes lacked both the political organization and capacity for expression necessary for a coherent national political program.

To a large extent, the Sandinista Front was a manifestation of the vacuous nature of this political culture. The Front mirrored the limitations of the broader society's poor social organization and political participation. The FSLN world view was ideologically narrow. Perhaps Nicaragua's geographical isolation and U.S. tutelage made it inevitable that the Sandinista Front founders would adopt an exaggeratedly pro-Soviet stance. Both Carlos Fonseca and Tomás Borge, founders of the FSLN, had learned their elementary Marxism from Soviet handbooks. This is exemplified by Fonseca's idealistic, almost utopian book *Un Nicaragüense en Moscú*, which parroted the Soviet interpretation of the Hungarian invasion in 1956.[5]

Due to the poverty of the country's political culture, at the end of the 1950s the Nicaraguan Socialist Party (PSN)—the pro-Soviet communist party— was the only party of substance for the Nicaraguan left. Its political passivity notwithstanding, the PSN gave the new militants their primary ideological reference and rudimentary theoretical tools. The real dispute between the PSN and the Front in subsequent years concerned tactics, specifically the advisability of armed struggle. The differences grew over time, particulary since the Front and the Socialist Party were competing for a very small political constituency.

Most of the Front members had studied at the Nicaraguan National University. Those who had left the country in the 1960 had spent most of their time in Cuba and, in some cases, in the Soviet Union. Therefore, Cuba remained the revolutionary paradigm for the Front. Just as the Nicaraguan bourgeoisie vulgarly imitated the Americans, the Sandinista Front indiscriminately mimicked the rhetoric and tactics of the Cuban revolution. Spurred by the memory of the American interventions in Nicaragua in 1912 and 1927, young people in Nicaragua readily adopted an anti-American position while lauding Cuba's valiant efforts at achieving automony from the United States. The idealism of Castro's revolution represented an attractive challenge to the arrogance of U.S. hegemony in Central America.

Interestingly, even during periods of great tension between Cuba and the Soviet Union, the more sophisticated cadres of the Sandinista Front were not willing to adopt a critical posture towards the Soviets. This despite the fact that they had adopted the Cuban tactics and methods for popular mobilization, and also despite that they had begun to have serious disagreements with the Soviet-aligned Nicaraguan Socialist Party. By the end of the 1960s, the Sandinista Front had "evolved" from the *foco* thesis to what came to be known as the strategy of the Prolonged People's War (GPP).

The *foco* approach was born out of the Cuban experience, in which priority was given to the armed guerrilla movement over and above the party. Regis Debray, in his classic effort at theoretical rationalization of the Cuban position, assumed that objectively, conditions in Latin America were ripe for a revolutionary process.[6] Debray wrote that the subjective conditions which were necessary for the initiation of the revolutionary movement would be created through the armed action of the guerrilla vanguard or *foco*, as Ernesto "Che" Guevara called them. With the failure of "*foquismo*," not only in Nicaragua but throughout Latin America, the Sandinista Front was obliged to reassess its revolutionary theory.

Chinese revolutionary rhetoric was found useful in justifying the Front's continuing presence in the mountains and the role of the city as the starting point of guerrilla warfare. This was, in other words, Fonseca's military strategy—that the war should be fought primarily in the countryside with logistical support from the cities. "*Foquismo*" was revived in a new form—the ideal of the "Prolonged People's War."

At the beginning of the 1970s there emerged among the rank and file of the Front a novel Marxist tendency. A new generation of Sandinistas who provided the ideological foundations for the Proletarian Tendency had been educated in Chile during the Allende years. They had close links with the MAPU militants (the Unitary Movement for Popular Action), a leftist splinter group with a peasant base that split from the Christian Democrats in the early 1970s.

They returned from Chile with new "dependency" theories suggesting that a total break with the developed metropolitan centers of capitalism was necessary for development to occur in the third world periphery.[7] They also brought back a new strategy that favored moving the struggle from the countryside to the city. This strategy would organize a Sandinista Party among the Nicaraguan working class and the rural proletariat in the cotton fields of León and Chinandega, the only regions where a rural proletariat proper, rather than a peasantry, existed in Nicaragua.

The ideological divisions between adherents of the Protracted People's War faction and the Proletarian Tendency crystallized in a struggle for power that had been latent for years within the Sandinista Front. One result was the emergence of what came to be known as the "insurrectionist tendency," or the "*Terceristas*".[8]

The GPP, led by Tomás Borge, Bayardo Arce and Henry Ruiz represented the old guard. The Proletarian Tendency, under the control of Jaime Wheelock, Carlos Núñez and Luis Carrion, represented the new generation, those who were unhappy with being in the second echelon, yet who in many respects were just a dogmatic as those of the GPP. The *Terceristas*—Humberto Ortega, his brother Daniel, and Victor Tirado—looked imaginatively toward a more gradual transition to socialism, and had a much broader concept of class alliances. Not only did they bring together a group of progressive bourgeois supporters *"Los Doce"* (the Twelve),[9] but they also linked up with a powerful faction known as the *Frente Sur* (the "Southern Front"), which included Eden Pastora (*Comandante Zero*), Germán Pomares and José Validivia. This group was associated with Omar Torrijos' line in Panama, which favored a nationalist third option for Central America.

While there was a general consensus among those who would eventually become the Sandinista national leadership on the socialist objectives of the revolution, there remained disputes about revolutionary strategy. There were also differences in generation and personality. Before the victory, there was no real conflict concerning the socialist objective between hard-liners and moderates. It was the *Terceristas* who proved to have the most pragmatic and appropriate strategy. Having earned support from the Cubans, Torrijos, and the Venezuelans the *Terceristas* were able to convince the other groups within the FSLN to follow their line. When the revolution triumphed, the *Terceristas* were the main force inside the Sandinista Front.

There were two factions within the *Terceristas*, mediated by the Ortega brothers who provided the point of equilibrium. One of these groups was the so-called "Young *Terceristas*," who had been in the Internal Front. This group had the support of the top guerrilla *comandantes*. The members of the Internal Front mistrusted the "petit bourgeois" intentions of the Southern Front, and remained within the *Tercerista* movement only because of their confidence in Humberto Ortega's strong ideological line.

Once in power, the *comandantes* who became members of the national leadership — the National Directorate — including the *Terceristas*, rejected the broad coalition that had brought them victory. The Southern Front was relegated to a secondary role, and the Ortegas favored the Young *Terceristas* within their own faction. The split within the *Terceristas* weakened the group in its post-revolutionary struggle with the other factions within the Front. In addition, most of *Los Doce*, who originally had called for moderation and balance in the new government, began to portray themselves as radicals in order to gain ideological credibility and thus secure key posts from their more radical Sandinista superiors.

The Sandinista Front did not observe the pluralistic political platform that had helped to bring them their initial popularity and legitimacy. They also failed to acknowledge to the world that the three tendencies had been reunited not only because of Castro's authority, but also because of the efforts of Panama's Torrijos and the social democratic former president of Venezuela, Carlos Andrés Pérez. During the first months after the victory, some of the *comandantes* adopted the extreme view that the United States had not intervened militarily in Nicaragua in 1979, although imperialist logic would have demanded it, because of the shift in the world balance of power between the United States and the Soviet Union. They even claimed that the

United States actually had been constrained by fear of Cuba, which, according to the *comandantes*, had demonstrated its military superiority over the South African Army in the liberation of Angola. As far as the Sandinista Front was concerned, the world was necessarily bipolar, and they could not conceive of their victory as partly the expression of a worldwide movement toward multipolarity. Similarly they did not differentiate among branches of the U.S. government, between U.S. public opinion and the administration, or among the various currents within the Carter administration itself. As far as they were concerned, imperialism could only act as a single person, with a single will.

The *comandantes* trusted neither the European socialists nor their Latin American supporters such as Torrijos or Andrés Pérez. According to the FSLN, these people were seeking only to dilute Nicaraguan socialism by co-opting their revolution and transforming it into social democracy. In the *comandantes'* vision of socialism, Cuba and the Soviet Union were necessarily strategic allies of the Sandinistas. The leaders of the Front—both the old and the new generations—saw the struggle between capital and labor as the central contradiction of all capitalist societies. They then mechanically projected outwards this single contradiction as if the world could be reduced to a struggle between imperialism and the socialist camp.[10]

As for Central America, the *comandantes* argued that an independent socialism was impossible in light of the open, dependent nature of the Nicaraguan economy. If Nicaragua was to become socialist, there was not an alternative to full integration with the Soviet bloc. The immediate challenge was to retain the support of their Western allies while forging permanent relations with the socialist camp. For this reason, within days of its victory, the Sandinista Front began to offer clear signals of devotion to the Soviets, which hampered their immediate relations, particularly economic ties, with the West.

Moscow had to be shown that the FSLN was not a truly non-aligned, hence untrustworthy, Third World movement. It was essential to demonstrate that its leaders had learned from the Cuban example and that the errors of the 1960s, when relations between Cuba and the Soviet Union had been tense and difficult to manage, would not be repeated.

The Cubans, however, who enjoyed unparalleled prestige among the Sandinista militants, acted in a complex and often contradictory manner. On the one hand, they reminded the Nicaraguans that all revolutions are different and theirs should therefore find its own solutions. But on a more political level, they simply projected their own economic and military experiences onto Nicaragua.[11]

The Cubans contradicted themselves in other ways. They were the first to point out that Moscow was not ready to subsidize the Nicaraguan economy. But concurrently, in the inter-*comandante* conflict, they supported those members of the National Directorate who were the most pro-Soviet and least flexible, such as Tomás Borge and Bayardo Arce. While the Cubans did recommend a certain tactical moderation, they could not see the importance of the third option as a strategic alternative for the Sandinista revolution. For this reason, many Nicaraguans, including those who sympathized with the revolution, thought that Cuba showed little imagination in its policy toward Nicaragua. This may have resulted from the Cubans losing touch with the dynamics in Central America during their twenty years in isolation or perhaps from their inability to conceive an alternative to their own model. In any event, Fidel Castro had little, if any, room for maneuver vis-à-vis Nicaragua, particularly in light of Cuba's enormous financial dependence on the Soviet Union and the pro-Soviet attitude already present among the National Directorate.

SANDINISTA FOREIGN POLICY

According to the Sandinistas the security of the revolution lay almost exclusively in the acquisition of military hardware, and in building up an army capable of a strong defense. In part, this concern for a strong military presence originated from the fear of U.S. intervention. However, it was also due to the *comandantes'* perception of the necessity of maintaining adequate protection against the joint forces of other Central Ameican countries.

According to the National Directorate, a region as small as Central America allowed for only one of two options: a revolutionary solution for the entire region, given the "ripple effect" of the Sandinista Revolution, or the eventual defeat of Nicaragua. Thus, the détente with Honduras at the beginning of the revolution could only be temporary. To the *comandantes*, it was not even certain that friendly relations would continue with Costa Rica and Panama. The new Nicaragua could not expect favorable international opinion indefinitely. The Nicaraguan advance toward socialism, and the country's ties with the Soviet Union and Cuba would, sooner or later, alienate the European social democrats, American liberals, and even regional governments such as Venezuela and Mexico.

The Sandinista Front therefore decided to augment its armed forces to match the Central American armies, using Soviet equipment and Cuban advisors. Managua never made a genuine effort to diversify the sources of its military aid. For example, Panamanian advisors who had arrived at the beginning of the revolution were assigned to train traffic police. Tactically, everything was negotiable for the *comandantes* — except the final objectives of the revolution and the Soviet-backed military build-up. Internal working papers of the Sandinista Front on possible negotiations with the United States stressed that anything that might affect the vital decision to go ahead with this military build-up should be rejected. Even more importantly, negotiation was not a foreign policy objective; it was a means for buying time and gaining strategic advantage.

Paradoxically, this view was advanced only after U.S. Under Secretary of State for Latin American Affairs Thomas Enders visited Nicaragua in August 1981 to offer the *comandantes* a *Pax Finlandia*. This proposition clearly emerged in February 1982 when Mexican President Lopez Portillo offered a quid pro quo publicly in Managua:

> . . . the government of the United States should reject threats or the use of force against Nicaragua. And if the Somocista bands operating along the border between Honduras and Nicaragua could be disarmed, and if similar groups stopped training in the United States — thus removing a real threat to the country's integrity — it was possible to think that the government of Nicaragua would simultaneously renounce the procurement of arms and aircraft, and stop channeling its scarce resources into maintaining a standing army that was of a size to be of concern to neighboring countries and others close by.[12]

To the *comandantes,* this offer of disarmament proved that Mexico had betrayed their revolution.

With Enders' visit to Managua, the Sandinista leadership concluded that, as far as the Reagan administration was concerned, freedom of press, political pluralism and the future of the bourgeoisie were irrelevant. Washington's central concern seemed to be the geopolitics of the revolution — its relations with the guerrillas in El Salvador, and its military ties with the socialist camp.

Enders' proposal was very simple: the Sandinista program would be tolerated within Nicaragua's borders, but, in exchange, Nicaragua would have to adjust its foreign policy to accommodate the United States' interests.

When Enders visited Managua in August 1981, the leaders of the Sandinista Front felt that their future was secure. The threat of a U.S.-backed counterrevolution was even useful to justify the clamp-down on domestic opposition. In addition, the economy had experienced a second year of growth, and the Salvadoran guerrillas seemed to be on the verge of victory. However, the importance that the socialist camp would later attribute to Nicaragua, and the real scope of the Reagan administration's policy toward the Sandinista Revolution, were yet to be seen.

By mid-1982, however, this sense of security had dissipated. The Reagan administration managed to persuade Congress, the U.S. public, and the European allies of the threat of a creeping, Nicaraguan-spurred communism in Central America. By this time it had also become apparent that sufficient economic aid from the socialist bloc would not be forthcoming. With the Nicaraguan economy in crisis as a result, among other things, of the drastic reduction in Western economic assistance, Daniel Ortega traveled as head-of-state to Moscow, to solicit support for Nicaragua's ailing economy. His sole achievement was an agreement for the transfer of the equivalent of $150 million in farm machinery and other technical aid over the next five years. However, for some Sandinistas, symbols apparently compensated for the lack of tangible resources. Some of the Front leaders insisted that the more significant fact was that *Comandante* Ortega stayed overnight in the Kremlin itself, while Nixon, during his historic trip in 1972, had slept only in the outskirts of Moscow.

The optimism of the Sandinistas proved unjustified. The balance of payments forecast displayed the true magnitude of the economic crisis of the revolution; the country would need a minimum of $450 million in hard foreign exchange to cover its foreign deficit, and another $500 to 600 million annually for the next five years.

THE FUTURE

To claim that the Reagan administration's policies were solely responsible for radicalizing Nicaragua and aligning it with the socialist camp would mean ignoring the behavior of the Sandinista Front during the Carter years, and neglecting its origins and ideological bent. However, the Reagan administration did force a premature radicalization of the revolutionary process. The administration's excessive rhetoric and logistical support for the counterrevolution gave the *comandantes* the opportunity to justify their radical inclinations, thereby transforming U.S. concerns into a self-fulfilling prophecy. This U.S. approach particularly suited the more dogmatic of the National Directorate. A symbiotic relationship eventually developed between the hard-liners of the National Directorate and the ideologues of the Reagan administration. The actions of one side were used to jutify the actions of the other. Both offered tactical concessions while remaining intransigent in strategic matters.

While at the beginning of the revolution there was a pro-Soviet consensus among the *comandantes*, this does not mean that initially there were not some *comandantes* who questioned the value of such an alliance — one which has ensured a large supply of weaponry but which has not delivered the economic means to overcome the crisis. Thus, while it is true the the Reagan administration was not directly responsible for the resulting close ties between Managua and Moscow, U.S. policy toward the revolution may be blamed for complicating the dynamics of the National Directorate. The continuation of these policies may hinder or even destroy any possibility of a redefinition of relations between the Sandinista Front and the socialist camp.

Indisputably, some *comandantes* have become further radicalized while in power. Yet others have adopted more flexible positions due to the constraints imposed by policy and governing. The *Terceristas*, who earlier demonstrated tactical moderation, and Jaime Wheelock, a leading member of the Proletarian Tendency, have been responsible for state affairs and economic policy. On the other hand, the members of the Prolonged People's War faction, such as Tomás Borge and Bayardo Arce, in charge respectively of the Ministry of the Interior (the state security apparatus) and the Sandinista Party structure, have never had to negotiate with a multilateral agency for a loan to prop up the country's balance of payments. Nor have they ever had to seek technical assistance for the development of Nicaragua's agrarian sector. Spared the necessity of compromise, they have retained their political infantilism.

The struggle for power among the faction has proven to be the driving force of the new regime. At the beginning, there was merely a power struggle within the Sandinista Front, and a contest among the *comandantes* of the National Directorate to be the first among equals. This eventually acquired substantive ideological ramifications that could affect the political orientation of the revolution. For Comandantes Borge, Arce, and Ruiz, quick radicalization of the revolution is essential however premature it might be. Ruiz's Ministry of Planning has limited powers in a mixed economy, while Borge's state security system and Arce's party organizations can gain hegemony only through increased radicalization. On the other hand, Daniel Ortega, a *Tercerista* leader, tends toward a less ideological and more pragmatic view partly because of his responsibility for policy within the state apparatus. Jaime Wheelock, the leader of the *proletarios*, who is involved in agrarian planning and decentralizaion of the economy, favors a slower transformation of the country. [13]

Paradoxically, both Tomás Borge and Bayardo Arce would be ready to negotiate an agreement with the Reagan administration, based on a trade-off: Managua's support for the Salvadoran revolutionaries would cease in exchange for the termination of Washington's support for the Nicaraguan counterrevolutionaries on the Honduras border. Further, Nicaragua should not be asked to make concessions at home of a *strategic* nature. This option of a *Pax Finlandia* would be acceptable to some in the Reagan administration. It would be equally attractive to the more dogmatic among the members of the National Directorate for it would permit their uncontested move to an orthodox domestic socialist model.

On the other hand, the Ortegas and Jaime Wheelock may be willing to promote an opening in Nicaragua while still insisting that Nicaragua provide some support and refuge to the Salvadoran resistance. The real hope for the Sandinista revolution is if the *Tercerista* positions that prevailed in the war against Somoza were to prevail under the present, albeit changed, conditions, that is, if room were made for centrist forces and democratic dissidents. If the Nicaraguan center or the Salvadoran left are not permitted effective participation in Central American political life, prospects for a regional solution are practically nonexistent.

NOTES

1. On the difficulties of a direct transition to socialism under conditions such as those inherited by the Sandinista Revolution (and taking into account the limits imposed by the agro-export model), see the paper by Mario DeFranco, "Aspectos del desenvolvimiento económico de Nicaragua," delivered to the Friedrich Ebert Foundation in Bonn, F R Germany in March 1981. See, also, the essay by Arturo Cruz Sequeira, "Nicaragua: Crisis económica, radicalización o moderación?" in *Centroamerica: Más allá de la crisis*, edited by Donald Castillo Rivas, Mexico City, SIAP, 1983. For a discussion of the possibility of a more immediate transition to socialism, see the article by E.V.K. FitzGerald, "The Economics of the Revolution," in *Nicaragua in Revolution*, edited by Thomas W. Walker, Praeger, New York, 1982.
2. Division of Planning, Studies and Control, International Fund for the Reconstruction (FIR), Managua, 1982.
3. See the article by Dan Jakobson, Permanent Representative of Finland to the United Nations, 1965-72, in *Foreign Affairs* (Summer 1980), "Finland: Substance and Appearance." In this article he suggests that Finnish policy was designed to avoid antagonizing any important power: "This surely is the course of wisdom for a small neutral nation which is heavily dependent on foreign trade. But of course it is especially important for every Finnish government to consider what effect its actions might have on its powerful neighbor. In any international crisis Finnish security may depend on whether Moscow beieves it can trust Finland not to help its enemies. Such trust can only be secured by consistent behavior over a long perid of time. It is therefore not only unrealistic but also irresponsible to make overt hostility to the Soviet Union a criterion of Finnish independence."
4. The propaganda machinery of the Sandinista Front in fact drew a parallel between the dissident trade unions in Nicaragua and Solidarity in Poland, portraying both as agents of imperialism. See the speeches by Daniel Ortega to the Conference of the Non-Aligned Nations in Havana, Cuba in September 1979, and to the United Nations General Assembly in October of the same year.
5. Carlos Fonseca, *Un Nicaragüense en Moscú*, reprinted in 1980 by the Departamento de Propaganda del FSLN, Managua, Nicaragua.
6. Regis Debray, *Revolution in the Revolution? Armed Struggle and Political struggle in Latin America*, New York, Monthly Review Press, 1967.
7. The most popularized works on the theory of dependency were: *Dialectica de la dependencia*, by Ruy Marini; *Socialismo o fascismo: El nuevo carácter de la dependencia y el dilema latinoamericano* by Teotonio Dos Santos; the essay of Vania Bambirra; and the writings of André Gunder Frank. These were works that gained the ideological acceptance of the militants of the Sandinista Front, but other major theoretical contributions of the time, such as those by Celso Furtado and ECLA, were not assimilated.
8. The Proletarian Tendency was the only one that bothered to find a theoretical framework in which to rationalize the divisions within the Sandinista Front, in the paper "La Crisis Interna y las Tendencias," from the *Colección 4 de mayo* in early 1978. However, long before this theoretical exercise was developed, Carlos Fonseca, in his last writings (now considered as his political testament) supported the positions of Tomás Borge, and violently criticized Jaime Wheelock for divisionist tendencies and for his arrogance toward the efforts of the old militants of the Front. In the absence of Carlos Fonseca, Tomás Borge

became the defender of Sandinista orthodoxy, while Jaime Wheelock represented the revisionist view which, nonetheless, remained within Marxist parameters.

9. *"Los Doce"* was a group formed in late 1977 by distinguished intellectuals, technocrats and businessmen, who were widely respected in Nicaragua and who endorsed the position of the *Tercertistas*. After the victory, they assumed important positions in the state apparatus, such as the foreign minister, the president of the Central Bank, and member of the Junta of National Reconstruction.

10. This position was clearly reflected in the speech given by Commander Humberto Ortega to the officers of the Sandinista Popular Army (EPS) on August 25, 1981, when he asserted that at the moment of victory of the Sandinista People's Revolution in July 19, 1979, society had developed into two polarized camps: on the one hand, the imperialist camp, headed by the United States and other capitalist countries of Europe and the world; and on the other, the socialist camp, made up of a number of countries in Europe, Asia and Latin America, and spearheaded by the Soviet Union.

11. Examples of Cuban influence extended from the smallest detail to the most important. Accounting bodies and statistical centers, charged with gathering information on the national accounts and balance of payments, have changed their methodology to conform to the Cuban system. On the Atlantic Coast, the Cubans have insisted on handling the Miskito Indian question as a security problem, recommending policies similar to those which they used in El Escambray at the beginning of the 1960s.

12. A copy of the Mexican President's speech was provided to the author by the Mexican Embassy in Nicaragua.

13. See the author's forthcoming article "Nicaragua: A Revolution in crisis" in the *SAIS Review* (Winter 1984).

5

THE SALVADORAN LEFT

Robert S. Leiken

There is some reason to fear that the triumph of the guerrillas of the Salvadoran Farabundo Martí National Liberation Front (FMLN) would reproduce all the negative features of the Sandinista regime. Indeed, many believe that an FMLN regime would be far worse. After all, the Sandinistas never engaged in kidnapping campaigns or economic sabotage. Their military actions were always calculated — to win the sympathies and indeed embolden the Nicaraguan masses. Their history was not scarred by murderous fratricide, and they never professed themselves to be Marxist-Leninists.

To some, this last difference between the FMLN and the Sandinistas is approximately that between a confessed criminal and one who covers up his crime. But if the FMLN groups are explicitly, not covertly, Marxist-Leninist, the fact that the FMLN is a known quantity to the Salvadoran people is a positive reflection of its own history and of Salvadoran political life. For if it is true, as Arturo Cruz Sequeira asserts in the previous essay in this volume, that the Sandinista Front was a "manifestation" of the impoverished "political culture" of Somoza's Nicaragua, the FMLN, and especially the FMLN-FDR (Revolutionary Democratic Front), is a reflection of the very different political and cultural conditions of El Salvador.

I would like to thank David Weiner and Lawrence R. Thomas for their superb research assistance.

Much of this essay is based upon interviews the author conducted beginning in 1980, through December 1983, with members on all levels of the FMLN-FDR in Managua, Nicaragua; San Salvador and Corinto, El Salvador; San José, Costa Rica; Mexico City; and Washington, D.C. In order to preserve the anonymity of the subjects, these interviews will be cited in the chapter notes as "author's interview" followed by the particular organizational affiliation of each given subject.

Portions of this essay originally appeared in the June 1983 edition of the journal *Worldview*.

The FMLN's coalition with the FDR is the first salient difference with the Sandinistas. During the Nicaraguan revolution an alliance with the moderate left was formed within the last months of the fighting, but it was "tactical" and short-lived. The alliance was never tested by prolonged struggle, nor consolidated by joint work and joint risk. It was seen by most of the Sandinista leadership as an enforced requirement of the war against Somoza, not as a strategic alliance for building a modern Nicaragua.

The members of *Los Doce*—the twelve distinguished Nicaraguan businessmen, clergymen, professionals, and intellectuals who comprised something like a Nicaraguan counterpart of the FDR leadership — were as inexperienced politically as the Sandinista *comandantes*. The latter had spent most of their lives in exile or in jail. Unlike the leaders of the FMLN-FDR, they had not led labor and peasant unions, teachers' organizations, or broad political coalitions, nor been ministers of state or army officers. This was another reflection of what Arturo Cruz Sequeira has called Somoza's "populist" depoliticizing of Nicaraguan society.

In the 1960s and 1970s Salvadoran political life swarmed with broad-based political parties, grass root movements, coalitions, demonstrations, popular organizations, and contested—if often fraudulent—elections. Guillermo Ungo, the President of the FDR, headed the social democratic National Revolutionary Movement (MNR). Although miniscule, that party was the linchpin of a successful national coalition (until victory was snatched away by a military coup). The coalition included the Christian Democrats to the right and the communists to the left. It was no mean political feat to keep such a coalition together and bring it to victory.

During the 1970s the universities of San Salvador were hotbeds of political activism and debate. The intellectual hegemony of the Salvadoran Communist Party (PCS), the main organ of Soviet influence in the left, was challenged by a number of pretenders, many of whom are now joined with the Communist Party in the FMLN. Their ferocious polemics brought to El Salvador the storm raging within the international communist movement. While the Salvadoran militants interpreted the views of the Cuban, Chinese, Albanian, North Korean, Italian, and Soviet parties in their own way and for their own purposes, the disputes meant that Salvadoran Marxism-Leninism, unlike its Nicaraguan counterpart, was exposed to winds of fundamental ideological contention. Of all these differences, none was more important and more acrimonious than the controversy over whether the Soviet Union was a socialist ally or an imperialist enemy camouflaged behind a socialist rhetoric.

The Salvadoran revolutionaries' ability to entertain a fundamental questioning of the Soviet Union (and Cuba) was itself a function of Salvadoran "political culture" and history. In Nicaragua, the intimate identification of the United States with the Somoza tyranny and the *Somocista* National Guard created a deep-rooted animosity toward the United States.

The Salvadoran Opposition (FMLN-FDR)

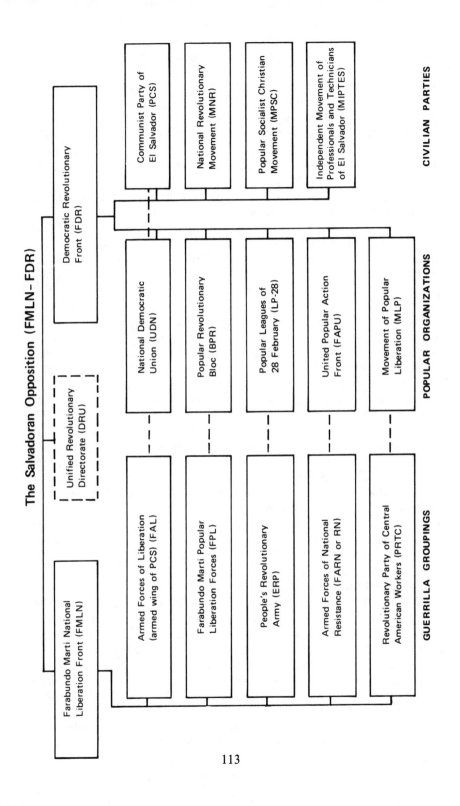

Farabundo Marti National Liberation Front (FMLN)

Unified Revolutionary Directorate (DRU)

Democratic Revolutionary Front (FDR)

CIVILIAN PARTIES

Communist Party of El Salvador (PCS)

National Revolutionary Movement (MNR)

Popular Socialist Christian Movement (MPSC)

Independent Movement of Professionals and Technicians of El Salvador (MIPTES)

POPULAR ORGANIZATIONS

National Democratic Union (UDN)

Popular Revolutionary Bloc (BPR)

Popular Leagues of 28 February (LP-28)

United Popular Action Front (FAPU)

Movement of Popular Liberation (MLP)

GUERRILLA GROUPINGS

Armed Forces of Liberation (armed wing of PCS) (FAL)

Farabundo Marti Popular Liberation Forces (FPL)

People's Revolutionary Army (ERP)

Armed Forces of National Resistance (FARN or RN)

Revolutionary Party of Central American Workers (PRTC)

This, coupled with the unquestioned ideological hegemony of Moscow and Havana over the Nicaraguan left, made it axiomatic to the Sandinistas that the enemy of their enemy was their "natural ally." It predisposed them to view the world in the words of Sandinista Defense Minister Humberto Ortega, as "polarized into two great camps: on one side, the imperialist camp, the capitalist camp headed by the U.S. . . . and on the other side, the socialist camp . . . vanguarded by the Soviet Union."[1]

The U.S. presence in El Salvador was more diffuse. Salvadoran revolutionaries concentrated their fire on the "fourteen families," the "oligarchy." The internal contradictions of Salvadoran society received the major attention. The fact that many Salvadoran revolutionary leaders were refugees from the bitter internal struggle inside the pro-Moscow PCS further complicated matters. By the early 1970s most of the emerging leaders of the Salvadoran revolutionary movement regarded the PCS as having sold out to the Salvadoran establishment. They attacked it as "chauvinist" for supporting El Salvador in the war against Honduras in 1969, as "reformist" for opposing revolutionary armed struggle, and "revisionist" for its fidelity to Moscow.

The differences between the Salvadoran and the Nicaraguan left in political experience, ideological diversity, and attitudes towards the superpowers, to some degree reflect broader differences between Nicaraguan and Salvadoran society. El Salvador is far more industrialized and cosmopolitan than Nicaragua. Its working class is larger, and it has a long history of labor activism and unionization. The Salvadoran countryside is more polarized than the Nicaraguan where the existence of an agricultural frontier, among other things, has given a wider berth to the individual producer and indigenous community. In tiny Salvador's countryside, patron-client relations prevail. As a result the Salvadoran peasantry is more passionate when roused and more accustomed to social organization. Salvadoran society has been paradoxically both more violent and better organized than that of Nicaragua.

These cultural differences suggest why, on the one hand, Sandinista leaders complain of the violent, even fratricidal, nature of the Salvadoran guerrillas, while the latter speak with disdain of the "infantilism" of the Sandinista leadership. Some of this can be chalked up to national rivalries. A more advanced economic and political organization does not guarantee political sanity. We recall Germany in the 1930s. Yet it is obviously not the case that the FMLN is a Salvadoran reincarnation of the Sandinistas, nor that the fate of El Salvador with the guerrillas sharing power must necessarily mimic that of Sandinista Nicaragua. Such assumptions descend from the 1950s view that "the Communist bloc" was monolithic — that Russia, Yugoslavia, China, and Eastern Europe were all inseparable and natural allies. The FMLN bears the birthmark of its formation within the specific framework of Salvadoran society and history. We cannot understand its by analogy — whether to Nicaragua or to Vietnam. A more fruitful course is to analyze the singular and intricate history of the FMLN itself.

GENEALOGY

The FMLN has two main sources: radicalized religious activists, and the Salvadoran Communist Party. Vatican II and the 1968 Conference of Latin American bishops in Melellin, Colombia, had an especially powerful impact on the Salvadoran clergy.[2] "Christian base communities," small Bible-study groups disseminating liberation theology's message of Christ's "preferential option for the poor," were formed in many parishes which later were to serve as rear-guard zones for the guerrillas.[3] The guerrilla-led mass "popular organizations" formed in reaction to the electoral frauds of the early 1970s drew many of their activists and leaders from these Christian communities.

The same was true for the "political-military fronts" that split off from the Salvadoran Communist Party. In 1970, Salvador Cayetano Carpio, a former seminarian and the secretary-general of the party, resigned and took underground the first cell of the Popular Forces of Liberation (FPL). They quickly recruited radicalized members of the Christian base communities and persecuted union activists. Shortly thereafter an amalgam of ex-party members, young Christian Democratic Party dissidents, religious activists, and student revolutionaries known as *El Grupo* ("The Group") publicly announced the formation of the the the People's Revolutionary Army (ERP). Two more organizations, the Armed Forces of National Resistance (FARN or RN), and the Revolutionary Party of Central American Workers (PRTC), were later to split from this grouping.[4] The fifth guerrilla organization, the Armed Forces of Liberation (FAL), was formed by the Communist Party between 1977 and 1979.[5] Thus, in varying degrees, all of the guerrilla organizations are products of the prolonged and turbulent struggle within the Salvadoran Communist Party.

The first apple of party discord, dating back to the Cuban Revolution, was the question of armed struggle. During the 1960s there developed in the PCS currents that favored the Cuban and Chinese criticisms of the Soviet line of "peaceful transition to socialism" which had repudiated armed struggle.[6] Sympathizers of the Cubans gravitated to the FPL; of the Chinese to the ERP. The Soviet invasion of Czechoslovakia and enunciation of the Brezhnev Doctrine—each in turn endorsed by Fidel Castro and repudiated by the Chinese—sharpened the divisions in the party as well as among its dissidents. By the early 1970s the FPL, like the Cubans, was lining up with Moscow on international questions. The revolutionary groups engaged in ferocious polemics in their newspapers, in the National University, and in the "popular organizations" then beginning to form.[7]

The first of the popular organizations was the United Popular Action Front (FAPU), a broad coalition of peasant, trade union, teacher, and student organizations, professors, radicialized clergy, and members of the Communist Party, the FPL, and the ERP. By then the ERP itself was beginning to subdivide into a "military" and a "political" wing. The latter, which eventually would become the National Resistance (RN), was responsible for work inside the FAPU. The differences within the FAPU between what was to become the RN and the FPL were to reemerge years later, after the formation of the FMLN, on the key question of political and military strategy for the revolutionary war.

In 1974-75 the two FAPU factions diverged on the role of reform versus revolution, the working class versus the peasantry, popular insurrection versus "protracted war," and on the matter of alliances with the middle class. The ERP-RN conceived the revolution as unfolding in stages leading to mass insurrection. Actions should correspond to "the historical moment," especially the level of awareness and organization of the masses. The struggle for reforms was necessary to consolidate the mass organizations, to create a political space in El Salvador, and for the masses to learn "from their own bitter experience" the futility of reformism.[8] The same flexibility applied in choosing allies. All "democratic sectors" should be fused in a broad "anti-fascist united front." This would include not only those directly "represented," the workers and the peasants (with emphasis on the labor unions), but also ample sectors of the middle class and "democratic army officers."[9]

The FPL considered the peasantry the key element in a worker-peasant alliance for a "protracted people's war." The FPL rejected the "anti-fascist united front" because it "liquidated class contradictions." The reform struggle and alliances with the middle class and military reformers would lead to co-optation. The mass organizations should provide the recruits for protracted war. Partly because of the large number of radicalized Christian militants, the FPL leadership inculcated a messianic spirit of self-sacrifice — in Cayetano Carpio's words, "a mystique . . . so that the members . . . are disposed to sacrifice their life . . . in any moment." The RN, by comparison, was a body of irresolute "politicians," disposed to compromise with the enemy.[10]

As a result of these differences and the bitter rivalries among member organizations, the FAPU split, and, in July 1975, the FPL formed its own popular organization, the Revolutionary Popular Bloc (BPR). But even as this split was developing, the ERP itself was splitting. In 1975 its "Military Staff" tried and executed the group's leading intellectual, Roque Dalton, charged as a "Soviet-Cuban and CIA double agent." Dalton's supporters, members of the political faction of the ERP, subsequently left the group to form the RN.[11]

By 1978 each of the three main guerrilla groups headed a "popular organization." The FPL-led BPR was the largest, with nine affiliated organizations and a membership of sixty thousand. Its main base was among the agricultural workers and peasants demanding wage hikes, reductions in land rents, and credits. The BPR frequently led peasant occupations of haciendas and uncultivated land. The RN-led FAPU (about half the size of the BPR) was strong among the urban trade unions of the National Federation of Salvadoran Workers (FENASTRAS). Belatedly, in February 1978, the ERP organized its own popular organization, the Popular Leagues of February 28 (LP-28). In late 1979 the PRTC founded the Popular Liberation Movement (MLP). By this time the Communist Party had formed a guerrilla wing, the Armed Forces of Liberation (FAL). Back in the 1960s the Party had gained control of the National Democratic Union (UDN) and organized it as an electoral front. With the affiliation of trade unions and teacher organizations, it too gradually took on the character of a popular organization. By May 1980, all five popular organizations had united in the Revolutionary Coordinator of the Masses (CRM). At this time these mass organizations, capable of organizing truly massive street demonstrations in the capital, were the foundation of the guerrillas' power.[12]

In 1975, FAPU demonstrators were gunned down in San Salvador. Thereafter mass demonstrations and meetings were accompanied by small contingents of discreetly armed militants. Government repression solidified the links between the popular organizations and the guerrilla groups. The former came to constitute recruiting ground for the latter.[13] Demonstrations grew steadily in size and, in January 1980, four popular organizations announced a demonstration to celebrate their unification. Most prominent among the demands advanced by the organizers of the demonstration were calls for land reform, the creation of a "new people's army to replace the old," a national health care system, and a campaign against illiteracy.[14] Estimates of the size of this demonstration vary widely, but it certainly was the largest in Salvadoran history.[15] It was fired upon by the Salvadoran security forces, leaving dozens dead and hundreds injured. This and the massacre that accompanied the funeral of Archbishop Oscar Romero in March ended the epoch of large street demonstrations in San Salvador. The center of activity of the revolutionary organizations shifted to their rear-guard bases in the mountains. In May 1980 they announced the formation of the Unified Revolutionary Directorate (DRU), the precursor of the FMLN.[16]

The revolutionary organizations had reacted in different ways to the reformist military coup of October 1979. The Communist Party welcomed the coup and prepared to join the government. The ERP called for an insurrection and set up barricades in San Salvador's suburbs. Later, in an about-face, it agreed to "study" any offer of participation in the junta. The FPL called the ERP's insurrections "suicidal" but opposed the junta as a U.S. plot. Its BPR occupied the headquarters of the economic, planning, and labor ministries, taking three hundred hostages to exchange for political prisoners, wage increases, and price controls. The RN favored "dialogue" between the junta and the popular organizations.[17]

The October junta was composed of reformist and traditional military officers as well as Christian Democrats, Social Democrats, and Communists who later were to join the guerrilla-led popular organizations in the FDR. The revolutionary organizations' attitudes toward the junta were consistent with past and future divergencies. The ERP leapt at the prospect of armed insurrection. The FPL was cautious militarily but intransigent politically. The RN perceived an opening toward an "anti-fascist front" and sought an understanding with the reformist middle class politicians and military officers. When the junta collapsed under the weight of its own internal contradictions, all sides could claim vindication. But Cynthia Arnson's assessment is more accurate:

> By failing to appreciate divisions within the military and between the civilian and military representatives of the junta, the left played into the hands of the coup's betrayers. The High Command and sectors of the Army security forces furthest to the right ordered a stepped up campaign of violence and repression on the premise of restoring "law and order." The junior officers acquiesed to their superiors. . . . The attitude of the left caused the younger officers to feel that they, too, were regarded as the enemy.[18]

AT WAR

The legacies of the FMLN's prehistory were smoldering, and sometimes violent internal struggle and an organic linkage with significant mass organizations. The latter have provided not only a reserve of guerrilla fighters and sympathizers but also the bulk of the "militias" that now play a key role in the FMLN military structure. Along with 6,000-8,000 guerrillas, the FMLN claims to have up to a million sympathizers, including one hundred thousand militia members. The latter provide food, storage, a postal service, intelligence, and back-up support in military operations. Militia members "keep a gun and some ammunition in their hut or farm" and "follow a certain discipline." In the cities they are supplemented by block and neighborhood committees that stockpile arms, ammunition, food, water, and medicine and provide logistical support, erect barricades, and dig trenches during conflicts.[19]

As the war has deepened, the guerrillas have consolidated their support system, but their reservoir of popular sympathy seems to have diminished significantly, especially in the capital. According to ERP commander Joaquín Villalobos, the guerrillas failed to earn sufficient popular support early in 1981, just when their military capacities appeared to have matured and they undertook the "final offensive." "What happened was that we lost the propitious moment."[20] In fact, they have consistently overestimated the readiness of the masses to support their tactics and heed their calls for strikes and insurrections. The guerrillas' onslaught on the economy has destroyed factories, stores, buses, private cars, and public utilities, causing widespread disruption, unemployment and misery.[21] In January 1982, trade union leaders sympathetic to the guerrillas' moderate program, if not their immoderate methods, told me that three years before, at the time of the great street demonstrations in San Salvador, "the guerrillas spoke for all people." Now they believed that no longer was the case. This alienation is one reason why an incipient "third force" has emerged in El Salvador from among the unions and other sectors. It supports neither the FMLN nor the government but peace talks between them.[22]

However, the elections of March 1982 should not so much be interpreted as a repudiation of the guerrillas as of the war. When elections are carried out under conditions of civil war, such as those held in Algeria between 1948 and 1954, in South Vietnam in 1967 or Zimbabwe-Rhodesia in 1979, the results can be deceptive. In the case of El Salvador the elections reflected, among other things, the changing conditions of the war.[23] As is customary in Third World revolutionary wars, the locus of guerrilla power had shifted to the countryside. The government controlled most of the major cities (though they remain subject to guerrilla incursions), the guerrillas much of the eastern and northern countryside. The election turnout was heavy in the government-controlled cities and quite light in areas dominated by guerrillas.[24]

Since the failed "final offensive" of early 1981, the guerrillas have carried out several offensives, each larger, better coordinated, and more damaging than the last. Guerrilla assessments of the war tend to correspond to the divergent approaches of the major groups.

The ERP has been inclined to triumphalism. After the FMLN's successful January 1983 offensive, leading ERP *comandantes* were predicting the Salvadoran army's collapse by the end of the year.[25] The ERP is also by far the FMLN's most effective military force. This summer it inaugurated a full-size brigade, the Rafael Arce Zablah, capable of undertaking a variety of strategic missions. It was apparently trained in the ERP's "zone of control" in northern Morazán province, where the ERP runs two "military academies." These are directed by former Salvadoran army captains.[26] In early September the Arce brigade initiated the latest, and spectacularly successful, guerrilla offensive by taking and holding for the better part of one day, the country's third largest city, San Miguel.[27]

The other two major groups have been more restrained in their analyses. The RN and the FPL stress that although the government's new "National Pacification Plan" failed as soon as the guerrillas pushed against it, the army still retains "relative control over the strategic economic zones" and "abundant tactical resources." Above all "the masses are not insurrectionary." Nonetheless they stress that the nature of war is changing from one of isolated guerrilla attacks to a "war of movement" utilizing ever larger guerrilla contingents able to move freely and openly through greater areas of the countryside.[28]

The guerrillas assert that their military successes have increased their numbers, leading in turn to grander exploits. The widening of their "zones of control" in 1982-83 enables them to incorporate more peasants into their ranks. The expansion of the areas of conflict, from which the guerrillas withdraw upon arrival of the army, allows them to create clandestine networks. This, in turn, facilitates travel from areas of conflict into controlled zones where recruits can undergo military training. With each temporary occupation of a village—they claim seventy were taken in their offensive of fall 1983—the guerrillas are able to propagandize and to establish an underground organization.[29]

TAKING SIDES

The RN and ERP have shown the greatest independence in developing their international views and in their international dealings. Among RN intellectuals and political leaders genuine non-alignment has been a basic ideological tenet. Among many lower-level RN cadre, however, strong sympathies for Cuba prevail. The ERP is fiercely nationalistic, impatient with ideology, and suspicious of "socialist" solidarity. Both the ERP and the RN have been quite critical of the Cuban presence and influence in Managua. ERP leaders have said that they would not want to see "so many Cuban doctors, teachers, and advisors in El Salvador." A leading RN official considers Nicaragua's press censorship a grave error. "If they didn't like *La Prensa*, they should have created a better newspaper." He was critical too, of the Cuban role in Sandinista economic planning and thought that together they were leading the country toward economic disaster. But the Sandinistas' greatest error has been their sectarianism, "not incorporating the masses into the revolutionary process."[30]

Historically, the FPL has been the group closest to Cuba and Nicaragua. It is especially intimate with the Protracted People's War (GPP) faction of the Sandinistas, which has proved to be the most proficient at infighting in Managua. Cuban officials consider the FPL to have "the most developed Marxist-Leninist analysis of Salvadoran reality."[31] But the FPL's former leader Cayetano Carpio's intransigent opposition to a political settlement had led to frequent tensions with Havana. With respect to the Soviet Union, the FPL has had two orientations over the years. The old leadership from the Salvadoran Communist Party retained few criticisms of Moscow once the USSR had abandoned its line of "peaceful transition." Characteristically they defended the invasion of Afghanistan and martial law in Poland. Younger leaders and militants with Christian activist origins, on the other hand, consider the Soviet Union corrupt and oppressive. Like others in the FMLN, they criticize Moscow not from an East-West perspective, but from a North-South perspective.[32]

The Salvadoran Communist Party, with its Armed Forces of Liberation (FAL), remains firmly in the Soviet camp. It has gained some measure of influence within the PRTC, hitherto quite independent. Nonetheless, a PRTC congress in the spring of 1983 reaffirmed its independence.[33]

The FPL is the largest of the FMLN groups in membership but not in armed guerrillas. As of early 1983 the ERP, with close to 40% of the guerrillas, was, by far, the biggest and most effective fighting force. The FPL is next largest with about 20%, followed by the FARN with 15%. The FAL and the PRTC each have less than 10% of the guerrillas, and the remainder is not permanently attached to any single group.[34] A major argument against negotiations with the FDR-FMLN is that "the Marxist-Leninists have the guns." Yet among these "Marxist-Leninist" guerrillas, it is the organizations that stand at the greatest distance from the Soviet Union which control nearly two-thirds of the fighting force.

It is not certain that the FMLN will pursue real non-alignment. The Cubans have been assiduously courting the ERP, with whom they share a militarist orientation. The PRTC, as we have seen, is vulnerable to penetration by the Salvadoran Communist Party. Furthermore, as the war drags on and threatens to regionalize, the FMLN must perforce draw closer to its Nicaraguan and Cuban allies.[35] On the other hand, the recent events within the FPL disclose this group as a rather unreliable wedge for Cuban-Soviet penetration.

NEGOTIATIONS AS STRATEGY

The most neuralgic point of difference within the FMLN has been the question of negotiations. As we have seen, all of the groups now comprising the FMLN—with the exception of the RN—refused to negotiate with the reformist October 1979 junta which included many of their current colleagues of the FDR. After the failure of the "final offensive" in February 1981, the political diplomatic commission of the FMLN-FDR approved an internal document which committed it for the first time to negotiations. Yet the document supported negotiations only as a "tactic," a "maneuver" for "gaining time and diplomatic initiative." These reservations were the price exacted by Cayetano Carpio's FPL hard-liners from the rising number of FMLN-FDR members who supported a political solution.[36]

In the second half of 1981 the FPL became increasingly isolated on this issue as the other guerrilla groups and even the FPL's main outside backer, Cuba, endorsed "negotiations as a strategy." In late 1982 and early 1983 the latest round in the struggle for "negotiations as strategy" was fought inside

Subsequent revelations from Managua and from the FPL itself have made it possible to reconstruct broadly the series of events leading to and issuing from those assasinations.

Under Cayetano Carpio's leadership, the FPL had become an increasingly isolated, recalcitrant opponent both of negotiations and of the military and political unification of the FMLN. The other FMLN groupings bitterly complained of the FPL's refusal to coordinate military actions with the other groups. They regarded this as a major reason for the failure of the guerrillas' March 1982 election offensive.[37]

Carpio's intransigent, fiercely independent attitude eventually created dissension in his own organization. Second-in-command Melida Anaya Montes (a.k.a. "Ana María"), became the voice of the opposition. In October of 1982 Ana María supported the decision of the other FMLN groupings to present a concrete negotiating proposal to the government. Cayetano Carpio balked, but was forced to go along when the other groupings threatened to present the proposal without him.[38]

Cayetano Carpio's line was finally and decisively overthrown at a meeting of the FPL's central command (Co-Cen) in January 1983. There, the FPL accepted negotiations as "an auxiliary but strategic factor in our struggle"; approved "unity of the FMLN" as a "strategic objective" and pledged to "eliminate from our vocabulary all objectives which offend the other organizations"; and accepted that alliances were now to include all "non-oligarchal" sectors.[39] The document was approved overwhelmingly by the Central Command, signifying that Ana María was now the de facto leader of the organization.

Less than three months later, Ana María was repeatedly and grotesquely stabbed to death by Cayetano Carpio's closest comrades. According to an official communiqué of the FPL, Cayetano himself, resentful at his "political and moral defeat" in the Co-Cen meeting became "the principal initiator responsible for the assassination. . . . "[40]

It has been rumored by unofficial FMLN sources and diplomats in Managua that Tomás Borge, a leader of the Sandinista's National Directorate and Minister of the Interior, went personally to Cayetano Carpio's house three days after Ana María's murder. Borge is reported to have told Carpio that he had to choose between suicide and public disclosure of his own and his comrades' involvement in Ana María's murder. Suicide would assure that the murder would remain an internal FPL affair.[41]

Borge had originally denounced Ana María's assassination as a "CIA plot."[42] Subsequently, both Managua and the FMLN quietly dropped that allegation, but there has been speculation of international involvement from another source. Historically, Borge's own GPP faction of the Sandinistas had been close to Cayetano and the FPL. This was especially true of

National Directorate *comandante* Bayardo Arce of the GPP and his assistant Julio López. These two head the international section of the Sandinista Party and are charged with relations with fraternal organizations. According to Sandinista defector Miguel Bolanos Hunter, his former superior in the Interior Ministry accused Julio López of having failed to guarantee Ana María's security. Bolanos claims she was killed for "political reasons – she was just back from Cuba and wanted to have more dialogue between the guerrillas and the Salvadoran government."[43] The GPP is reported to be the most intransigent of the Sandinista factions, though Borge himself, after a sharp turnabout this summer, now champions the Nicaraguan negotiation campaign. (See Arturo Cruz Sequeira's essay in this volume.)

The international reverberations of the deaths in Managua do not stop here. On May 25, U.S. Navy Lieutenant Commander Albert A. Schaufelberger, a military adviser in the American embassy, was killed in San Salvador. The FPL, and later the FMLN as a whole, took responsibility for the action,[44] but the manner in which they did it raises questions. The FPL "communiqué" was delivered to a commercial Salvadoran radio station on stationery without the group's customary letterhead. Moreover, normally such communiqués are read over the guerrillas' own radio stations. The FMLN delayed in acknowledging responsibility for the action. Subsequent events were to suggest that this and other urban terrorist actions carried out during the same period were committed by a breakaway group of Cayetano Carpio's supporters within the FPL.

In August, the FPL held a "unity congress" dedicated to Ana María and reaffirming the hegemony of her line.[45] But the unity was short-lived. Three months later, Cayetano Carpio's closest followers had split from the FPL, repudiating its new leadership. In early December a new faction, the Revolutionary Workers' Movement – Salvador Cayetano Carpio (MOR), claimed responsibility for several bombings in San Salvador. The split and the terrorism confirmed earlier speculation that there had been a dissident terrorist faction inside the FPL since April. Within days of the MOR declaration, the FPL issued a communiqué denouncing Cayetano Carpio and the "backward, sectarian and anti-unity position of MOR."[46]

Certainly for the FPL, violence has been "the midwife of history." The main result of their fratricidal struggle has been the consolidation of positions favoring negotiations and unity with the other FMLN groups.[47] According to FMLN and FDR sources the FPL now cooperates militarily and politically with the other groups. The spectacular military successes of the guerrillas in the latter part of 1983 appeared to corroborate this claim. Politically, the guerrillas now appear firmly united around the FMLN-FDR October 1982 proposal for unconditional negotiations.

What has led these guerrilla organizations down the path from no dialogue with the reformist October junta – which included their current associates in the civilian wing of the FDR – to unconditional negotiations with the present right-of-center government? In the light of the guerrillas' steady military progress, weakness cannot be the explanation. The guerrillas do acknowledge war-weariness, but they give more stress to the toll on the civilian population. The importance of the FMLN's links with the popular organizations has never been properly understood in Washington. The popular desire for peace is one reason the majority of organizations in the FMLN have rejected the strategy of protracted war.

The FMLN holds that a military victory over the Salvadoran armed forces is possible, but recognizes that a government produced by a military victory would have serious internal and external problems. Among the external problems would be the hostile attitude of the United States. The reconstruction and development of the war-devastated economy would become insuperably difficult should the U.S. seek to embargo the Salvadoran economy – one far more industrially developed and hence more dependent on foreign imports than that of Cuba or Nicaragua.[48]

These factors help explain why the FMLN-FDR has progressively softened its negotiating position even as it has gained ground militarily. The FMLN has now agreed to the preservation of the "institutionality of the army" in a negotiated settlement. They are also prepared to participate in elections, and to guarantee a non-aligned foreign policy, and a mixed economy.[49]

These concessions could form part of a framework for negotiations that could safeguard legitimate U.S. security interests. In this framework the security forces would be cleansed, professionalized, and placed under the effective jurisdiction of the Interior Department, where they could be integrated with FMLN forces into a territorial militia. The Salvadoran army's officer corps would be preserved, and only individual officers guilty of major abuses and convicted after proper investigation and due process would be retired with compensation. The same would be true for members on both sides of the territorial militia.

When Sandinistas came to power in Nicaragua, the failure of previous mediation efforts led to their enjoyment of a vital monopoly of military and political resources. This has been a major factor in the country's evolution toward a monolithic political apparatus and alignment with the Soviet bloc. Should there be negotiations in El Salvador, a multiplicity of political actors, each with military and political resources, will contend for power. Among them will be the moderate pro-government political parties; the civilian parties in the FDR; the different FMLN groupings with their conflicting agendas; military reformers and more conservative military officers; the church; and the trade unions. Negotiations will not end the struggle but they will shift it to different terrain – the political and economic. On this terrain the Cuban-Soviet bloc is at its weakest.

As we have seen, conflict in the FPL does not seem to prefigure fissures within the FMLN. It is unlikely that the FMLN will split *before* a political settlement is achieved in El Salvador. However, there is danger that if the sectarian past reasserts itself, internal conflict could develop after a political settlement. It is also unlikely that the "democratic elements" of the FMLN-FDR would split off from the guerrilla organizations before the end of the war. Both the Carter and Reagan administrations have endeavored to lure the FDR away from the FMLN via elections. This has little chance of succeeding as long as its civilian adherents believe that a rupture of their alliance with the FMLN would deliver them into the hands of the armed oligarchy. After the October 1982 disappearance from San Salvador of several leaders of the FDR just as the latter was proposing negotiations, such fears seemed warranted.[50]

Furthermore, the drawing of hard and fast distinctions between the "democratic" and the "violent" members of the opposition is not always useful. This is not only because the "democrats" support the armed struggle but also because the integration of the FMLN and the FDR's civilian organization is horizontal as well as vertical. The FPL has gained a certain measure of influence in the Social Democratic MNR of Guillermo Ungo. Ruben Zamora of the Popular Social Christian Movement — split off from the Christian Democratic Party — is highly respected and trusted by the ERP and the RN. The immanent line of demarcation within the FMLN-FDR is not so much between democracy and revolution but between non-alignment and Soviet alignment.

SOCIALISM AND SOVIETISM

In Central America, as in the rest of the Third World, revolutionary groups display a variety of attitudes toward the Soviet bloc. But in the American "backyard" the left is more inclined to Soviet alignment than in other parts of the Third World. Many, but certainly not all, Central American dissidents have come to regard world events as a contest between "reactionary forces" led by "Yankee imperialism" — of which they have had firsthand experience — and "progressive forces" led, or at least assisted, by the Soviet Union — of which they have had none. A history of U.S. opposition to legitimate change in Central America, revolutionary or otherwise, has been the main propagator of this view. Currently the principal justification for resumption of such policies has been the assumption that revolutionary movements eventually must link themselves to Soviet expansionism. Yet the diversity and even collision of views among the Salvadoran revolutionary groups in particular, and Central American groups in general, should force us to examine this assumption.

Salvador is only the most graphic example of the division between non-alignment and Soviet alignment within the Central American left. Many of the *Terceristas* in Nicaragua envisioned a non-aligned course for the revolution in which the country would stand equidistant from the two superpowers. Between 1979 and 1983 a line similar to the old FPL line in El Salvador — that of the GPP tendency — seemed to have prevailed in Managua. There is reason to hope that the old *Tercerista* positions may reassert themselves in Managua.

In Guatemala and Costa Rica similar divisions exist among leftist groups. The Guatemalan Revolutionary Organization of the People in Arms (ORPA) and the Rebel Armed Forces (FAR) replicate some of the RN and ERP agnosticism toward Moscow. The People's Guerrilla Army (EGP) is closer to the Salvadoran pro-Cuban FPL while the Guatemalan Workers' Party (PGT) is directly backed by Moscow. In the summer of 1982, the Costa Rican electoral front, *Pueblo Unido* (People United), split twice over the issues of broad alliances and the Soviet Union. Eric Ardon, the leader of the Revolutionary Movement of the People (MRP) declared that a major reason for separating from the *Vanguardia Popular*, the pro-Soviet party, was that "they are permanently aligned with the Soviet Union."[51] This same Eric Ardon was accused of Sovietism after he interrupted President Reagan during his visit to Costa Rica in December 1982.[52]

Over the past decade, U.S. political leaders and policymakers have learned to distinguish leftism, even some varieties of Marxism-Leninism, from Sovietism. In other parts of the Third World non-Soviet and pro-Soviet insurgent groups have parted company after the winning of power. This has been the case in Angola, Zimbabwe, Egypt, China, and Indochina, among others. Recently, a virulently anti-Soviet guerrilla group emerged in Peru.[53] In a number of Asian and African countries, revolutionary regimes have spurned alignment with the Soviet Union. Marxist-Leninist China, with one quarter of the world's population, remains a bulwark against Soviet hegemonism. Marxist-Leninist Yugoslavia receives U.S. aid.

Nonetheless, we have been reluctant to apply these distinctions in the U.S. "backyard." These distinctions will have to be made if the U.S. is to live peaceably with its southern neighbors. By ignoring them and by its wholesale opposition to the entire Central American left, U.S. policy pushes the non-aligned left into the arms of those who are pro-Soviet. U.S. national security would indeed be threatend by Soviet-aligned regimes in the Caribbean Basin, but not necessarily by independent leftist regimes — even if they do speak the language of Marxism and seek to practice socialism. This discrimination will be fundamental to developing future U.S. policies for the region.

NOTES

1. Humberto Ortega, "La principal tarea del pueblo es prepararse militarmente para defender su poder" [The principal task of the people is to prepare itself militarily to defend its power], speech delivered in Managua on 25 August 1981.

2. Vatican II elaborated Pope John XXIII's 1961 and 1963 encyclicals concerning the human right to a decent standard of living, education, and political participation. Vatican II set forth two key principles. First, that the Church was of this world, and second, that it was a community of equals. Pope Paul VI inaugurated the Medellin meeting, where Latin American bishops adapted these principles to Latin reality. Lernoux noted that Medellin was "one of the major political events of the century: it shattered the centuries-old alliance of Church, military and the rich elites" (Penny Lernoux, *Cry of the People*, Garden City, N.Y., Doubleday, 1980, pp. 31-43.) To the chagrin of traditionalists in the Latin Church, Medellin provided justification for the growing number of lower-level clergy who wanted to move beyond purely religious concerns to political issues. Tommie Sue Montgomery explains that "while 4 of the 6 members of the Salvadoran hierarchy adhered to an institutional, sacramentalist view of the Church's role in society, the 2 remaining prelates, both in the archdiocese of San Salvador (and Archbishop Oscar Romero before his death) accepted and promoted the positions of Medellin from the beginning. (Tommie Sue Montgomery, *Revolution in El Salvador*, Boulder, Colorado: Westview Press, 1982, p. 100).

3. The "preferential option for the poor" included obligations on the part of the Church "to defend the rights of the oppressed, to denounce the unjust actions of world powers that work against self-determination of weaker nations." Lernoux, *ibid.*

4. Author's interviews with FMLN leaders. See also Dickey, C.: "Unruly Salvadoran Left Appears to Coalesce" *Washington Post*, July 8, 1983. p. Al; Tirado, Manilo, *La Crisis Politica en El Salvador*, Ediciones Quinto Sol, SA, Mexico, 1980. pp. 37-72; Montgomery, *Revolution*, pp. 119-58.

5. Salvadoran Communist Party leader Shafik Jorge Handal wrote in 1980: "We have never encouraged the people to pin their hopes on a way [elections] that was clearly unrealistic in our country. But when legal possibilities were exhausted, it did not prove easy to follow Lenin's wise advice: to be ready to employ the most diverse forms of struggle, to go over from one form to another in accordance with political situation. During these 2 years, other revolutionary organizations, despite propounding some concepts which we felt were ill-advised, acquired considerable influence and the armed struggle assumed a mass character." Handal, S.J., "We Have No Alternative to Armed Struggle," *World Marxist Review*, October 1980, p. 14.

6. For a more detailed discussion of the concept of peaceful transition and the divisions within the international communist movement concerning this question, see Leiken, R., *Soviet Strategy in Latin America*, The Washington Papers No. 93, Praeger: 1982, chap. 3.

7. Author's interviews with leading members of ERP, FPL, PRTC, FARN, and FDR. See also Tirado, *La Crisis*, pp. 47-66; Montgomery, *Revolution* pp. 120-28.

8. V.I. Lenin, *Left-Wing Communism: An Infantile Disorder*.

9. Author's interviews with members of FMLN-FDR; also see Montgomery and "Armed Forces Prepare to Face 'War of Attrition' Test," *Latin American Weekly Report*, September 5, 1980, p. 5.

10. Author's interviews with FARN and FPL leaders; cf. Mario Menendez Rodriquez, *El Salvador: Una Autentica Guerra Civil*, San José, Costa Rica, 1981, pp. 23-116.

11. "Dalton, Fusilado por Espia de la CIA: FPL," *Excelsior* (Mexico City), 10 March 1980, p. 30A; also see, Manlio Tirado, *La Crisis Politica en El Salvador* (Mexico City: Ediciones Quinto Sol, 1980), pp. 49-60; cf. Gabriel Zaid, "Enemy Colleagues: A Reading of the Salvador Tragedy," *Dissent* (Winter 1982), pp. 17-27, for a slightly different version of the same events.

12. Christopher Dickey, "Unruly Salvador Left Appears to Coalesce," *Washington Post*, 8 July 1983, p. Al.

13. Tirado, *La Crisis*, pp. 66-72.

14. Robert Armstrong and Janet Shenk, *El Salvador: The Face of Revolution*, Boston, 1982, p. 133.

15. Montgomery estimates that 200,000 participated in the march (*Revolution*, p. 129); Tirado estimates that "more than 100,000 people" demonstrated; (*La Crisis*, p. 98.); Drawing upon newspaper accounts immediately following the demonstration, Cynthia Arnson maintains that "at least 80,000" marched (Cynthia Arnson, *El Salvador: A Revolution Confronts the United States*, Washington: Institute for Policy Studies, 1982, p. 48)

16. "Comunicado de la Dirección Revolucionaria Unificada (DRU-PM) Anunciando la Formación del Frente 'Farabundo Martí' para la Liberacion Nacional (FMLN)" in *Estudios Centroamericanos*, Oct.-Nov., 1980, pp. 1092-1093.

17. Tirado, *La Crisis*, p. 91.

18. Arnson, *El Salvador*, p. 44

19. Author's interviews with Ferman Cienfuegos, the commander of the FARN, and other FMLN leaders. On the estimated size of current FMLN forces, see: McCartney, Robert, "Salvador Guerrillas Consolidate their Hold on Rural Towns," *Washington Post*, December 13, 1983, p. A1.

20. Villalobos' analysis is drawn from an interview conducted by Chilean journalist Marta Harnecker in 1982 ("De la Insurrección a la Guerra," *Punto Final* [Mexico City], No. 204, November-December, 1982, pp. 1-24). The quote, also from this interview, was cited by Christopher Dickey ("Unruly Salvadoran Left Appears to Coalesce," *Washington Post*, 8 July 1983, p. A1).

21. In an early 1983 communiqué, the ERP sought to explain the rationale behind the FMLN's strategy of economic sabotage:

    "The Salvadoran dictatorship, its armed forces and imperialism know perfectly well that the economy is the basic pillar of political and military power and that in every way the basic economic areas are military objectives. The dictatorship is always crying about the effects of economic sabotage and what advantages it gives to the revolutionary movement.

    "1. Sabotage has a strong impact on the economy, which reduces the dictatorship's capacity for continuing the war. Therefore, it reduces the offensive potential of the armed forces.

    "2. It forces the army to disperse widely, deploying many units to guard highways, bridges, transportation routes, communications media, electrical wires and installations, estates, etc. Thus we are also reducing the army's offensive potential in this way.

    "3. The army's inability to control the situation is demonstrated, and thus the state apparatus of the dictatorship is destabilized.

    "Sabotaging the economy within the framework of a war is not terrorism. It is a weapon used in any military confrontation." (Daily Report: Latin America, 15 March 1983, Foreign Broadcast Information Service (FBIS), U.S. Dept. of Commerce. Hereafter all citations from the Latin America Daily Reports will be designated by the familiar acronym, FBIS, followed by the date of the Daily Report in which the translated item was printed.

22. Author's interviews with Salvadoran trade union leaders.

23. See the "Prepared Statement" of Robert S. Leiken before the Committee on Foreign Relations of the U.S. Senate, 1 April 1982 for a more detailed interpretation of the significance of the March 1982 Salvadoran elections.

24. For the positions taken by various political forces in El Salvador on the 1982 elections, see the section entitled "Posturas Ante Las Elecciones" in *Estudios Centroamericanos*, April, 1982, pp. 307-323. For returns by department, see "Resultados Electorales por Departamento" in same, p. 324.

25. Author's interview with Ana Guadalupe.

26. For ERP reports on some of the more daring early operations of its Arce brigade during the summer of 1983, see the translations of ERP radio dispatches over the official *Radio Venceremos* broadcasting system, in: FBIS, 6 June 1983, 17 June 1983, and 21 July 1983.

27. Lydia Chavez, "Salvadoran Guerrillas Attack Nation's Third Largest City," *New York Times*, 5 September 1983, p. A1; and "Informers Aiding Salvador Rebels," *New York Times*, 6 September 1983, p. A3.

28. Author's interviews with RN and FPL cadre.
29. McCartney, Robert, "Salvadoran Guerrillas Consolidate Hold Over Rural Towns," *Washington Post*, 13 December 1983, p. A1.
30. Author's interviews with RN leader.
31. Author's interviews with FMLN leaders.
32. Author's interviews with FPL leaders.
33. Author's interviews with PRTC leaders.
34. Author's interviews with FMLN leaders.
35. According to the ERP in a March 1983 communiqué (FBIS, March 15, 1983), the FMLN unwillingly participates in the regionalization of the Salvadoran conflict. The guerrillas seek external assistance only because their adversaries have already done so:

    "However, in dealing with our country's situation, imperialism has designed a regional strategy, uses economic pressure on Latin American governments in order to force them to support U.S. plans, violates the Panama Canal treaties, threatens Panamanian stability, foments coup d'etats in Guatemala, places General Álvarez in power in Honduras, and makes this country the main instrument for its military plans in Central America. It also uses economic pressure to force Costa Rica into becoming its diplomatic pawn, supports Somozist bands based in Honduras, threatens to invade Nicaragua, tries to isolate Cuba from the rest of Latin America and puts enormous economic pressure on Mexico, in an effort to have it change its foreign policy.

    "In the midst of this panorama, these kinds of aggression, the enemies of humankind are denouncing us because according to them our struggle is not a national struggle and we are instruments of Cuba and Nicaragua. Our struggle is and will continue to be a national struggle, but we are not naive and realize that we cannot and should not fail to include our plans within the framework of a regional conflict, in which the interests of the peoples of Central America, the Caribbean, and Latin America in general are at stake. Our struggle in the diplomatic and political field already has a regional context, and if the imperialists insist on their policy of aggression, the open regionalization of the war will become a necessity and we will participate in it.

    "It is in this context that the forces that form the FMLN maintain and strengthen relations with all the forces and governments interested in the peace of Central and Latin America. That is why we reply to imperialism: We are and will continue to be friends of the peoples and Governments of Cuba and Nicaragua and we are not ashamed of this. On the contrary, we are proud to maintain relations with those peoples, who are bastions of the anti-imperialist struggle."
36. Author's interviews with FDR leaders; cf. Zoilo G. Martínez de la Vega, *Centroamerica Alarma Mundial* (Mexico City: Compania General de Ediciones, 1981); cf. Shirley Christian, "The Other Side," *The New Republic* 24 October 1983, pp. 13-19.
37. Author's interviews with FMLN cadre.
38. Christopher Dickey, "Salvadoran Rebel Intrigue: Dispute Leads to Death of Two Guerrilla Leaders," *Washington Post*, 27 June 1983, p. A16.
39. These references come from a captured document acknowledged to be authentic by the FPL: *"Circular Estrictamente Internal del Comando Central de las FPL Farabundo Martí a todos los organismos y miembros de las FPL Farabundo Martí"* also see Christopher Dickey, *Ibid.* In March 1983, one month before he committed suicide, Carpio was reported to have told Managua's Radio Sandino that the "Salvadoran opposition is willing to start negotiations without conditions at any moment." (FBIS, 8 March 1983, p. P3)
40. "Comunicado Oficial de las Fuerzas Populares de Liberacion (FPL) 'Farabundo Martí,' " 12 December 1983; also see, Stephen Kinzer, "Salvador Rebels Revile Late Chief," *New York Times*, 14 December 1983, p. A21.
41. Author's interviews; cf. Christian, "The Other Side", p. 13.

42. See excerpts from news conference with Borge broadcast over Managua Domestic Service on 8 April 1983 (FBIS, 8 April 1983); also see the "Official Communiqué" from the Ministry of the Interior of Nicaragua, April 1983. Tomás Borge heads this ministry.

43. Joanne Omang and Don Oberdorfer, "Defector: Salvadoran Rebels Closely Tied to Sandinistas," *Washington Post*, 19 June 1983, p. A15.

44. Arthur Allen, "Rebels Say They Killed U.S. Adviser," *Washington Post*, May 27, 1983, p. A1.

45. See FPL communiqués on the August 1983 "unity congress" in FBIS: 13 September 1983, p. P10-11 and 14 September 1983, p. P4. On the ERP's view of the congress, also see FBIS 14 September 1983, p. P4.

46. "Comunicado Oficial de las FPL," 12 December 1983; also see, Robert McCartney, "Dissidents Form New Rebel Unit in El Salvador," *Washington Post*, 12 December 1983, p. A21.

47. Stephen Kinzer, "Salvador Rebels Revile Late Chief," *New York Times*, 14 December 1983, p. A21.

48. In a letter to House Speaker Tip O'Neill 20 February 1982, RN Commander Ferman Cienfuegos asserted: "We are convinced also that the reconstruction of the country and its fair development demand the assistance of private resources and foreign investments; we hope to share our efforts with these investors. It will not be possible to build a new society through arbitrary political impositions."

49. See the "Proposal of the Farabundo Martí National Liberation Front and the Democratic Revolutionary Front (FMLN-FDR) for a Political Settlement to the Armed Conflict in El Salvador," December 1981; also see Christopher Dickey, "Salvadoran Left Widens Talks Offer," *Washington Post*, 3 December 1981, p. A1. For a more detailed discussion of the necessity of a non-aligned foreign policy from the perspective of the FMLN, see Fabio Castillo's officially sanctioned (by the FMLN) piece, "The National Security Interests of the United States and of the Central American and Caribbean States." In 1982 Ferman Cienfuegos told a *Washington Post* reporter that the guerrillas understood that the best possible outcome of the war would be a coalition government, a mixed economy, and a non-aligned foreign policy. Interestingly, this "unified conclusion" was demanded by "this historical stage. It may not be born from one's wishes, but it is the result of our analysis of the war. It is the Salvadoran people who are demanding unity, and we represent our people. There is [also] a change in the world situation, and we must respond." These remarks strongly imply a Cuban and/or Soviet hand in the shift in the FMLN's position. (Jim Hoagland, "Guerrilla Attempts to Allay U.S. Fears," *Washington Post*, 8 March 1982, p. A1)

50. Richard Meislin, "5 Key Leaders of the Opposition Reported Kidnapped in Salvador," *New York Times*, 23 October 1982, p. A1; and "U.S. Envoy Assails Salvador Seizure," *New York Times*, 24 October 1982, p. A9.

51. *La Nación* (San José, Costa Rica), 8 August 1982, p. 4A.

52. Steven Weisman, "Reagan Denounces Threats to Peace in Latin America," *New York Times*, 5 December 1982, p. A1.

53. For an excellent study of the *Sendero Luminoso* guerrillas in Peru see, Cynthia McClintock, "Democracies and Guerrillas: The Peruvian Experience," *International Policy Report* (Washington: Center for International Policy, 1983).

6

THE SOVIETS AND CENTRAL AMERICA

Morris Rothenberg

The victory of the Sandinista revolution in Nicaragua heightened Soviet hopes for increased influence in Latin America. The Kremlin sought to make this hope a reality through intensifying ties to the new Nicaraguan regime and by encouraging the emulation of the Nicaraguan experience elsewhere in the region. Nicaragua was particulary important for Moscow because it raised the possibility of widening Cuba's breach in the doctrine of "geographic fatalism" — which had held that the U.S. would not permit leftist governments or strong Soviet influence close to the United States.

Nonetheless, a variety of constraints remain on Moscow's commitments and the directness of its involvement in the region. Some stem from the limits on Soviet resources, the greater importance of other areas, and U.S. proximity. Others are a function of specific regional developments: a newly activist U.S. policy; the failure of the Salvadoran guerrilla's 1981 "final offensive"; and the growing problems caused by anti-Sandinista efforts in Nicaragua. Several factors seem to obviate Moscow's need for a high-profile policy: the existence of proxies; domestic uncertainties about U.S. Central America policy; Latin American concerns about that policy; and perceived trends in U.S.-Latin American relations and the region itself. In accord with these constraints, Moscow has combined propaganda and diplomatic campaigns with carefully modulated military aid in an effort to ease the pressures on Nicaragua and the Salvadoran left and to deter the United States from drastic actions.

Prior to Castro's victory in Cuba, Latin America as a whole, and Central America in particular, was an area of extremely limited interest to the Soviet Union. Soviet attention in the Third World centered almost exclusively on Asia and Africa. Soviet ideologists saw Latin America as neither full-fledged capitalist states nor areas ripe for national liberation. U.S. actions in Guatemala in 1954 confirmed for Moscow and Latin American communists the validity of the doctrine of geographic fatalism.

Soviet attitudes were changed by Castro's survival and by U.S. acquiescence in the development of Cuba as a communist state and the steady growth in Soviet-Cuban military relations. Moscow has accumulated an enormous strategic stake in Cuba and to that degree in Latin America. The establishment and consolidation of this "first socialist state" in the Western hemisphere has been vital to the Soviet leadership's claim of legitimacy as the special representative of world history. Moscow's military position in Cuba has strengthened the image of Soviet power in the overall East-West context. Cuba is an important adjunct of Soviet political, military, propaganda and intelligence activities not only in Latin America but in Third World areas far afield. Current and potential Soviet military threats are examined in some detail in the Cirincione and Hunter essay in this volume. Five percent of total Soviet foreign trade is directed to Cuba. Maintaining this relationship with Cuba is a major factor determining Soviet policy toward Central America.

Despite its success in Cuba, Soviet involvement in Central America remained negligible throughout the 1970s. The USSR had diplomatic relations only with Costa Rica. It sought, without success, to establish relations only with Panama. American emphasis on "no more Cubas" culminating in the Dominican intervention, Soviet insistence that Havana cool its revolutionary ardor and the failure of revolutionary situations to develop in the area placed Central America near the bottom of Soviet international priorities. Furthermore, opportunities for the Soviets arose elsewhere in Latin America, most notably with Allende's victory in Chile in 1970.

In the early 1970s, growing Soviet interest in "progressive" military regimes found their reflection in Soviet approval of Torrijos in Panama and the regime of General Oswaldo López Arrellano in Honduras. Torrijos' focus on the return of the Panama Canal earned him Soviet plaudits, although Moscow and Torrijos exercised care to avoid too close a Soviet embrace which would jeopardize U.S. ratification and implementation of the terms of the August 1977 treaty. Defiant actions either against right-wing governments or U.S. firms in Central America brought expressions of delight from Moscow, but these came and went with no appreciable impact on Soviet policy.

THE SANDINISTA WATERSHED

The 1979 Sandinista revolution decisively activated Soviet interest and involvement in Central America. While the revolution was basically not of Soviet making, Moscow and some of its closest allies did play a marginal role. Castro has emphasized that the Soviet leadership had no personal ties with the Sandinistas before their victory. However, the Soviets have made a great deal of the fact that Carlos Fonseca, the founding father of the Sandinistas, attended the 1957 World Youth Festival in Moscow and a year later wrote a highly sympathetic book entitled "A Nicaraguan In Moscow." However, there has been no denying the long and close ties that existed between the Sandinistas and Cuba, which undoubtedly served as a vital channel for Moscow as well. The Cubans played a major role in uniting Sandinista factions and facilitating the receipt of Cuban arms. Moscow's most direct role probably took the form of forcing the pro-Soviet Nicaraguan Socialist Party to switch (as it did in April 1979) from rivalry to collaboration with the Sandinistas, from an emphasis on political to military action.

The Soviet Union portrayed the Sandinista victory as a historic watershed reversing the downturn in communist fortunes following the 1973 overthrow of Allende in Chile, and heralding a new revolutionary upsurge, not only in Central America, but throughout Latin America. Several Soviet spokesmen put Nicaragua within the context of world-wide anti-American developments. Thus, Andrei Kirilenko, in his address on November 6, 1979 honoring the 62nd anniversary of the October Revolution, asserted that "the Soviet people rejoice that in recent years the people of Angola, Ethiopia, Afghanistan, Nicaragua and Grenada have broken the chains of imperialist domination and have embarked on a road of independent development."

In the immediate aftermath of the Sandinista victory, Soviet commentaries emphasized that this development, like Castro's victory in Cuba, demonstrated the possibility of anti-American revolutionary transformations in the "strategic rear" of the United States. For example, a Nicaraguan communist wrote in the Prague-based *World Marxist Review* that the Nicaraguan triumph constituted "a further setback of imperialism that has, moreover, affected a most sensitive area traditionally regarded by imperialism as its most dependable 'hinterland.' "[1] A 1983 Soviet pamphlet on Nicaragua was still similarly stating that "the Sandinista revolution, being an integral part of the world revolutionary process, serves as yet one more convincing confirmation of the helplessness of imperialism to restore its lost historic initiative and to turn back the development of the modern world."[2]

The USSR moved even more rapidly. It had in Castro's case to establish diplomatic, economic and other relations with the Sandinista regime. Responding immediately to the declaration of a Provisional Democratic Government of National Reconstruction, Brezhnev on July 20, 1979 expressed Soviet willingness "to develop multifaceted ties with Nicaragua."

Moscow has also worked assiduously to strengthen its relationship with virtually the entire ruling junta, particularly the military, intelligence and security apparatuses. On March 17, 1980 the first major Sandinista delegation arrived in Moscow, on a journey that also took them to Bulgaria, East Germany and Czechoslovakia. The delegation included Minister of Interior Tomás Borge, Minister of Economic Planning Henry Ruiz, Minister of Defense Humberto Ortega, and junta member Moisés Hassán.

Top Sandinista leaders made a remarkable number of trips to the Soviet Union between May 1982 and mid-1983. In May 1982, Daniel Ortega came for the conclusion of a series of economic agreements. In a September visit publicized by Managua but not by Moscow, Borge discussed bilateral relations in the Soviet capital. Daniel Ortega represented the Sandinistas at Brezhnev's funeral in September; Minister of Agriculture Jaime Wheelock at the USSR's 60th anniversary celebrations in December. In February 1983, Planning Minister Ruiz met with his Soviet counterpart. In March 1983, Daniel Ortega passed through Moscow en route home from the non-aligned conference in New Delhi long enough to be received by Andropov. In June, Political Coordinator Bayardo Arce visited to implement the 1980 party-to-party agreement. In July, Wheelock was back for the signature of an agricultural pact.

Perhaps most significant has been the military relationship established between the USSR and Nicaragua. The presence of Defense Minister Humberto Ortega suggests that military aid may well have been explored during the visit of the March 1980 delegation. Several factors support this supposition. Soviet postmortems on Chile emphasize that one of the USSR's major lessons is that revolutions must be able to defend themselves, both by seizing control of a country's armed forces and by obtaining all the military aid they can. Soviet analyses especially praise the Sandinista regime for having learned these lessons.

In November 1981, Ortega visited the Soviet Union again for more than a week, and this time it may be presumed that military aid was at the top of the agenda. The Soviet military newspaper *Red Star* on November 21 announced that Ortega had had "a friendly conversation on matters of mutual interest" with Moscow's three top military officials, Defense Minister Ustinov, Chief of Staff Ogarkov and head of the Armed Forces' Main Political Administration, General Yepishev.

According to Nicaraguan defector Miguel Bolaños, the army, the militia, the police (including security police), special troops, and commandos are now equipped with Soviet arms. He claims there are 100 Soviet tanks in Nicaragua (the Pentagon says 50), and 80 MIGs waiting in Cuba. Nicaragua is said to have received both radar-guided and heat-seeking ground-to-air missiles.[3] During Daniel Ortega's mission to Moscow, an agreement was signed for Soviet repair and use of the Pacific port of San Juan del Sur. In other countries, an agreement of this kind opened the way to use of these facilities for naval surveillance and other military purposes.

The unpublicized visit to Moscow in September 1982 by Interior Minister Tomás Borge at the invitation of Andropov and Soviet security officials underscored the growing military relationship between Moscow and Managua, although Cuba appears to play the main role. Bolaños states that there are 70 Soviet advisors involved in all aspects of Nicaraguan state security, along with 400 Cubans, 40 to 50 East Germans, and 20 to 25 Bulgarians. Training is said to be based on handbooks provided by Cuba and Bulgaria, while the USSR, he says, has built a school for state security.

In addition, Soviet economic ties with Nicaragua have steadily increased. *Pravda* thus declared on July 19, 1983 that "the Republic's fraternal relations with the USSR, Cuba and other socialist countries are of great significance in helping the Nicaraguan people to thwart imperialism's latest designs" aimed, it said, "to ring the country with an economic blockade and a trade boycott."

During the first official Sandinista visit to Moscow in March 1980, a variety of agreements of trade, technical cooperation, civil aviation and consular ties were signed. In September 1981, the USSR concluded further economic, technical, communications and fishery agreements with Managua. An economic protocol provided $50 million in Soviet credit, supplementing $100 million from Libya and $64 million from Cuba.[4] After his return from Moscow in May 1982, Daniel Ortega told a press conference that the USSR had granted an additional $150 million credit.[5] According to the Amercan embassy in Managua, during 1982 the Soviet bloc had become the source of 47% of assistance obligated for Nicaragua, as compared to 15% in 1981.[6]

Moscow and Managua have gone far to establish their ideological affinity. Indicative of their special relationship was the signing, during the March 1980 visit of the Sandinista leadership, of a party-to-party agreement between the Communist Party of the Soviet Union and the Sandinista National Liberation Front — generally a step taken by Moscow with regimes it labels "states of socialist orientation." Although the Sandinista Front was then not nominally a party, the agreement suggested Soviet expectations that the front would become one and, under Soviet guidance, take on the characteristics of a Soviet-style organization, much as Castro's organization had done in Cuba.

During this and other meetings which followed, the Sandinistas aligned themselves with major Soviet foreign policy positions. Beginning in January 1981, a succession of agreements provided for further enhancement of ideological ties, for example, agreements on education and radio cooperation. During 1981 and thereafter, substantial numbers of Nicaraguans were sent to the USSR for education and technical training.

Reinforcing this process is a formidable array of ties which have developed between Sandinista Nicaragua and other communist states. The Sandinistas have party-to-party agreements with at least East Germany, Bulgaria and Czechoslovakia. Other Sandinista bodies have formal ties with counterparts in Eastern Europe and most notably with the Cuban Committee for the Defense of the Revolution. Nicaragua is now affiliated with all major international communist front organizations and in May 1982 became affiliated with Intersputnik, the Soviet-sponsored telecommunications organization – Nicaragua's first such accession to a multilateral communist governmental body.

Between 1980 and early 1983, Moscow on occasion gave Nicaragua the enhanced ideological status reflecting these developments. In November 1980 and January 1981, leading Soviet ideologist Boris Ponomarev wrote that states of socialist orientation were emerging in Asia, Africa "and Central America." He named no names, but only Nicaragua fit the bill. For several months in 1982, Soviet journals as well as the May Day slogans that year used the term "people's democratic" to refer to Nicaragua, a term hitherto attached only to postwar regimes in Eastern Europe. In June 1983, a *Pravda* article included Nicaragua in a list of socialist orientation countries.[7] While this was an exception, Soviet commentaries frequently describe Nicaragua in the same terms as countries habitually given this designation.

Perhaps most symbolically significant was the agreement announced by Radio Managua on September 16, 1983 whereby Nicaragua became an observor country in the Soviet bloc's major economic organization, the Council for Economic Mutual Assistance (CEMA). At a summit meeting of the organization in Berlin the next month, Nicaraguan Planning Minister Henry Ruiz did in fact attend as an observer. As long ago as fall 1979, Nicaraguan officials had considered ties to CEMA, but these had been deferred on political and economic grounds.[8] Whatever the practical purposes of the move, Nicaragua's status in CEMA now places it on par with other observer countries, who are either "socialist" countries, such as Yugoslavia, or "socialist-oriented," such as Angola, Afghanistan, Ethiopia, and others.

MOSCOW'S DOMINO THEORY

The Soviets saw the Sandinista victory as producing a domino effect in Central America. Operating mainly through Cuba and local communists, Moscow sought to duplicate the Nicaraguan experience in El Salvador.

Reaffirming the position taken since the Sandinistas came to power, the 1983 Soviet pamphlet on Nicaragua states: "The victory of the Sandinista people's revolution has materially shaken the foundations of the system of American imperialism's sway which had taken shape in Central America."[9] The Soviet foreign policy magazine *New Times* wrote that "the strengthening of the Cuban socialist system and the growth of Cuba's international influence, the victory of the popular democratic and anti-imperialist revolution in Nicaragua . . . have given a powerful push to the revolutionary movement in Central America, directed against tyrannical military dictatorships set up and supported by the United States."[10] This perception led to a significant doctrinal shift among pro-Soviet communist parties in the area and was accompanied by growing Cuban efforts to unify contending guerrilla groups and to mount a program of military aid and training for these groups.

On the doctrinal side, a roundtable discussion in the first three 1980 issues of the Soviet journal *Latinskaia Amerika* contained several expressions of approval for the hitherto rejected views of Ernesto "Ché" Guevara on the primacy of armed struggle. The June 1981 issue of the international communist journal *World Marxist Review* reported that a "study commission" had concluded that "far from impeding armed struggle, as some petty bourgeois theorists contend with reference to the experience of the 1960s, the present international situation largely predetermines its favorable outcome."[11]

Doctrine was soon backed by action. With respect to El Salvador, Cuba served as a host as three unified organizations were established in 1980: in April, the Revolutionary Democratic Front, a broad organization intended to present the Salvadoran guerrilla case abroad; in May, the Unified Revolutionary Directorate, a central executive arm; in October, the Farabundo Martí People's Liberation Front (FMLN), the coordinating body of the guerrilla organizations. Similar processes took place in Guatemala and Honduras in 1982.

Unification of the Salvadoran guerrillas was evidently the precondition for military aid which came from a variety of sources by way of Cuba and Nicaragua. The Soviets apparently acted as the go-between but have exercised great care to avoid direct involvement. When Kremlin press spokesman Leonid Zamiatin was asked by foreign newsmen during the 26th Soviet Party Congress in 1981 about State Department charges regarding the Soviet role in arms aid to Salvadorn guerrillas, he contended: "The Soviet Union does not provide El Salvador with arms. It never has. It never will." [12] This disavowal and the failure of the Salvadoran party to be included among foreign party delegations at the time presumably stemmed from a desire not to undermine Secretary General Brezhnev's proposed summit with the new American president.

An important feature in Moscow's relationship with the Salvadoran guerrilla struggle — which distinguishes it from the Sandinista situation — has been the role of the orthodox pro-Soviet Salvadoran Communist Party. As indicated by the State Department press release in February 1981, the head of that party, Shafik Jorge Handal, led the shopping expedition for arms in Moscow, East Berlin, Hanoi, and other communist capitals in June-July 1980.[13] Handal was given the unusual honor of contributing an article in November 1980 in the Soviet Communist Party's principal ideological journal *Kommunist*. There Handal proclaimed that his cause "will win through the use of arms because, objectively, no other path exists." While not mentioning the question of arms deliveries, Handal hinted at the possibility when he stated that "We believe that in today's world there are moral, political and material forces that are in a position to curb the imperialists." In return, he indicated "we take this into consideration in our activities, linking more tightly our internal political and military struggle with the political struggle in the international arena."[14]

However in July 1982 a Soviet article on El Salvador noted "that the attainment of the unity of the revolutionary organizations will be quite painful."[15] In a hint that members of the Communist Party were balking at a subordinate role, the article pointedly recalled the "sad experience" of the Nicaraguan Socialist (i.e., Communist) Party, which preferred purity to unity with the radical Sandinista front. Later, an October 1983 article noted the party's successful "determining role" in the formation of the Farabundo Martí organization.[16]

Soviet attitudes toward El Salvador have varied in accordance with the situation on the ground and estimates regarding possible U.S. actions. Perhaps the high point of Soviet hopes came with the guerrillas' "final offensive" of January 1981. Subsequent Soviet accounts fluctuated according to guerrilla successes (which are emphasized) and setbacks (which lead to periods of Soviet media silence).

A Soviet postmortem on the failure of the "final offensive" suggests that it was launched prematurely because of concern about increased U.S. involvement under the new American administration. In the words of the Soviet author:

> The absence of political paths to resolve the most acute internal political crisis in essence pushed the left forces to an activization of military actions. A catalyst of this [was] the victory in the U.S. presidential elections of Ronald Reagan, insofar as all ultra-rightest forces in Latin American pinned their hopes, with his coming to power, on more active participation by the United States in putting down popular movements of a democratic character. It is possible that this prospect also exerted an influence at the beginning of 1981 in hastening the time periods for the start of the big offensive.[17]

THE THREAT TO CUBA

One of the most serious consequences for Moscow of events in Central America has been the perceived threat of U.S. actions against Cuba—a prospect Moscow thought had been laid to rest in the 1970s. To maintain and strengthen its stake in Cuba, the USSR has significantly stepped up military aid and upgraded its security commitments to Havana. The steps began during the Carter administration, when charges of Cuban involvement in Central America generated Soviet countercharges of U.S. intentions to intervene in Cuba. These countercharges evidently led to the signature on May 31, 1980 of a friendship treaty between Cuba and East Germany, the only such treaty between Cuba and a member of the Warsaw Pact. Although the treaty contains no military clauses, the Soviets emphasize the treaty's importance as evidence of bloc support for Cuba against "imperialist" threats.

The coming to power of a U.S. administration defining issues in East-West terms, placing greater emphasis on the role of military power, and defining Central America as a test case of U.S. foreign policy brought the issue of intervention to the forefront of Soviet considerations in the region. In 1981 the 26th Soviet Communist Party Congress in February 1981 Brezhnev raised Cuba's ideological status by formally including it in a listing of members of the "socialist community." Soviet pronouncements define this status as linking a country "indissolubly" to the Soviet bloc under the aegis of the Brezhnev Doctrine.

In the fall of 1981, Moscow responded to the Reagan administration's accusations of Cuban involvement, via Nicaragua, in El Salvador with a series of warnings about the "serious consequences" of any punitive U.S. actions against Cuba. To reinforce these warnings, the USSR stepped up military deliveries to Cuba. Defense Minister Ustinov's participation in meetings between Andropov and Fidel and Raúl Castro in November and December 1982, as well as subsequent Soviet references to the "combat solidarity"[18] between the two countries and the "indissoluble"[19] links between their two armies were designed to underscore the Soviet-Cuban military relationship. The hope was to deter the United States, reassure Havana and to remind Latin Americans of the USSR's role.

To what extent the USSR would respond militarily to U.S. "punitive action" is an open question. The involvement in combat of Cuban "advisers" and "workers" in Grenada may be a model of the obligations which would be assumed by the Soviet brigade in Cuba. Unlike most other members of the socialist community, Cuba does not have a formal Soviet military commitment embodied in a mutual aid or friendship treaty. Moscow's preferred option is not to be put to the test.

THE THREAT TO NICARAGUA

As in the case of Cuba, the USSR responded to perceived threats of U.S. intervention — U.S.-supported *contras* and the U.S. Big Pine exercises — with increased military aid, but a great deal more circumspection about long-term security commitments.

According to U.S. Defense Department officials, there has been a steady rise in Soviet military deliveries to Nicaragua in 1982 and 1983. As reported by the *New York Times* on August 2, 1983, five ships from the USSR or Eastern Europe with military supplies docked in Nicaragua in 1982; ten had already arrived by August 1983, with another ten on the way. Deliveries in 1981-1982 were said to include smaller transport planes, helicopters, and trainers, while 1982-1983 deliveries concentrated on heavy weapons, including tanks, armored personnel carriers, artillery and aircraft.

However, Moscow has exercised care in the kind of weapons it has supplied and its declaratory policy about this aid. The weapons appear exclusively for defense purposes and are supplied by third parties. MIG planes, which Nicaraguan pilots have been trained in Bulgaria to fly, are said to remain still in Cuba.

Moscow has never publicly acknowledged its military aid program to Nicaragua and has avoided the appearance of any direct commitment. Thus TASS denounced as a "fabrication" Secretary of State Haig's speculation that 17 Soviet MIG-21 planes in Cuba were intended for transshipment to Nicaragua. In August 1983, Moscow denied that its ship, the *Aleksandr Ulyanov*, detained by the U.S. en route to Nicaragua, was carrying military supplies. The closest Moscow has come to acknowledging Soviet aid has been in its occasional citation of Sandinista statements about Managua's right to get weapons from any source. The Soviet military newspaper *Red Star*, on May 4, 1983, for example, reported an assertion by National Directorate member Bayardo Arce that, "faced with the Reagan Administration's aggressive intrigues and threats, we will continue to exercise our sovereign right to ask any country, regardless of its political and social system, for military aid in order to defend the motherland." No specific country is ever mentioned.

Soviet spokesmen are most evasive in their response to questions as to what actions the Soviet Union would take if the United States did invade Nicaragua. When this question was put to Yuri Fokin, General Secretary of the Soviet Foreign Ministry, at a press conference in Managua on August 3, 1983, he replied: "We will support Nicaragua *politically* in every way"[20] [emphasis added]. When the Soviet ambassador to Nicaragua was asked in November 1983 how the USSR "would express its solidarity" in the event, he responded that Soviet solidarity already "has been one of the most powerful deterrents to U.S. aggression against Nicaragua" and that "U.S. invasion of Nicaragua must be nipped in the bud."[21] In an otherwise lengthy treatment, Moscow omitted that portion of Fidel Castro's October 1983 press conference in which he said Cuba would be unable to aid Nicaragua if it were attacked by the United States.

In the face of *contra* activity, Moscow's public position is that the Sandinistas are handling the situation successfully. Such was the gist of the exchange between Andropov and Daniel Ortega on March 25, 1983. The Soviet leader was quoted by TASS as having "expressed the conviction that Nicaragua will be able to uphold its freedom and independence," while Ortega "emphasized that the revolutionary government of Nicaragua has all the necessary resources to defend the motherland." A November 1983 Soviet article concluded that the "CIA mercenaries are meeting a crushing rebuff" and Washington is well aware that the "*Somocista* cutthroats . . . are not in a position to overthrow the Sandinista government."[22]

Despite the potential significance of Nicaragua's joining CEMA as an observer, it seems to imply a Soviet economic commitment which is less than the USSR is willing or able to give. Moscow has been reluctant to take on the economic burden of Nicaragua as it did in Cuba. The USSR's failure to rush in as it had in Cuba to take up Nicaragua's sugar quota when it was dropped by the United States is symbolic of Moscow's reluctant approach. Soviet analyses of the Sandinista regime have indicated satisfaction with its ability to get aid from a variety of donors.

Thus, while it has increased, the weight of bloc trade in the total Nicaraguan picture remains limited. According to *Pravda*, on July 19, 1983 Nicaraguan imports from socialist states increased to 11.5% in 1982 as opposed to 3.3% in 1981. A later Soviet article stressed the diversification of Nicaraguan trade "in response to the economic war on the part of the U.S."[23] According to the article, Nicaraguan imports in 1983 are to be divided as follows: 15% from Central America, 27% from other Latin American countries, 14% from the Common market, 19% still from the United States, 8% from other developed capitalist countries, 12% from socialist countries.

Drawing upon the lessons of its Cuban experience, Moscow has in recent years been cautioning countries with which it has close political sympathies such as Nicaragua not to pin excessive hopes on economic support from the Soviet Union. In his June 15 Central Committee plenum speech, Andropov graphically expresses the primacy of political and military support over economic aid in the Third World:

> It is one thing to proclaim socialism as one's goal and another thing to build it. A certain level of productive forces, culture and social consciousness are needed for that. Socialist countries express solidarity with these progressive countries, render assistance to them in the sphere of politics and culture, and promote the strengthening of their defense. We contribute, to the extent of our ability, to their economic development as well. But, on the whole, their economic development just as the entire social progress of those countries, can be, of course, only the result of the work of their peoples and of a correct policy of their leadership.[24]

THE SOVIET POLITICAL COUNTER-OFFENSIVE

To ease pressures on Cuba, Nicaragua and the Salvadoran left, Moscow has repeatedly warned Washington about the repercussions of U.S. intervention in any or all of the three and has increasingly focused on the virtues of a political settlement. These efforts reflect not only Moscow's desire to avoid military confrontation but its belief that a long struggle lies ahead requiring subtler military and political means than those employed during the Sandinista's accession to power and early Salvadoran military successes.

Soviet emphasis on U.S. intervention serves a number of purposes. By focusing attention on U.S. policies, Moscow may hope to generate world opposition and to deter intervention. Soviet warnings about Central America are designed in particular to play on fears both in Europe and Latin America about U.S. attitudes toward the use of force.

Moscow, of course, recognizes the potential of the intervention issue as a major source of contention between the United States and Latin America. On the eve of Secretary of State Shultz's visit to Mexico in April 1983, a Soviet television commentary reported "acute disagreements between the United States and Mexico on relations with El Salvador and Nicaragua." When Venezuelan Foreign Minister Zambrano came to Moscow in April, Gromyko lectured him about "the threats, provocations and pressure against Cuba, Nicaragua, Grenada and other countries" by unnamed "imperialist forces."[25]

While exploiting these opportunities to isolate the United States, Moscow also thus increased its declaratory support, first for Mexican and then for Contadora efforts at a peaceful settlement in the region. Soviet interest in these proposals appeared more for their utility as a source of pressure on the United States and a deterrent to strong actions on its part, than a willingness to make them the centerpiece of a settlement. Soviet references to Mexican and early Contadora proposals usually focused on those aspects which would lead to a U.S. withdrawal from Central America. Soviet professions of support for Contadora efforts invariably gave equal if not greater place to proposals by Nicaragua and later, the Salvadoran left.

In March 1982, when both Nicaragua and Mexico presented negotiating proposals, Brezhnev declared that peace in Central America would be "best served, in our view, by the peace-loving proposals which were recently put forward by the government of Nicaragua." Almost as an afterthought, he added that "in the same vein are the ideas which were expressed by the president of Mexico". When Venezuelan Foreign Minister Zambrano visited Moscow in April 1983, Foreign Minister Gromyko, as reported by *Pravda*, declared that "we assess positively the proposals of Venezuela, Mexico, Nicaragua and certain other countries aimed at a political settlement," but that "it would be an exaggeration to assert that our approach to all questions is identical"—indicating that significant disputes must have arisen on matters of substance.

In a conversation with American senators in August, Andropov "emphatically advocated a political settlement in Central America" and "that everything be done to prevent the situation in that region from getting out of control." As before, he gave priority to the Nicaraguan and Cuban proposals which had been made during July. According to the Soviet announcement, Andropov was said to have "positively" evaluated "the efforts of Latin American countries which are trying to assist in finding mutually acceptable solutions" but to have "expressed the Soviet Union's full support for the constructive proposals set forth by Nicaragua and Cuba."[26]

Whether Moscow acquiesced in the Sandinista moves in early November to mollify the U.S. and Western European critics—withdrawal of Cuban and Salvadoran insurgent personnel from Nicaragua, eased censorship, overtures to business and church circles—is not clear. Despite Soviet insistence that the Sandinistas are weathering the pressures on them, Soviet commentaries concede that the actions of the *contras* have harmed the economy. There is also less attention in Soviet analyses to its economic successes than during the first years of the Sandinista regime.

While it probably welcomes talks insofar as they deter the U.S. from taking military action and complicate U.S. relations with Latin America, Moscow may also be apprehensive about how far the Sandinistas will be required, or willing, to go. In the early years of the Sandinista regime, Soviet analysts praised the Sandinista leadership for its flexibility in dealing with what they called the "middle strata" but emphasized the overriding need for maintaining control over the main levers of power.

Moscow would most likely draw the line on any concession that jeopardizes the Sandinista monopoly of power. A 1983 Soviet article argued against demands that Nicaragua hold Western-style elections. The Soviet author called such demands an attempt "to discredit the Sandinista leadership, above all in the eyes of Latin American public opinion" and quoted Tomás Borge to the effect that elections "cannot serve as a theme for negotiations with a foreign power."[27] The article stated further that the Sandinista leadership had "by no means usurped political power" but that Sandinista primacy is the "legitimate result" of popular support for them. In this connection it is of interest to recall that Castro had suggested shortly after the Sandinistas assumed power that it might be a good idea for the Sandinistas to hold free elections because they would win "by a very wide margin," while Soviet analysts strongly supported Sandinista leaders who opposed such elections.[28]

Possibly reassured by how the Sandinistas intend to manage their elections, Moscow recently gave a special accolade to the Sandinsta announcement on electoral preparations. *Pravda* said that the relevant decree had evoked "tremendous political resonance" at home and abroad, and that it had "inflicted a crushing blow to fabrications by imperialist propoganda that the Sandinistas are afraid of a free expression of the will of the people."

Moscow has been particularly dubious about prospects for talks on El Salvador. In 1982, the Soviet media completely ignored Mexico's call for a settlement between the parties in El Salvador.

There is little which suggests belief by Moscow in the feasibility of meaningful negotiations with the U.S. or the Salvadoran government. One Soviet journal noted that the idea of a dialogue with the Salvadoran rebels was supported by "definite circles of the [U.S.] Democratic and Republican parties, the U.S. Catholic Church, the governments of Mexico, Venezuela, Colombia, Panama and other countries of Latin America and Western Europe, the leadership of the Socialist International, the non-aligned movement, the majority of UN members."[29] Under such pressures, Washington was said to be "maneuvering" by pretending to favor a peaceful settlement. This, like several other Soviet commentaries on the subject, focused heavily on the unacceptability of any proposal calling for the guerrillas to participate in an election. Such proposals were merely designed to get the guerrillas to lay down their arms and participate in an election whose results were foreordained.

Moscow apparently has accepted negotiations between the Salvadoran left and U.S. Ambassador Stone, but has been consistently dubious about the ambassador's motives. The Soviet newspaper *Sovetskaia Rossiia* on August 11, 1983, for example, seized on Stone's meeting with a leftist representative "as U.S. recognition of the Salvadoran revolutionary organization's real strength" but expressed "fear that this move is purely propagandist in nature."

BROADER SOVIET PERSPECTIVES

A basic tension exists between Moscow's ideological self-image and geopolitical realities. Soviet ideologists claim that the USSR's achievement of strategic parity with the United States has put a brake on "imperialism's" freedom of maneuver and that the USSR's emergence as a world power gives it a crucial voice in all world problems.[30] Since the early 1970s the Soviet military establishment has expanded the mission of the Soviet armed forces to include not only the traditional defense of the Soviet Union, but the defense of friends and allies, as well as "rendering aid to all those struggling against imperialism."[31] Moscow also emphasizes its role as head of the world revolutionary process. Soviet preoccupation with U.S. threats carries the risk of forcing Moscow to take actions to fulfill its ideological claims. In this context, Moscow can be expected to probe the depths of Washington's tolerance and to take advantage of the turmoil in Central America.

At the same time, the limits already evident in its commitments indicate that Moscow will proceed with caution. While eager to undermine further the doctrine of "geographic fatalism," other areas of the world clearly have greater priority. Moscow has also had to devote significant military forces to Afghanistan, and is preoccupied by Poland, the issue of U.S. nuclear missile deployments in Europe, and the Middle East. (For example, the quantity and sophistication of weapons supplied to Syria after the Israeli invasion of Lebanon far outweighed those to Nicaragua.)

Moscow will continue to respect U.S. power and geographic advantages in Central America. Despite its ideological view that all foreign policy problems impinge on the superpower struggle, Moscow has consistently muted the East-West aspects of the Central American conflicts. Indeed the Soviets deny that the USSR, Cuba or Nicaragua are involved militarily in El Salvador, presumably so as not to lend credence to administration arguments about the nature of these conflicts or to provide justification for increased U.S. intervention. The minimal treatment given the *Aleksandr Ulyanov* hailing incident was clearly designed to avoid transforming the Nicaraguan issue into a U.S.-USSR confrontation. The strategic importance attached by the United States to the region makes the extension of Soviet influence an attractive target, but also convinces the USSR to exercise caution in pursuing such an objective.[32]

Moscow's low profile also serves Soviet regional objectives. By relying on proxies indigenous to the area, the USSR avoids an interventionist appearance which might drive Latin American countries back toward the United States and jeopardize Soviet interests elsewhere on the continent. In this connection, Moscow has adopted a differentiated policy toward countries like Costa Rica and Panama as well as the rest of Latin America where it sees no prospects for insurgencies. Regarding these countries, the USSR encourages government support for Cuba, Nicaragua and the Salvadoran left, or for diplomatic efforts designed to reduce the chances of U.S. intervention. The presence during 1981 of 675 students from Costa Rica in the USSR and Eastern Europe suggests long-term Soviet interest and support in Central and Latin America.[33]

Over both the short and long run, indeed, Moscow may calculate that major forces are at work in the United States and in the region which make unnecessary either significant Soviet inputs or too forward a Soviet policy.

U.S. DOMESTIC ATTITUDES

Despite its warnings, Moscow perceives effective limits on Washington's willingness and ability to take direct military action. American sponsorship of the *contras* and moves to strengthen the capabilities of Honduran and Salvadoran military forces indicate to Moscow U.S. unwillingness to incur the military costs and risks of direct involvement. A March 1983 *Izvestiia* editorial on U.S. policy in Central America remarked that "in our day you cannot so readily send gunboats and Marines south of the Rio Grande." An April *Izvestiia* article defined U.S. views as follows:

If it is not possible, as in the old days, to send in an armada of dread-noughts, then let their place be taken instead by Pentagon advisors actively involved in the Salvadoran military's affairs; and if the Marines can no longer immediately be put into the field, maximum use must be made of the remnants of the dictator Somoza's guards—arming them and, under CIA supervision, drilling them in how to stage an invasion of Nicaragua.

The Soviet media has featured internal U.S. political opposition to military intervention in either Nicaragua or El Salvador. Moscow closely followed congressional votes on covert aid to Nicaragua and military assistance to El Salvador. Frequent citations were made of American fears that the U.S. might be repeating the Vietnam experience. The Soviet foreign policy journal *New Times* reported, in connection with the debate on covert operations in Nicaragua, that "there is resistance to a policy of intervention in Central America even among the military,"[34] citing a statement by retiring U.S. Army Chief of Staff General Edward Meyer that the dispatch of the 82nd Airborne Division, for example, would not be sufficient to solve the problem.

The need to take into consideration wide domestic opposition was said to explain the Reagan administration's support for elections in El Salvador, its willingness to talk to the Sandinistas and the Salvadoran left, and its resort to the Kissinger Commission. Soviet speculation in mid-1983 about the 1984 elections suggested that Reagan would adopt a peace-making posture in Central America for the purposes of his reelection campaign. Although the U.S. invasion of Grenada reinforced Soviet charges about U.S. willingness to use its own forces in Central America, the invasion may have shaken Soviet views about the strength of domestic U.S. opposition to such a policy. A major Soviet foreign policy journal in November, for example, quoted U.S. television about the "astounding support across the U.S." for the Grenada operations, support which the Soviet author saw as reflecting a "deep going imperial chauvinism that prevails in the United States."[35]

U.S. REGIONAL PROBLEMS

Moscow believes that U.S. involvement in Central America will inevitably run head on into the long-term trend of Latin American assertiveness, independence and anti-Americanism. Thus, the United States may win in Central America but jeopardize important positions elsewhere on the continent. The main arena of struggle in the hemisphere will not be in Central America or in the Caribbean but in the major Latin American countries. According to a leading Soviet foreign policy journal:

The U.S. ruling elite calculates that however important in strategic or political relations the individual small countries of the region are, the outcome of the opposition between the forces of progress and reaction on the soil of Latin America is being decided in key countries — Brazil, Mexico, Argentina.[36]

In this context Soviet analysts also predict a steady breakdown of the inter-American system, citing for example, the inability of the United States to secure joint action to replace Somoza and more recently the Falklands crisis. Cleavages between the U.S. and Latin American countries on Central American policies are considered further indications in this direction.

Soviet analysts believe that neither U.S. conservatives nor liberals have the answer to Central America's problems or the proper U.S. role in the area. A Soviet think-piece, while crediting the liberals with greater "realism" in their approach, declares that the "liberals" conception is not a new one. U.S. liberals want to counter Cuba "not with an armed response but with a financial one." This has been tried, the writer states, but "every time obstacles have arisen which could not be overcome, either by massive injections of dollars or by reformist plans."[37]

As in other areas, Moscow foresees "ebbs and flows, successes and temporary defeats" in Central America, an approach which makes it possible for Moscow to accept leftist setbacks, if not with equanimity, then at least with a belief of ultimate reversal. The Kremlin has borne Allende's overthrow, Manley's defeat in Jamaica and most recently Bishop's demise in Grenada. Presumably the Soviet Union could digest setbacks in El Salvador or in Nicaragua.

In Central America, in particular, Moscow clearly foresees the political and economic situation remaining fragile for so long that the soil for leftist movements and anti-American sentiments will remain fertile. With the retention of Cuba and the maintenance of a sympathetic relationship with Nicaragua, Moscow sees itself continuing to have important bases of operation in the area.

Moscow undoubtedly welcomes the extent to which U.S. military involvement in Central America stretches U.S. military resources and diverts attention from areas of greater direct interest to the Soviet Union.[38]

More broadly, Moscow regards U.S. involvement in Central America as the correction of a global asymmetry in which unlike the U.S. the USSR has had to show special concern for areas contiguous to itself.

NOTES

1. Alvaro Ramirez, "Nicaragua: From armed struggle to construction," *World Marxist Review*, No. 1, January 1980, p. 52.

2. I.M. Bulychev, *Nicaragua Today*, Moscow, Mezhdunarodnye Otnosheniia, 1983, p. 13.
3. *Inside Communist Nicaragua: The Miguel Bolaños Transcripts*, Heritage Foundation Backgrounder, September 30, 1983.
4. TASS, September 4, 1981, in U.S. Foreign Broadcast Information Service, Daily Report-Soviet Union (FBIS-SU), p. K-2.
5. Radio Managua Domestic Service, May 10, 1982 in FBIS-Latin America (LAM), May 11, 1982, pp. P8-P10.
6. American Embassy Managua, *Foreign Economic Trends Report 1983*, p. 3.
7. *Pravda*, June 16, 1983.
8. A. Kuzmin, "Nicaragua Defends Freedom and Independence," *Mezhdunarodnaia Zhizn*, No. 11, November 1983, p. 18.
9. I.M. Bulychev, *op. cit.*, p. 56.
10. Yu. Antonov, "Epicenter of Storms," *New Times*, March 19, 1982, p. 8.
11. "Latin America: A Continent in Struggle," *World Marxist Review*, June 1981, p. 47.
12. *New York Times*, February 26, 1981.
13. *Ibid.*, February 24, 1981.
14. Robert Rand, "The USSR's Stake in El Salvador," Radio Liberty Research Report, RL 1261/81, March 21, 1981.
15. E. Vorozheynika, "The Revolutionary Organizations of El Salvador and the Popular Movement," *Latinskaia Amerika*, July 1982, p. 33.
16. E. Nadezhdin, "El Salvador: In a Struggle for the Right to Live," *Politicheskoie Samoobrazovaniye*, No. 10, October 1983, p. 114.
17. N.S. Leonov, "Salvadoran Drama," *Latinskaia Amerika*, August 1981, p. 14.
18. B.I. Gvozdarev, "Washington's Anti-Cuban Policy – A Threat to the Peace and Security of the Peoples," *USA: Politics, Economics, Ideology*, No. 5, May 1983, p.15.
19. In *New Times*, No. 47, November 1983, p. 7.
20. Radio Havana, August 3, 1983 in FBIS-LAM, August 4, 1983, p. P-10.
21. Radio Managua Domestic Service, November 4, 1983 in FBIS-LAM p. P-23.
22. Dmitry Volsky, "Under the Jolly Roger of Violence," *New Times*, No. 47, November 1983, p. 6.
23. Volsky, "Shield for Democracy or Sword of Imperialism," *New Times*, No. 32, August 1983, p. 8.
24. *Pravda*, June 13, 1983.
25. FBIS-SU, 14 April 1983, p. K-2.
26. *Pravda*, August 19, 1982.
27. Kuzmin, *op. cit.*, pp. 13-16.
28. Castro speech, July 26, 1979 in FBIS-LAM, 27 July 1979, p. Q-10; For Soviet discussions, see symposium in *Latinskaia Amerika*, No. 3, March 1980.
29. Nadezhdin, *op. cit.*, p. 116.
30. "The Working Class and the Development of the World Revolutionary Process," *Obshchestvennye Nauki*, No. 5, 1983, p. 50.
31. Marshal A.A. Grechko, Speech at 24th CPSU Congress, *Pravda*, April 3, 1971.
32. Yu. Shvetsov, *Sovetskaia Rossiia*, September 13, 1983.
33. U.S. Department of State, *Soviet and East European Aid to the Third World, 1981*, February 1983, p. 23.
34. Volsky, *op. cit.*, *New Times*, No. 32, August 1983, p. 8.
35. For example, in an editorial in *Kommunist*, No. 15, October 1983.
36. A. Glinkin, P. Yakovlev, "Latin America in the Global Strategy of Imperialism," *Mirovaia Ekonomika i Mezhdunarodnye Otnosheniia*, October 1982, p. 79.
37. A. Matliana, "Disagreements within U.S. ruling circles on Latin American policy issues," *Latinskaia Amerika*, No. 3, March 1983, pp. 2-5.

38. While the majority of Soviet commentaries attacked U.S. Big Pine maneuvers in the Caribbean as evidence of U.S. gunboat diplomacy, one journal noted that the maneuvers required a shifting of forces from other areas.

ECONOMIC AND MILITARY REALITIES

7
THE COST OF ALTERNATIVE U.S. POLICIES TOWARD EL SALVADOR, 1984-1989

Theodore H. Moran

I. OVERVIEW AND SUMMARY RESULTS

The debate about American policy options toward El Salvador has been carried out largely in an economic vacuum. Proposals about what the United States should or should not do are being advanced without a realistic appraisal of what they would cost or, alternatively, whether they are being supported with sufficient resources to make them plausibly viable.

On the one hand there are painstaking appraisals of fragments of the administration's budgetary proposals for the region — $60 million in reprogramming of last year's aid, $50 million in supplemental assistance to last until next year. On the other hand, there are vast speculations about the construction of a "Marshall Plan" for the development of Central America, predicated upon an end to hostilities and the restoration of stability. But how much is it likely to cost in terms of U.S. assistance to get from here to there? And how much will the costs vary depending upon the policy scenario the United States chooses to try to accomplish its objectives?

This study attempts to determine the costs of four alternative scenarios for U.S. policy toward El Salvador. It does not try to judge which scenario is preferable, or which offers the greatest benefits (to weigh against the cost) in terms of America's larger national interests. And it does not mean to suggest that decisions affecting U.S. policy-making toward Central America will be taken primarily on economic grounds. Rather, it hopes to provide some base-line cost estimates to serve as an input to the larger debate on political and security issues. Each scenario runs for five years.

Scenario I: Continuation of Current U.S. Policies

U.S. economic and military policies toward El Salvador continue at 1984-request levels, with protracted struggle but no political breakthrough over the course of the five years.

Scenario II: Moving Toward a Negotiated Solution

Significant guerrilla groups participate with the Salvadoran government in a joint effort at reconstruction, whether through elections or through "power-sharing." The reconciliation begins with great mutual suspicion in the first year, and proceeds very cautiously during the next four with large sections of the local elite unwilling to stake large new investments on the outcome. Throughout the period U.S. aid attempts to stabilize domestic economic activity at 1982-1983 levels and begin to produce a growth rate of approximately three percent per year (zero percent per capita).

Scenario III: Military Escalation Without U.S. Combat Troops

U.S. military assistance is stepped up to give Salvadoran troops the equipment and training they most need in the largest amounts they can absorb effectively without American advisers participating in combat. At the same time domestic economic activity is stabilized and strengthened with equal U.S. assistance as in Scenario II.

Scenario IV: Reaching Beyond El Salvador with an Invasion and Occupation of Nicaragua

To isolate the struggle in El Salvador, the United States moves against Nicaragua. American troops with representative CONDECA contingents establish beachheads and airheads in Nicaragua, take over the principal cities of Nicaragua, extend a presence throughout the countryside, and proceed to deal with sabotage and insurgency after the high-intensity warfare has died down. The United States reinforces the Salvadoran military effort as in Scenario III, leaving it to the Salvadorans to deal with their own insurgency.

This study does not attempt to specify policies, or put a price tag on a "Marshall Plan" to develop the region over the longer term. Nor does it seek to specify the longer run economic, political, or security costs, or benefits, of choosing one alternative rather than another. Moreover, it is important to underscore the limitations of this kind of analysis. At the most basic level, one must remember that any construction of cost estimates is only as good as the assumptions that go into them. Once the assumptions are made explicit, however, anyone who disagrees with the analysis can more easily prepare his own forecast. Furthermore, not only do the estimates contain great uncertainties, but these uncertainties grow, perhaps exponentially, as the scale of the scenarios increases. At the same time the "costs" that accrue to the United States from choosing one policy over another come in many forms, from the loss of human lives to a threat to the security of the United States, against which the dollar figures calculated here have dramatically small meaning.

Nevertheless, despite these caveats, there are several rather clear conclusions from this study.

First, no solution will come cheap, not even a hypothetical *Negotiated Solution* agreed to as early as in 1984. That will cost nearly $4 billion over five years.

Second, while *Continuation of Current U.S. Policies* is the cheapest course, requiring between $3 billion and $4 billion over the same period of time, this course almost surely lacks the resources needed to turn economic activity in El Salvador around from the relatively depressed 1982-83 levels (already no more than three-fourths of 1978 levels). Indeed, over a five-year period, there will be a further drain on the country's already dwindling capital stock of approximately half a billion dollars. At the same time current funding patterns seem likely to undermine political support for the central government from either the peasants and small farmers or from the upper classes. Finally, present assistance efforts fail to meet the main technical needs of the Salvadoran military in its confrontations with the guerrillas. All suggest that this policy would not fulfill U.S. economic, political and military objectives.

Third, *Movement Toward a Negotiated Solution,* with more ample resources to make it economically and politically viable despite an assumed on-going suspicion and hostility on the part of Salvadoran economic elites, will cost only marginally more than the continuation of current U.S. policies.

Fourth, *Military Escalation Without U.S. Combat Troops* will cost almost twice as much as either of the two preceding scenarios, between $6 and $7 billion over five years. The higher aid levels in this scenario reflect U.S. Department of Defense priorities, but are capped as indicated because the marginal utility of supplying increased U.S. weaponry declines sharply (according to American military assessments) unless U.S. combat advisers and/or troops are inserted along with it. But these expenditures do not necessarily ensure against the introduction of U.S. combat troops. On the contrary, they create a need for U.S. forces to protect the added equipment (especially the concentration of helicopters) and to provide training, thereby setting the stage for a catalytic attack by the guerrillas.

Finally, it must be reiterated that *Reaching Beyond El Salvador with an*

Invasion and Occupation of Nicaragua incorporates much larger and much graver uncertainties than any of the other scenarios, and would hardly be contemplated solely or principally as an action focused at stabilizing the situation in El Salvador. It costs approximately $16 billion, or four times more than the Continuation of Current U.S. Policies or the Moving Toward a Negotiated Solution, and is likely to result in between 2,000 to 5,000 American dead and between 9,000 to 19,000 American wounded.

It should be stressed that these basic compilations of cost figures do not provide any assurances that the expenditure of greater resources alone in Moving Toward a Negotiated Solution, or Military Escalation Without U.S. Combat Troops, or Invasion and Occupation of Nicaragua will achieve the political and military objectives of the United States. In contrast one can be certain, however, that the less expensive Continuation of Current U.S. Policies will not accomplish its objectives.

II. THE ECONOMY OF EL SALVADOR

El Salvador is a small country with limited resources and a large population (almost five million) which is increasing at a rate of 2.9% per year. Despite these obstacles, its economic performance prior to 1979 was impressive.[1] From 1960-1978 the Salvadoran economy grew at 5.4 % per year with investment rising faster that GDP. The investment GDP ratio climbed from 14% in the early 1960s to 23% in 1976-78. Of this, most came from domestic savings, which rose from 12% to 20% of GDP. The export performance of the economy was strong, growing from 22% of GDP to 36% of GDP over the same period. Within this, manufacturing exports became significant, rising to one-third of the total in 1976-78. In general, the labor force has shown itself to be productive and adaptable. There are relatively proficient technical and managerial groups.

On the other hand, the country's wealth has remained very poorly distributed, with the upper 20% of the population capturing 66% of total income and the bottom 50% of the population having only 12% (the most skewed income distribution in all of Central America). Even at the height of economic growth, two-thirds of the Salvadoran households lacked piped water, over one-half were without electricity, and malnutrition was frequent among small children.[2]

Since 1978 the economy has been deteriorating dramatically. International prices for El Salvador's principal export crops — coffee, sugar, and cotton — have dropped, with terms of trade falling approximately 40%. The internal political-military conflict has resulted, according to the U.S. embassy in El Salvador, in approximately $235 million lost in agricultural production.[3] Infrastructure has been repeatedly attacked. In 1982, Planning Ministry records showed 1,285 buses, more than one-third of all those in the country, damaged or destroyed. Seventy bridges were blown up, 11 of 18 railroad engines put out of commission, and 285 high-voltage towers knocked over. While factory sabotage in urban areas has been relatively light, recurrent loss of power and transportation facilities has greatly reduced efficiency. Factories require back-up diesel generators, extra security guards, spare parts, and larger inventories to ensure against delays in delivery.

While there are some much publicized examples of investment, the aggregate disinvestment in the economy has been large. A Central Bank survey in 1981 found that, in a sample of 58 firms employing 100 or more workers and including nearly one-third of all enterprises of that size, total investment was less than one-tenth the level of 1978-79. Foreign investment dropped to very low levels. Capital goods imports declined from $87 million in 1978 to approximately $32 million in 1982.

With the deterioration of physical plant and equipment, a study prepared for U.S. AID in 1981 showed that even then more than $243 million would be required to raise production to 80% of the 1978 level.[4] But rather than inflows of new capital, the reverse has occurred with capital flight amounting to at least $779 million from 1978 through 1983 (and probably more).

Table 7.1. Capital Flight from El Salvador, 1979-83[5]
($ million)

1979	1980	1981	1982	1983
$233	$413	$83	$30	$20 (est.)

In total, the deterioration of the Salvadoran economy since 1978 has amounted to nearly one-fourth (23%) of the country's GDP. All sectors have been affected, with manufacturing down over 30%, construction down 40%, commerce down 29%. Agriculture has lost 14% of value-added. The open unemployment rate jumped from 3.7% in 1977-78 to 26% in 1982. Between June 1979 and the beginning of 1982 work was suspended at 236 companies.

At the same time government expenditures have increased sharply, rising by more that 50% between 1978 and 1982. Of all categories, military outlays naturally have accelerated the fastest, 132% between 1978 and 1981.[6] As recently as 1975 the defense budget was $26 million; by 1981 it was $138 million (including items for interior and public safety). Despite efforts to boost tax revenues, the government has faced recurrent large deficits.[7]

One result of these large deficits has been a significant drop in real public investment (-35% in 1982) as more funds go to cover operating costs despite the accumulation of damage to public infrastructure.

The fiscal crunch has been accompanied by a severe balance of payments squeeze. Despite a cutback on imports, the trade and services balance has

Table 7.2. Public Sector Fiscal Deficits, 1979-82[8]
($ million)

	1979	1980	1981	1982
1. Revenues	800	831	805	1030
2. Expenditures	941	1063	1208	1341
3. Surplus/Deficit	-141	-232	-403	-311

suffered a cumulative deficit of $1.1 billion between 1979 and 1983, with a loss of reserves of $413 million. There has been a "virtual disappearance," according to the Inter-American Development Bank, of international commercial sources of finance that previously provided working capital to agriculture, and a three-quarters decline in the amount of short-term import credits to agriculture and industry which totalled $750 million in 1978.[9] Manufacturers must now place prior deposits of 100-200% on imports. This burden is quite heavy on the industrial sectors since imports of semifinished goods represented 56% of imports and 55% of exports in 1979-82.

This has created a large, and growing, resource gap in El Salvador's international accounts.

Table 7.3. Resource Gap, 1981-83[10]
($ million)

	1981	1982	1983 (est.)
1. Merchandise Exports	$794	$700	$710
2. Merchandise Imports	-986	-883	-940
3. Trade Balance	-192	-183	-230
4. Services (net)	-128	-147	-151
5. Transfers (net)	51	53	62
6. Balance of Current Account	-268	-277	-319
7. Reduction of Past Arrears	—	- 21	- 21
8. Amortization of Short-term Debt	—	—	- 60
Resource Gap	-$268	-$298	-$400

The United States has attempted to establish something of an equilibrium for El Salvador through rising amounts of American assistance.

It is difficult to conclude, however, that the attempted "equilibrium" in the 1983 international accounts represents a real equilibrium for the Salvadoran economy. A projection of the economic trends of 1983 over the next five years with political and military conditions unchanged suggests that capital-flight in the private sector, even after falling off from 1979-81 levels, will still reduce domestic capital stock by a further $100 million, and that international reserves will decline in theory by another $243 million (sending

Table 7.4. Financing of the Resource Gap, 1981-83[11]
($ million)

	1981	1982	1983 (est.)
1. Official Financing (net)	$216	$337	$358
U.S. Government	111	190	232
Non-U.S. Government	105	147	126
(IBRD, IBD, France, Canada, etc.)			
2. Private Commercial Banks (net)	56	40	13
3. Private Capital (net)	-83	-30	-20
4. Reduction in International	79	-49	49
	$268	$298	$400

Note: A positive figure indicates reserves were drawn down to finance the gap.

them to a level of minus $438 million). It is probable that the international commercial banks, now in a modest net positive position ($13 million in new loans above debt service in 1983) will at best merely roll-over their loans but not increase their exposure. Finally, non-U.S. government sources of official funding have been declining. The 1983 level may itself be difficult to maintain. In sum, the continuation of the "balance" of 1983 is likely to produce a growing drain on the Salvadoran economy that will amount to nearly half a billion dollars over the next five years. It is improbable under such conditions that the economy can stabilize itself, let alone turn itself around (barring a highly unlikely boom in prices for coffee, cotton, or sugar, which are all forecast to be in structural oversuppply in the medium term). The likely outcome from projecting the "balance" of 1983 into the future is a continuing decline along the current trend line of minus 3% per year, resulting in a level of economic activity roughly 15% lower at the end of the five-year period than in 1983. Given the 1983 unemployment rate of 25-27%, and the faltering level of production in both the agricultural and industrial sectors, the outlook for 1989, in the absence of a decisive change in the political-military situation, is quite dismal.

III. STABILIZING THE SALVADORAN ECONOMY

To counter the continued deterioration of economic conditions in El Salvador, there are four areas in which greater public assistance is clearly needed.

1. Industrial Assistance

It is difficult to know with any precision what would be required to reverse the decline in industrial production and industrial employment, and provide the underpinning for a real growth rate of approximately 3% per year (still zero growth in per capita terms). At a minimum it should require at least $100 million in additional capital inflows to help recapitalize small-to-medium sized industrial projects and to help rebuild infrastructure. It must be recognized that this will have a net impact well below the face value of the incremental supporting funds; realistically, 20% to 40% percent should be expected to be converted into additional capital flight on the part of the Salvadoran elite.

2. Agrarian Reform[12]

Agriculture continues to be the most important sector of economic activity in El Salvador, generating one-fourth of GDP and employing more than one-half of the active labor force. The land has been very unequally distributed, however, with approximately 2,000 farms of more that 100 hectares occupying 40% of the farm area. Moreover, 60% of the farming units and 24% of the land has been under the control of absentee landlords. In 1980 the government launched a land reform of three phases: Phase I, which provides for the expropriation of farms (with equipment and livestock) above 500 hectares; Phase II, which similarly provides for the expropriation of farms from 100 to 500 hectares; and Phase III, which provides for the transfer of land to tenant farmers who work it. In the first two years, 1980-82, a total of 328 Phase I properties were expropriated and turned into cooperatives. By 1983, however, Phase I reforms had come to a standstill. Phase II never got underway. Phase III operations have been largely suspended, with many tenant beneficiaries evicted from lands to which they had a right.

The Salvadoran government faces a complex mix of objectives in the Agrarian Reform Program: to build political support among the poorer farmers; to maintain agricultural production; and to avoid disruption and disinvestment on the part of the landholding classes. To accomplish all three will require a steady stream of production and investment credits, the provision of technical services and marketing assistance, and a dependable compensation schedule. In the first two years of Phase I activities alone, $167 million was extended in production and investment credits and $78 million in compensation payments. Both of these have to be continued, and expanded, despite the pressure on the government to divert its available funds to the military sector. In addition, to ease upper class resistance to the agrarian reform a larger proportion of the compensation will probably have to be paid in cash (currently Phase I land is paid for entirely with bonds, while livestock and machinery are bought with 25% cash and 75% bonds). In all, at least $50 million per year in additional support should be included to help ensure support for the agrarian reform in the Constituent Assembly and make it viable for the farmers in the countryside.

3. Trade Financing

As indicated in the earlier analysis of the deterioration of the Salvadoran economy, economic stabilization and the beginnings of recovery will require the creation of a $200-300 million short-term credit facility to finance (or guarantee finance for) the imports needed to produce the projected industrial and agricultural exports.

4. Additional Balance of Payment Support

According to the U.S. AID model of the Salvadoran economy, a shift in the domestic growth rate from minus 3% to plus 3% will add a net $66 million to the trade deficit (additional exports minus additional imports).[13]

In total, additional assistance in these four areas raises the resource gap from the 1983 level of $400 million to at least $616 million per year. (Export prices are held constant for this calculation. If, as State Department economists expect, coffee prices fall in real terms over the period, the resource gap will be larger than figured here.) Concomitant with the higher aid levels, the Salvadoran government will have to improve its macroeconomic performance, especially with regard to exchange rates.

Table 7.5. Resources Required to Stabilize the Salvadoran Economy
($ million per year)

1. 1983 Resource Gap (see Table 7.3)	$400
2. Additional Project Capitalization	100
3. Additional Support for Agrarian Reform	50
4. Additional Balance of Payments Support	66
Total	$616*

*Plus the establishment of a $200-300 million short-term credit facility, or a credit-guarantee facility.

Table 7.6 specifies how the resources required to stabilize the Salvadoran economy might be supplied under the hypothesized Moving Toward a Negotiated Solution, and Military Escalation Without U.S. Combat Troops scenarios. The alternative scenario of Reaching Beyond El Salvador with an Invasion and Occupation of Nicaragua will be considered latter.

Non-U.S. government official support has been declining, from $147 million in 1982 to $126 million in 1983. In comparison, it is assumed that a reconstruction effort for El Salvador based upon a negotiated solution will be able to attract support from European donors (France, West Germany, Great Britain, the Scandinavian countries) and Canada, plus from the World Bank and the Inter-American Government Bank, at a level of $160 million

Table 7.6. Financing of Resources
Required to Stabilize the Salvadoran Economy
($ million)

	Negotiated Solution	Military Solution for El Salvador (No U.S. Combat Troops)
1. Official Financing	$576 to 626	$636
U.S. Government	416 to 466	566
non-U.S. Government	160	80
2. Private Commercial Banks	10 to 60	0
3. Private Capital	-20	-20
4. Reduction in International Reserves	0	0
Total	$616	$616

per year. With a Military Escalation in El Salvador Without U.S. Combat Troops scenario, that level of non-U.S. support may drop to $80 million.

As for lending from private international commercial banks, it is assumed that with the Moving Toward a Negotiated Solution scenario private international commercial banks will continue net lending at about the 1983 level ($12 million) for the first two years, and then raise it to approximately the 1981 level ($56 million). In Military Escalation in El Salvador, they may not increase their net exposure, and could in fact reduce it.

In both the Moving Toward a Negotiated Solution and the Military Escalation Without U.S. Combat Troops scenarios it is assumed that local business groups will be as cautious and mistrustful of the final outcome as they have been in 1983 (at least $20 million per year in capital flight). There are many analysts who believe that the prospect of peace through negotiations will have a broadly stimulative effect on the economy. The Negotiated Solution scenario here is constructed more cautiously.

IV. MILITARY SUPPORT FOR EL SALVADOR

In the Continuation of Current U.S. Policies scenario, U.S military support to the Salvadoran armed forces is extended for five years at the 1984 request figure of $86.3 million for a total of $432 million. In the Moving Toward a Negotiated Solution scenario, U.S. military support is continued at the 1983 level ($26.5 million) to provide on-going training and modernization, to assist the integration of fighting forces, and to counter any dissident factions that might hold out against the negotiation process. This will total $133 million.

For Military Escalation Without U.S. Combat Troops, the United States makes a determined effort to improve Salvadoran military effectiveness. There is common agreement among military analysts that the Salvadoran armed forces will have to show substantial progress in their ability to project force into the field if they are to prevail over the guerrillas.[14] While opinions vary about the order of priorities for expanding Salvadoran capabilities the principal needs include:

1. Medevac helicopters and facilities (30% of Salvadoran battlefield casualties die, many due to bleeding, which depletes troop strength, saps morale, and makes commanders understandably leery about deploying forces).

2. Logistical facilities to support troops during operations, especially the provision of food and ammunition in the countryside by air and road.

3. Air mobility for troop transport (for example, helicopters to provide mobility for two companies of troops).

4. Communications equipment, especially secure field radios.

5. Modern howitzers to replace Salvador's antiquated artillery pieces.

6. Expanded training programs at all levels, including maintenance and logistical personnel as well as officer and troop training.

7. Reenlistment pay incentives. Currently as few as 15% of the Salvadoran graduates of U.S. training programs reenlist. Many move instead into the security forces, where pay is higher. At a minimum, army pay scales need to be brought up to security force levels.

8. A dependable provision of consumables, especially ammunition and fuel. Each year the Salvadoran military suspends combat operations toward the end of the American fiscal year while the U.S. government debates the supplemental defense funding request.

To meet these needs would require equipment expenditures of approximately $60 million for 30 Huey helicopters, $40 million for base, hangar, and logistical facilities for the helicopters, $10 million for six towed howitzers, $2 million for land-mobile vehicles and $1 million for communications. To this should be added annual expenses of $20 million for helicopter maintenance and replacement (5 per year) and $1.3 million for artillery maintenance. To provide reenlistment incentives will cost $2 million per year. To ensure the pipeline for consumables (fuel and ammunition) will require $20 million per year above the 1984 request. Similarly, to provide the necessary training for maintenance as well as combat personnel (including pilots) will require $15 million per year above the 1984 request.

Over a five-year period, augmenting the administration's 1984 request with the expenditures listed above will cost $827 million.[15] This expenditure level is constrained because there appears to be a consensus within the U.S. government that there would be sharply diminishing returns above these levels without the insertion of U.S. military personnel to manage local combat operations.

The above estimates are constructed on the assumption that American troops continue to play no direct combat role in El Salvador. How realistic this assumption is, however, is open to question. The additional equipment, especially helicopters, will offer attractive targets for guerrilla rocket attacks. That will offer a strong rationale for American troops to protect the airfields. That task can be effectively performed only if those U.S. troops are allowed to patrol actively into the countryside around the airfields.

V. REGIONAL ASSISTANCE

In the Continuation of Current U.S. Policies scenario, U.S. economic and military assistance to Honduras, Panama, Costa Rica, and Guatemala is projected at the 1984 request level for each year ($284 million for economic support, $59 million for military support) plus $80 million for "covert" operations against Nicaragua and $60 million as the incremental cost for regional military exercises. In Moving Toward a Negotiated Solution, economic assistance to this regional group is continued at $284 million per year while military assistance is cut in half, "covert" support is stopped after the first year and regional military exercises return to normal levels.

In Military Escalation Without U.S. Combat Troops, economic and military funding for Panama and Guatemala is maintained at the 1984 request levels. With regard to Costa Rica, military assistance is increased by $30 million per year (from $2.2 million) to reflect the wish of many in the U.S. administration that the country start to build up national military facilities and forces. Economic assistance for Costa Rica is held constant at $106 million per year. "Covert" funding is continued at $80 million per year as is the incremental cost of U.S. military exercises at $60 million per year.

For Honduras, the United States acts to modernize the country's aging force of Super Mystères by providing 12 F-5Es as well as 7 additional A-37s to ensure air superiority over Nicaragua over the next five years. This increases the annual 1984 request figure of $41 million by $200 million spread over the period 1984 to 1989. (If MIG-23s or MIG-27s were introduced into Nicaragua, a larger and more sophisticated improvement in the Honduran Air Force would be necessary.) At the same time annual economic assistance for Honduras is increased by $50 million above 1984 request levels. This reflects the severe economic needs of the country. It also reflects the bargaining leverage of the government. The country's fiscal deficits and balance of payments gaps have both been augmented by its efforts on behalf of American military objectives in the region.

Stopping short of the Reaching Beyond El Salvador with an Invasion and Occupation of Nicaragua scenario, the comparative cost of the other three options is shown in Table 7.7.

Table 7.7. Comparative Cost of the
First Three Scenarios, 1984-1989
($ million)

	Continuation of Current U.S. Policies	Moving toward A Negotiated Solution	A Military Solution Without U.S. Combat Troops
1. Economic Support for El Salvador	978	2,180	2,780
2. Military Support for El Salvador	432	133	827
3. Regional Economic and Military Support	2,415	1,648	3,015
	$3,825	$3,961*	$6,622*

*Plus the one-time creation of a $200-300 million short-term trade credit facility, or trade credit guarantee program.

Many analysts believe that progress in negotiations in El Salvador could be part of a broader regional movement toward reconciliation and reconstruction, resulting in greater domestic and foreign investment throughout Central America thereby reducing the need for external assistance. The estimates here are more cautious. Also, for purposes of comparison, no aid to Nicaragua is included in any of these three scenarios. In fact, the U.S. government might want to include substantial reconstruction aid to induce Nicaragua to cooperate with a negotiated solution in El Salvador. Estimates of U.S. economic assistance prepared for the National Bipartisan Commission on Central America are very close to the economic support component of the above calculations, ranging from $3.3 billion to $6.1 billion. The commission's framework extends, however, for two additional years, to 1990, includes $2 billion in net loan paybacks to the private commercial banks, and hypothesizes $3.4 billion in external assistance for Nicaragua. In total this brings U.S. economic assistance to $10 to $12 billion over seven years.

VI. REACHING BEYOND EL SALVADOR WITH AN INVASION AND OCCUPATION OF NICARAGUA

The following scenario is drawn from three separate analyses by military analysts and consultants.[16] Calculations of fundamental requirements — between two and three divisions of American troops backed by appropriate air support and logistics facilities — does not vary widely. The scenario presented here is, in effect, a median estimate. It should be emphasized, however, that the uncertainties with regard to the pace of the occupation, the rate of American losses, and the endurance of Nicaraguan resistance are enormous.

In the base scenario, one Marine division, one U.S. Army air mobile division, one Army light infantry brigade, and one Ranger battalion take airports and beachheads, link up, and occupy the four major Nicaraguan cities in twelve days. For representational purposes, other CONDECA contingents may be included, but U.S. forces conduct the main fighting. Over the next twenty days they establish a presence throughout the countryside, with a relatively high level of insurgency continuing over the following three months as Sandinista resistance draws down accumulated military supplies. After the initial 122 days of high tempo fighting, approximately one division withdraws, leaving a one-and-a-half division American occupation force as well as CONDECA troops to deal with sabotage and insurgency over the remainder of the five-year period.

With regard to the Nicaraguan economy, exports drop 80% during the first year while American assistance allows imports to remain constant. Tax revenues similarly drop 80%, while American assistance maintains government expenditures at constant levels. Additional U.S. aid for reconstruction and development comes to $500 million. Over the remaining four years, exports reach no higher than 60% of 1982 levels due to on-going sabotage while imports are held constant. Tax revenues reach 60% of 1982 levels while expenditures are held constant. Additional U.S. reconstruction and development assistance is held at $300 million per year.

The invasion force of a Marine division, Army air mobile division, Army light infantry brigade, and Ranger battalion, together with Air Force and Navy air support and appropriate logistics total approximately 61,000 men (of whom an average of 25,000 are directly involved in combat as casualties are replaced), the equivalent of three air wings (216 planes), 734 helicopters, and miscellaneous tanks, armored personnel carriers, trucks, and other equipment.

In the initial thirty-two days of high intensity warfare the attrition rate for helicopters is 20% (148 helicopters), and for aircraft 3% (7 planes, half due to enemy gunfire and half due to accidents especially with an early preponderance of carrier sorties). American casualties in the first twelve days of city-fighting are 50 to 100 dead per day, with 300 to 600 wounded.[17] (The Vietnam ratio of wounded to dead was 6 to 1; some U.S. military officers estimate that a ratio of 8 to 1 or 10 to 1 might be more realistic in Nicaragua. The more conservative 6 to 1 ratio is used here.) During the next twenty days of occupying the countryside, American casualties are 15 to 30 dead per day with 120 to 180 wounded.[18] Taken together, battlefield casualties during the initial period of relatively high intensity warfare is 900 to 1800 killed, and 5400 to 10,800 wounded. In addition, the number of accidental deaths among U.S. forces not directly due to enemy action is 161 to 322 during the same period (in Vietnam the ratio of deaths due to enemy action versus accidental death was 5.6 to 1). The result is 1061 to 2122 Americans killed, and 5400 to 10,800 wounded. For an operation moving at this pace, casualties among the Nicaraguan population are likely to be very much higher.

For the next three months of lower intensity warfare the attrition rate for helicopters is 2% (15 helicopters), for aircraft 1% (3 planes). Among American soldiers 5 to 10 are killed per day for a total of 450 to 900 battlefield deaths, 81 to 161 accidental deaths, and 2700 to 5400 wounded.[19]

For the subsequent two years, the attrition for equipment is the same each year as the preceding three months (a total of 30 helicopters, 6 aircraft, with American soldiers killed at a rate of 200 to 600 per year, plus 300 to 900 wounded) assuming that *contras* and CONDECA troops carry the burden of pacification.

For the final two years and eight months, the attrition is 15 helicopters, 2 aircraft, and 400 American dead and 600 wounded. This assumes, perhaps unrealistically, that the opposition to the American occupation diminishes dramatically over time, and that the internal resistance is effectively prevented from receiving support from outside the country.

Over five years, the total is 208 helicopters, 18 aircraft, miscellaneous other equipment, and between 2,392 and 4,783 dead with 9,300 to 18,600 wounded. The specificity of these numbers should not be taken, of course, to indicate precision in these calculations.

For purposes of estimating the replacement cost of the materiel losses the figure for the helicopters is $2,306 million (75% of the losses being attack helicopters at $7 million per Blackhawk and $10 million per Apache, 20% observation helicopters at $4 million each, and 5% heavy lift helicopters at $27 million each), $222 million for the aircraft (70% of the losses being replaced by F-16s at $22 million each, 10% Harriers at $24 million each, 10% F-15s at $27 million each, and 10% A-6Es at $36 million each), and $80 million for the miscellaneous tanks, armored personnel carriers, trucks, and other equipment. The total for the materiel losses is $2,608 million.

In terms of operating expenses above and beyond those that would be incurred by similar troops in a training status, a more complicated and also inexact methodology is required. It costs $2.192 million per day in 1983 to maintain one infantry division in the United States in a training status. It cost $4.705 million per day in 1983 dollars to support one division in Vietnam in 1968.[20] In a rough sense, the incremental cost of combat is $2.513 million per division per day. For the first thirty-two days of the invasion the cost of the assault is 140% the average Vietnam rate per division, for the next three months 80%, for the next two years 30%, and for the final two years and eight months 10%. From this, the total incremental operating cost of the invasion and occupation is calculated to be $1,938 million.

With regard to the need for U.S. economic aid to support the Nicaraguan economy, the requirement in the first year for budgetary, balance of payments, and reconstruction assistance is $1,700 million, and for the next four years $1,100 million, or a total of $6,100 million.

Table 7.8. Economic Cost of Invasion
and Occupation of Nicaragua, 1984-1989
($ million)

1. Equipment Losses	$2,608
2. Operating Costs	$1,938
3. Economic Assistance	$6,100
Total	$10,646

COMPARATIVE COSTS FOR THE FOUR SCENARIOS

An invasion and occupation of Nicaragua would, in all probability, reduce certain U.S. government expenses associated with the Military Escalation Without U.S. Combat Troops scenario. For purposes of comparison here it is assumed to have an economic stimulative effect on El Salvador, cutting the need for economic assistance by $100 million per year. The requirement for military assistance may also be reduced by $50 million per year. In the case of Honduras, economic and military assistance may be cut in half from 1984 request levels, shelving the idea of supplying F-5Es and additional A-37s. In the case of Costa Rica, economic assistance may also be halved, and the idea of building up national armed forces abandoned. Special U.S. military training exercises in the region will be eliminated and "covert" assistance can be stopped. The United States will have to underwrite, however, the costs of CONDECA and the *contra* contingents participating in the invasion and occupation of Nicaragua.

Table 7.9. Total Economic Cost of U.S. Expenditures
in the Region with the Invasion and Occupation
of Nicaragua, 1984-1989
($ million)

1. Economic Support for El Salvador	$ 2,380
2. Military Support for El Salvador	577
3. Regional Economic and Military Support	2,381
4. Invasion and Occupation of Nicaragua	10,646
Total	$15,984

From these calculations, the costs of the four scenarios can be compared directly:

Table 7.10. Comparative Costs of the
Four Scenarios, 1984-1989

Scenario	Cost
I. Continuation of Current U.S. Policies	$ 4 billion
II. A Negotiated Solution	$ 4 billion
III. A Military Solution Without U.S. Combat Troops	$ 7 billion
IV. Reaching Beyond El Salvador with an Invasion and Occupation of Nicaragua	$16 billion

It should be reiterated how uncertain many of the key assumptions in this study are, and must remain. In general, however, these estimates are likely to err on the low side if only because the study holds waste, inefficiency, and corruption constant, yet expansion of foreign assistance frequently is accompanied by an increase in these phenomena. Moreover, the magnitude of the uncertainties mounts with the escalation of the scenarios. A variation of a few hundred million dollars in Scenario II might be considered large. A variation of several billion dollars in Scenario IV might be considered small.

Finally, the construction of these (or any other) scenarios involves an abstraction from reality, a static perspective, and artificiality. The Continuation of Current U.S. Policies scenario will almost certainly lead to further deterioration in Central America, and require new U.S. initiatives. A Negotiated Solution may be undermined, and disintegrate. A Military Escalation Without U.S. Combat Troops may in fact bring irresistable pressures for American soldiers to protect the new equipment, to train the Salvadoran forces, and to accompany Salvadoran soldiers into the field. And Reaching Beyond El Salvador with an Invasion and Occupation of Nicaragua implies embarking on a course of events that cannot easily be reconsidered, or terminated, when the costs pass $16 billion or the American casualties exceed five thousand American dead.

NOTES

1. The data in this study come from the Central Bank of El Salvador, the Ministry of Finance, the IMF, the World Bank, the Inter-American Development Bank, U.S. AID, the U.S. Embassy, the U.N. Economic Commission for Latin America, and private U.S. commercial banks.
2. *El Salvador: Updating Economic Memorandum,* Report No. 4054-ES, January 21, 1983 (Washington, D.C.: World Bank), p. 2.
3. These assessments are found in Christopher Dickey, "El Salvador: Economy of War, *Washington Post,* October 2, 1983; and *Economic Report: El Salvador,* GN 1474, August 1983 (Washington, D.C.: Inter-American Development Bank).
4. Checchi and Company, "Maintaining El Salvador's Private Sector: Industrial Recovery," prepared for U.S. AID (December 1981). The report was based on a survey of 94 of the 250 members of the Salvadoran Assocation of Industrialists and 86 of 100 members of the Merchants and Industrialists Society of El Salvador.
5. The figures for 1979 and 1980 come from Inter-American Development Bank estimates. The figures for 1981-83 from the Central Bank of El Salvador.
6. World Bank, "El Salvador: Central Government Cash Expenditures by Ministries," Table 5.4 in *El Salvador: Updating Economic Memorandum,* January 21, 1981.
7. El Salvador has a relatively regressive tax system, with more than 90% of the taxes levied on production, on business property, and on foreign trade, most of which, according to the Inter-American Development Bank, are passed on to customers. There is very little tax burden on income. With the decline in coffee, cotton, and sugar exports, and in industrial production, tax collections have declined. *Economic Report: El Salvador,* August 1983, *op. cit.,* p. 3. Tax reform efforts in the first half of 1983 were substantially weakened in the Assembly.
8. Central Bank of El Salvador.
9. *Economic Report: El Salvador,* August 1983, *op. cit.*
10. Figures from the Central Bank of El Salvador, as compiled for the U.S. government in "El Salvador: Macroeconomic Assessment for 1983," May 31, 1983.
11. *Ibid.*
12. On the Agrarian Reform, see Checchi and Company, "Agrarian Reform in El Salvador" (U.S. AID, December 1981); "Agrarian Reform in El Salvador: Process and Progress" (U.S. AID, August 1982); and Inter-American Development Bank, *Economic Report: El Salvador,* August 1983, *op. cit.*
13. *El Salvador: Macroeconomic Assessment for 1983,* May 31, 1983, *op. cit.*
14. This assessment reflects the predominant judgement of officers within the operational military commands, as well as analysts in the Department of Defense, the Central Intelligence Agency, and the Department of State.

15. The list included here is by no means exhaustive. Some military analysts would add: (1) Small patrol boats for coastal surveillance and interdiction. The Salvadoran navy now has less than 20 officers, and almost no repair facilities. In joint operations, the navy is the weakest link; (2) Fixed-wing spotter planes; (3) A more sophisticated C^3I grid for the Salvadoran command.

16. In addition I would like to acknowledge the help of Edward Swoboda, Chief, Defense and International Affairs, Cost Estimates Unit, Congressional Budget Office; Richard Millett, Professor of International Relations, U.S. Air War College; Colonel Thomas H. Harvey, USA, Visiting Military Fellow, Council on Foreign Relations; and Peter A. Wilson, defense consultant.

17. The principal variables concern the amount of warning the Nicaraguan armed forces receive, their capability to defend against airborne assault, and the decision of the government to resist the occupation of the cities.

18. These estimates could vary greatly with the amount of supplies and the degree of preparation and training Nicaraguan forces, and the Nicaraguan populaion, receive to resist in the countryside.

19. The main variables are the amounts of weapons and other materiel stockpiled in the rural areas, the extent of organized military operations and the ability of American forces to seal off the border against resupply.

20. *Strategic Survey, 1972* (London: Institute for Strategic Studies, 1972). To convert 1968 operating costs to 1983 prices, the Implicit Price Deflator for U.S. Defense Expenditures has been used. That goes back only to 1972; from 1968 to 1972 the U.S. Federal Deflator has been employed. In all, a 1968 operating figure of 100 would be 286 in 1983. This is imprecise because, on the one hand, military operations are more sophisticated in 1983, making them more costly. On the other hand, however, Vietnamese operations were conducted at much greater distance. Yet to help offset this, fuel costs in that pre-oil-crisis period were much cheaper.

21. The arithmetic totals are: Scenario I = $3.825 billion, Scenario II = $3.961 billion, Scenario III = $6.622 billion, and Scenario IV = $15.984 billion. Given the number of assumptions and the degree of uncertainty there is a danger these might convey a false sense of precision.

8
MILITARY THREATS, ACTUAL
AND POTENTIAL

Joseph Cirincione and Leslie C. Hunter*

Much of the current controversy over the role of U.S. military forces in Central America arises from vastly divergent perceptions of the regional threats to U.S. security. Proponents of an enlarged U.S. military presence emphasize the strategic implications of Soviet and Cuban regional involvement; advocates of disengagement dismiss this as so much Cold War rhetoric.

Obviously, no Central American country or insurgent movement in itself is a military threat to the United States. None is capable of jeopardizing U.S. survival or territorial integrity, nor of impeding, to any appreciable degree, a future wartime mission. But the Soviet Union and Cuba together have at least the potential to endanger U.S. security interests. And were Central American countries to align with Moscow, Central America could become a second staging area from which to threaten U.S. interests.

THE STAKES FOR THE UNITED STATES

As the former commander of the U.S. Southern Command, General Wallace Nutting, has noted, "in a geographic sense, at least, the Central America-Caribbean Basin area is our Afghanistan, and if push comes to shove in this region, the outcome is not in doubt. It would be very difficult for the Soviet Union to project the kind of conventional power into the Caribbean Basin that we can't deal with."[1]

It is more troublesome for the administration to rally consensus for a military solution to the guerrilla warfare (or "low-intensity conflict") presently raging across the isthmus and to prepare for the possibility that Cuba or Nicaragua may act as surrogates for the Soviet Union and intervene in these conflicts or actually invade neighboring states. "We are dealing with a form

*The ideas expressed in this essay are those of the authors, and do not necessarily represent the views of either the Department of the Navy or the Department of Defense.

of conflict which as a nation we don't understand too well," says Nutting, "and we are not certain as to how we should try to come to grips with it."[2]

The administration fears that American credibility would suffer if insurgent movements were successful in toppling the present U.S.-backed governments in Central America. "If Central America were to fall," asked President Reagan in his April 1983 speech to Congress, "what would the consequences be for our position in Asia and Europe, and for alliances such as NATO?" Such a question stems from the view that any left-wing government replacing a U.S.-backed regime would be irreconcilably opposed to U.S. interests and would align itself with the Soviet Union. Yet, the United States has been able to live with the negotiated victory of the insurgents in Zimbabwe and has cordial relations with Yugoslavia and economic and strategic relations with the People's Republic of China.

The real problem is not leftist regimes per se but that Soviet military facilities might be established in the wake of Soviet-aligned guerrilla victories. Vietnam is a case in point. As Ronald Steel has observed, U.S. security is not much affected by who rules Vietnam. "The same is true of El Salvador. It is an impoverished little country that does not endanger us regardless of who rules it."[3] What has affected U.S. security interests is the establishment of Soviet bases at Cam Rahn Bay and Da Nang. From there the Soviet Navy now patrols the South China Sea, sending clear messages to the nations of the region that Soviet power is now a force to be reckoned with in Southeast Asia. Could Nicaragua become another Vietnam, this time threatening the security of the United States' own borders? Even without Soviet bases, the adminstration fears that Cuba, Nicaragua, and other states in a Soviet-Caribbean Basin "axis" could use their military power to intervene in the region, challenging U.S. regional hegemony.

Finally, there is the danger that the U.S. could become bogged down in Central America, committing resources that would make the region America's Afghanistan in more than the geographic sense. Ahmed Shah Massoud, a well-known guerrilla commander in the Afghan resistance, recently complained that "America thinks the war in Afghanistan should continue like this — without loss or gain — irrespective of the Afghans who are being killed by the hundreds." In this way, he argued, the Soviets would remain bogged down in Afghanistan, the war burdening their economy, their international standing and their image in the Third World deteriorating, and their satellites growing more mistrustful.[4] More substantial commitment in Central America could create a similar quagmire for the United States.

To place these dangers in context, it is useful to examine briefly the Soviet-backed military build-up in Cuba and Nicaragua and to detail the military implications and limitations of these Soviet-linked states.

CUBA'S MILIATRY POTENTIAL

Cuba has the largest and best equipped military force of any nation in Latin America with the possible exception of Brazil. Its total armed forces stand at 153,000 troops, with a reserve of 190,000 and a territorial militia of 500,000.[5] There are also approximately 2,400 Soviet military advisors in Cuba providing training and support for the sophisticated array of new Soviet-built equipment which has poured into the island nation since 1975.

Cuba's ground and air forces include:

- 250 combat aircraft, including 200 MiG-21 and MiG-23 fighters

- 38 combat helicopters, including 18 new Hind-D gunships

- Over 650 tanks, including 60 powerful T-62 and 250 older T-54/55 heavy battle tanks

- 28 SAM battalions armed with 12 SA-6 mobile missile launchers and 200 SA-3 and SA-2 launchers

- 1,500 antiaircraft guns, including new shipments of the formidable ZSU-23-4 self-propelled antiaircraft guns

- More than 20 newly acquired AN-26 short range transport aircraft, which give Cuba the capability to transport supplies to most countries in Central America and to air drop troops on portions of Belize, Honduras, Jamaica and Florida

- Seven IL-62 long-range and some TU-154 medium-range jet transport aircraft, each capable of carrying 150 to 200 combat-equipped troops

Cuba also has a sizable expeditionary force. In 1983, this force was estimated to be about 40,000 troops, including 25,000 in Angola, 11,000 in Ethiopia, 750 in the Congo, 750 in Mozambique, 500 in other African countries, 300 in South Yemen, and over 1,000 in Nicaragua. As Robert Leiken notes, with its comparatively unspoiled revolutionary image, Cuba can do much in the Third World that Soviet troops cannot.[6]

The Cubans justify this build-up as a reasonable response to what they consider a constant threat of a U.S. invasion. They argue that the recent sharp increase in Soviet arms shipments to Cuba (69,000 metric tons in 1982; 66,000 in 1981, compared to an average of 20,000 from 1976 to 1980) is due to both the beginning of a five-year upgrading and replacement program and the more explicit threats from the United States to "go to the source," as former Secretary of State Alexander Haig stated on several occasions.

The Cuban build-up has largely achieved its defense objectives. A U.S. invasion of the island would now require an estimated 100,000 American troops and the deployment of more carrier battle groups than the U.S. could afford to commit. The U.S. would undoubtedly sustain heavy casualties in such an operation. This is probably not an option that the United States would be inclined to exercise except in the most dire emergency.

Despite the build-up, as a recent study done for the American Enterprise Institute concluded, "Soviet/Cuban conventional forces appear to constitute a low-level military threat to the United States in peacetime."[7] However, Cuba could interdict important sea lanes of communication (SLOCs) in a general war.

Cuban forces are essentially restricted to their island nation unless they are moved by air or sea. Here is where the Cuban troops confront the single most serious obstacle to their interventionist potential. Despite the recent acquisitions of modern transport planes, Cuba still does not have sufficient aircraft to sustain large-scale movements nor the amphibious assault landing craft and other naval vessels required to transport heavy armor. Cuban involvement in Angola and Ethiopia, for example, was predicated on Soviet approval and logistical support.

How seriously the present administration takes the threat of Cuban armed intervention in Central America is unclear. The State Department, for example, contends in one of its major statements on Cuba's military capabilities that "the Castro regime possesses a significant regional intervention capability. . . . Although this capability is modest by Western standards, it is impressive in the Central American or Caribbean context."[8] The report acknowledges, however, that this capability could only be effective "in aiding an ally in the region against an external invasion or in the suppression of internal conflict. Cuba does not have the wherewithal to conduct an outright invasion of another nation in the region except for the Caribbean micro-states."[9] It might be added that Cuban airlift and sealift operations could not succeed if opposed by U.S. naval and air forces.

This limitation could be partially overcome, of course, if armor and troops were already in place on the Central American isthmus. This is why the Sandinistas' warm embrace of Soviet military aid and advisors set alarm bells ringing throughout the U.S. defense community. For many, the arrival of Soviet tanks and armored personnel carriers in Nicaragua and the construction of airstrips capable of handling MiG-23s confirmed their worst fears that the Soviet Union intended to transform Nicaragua into a base for the military domination of the entire region.

NICARAGUA'S ARSENAL

The expansion and modernization of the Nicaraguan armed forces since the 1979 Sandinista revolution has been dramatic. The 7,500 to 9,000 soldiers of General Somoza's National Guard have been replaced by a standing army of 50,000 (including 25,000 reserves) which is twice the size of any other Central American army. There are 200,000 men and women in training for the popular militia.[10] The delivery of some 45 T-54 and T-55 tanks made Nicaragua the only country in Central America with heavy tanks. The Sandinistas have also acquired 12 BTR-60 armored personnel carriers, 12 105mm and several 152mm howitzers, 48 ZIS-2 57mm antitank guns, 2 Hip helicopters, and SA-7 surface-to-air missiles. These are all formidable weapons, and they account for most of the estimated $125 million in military equipment and supplies from the Soviet Union delivered during the 1979-1982 period.

Despite administration denials of any invasion intent, the Big Pine II exercises and the invasion of Grenada have been interpreted by the Sandinistas and many observers as thinly veiled threats of U.S. military intervention. "We are not a war machine," says Comandante Javier Carrion, commander of Nicaragua's north-central military region.[11] "We have tanks," he says, "possibly more than Honduras. But this is not the most important thing. It doesn't mean we have bad intentions."[12]

Nicaragua's military capabilities are still largely defensive. Its four-year arms build-up has made it unlikely that the country could be successfully invaded by any combination of Central American countries, even with the coordinated support of the insurgents battling in the north and south of the country. On the other hand, whatever intentions the Sandinista *comandantes* may have, their forces are not sufficient to invade even the relatively lightly-armed Honduras, let alone conquer an alliance of Honduras, El Salvador and Guatemala, backed by the United States.

NICARAGUA AS A REGIONAL THREAT

Honduras' 15,200-man armed forces and 4,500-man national police force are equipped only with 16 Scorpion light tanks and a few artillery pieces. Honduras is currently enlarging its army and acquiring new trucks, airplanes, communications equipment and arms.

Even with the Nicaraguan advantage in armor, troops and combat experience, the odds favor Honduras should the Sandinistas attempt to invade. In addition to the traditional advantage of the defending forces over the attacking army, the geography of the region favors Honduras. The most likely invasion route is through the relatively flat terrain due east of the Gulf of Fonseca, where Nicaraguan armor is now concentrated. Honduras could blunt any attempted armored thrust through this narrow gap with its superior air force. The 1,200-man Honduran Air Force is equipped with 26 combat planes, including four Korean War-vintage F-86E Sabres and 12 French-made Super Mystères which the Israelis have trained the Hondurans to repair and operate. Because of this equipment and American-Israeli training, Honduras has the top-rated force in the region. With its little air force and few antiaircraft weapons, the most the Sandinistas could accomplish by an invasion would be the capture of Choluteca, the biggest town in southern Honduras. Moreover, Nicaragua would have difficulty sustaining an invasion, given its limited fuel supply and logistical capabilities, particularly if the Honduran Air Force struck Nicaraguan fuel and supply depots and the United States blocked resupply by sea.

Thus, the Nicaraguan military threat to its neighbors (with the exception of defenseless Costa Rica) is currently limited to the shipment of military supplies to guerrilla forces and the possibility of military raids within 50 to 80 km of its border.

Whether Nicaragua can become the "mainland platform" for Soviet-Cuban expansionism depends in part on future shipments of arms. There are reports that South Yemen has sold the Sandinistas 10 Soviet-built, but outdated, MiG-17s. These aircraft, if delivered to Nicaragua, would mitigate the Honduran air advantage. A more significant arms transfer would involve 10 MiG-23s said to belong to Nicaragua but housed in Cuban hangars. Nicaraguan pilots have been trained to fly these aircraft, but delivery has been delayed possibly due to fear of strong U.S. reaction to their presence in Central America.

While the possibility of Cuban involvement in any regional war exists, Cuba's ability to intervene would be limited. The combat radius of Cuba's MiGs is too short to fly support missions from airfields in Cuba, but long enough to strike Honduran targets and then streak to airstrips at Puerto Cabezas and Bluefields on Nicaragua's Atlantic coast and to Montelimar on the Pacific, recently extended to accommodate MiG fighters. As noted above, transporting Cuban troops or any part of the substantial Cuban arsenal would be more difficult, particularly in the event of a U.S. blockade around Nicaragua. Fidel Castro may have had these realities in mind when he said, following the invasion of Grenada, that Cuba could not come to Nicaragua's aid if she were attacked.[13]

U.S. MILITARY OPTIONS IN NICARAGUA

The administration's growing displeasure with the Sandinistas has led it to consider military actions against Nicaragua. Among these are: emergency increases in the levels of aid and the introduction of hundreds of combat advisors; the imposition of a naval blockade of Nicaragua; limited air strikes on Nicaraguan positions; and, the full-scale invasion and occupation of

Nicaragua by U.S. troops. Each of these basic options has significant limitations.

Domestic political considerations argue for limiting direct American involvement in the conflict in order to prevent American casualties. However, the first option, simply increasing aid and advisors, could not overcome the major logistical and administrative shortcomings which plague all the Central American armies. Some Pentagon officials also fear that a gradual or partial increase in U.S. military forces would lead to a situation like Vietnam in which American troops would enjoy neither the backing of U.S. public opinion nor the operational freedom to accomplish their objectives. A July 1983 Pentagon study warned that, if a military commitment were "hobbled and trimmed back" by Congress, "the chances of failure are high."[14] Air Force Lt. Gen. John T. Chain, deputy chief of staff for plans and operations, affirmed that what the military does not want is "to get sucked into a Vietnam-type thing where we get nibbled to death."[15]

Pentagon doubts and even opposition to the use of military force as an instrument of diplomacy in Central America surfaced during the preparation for the invasion of Grenada. White House and State Department officials reportedly were dismayed to discover that the Pentagon had not developed a contingency plan for invading Grenada, despite several years of difficulties with the island.[16] "In the State Department, there is much talk that Defense Secretary Caspar W. Weinberger and the military are afflicted with 'the Vietnam syndrome': a reluctance to flex American military muscles without substantial, advance political backing at home."[17]

The success of the Grenadan invasion may overcome the military's reluctance to intervene. If so, there may be a greater U.S. willingness to undertake a naval blockade or quarantine of Nicaragua, possibly supplemented by air strikes. This would be a higher level of military involvement but would fall short of full commitment and would keep U.S. casualties low. The Navy practiced blockade techniques during the 1983 Big Pine II exercises in the Caribbean, and U.N. Ambassador Jeane Kirkpatrick has talked openly about the possibility of interdiction. When asked if the exercises were showing the Sandinistas that the U.S. could blockade Nicaragua, Kirkpatrick replied, "Maybe. Maybe we'll remind them of that."[18] However, there are several problems with this option.

First, the number of ships and troops required to do the job might strain U.S. capabilities. The blockade of Cuba in 1962 required 284 naval ships, including 8 aircraft carriers.[19] Blockading Nicaragua's Atlantic and Pacific coasts would require fewer platforms, but the entire Atlantic Fleet today has only 250 ships and 6 aircraft carriers. This raises one of the key concerns of Pentagon planners about U.S. operations in Central America and the

Caribbean. According to Admiral Harry Train II, then-commander-in-chief of the U.S. Atlantic Fleet, U.S. global forces were already committed elsewhere and "conflict in the Caribbean would require the diversion of U.S. resources, leaving other areas dangerously exposed."[20]

The 1983 Caribbean exercises involving two carrier task forces and the battleship *New Jersey* illustrate the problem. During these maneuvers, 43 warships, including support vessels, were stationed off Central America out of a total of 204 major U.S. surface combat vessels. Captain John Moore, editor of *Jane's Fighting Ships*, commented at the time that this stretched the U.S. Navy "desperately tight . . . the U.S. Navy simply does not have enough ships. NATO does not have enough ships."[21]

Second, a blockade against Nicaragua, to be successful, would take time. Even if the U.S. combat role were limited to air strikes while Central American ground forces took the casualties, public opposition could be expected if the blockade did not yield rapid results. Large sections of the anti-nuclear and civil rights movements might stage massive public protests. Congressional resistance to U.S. involvement could increase. Such opposition could not only prove to be a public relations disaster for the administration, particularly in an election year, it might also jeopardize the political support that military leaders have managed to win recently for large increases in defense spending for other programs. Public opinion thus figures substantially into the strategic calculus facing American defense planners.

If aid and advisors or a blockade fail to resolve the Central American situation in a manner favored by the administration, a third option could be an invasion of Nicaragua. Before the invasion of Grenada, some thought that this option had a good chance of initial success. There seemed to be some feeling among administration officials that with the proper preparation of public opinion and timely execution, a U.S. invasion of Nicaragua could be an accomplished fact before congressional and public opposition had time to organize itself. Even critics of Reagan administration policies, such as retired Rear Admiral Eugene Carroll, Jr., thought American forces were capable of winning a war in Nicaragua. Carroll estimated that U.S. forces could dominate the political and military situation in Nicaragua within ten days.[22] Some optimists had believed the 16,000-man Second Marine Division stationed at Camp Lejeune, N.C. could do the job alone.[23] Most likely, the U.S. would be invading in cooperation with troops from El Salvador, Guatemala, and Honduras, who have recently united in an anti-Nicaraguan military front, CONDECA (see Richard Millet's chapter in this volume). CONDECA would also provide a partial justification for the invasion, much as the Organization of Eastern Caribbean States did for the U.S. action against Grenada. Surrounded by hostile states, Nicaragua would be cut off from outside help. "We can shut them off without a supply siphon like the Ho Chi Minh Trail," observed one Pentagon land warfare specialist.[24]

If Cuba or the Soviet Union tried to intervene in the conflict, they would be blocked by superior U.S. naval forces of at least two carrier battle groups on each side of Nicaragua in support of the invasion. Cuba's recognition of the difficulties it would face were reflected in Fidel Castro's remarks to the press following the invasion of Grenada. The Soviet Union, in its campaign of invective after the Grenadan invasion, accused the U.S. of "international banditry" and of preparing an armed intervention in Nicaragua. Calling for an end to U.S. interference, Moscow expressed "unswerving solidarity" with the Nicaraguan people. In light of the military realities of the situation, however, the Soviet pledges of support sounded very similar to their "solidarity" with the PLO in 1982 as Yasser Arafat's forces were routed by Israel while Moscow stood by.

With a quick and successful invasion, the U.S. might avoid domestic and international condemnation. The Falkland Islands/Malvinas war, the Israeli invasion of Lebanon and the invasion of Grenada have demonstrated that public support can be created and maintained for short, decisive campaigns.

At the close of 1983, however, the Grenadan experience had cast some doubt on the idea of a quick and clean invasion. The casualty list from Grenada was 18 dead and 118 wounded in the face of only token resistance. The length of time U.S. troops remained on the island, despite the complete collapse of the Cuban and Grenadan forces within three days of the landing, forced a rethinking of the military and political costs of a U.S. invasion of Nicaragua.

The occupation of Grenada required 11 naval vessels, including the carrier *Independence* with its 90 aircraft, in support of 1,800 Marines of the 22nd Marine Amphibious Unit, two Army Ranger battalions of 600 men each, and 3,000 troops from the 82nd Airborne Division from Fort Bragg, N.C. This force overwhelmed the 800 Cubans on the island, 100 of whom were classified as regular military personnel, and the 1,000 to 1,200 members of the Grenadan Army, most of whom deserted their units at the beginning of the invasion.

An invasion of Nicaragua would be much more difficult. Alarmed by the Grenadan events, Nicaragua's leaders immediately began distributing small arms to the thousands of militia members already in training. U.S. troops would face much stronger resistance in Nicaragua, with a population 30 times that of Grenada, and highly motivated and skilled armed forces. The Grenadan people welcomed the arrival of U.S. troops, while the Nicaraguans would oppose a U.S. invasion of their country. Even Eden Pastora, commander of one guerrilla campaign against the Sandinista leadership, says that an American invasion would unleash a "national war, a patriotic war" in which all Nicaraguans would join together and fight.[25]

"We are ready," warned a Nicaraguan official, "we have half a million people in arms, young, old, peasants, city dwellers. If an invasion happens, it will have a very large cost — not just for us, but for the invading troops. Further, it could set off reactions in other Central American states, such as Guatemala, which are ready to explode."[26]

If reports of the extent of the Nicaraguan preparations are even partially true, U.S. forces could sustain daily casualties that approximate the Vietnam war figures. If successful at routing the defenders from the main cities and towns, occupying troops could subsequently face an experienced and dedicated guerrilla opposition, most likely enjoying the support of much of the population. U.S. domestic and international opposition would undoubtedly mount as U.S. forces were tied down in a war that drained men, money and resources away from areas of more vital concern.

NUCLEAR THREATS FROM THE SOUTH

At the other end of the threat spectrum is the prospect that the Kremlin might launch a nuclear strike from Cuba against the continental United States. Despite Soviet assurances after the 1962 Cuban missile confrontation and the Cienfuegos incident eight years later that no offensive weapons would be placed in the Western Hemisphere, numerous recent Soviet declarations have raised the possibility of a replay of the 1962 crisis.[27]

Although highly unlikely, the Soviets could attempt to use the Caribbean Basin region in several ways during a nuclear war:

- TU-26 Backfire bombers could conceivably use three or more airstrips in Cuba as recovery and relaunch platforms for strategic nuclear strikes.

- TU-95 Bears, which now fly regular reconnaissance missions from the Soviet Union over the North Pole and down the Eastern seaboard, could be fitted with nuclear missiles. Improved submarine servicing facilities in Cuba could permit existing ports to accommodate Soviet strategic nuclear submarines (SSBNs). Cuba now provides valuable facilities that extend the range of Soviet patrol submarines.

- Finally, Moscow has hinted that it might deploy intermediate-range missiles on the borders of the United States in retaliation for U.S. deployment of Pershing II missiles in Europe. While not adding significantly to overall Soviet megatonnage, these missiles would give the Soviets the same ability they claim the Pershing IIs give the United States: the option of launching a quick "decapitation" strike at military and political command centers and, with the pinpoint accuracy of both the Pershing IIs and the SS-20s, destroying even hardened military targets.

Some of these nuclear options are more feasible than others, although none is very likely in the near future. Backfire bombers, for example, could land and refuel in Cuba (or Nicaragua) only if airstrips located in these countries remained operational. In a nuclear war, these airfields, harbors and communications facilities might be obliterated either in a preemptive strike or at the first indication of a launch. Backfires would arrive to find only craters.

It is equally unlikely that the Soviets would succeed in emplacing nuclear weapons in Central America, either surreptitiously or openly. The 1962 missile crisis demonstrated that the United States would not tolerate such a flagrant attempt at intimidation. At that time, U.S. strategic and local conventional military superiority forced the Kremlin to back down. Although the United States no longer enjoys absolute strategic superiority, the Soviets are not apt to risk a superpower confrontation over missile deployments which would be of only marginal utility to them but highly provocative to the United States.

The Soviets do not have to place SS-20s in Central America to achieve a suprise attack capability. In fact, the most likely nuclear challenge confronting the United States is not missiles in Nicaragua or nuclear-armed MiG-27s in Cuba, but rather the possible deployment of Soviet SSBNs 100 miles off the eastern seaboard. At present, several Soviet Yankee-class SSBNs patrol the east and west coast 1,300 to 1,600 miles offshore. Missiles fired from these submarines could hit their targets within fifteen minutes from launch. If the "depressed trajectory" launch technique were implemented, the Soviets could strike targets within six minutes. With very little warning time, an SLBM attack could take out most soft command, control and communication (C3) centers, including the White House, and pose a substantial "pin down" threat to U.S. ICBM fields. However, the SLBMs on Yankee-class submarines patrolling off the U.S. coast probably lack the accuracy to "decapitate" hardened U.S. facilities. SS20s would pose such a threat, due to their accuracy, and multiple warheads.

From the Soviet perspective, deployment of strategic nuclear submarines close to the U.S. shoreline would merely be a response to U.S. deployment of Pershing IIs. Their submarine patrols would be easier to maintain if the Soviets breached the 1970 Cienfuegos agreement and began servicing their SSBNs in Cuban ports. Such a move would have an immediate impact on Western Europe. Europeans may perceive a reduced U.S. willingness to defend NATO Europe with U.S. nuclear missiles if there were a greater chance of a Soviet intermediate-range nuclear attack on the continental United States. Forward deployment of Soviet submarines might be used to exact concessions from the United States in the Geneva intermediate-range nuclear force negotiations. Finally, escalation of the nuclear arms race, even if Soviet-provoked, may push an already jittery Europe further in the direction of neutralism.

Ironically, while increased U.S.-Soviet tension in recent years has raised fears of an all-out war, both NATO and Warsaw Pact military planners appear to consider conventional war more likely.[28] The Caribbean region and Central America, although far removed from the main theater of battle, could play a critical role in the early stages of the conflict.

THE PROBLEM OF SEA LANE INTERDICTION

In a conventional war between NATO and the Warsaw Pact, the United States would bear the burden of reinforcing and resupplying the European theater with men and equipment. Some 1.5 million American troop reinforcements could be airlifted to Europe. Resupply, however, would require shipment by sea of some 12 million tons of military equipment and supplies, including fuel, ammunition, food, spares and replacement equipment, as well as the "minimum essential economic requirements of NATO nations for food, fuel, raw materials and manufactured goods to sustain the civilian population of some 300 million, the economies, and hence the war effort."[29] An estimated 3,000 to 6,000 sailings of ships would be required to move all these goods.[30] Protection of the sea lanes connecting the United States to Europe and the Pacific, several of which pass through the Caribbean, is obviously crucial to a successful Western defense strategy. It is not surprising then, that much of the Soviet military build-up and the upgrading and modernization of Cuban military capabilities are being reoriented toward missions of sea denial and against sea lanes of communication (SLOC).

The Soviet Union possesses the capability to mount a potentially damaging anti-SLOC campaign if it elected to do so.[31] According to one U.S. Navy admiral, SLOC interdiction is now "the dominant warfare capability built into the Soviet naval forces."[32] An asset of inestimable strategic value to Moscow in this mission is Cuba—an "unsinkable aircraft carrier that comes with a 200,000-man army."[33] Havana and Cienfuegos offer Soviet naval and air units an excellent vantage point from which to attack virtually all of the sea lanes connecting South America and Panama with gulf and east coast U.S. ports, as well as those which extend from the Panama Canal and the Gulf of Mexico to Western European harbors.[34] The use of Cuban airbases has enabled Soviet naval aircraft to extend their patrol of the northern and central Atlantic and greatly increase the time they can spend in mid-Atlantic ocean regions. Cuba also houses an intelligence collection center which intercepts U.S. communications and relays them back to Moscow. Soviet Bear-D aircraft regularly conduct reconnaissance missions from Cuba off the U.S. east coast. Cuba thus provides Moscow with many of the advantages of a forward base. In the opinion of one analyst, "Taken alone, the Soviet presence in the Caribbean is of sufficient significance to warrant serious apprehension in the United States, but when coupled with other Soviet initiatives — especially in the South Atlantic — the larger pattern thus disclosed assumes even more ominous dimensions."[35]

At present, Cuba possesses sufficient military capability to carry out limited interdiction missions in these sea lanes. Her MiG-23s could strike at convoys, supplemented by 2 Foxtrot submarines and the Koni-class frigate. Cuba also has 8 interceptor squadrons containing 78 MiG-21s and 40 MiG-19s which could be used for air defense of its naval operations and shore facilities. Less imposing, but perhaps more dangerous, are the 50 torpedo and missile attack boats, many equipped with Styx missiles, and the 8 Turya-class hydrofoil patrol boats. These boats could sink unarmed merchant ships and pose a serious, though not decisive, threat to modern armed vessels. The Cubans could also attempt to mine U.S. gulf ports. Their Navy's offensive mine warfare capability has been significantly upgraded since 1978.[36] Since 1976, joint Soviet-Cuban naval manuevers have been held yearly.[37] Thus, apart from Cuba's political role in the Central American-Caribbean region, the value of Cuba to the Kremlin should be viewed increasingly in light of its potential role in a conventional war.

Complicating matters, Soviet influence in Nicaragua raises the question of the potential military utility of Nicaragua to the USSR in interdiction scenarios. Some have posited that given the Soviet presence in Cuba, additional facilities in Nicaragua would be only of marginal value, while others fear that the Sandinistas' Soviet orientation, together with the recent expansion of airfields and upgrading of ports, add up to a greatly enhanced Soviet ability to imperil U.S. security.

From Nicaragua, MiG-23s could strike at Mexico, the southern United States and the Panama Canal. The canal remains important in NATO war plans, which rely on unimpeded access for the rapid transfer of amphibious forces, escorts and destroyers between the Atlantic and Pacific oceans as needed, as well as for trade and movement of raw materials and oil from coast to coast.[38]

The advantage to the Soviet Union of a Pacific port in Nicaragua can be assessed in the context of the numerous alternate shipping routes that may be employed by the United States precisely to avoid interdiction operations by Soviet forces. Some of these routes would pass by or near the west coast of Central America. For instance, U.S.-bound oil tankers might head eastward from the Persian Gulf to the U.S. west coast in order to circumvent a possible Soviet attack from submarines operating from support facilities near East Africa. A Soviet facility in western Nicaragua could expose them to attack as they neared their destination. Similarly, a westward route from the Persian Gulf, around the Cape of Good Hope, across the tip of and up the west coast of South America could render U.S.-bound tankers even more vulnerable to Soviet attack from a Nicaraguan base.

Thus, such a base, or basing rights, could enhance Soviet sea-denial capability and reduce the number of relatively safe shipping routes available to Western forces. Moreover, it could facilitate surveillance of west coast installations such as those at San Diego, California.

But Soviet and Cuban capability alone would not inevitably lead them to conduct SLOC interdiction missions in the Caribbean in wartime. Protection of Caribbean sea lanes has a proportionately higher priority for the United States than interdicting them has for the Soviet Union. Many analysts believe that, since the advent of nuclear weapons, SLOC interdiction has not figured high on the Kremlin's list of wartime missions.[39] Soviet military writings and weapons procurement patterns seemed to indicate that the Kremlin was planning for a "short and decisive war"[40] that would be over before NATO reinforcement and resupply efforts could spell the difference between success and defeat. Recently, however, considerable evidence points to a Soviet belief that a future war with NATO could be fought entirely on a conventional level. The Soviets have been readjusting their military forces, command structure, military exercises, strategy and tactics accordingly.[41] In conventional war contingency planning, because of the expected longer duration of the war, sea lane interdiction assumes a much higher priority.[42]

Soviet military force is not limitless, however. Like its U.S. counterpart, the Soviet Navy does not have sufficient capabilities to carry out all of its projected wartime missions simultaneously. Besides sea lane interdiction, Soviet naval missions also include: elimination of Western sea-based nuclear weapons through anti-carrier and anti-submarine warfare operations directed against NATO ballistic missile submarines, the protection of Soviet nuclear weapons based in their home ports and in coastal areas such as Murmansk, and assistance to the army on the northern flank.[43] Which mission would take precedence over the others in a war would depend on the character and course of the war.

If Moscow did decide to conduct strikes against Western shipping, a relevant question is where interdiction operations would be most effective — in the Caribbean or the North Atlantic. Obviously, all cargoes do not have equal strategic value. It is easier to select good targets at the departure point such as Beaumont or New Orleans, but operations farther away from home ports would require more Soviet support. Soviet deployment of some anti-SLOC submarines closer to the U.S. shoreline would oblige the United States to pull back its anti-submarine warfare (ASW) forces from Europe and tie them down on the eastern shore and in the Caribbean, giving the Soviets freer rein in the European theater. On the other hand, with the aid of the sophisticated intelligence monitoring facilities located in Cuba, suitable targets could be identified from this side of the Atlantic and the information transmitted to Moscow. The interdiction operations could then be conducted in the North

Atlantic where the United States does not have such a preponderant advantage. Moreover, USSR interdiction operations in north European waters would permit the USSR to conserve the forces needed to protect Soviet SSBNs closer to home. Indeed, there is evidence of a Soviet view that a sea lane interdiction campaign in the North Atlantic would both sink U.S. ships and prevent NATO anti-submarine forces from striking Soviet home-ported SSBNs.[44]

Leaving aside for a moment the probable U.S. military response that Caribbean interdiction operations would provoke, the Cubans face paradoxical choices when calculating the utility of interdicting U.S. shipping. In a NATO-Warsaw Pact war, Cuba would have much to gain by waiting out the initial phase of the war. It is better to attack a strong adversary after it has become weakened. By waiting, Cuba would maximize its own security and risk less grave consequences for its actions. On the other hand, Cuba's role in sea lane interdiction is time-relevant. Once U.S. or allied ships pass by the three choke points vulnerable to Cuban attack, Cuba's offensive capabilty is of negligible value. Cuba's security might then be severely threatened before it had inflicted appreciable damage.

The other side of the coin is that Cuba is highly vulnerable to any interruption of its own ship traffic.[45] Cuba has virtually no oil reserves and is entirely dependent on foreign supplies of petroleum and other materials. Modern war cannot be waged without petroleum. Military options, surely contemplated by Pentagon planners, include outright neutralization of Cuban offensive and intelligence capabilities, either by strikes against airbases and port facilities or by invasion. The operative question would then become when to do this — whether by a series of preemptive strikes at the outbreak of the war, or at some time during the course of the war, conserving resources for the European front but leaving Cuba as a thorn in the side of the United States for a period of time.

The Cubans are undoubtedly aware of these calculations. Some analysts feel that Cuba's most viable strategic option in wartime would be to declare armed neutrality. That is, its posture would be overtly neutral, but it might still carry out covert actions such as aid to insurgents, laying mines and other activities. Such a move would complicate American responses, since substantial U.S. forces would need to be diverted to the Caribbean while there would be little official justification for attacking an avowedly neutral country.

Thus, Cuban SLOC interdiction capabilities, even at their present modest levels, are an increasing threat to U.S. security interests and an additional option available to the USSR and Cuba, should they elect to use it. Countering Soviet-Cuban naval expansion in the Caribbean demands a diversion of scarce American resources, particularly anti-submarine warfare assets, needed elsewhere. According to one analyst, the apparent Soviet objective is, "progressively to tie up a part of the U.S. Navy's forces in the Caribbean, thus decreasing its presence in other sea areas."[46]

The United States could "fight through" a Soviet-Cuban interdiction campaign in the Caribbean. Secretary of the Navy John Lehman has noted that the costs would involve several days' delay in resupply, the probable loss of some 50 to 100 aircraft, some of the supplies destined for the western front and the diversion of valuable U.S. ASW forces.[47] The Pentagon has recently augmented American forces in the region and improved its crisis response capability through the creation of the U.S. Forces Caribbean Command,[48] enhanced presence and capabilities of U.S. air forces along the southeastern U.S. coast, and placing F-15s on air defense alert at Tyndall Air Force Base in Florida.[49] Other measures contemplated include selective reopening of old U.S. airbases in the Caribbean basin, periodic deployments to bases in the region subject to agreement by the host countries, and increased combined training exercises with friendly air forces.[50] Diversifying ports of embarkation and reducing the time-at-sea of U.S. ships are other possible ways to confront the SLOC interdiction problem.[51]

WHICH THREATS DESERVE WHICH RESPONSE?

There is a palpable difference between potential Soviet and Cuban nuclear or conventional threats to the United States, and conflicts in Central America. It is difficult to conceive that the Soviets would again risk war with the United States by emplacing nuclear weapons in Cuba or Central America, but the United States must continue to communicate the unacceptability of such an attempt. The Kremlin's ongoing efforts to upgrade its own and Cuba's capability to disrupt Caribbean shipping during a conventional war also require continued improvement of U.S. military plans, preparedness and regional cooperation.

On the isthmus itself, the picture is somewhat less clear. If Nicaragua and/or Cuba were to invade neighboring countries, the United States could not ignore requests for military help from Mexico and the Central American nations. Congress and the public would likely support the commitment of U.S. combat troops. At present, however, such a conflict is not likely.

The United States must prevent the introduction of powerful offensive weapons, such as MiG-23s, into Central America. It must also be vigilant against incremental steps, such as the Soviets have undertaken elsewhere, which could transform Nicaragua's ports and other military facilities into bases from which the USSR could operate. But is U.S. military action against Nicaragua justified in the absence of Soviet bases or sophisticated weaponry?

One of the issues raised by the Grenadan invasion is the propriety of militarily preempting a potential security threat before it has truly materialized. The resounding success of that nearly painless operation may make similar operations in Central America seem promising for those not troubled by their moral or legal dimensions. But the potential for success of a particular military option should not be the only yardstick by which to measure its appropriateness. The success of the Grenada invasion did not make it correct. Nor can it compensate for the detrimental impact this example of international lawlessness has had for the U.S. in Latin America and Western Europe.

Even if one feels that Grenada demonstrated U.S. resolve rather than poor judgment, the military costs of similar actions in Central America are serious enough to make even hardened Pentagon planners think twice. Central America is not Grenada. Military victories there cannot be won so cheaply. U.S. troops might eventually prevail, but the combat losses, domestic dissent, and damage to the U.S. alliance system could turn tactical victory into strategic defeat. Moreover, in Nicaragua it still seems possible to implement a policy capable of resolving the national security issues without incurring further losses or diverting military assets from other theaters.

In Nicaragua today, the legitimate security concerns of both nations might be addressed by a policy which combined a credible threat of U.S. retaliation if Soviet offensive weapons were introduced, with a U.S. pledge not to invade Nicaragua. It might eventually form the basis for a more comprehensive negotiated solution between the two countries. Short of an overall agreement, the United States might balance specific military threats (for example, the possibility that the United States would take out MiG-23s if they were flown to Nicaraguan airfields) with a commitment to proscribe the sale of equally sophisticated American conventional weapons to other Central American countries (such as the F-5Es which the Honduran government is currently seeking from the United States).

The United States can live with the Sandinistas as long as they refrain from acting as instruments of Soviet foreign policy. Thus the function of U.S. military force should be to remind Nicaragua of the consequences of facilitating a Soviet strategic threat to legitimate U.S. interests, not to overthrow the regime, however distasteful it may be to some Americans.

NOTES

1. *U.S. News and World Report*, June 13, 1983, pp. 25-25.
2. *Ibid.*
3. "How Vital is U.S. Stake in Central America?" *Philadelphia Inquirer*, May 29, 1983, p. 7.
4. Branigan, W., "Guerrillas Use Cease-Fire to Rearm," *Washington Post*, October 18, 1983, p. A13.

5. Military statistics in this essay are from: *Military Balance, 1983-1984*, International Institute for Strategic Studies, London; "Cuban Armed Forces and the Soviet Military Presence," *U.S. Department of State Bulletin*, September 1982; *SIPRI Yearbook, 1982* (Stockholm International Peace Research Institute, Taylor and Francis Ltd., London) 1982, pp. 400-404.

6. Leiken, R. S., *Soviet Stategy in Latin America*, The Washington Papers, No. 93, Praeger, 1982, p. 57.

7. Morris, C., "The United States-Caribbean Military Connection," American Enterprise Institute, Occasional Papers No. 7, August 1983, p. 11.

8. "Cuban Armed Forces and the Soviet Military Presence," *Department of State Bulletin*, September 1982, p. 64.

9. *Ibid.*

10. *SIPRI Yearbook*, 1982, p. 402.

11. Gutman, R., "U.S. is Holding Cards to Invade Nicaragua," *Newsday*, October 31, 1983, p. 4.

12. *Ibid.*, p. 29.

13. "Fidel Castro's Press Conference on Grenada," Foreign Broadcast Information Service, Latin America, 26 October 1983, p. Q14.

14. Woods, D., "U.S. Military Fears Costs, Effects of Latin Involvement," *Los Angeles Times*, July 27, 1983, p. 1.

15. *Ibid.*

16. Gelb, L., "Schultz, Pushing a Hard Line, Becomes Key Voice in Crisis," *New York Times*, November 7, 1983, p. 1.

17. *Ibid.*

18. McCartney, J., "A New Plan for Central America," *Philadelphia Inquirer*, July 31, 1983, p. 1-G.

19. Statement of Adm. Harry Train II, Commander-in-Chief, Atlantic, before the House of Representatives Committee on Armed Services, March 16, 1982 in *Hearings on Military Posture*, Committee on Armed Services, 97th Congress, p. 979.

20. *Ibid.*, p. 963.

21. *Chicago Tribune*, August 24, 1983, p. 5.

22. "No Military Solutions," *Dallas Times Herald*, 6 August 1983, p. 23.

23. "Pentagon: Once There, We'd Win," *Atlanta Constitution*, August 4, 1983, p. SA.

24. *Ibid.*

25. Interviews with Eden Pastora, Washington, D.C., November 16, 1983.

26. Interview with Dr. Mariano Fiallos Oyanguren, Secretary of the Board of Directors at the Nicaraguan Council of State and President of the Foreign Relations Committee at the Council of State, Washington, D.C., November 10, 1983.

27. For example, Soviet Defense Minister Ustinov said the Soviet Union will soon take steps "that will graphically demonstrate the illusory nature of U.S. calculations on its geographical isolation and the invulnerability of its own territory." Cited in *Soviet World Outlook*, November 15, 1983, pp. 3-4.

28. See McConnell, J. C., *The Soviet Shift in Emphasis from Nuclear to Conventional: The Mid-Term Perspective*, CRC490, Vol. 2, Center for Naval Analyses, Alexandria, Va., June 1983, pp. 23-39.

29. Rear Admiral S.A. Swarztrauber, "The Potential Battle of the Atlantic," U.S. Naval Institute, *Naval Review* 1979, p. 115.

30. *Ibid.*, p. 116.

31. See Nitze, P. H., and Sullivan, L., *Securing the Seas*, Westview Press, Boulder, Colo., 1979, pp. 75-76, 86-88; and Daniel, D. C., "Trends and Patterns in Major Soviet Naval Exercises," in Murphy, P. J., ed., *Naval Power in Soviet Policy*, Vol. 2, USAF Studies in Communist Affairs, GPO, Washington, D.C., 1978, pp. 230-231.

32. Swarztrauber, *op. cit.*, p. 112. Fully two-thirds of the Soviet Navy's 2,000-plus assets, including two-thirds of all submarines both nuclear- and conventionally-powered, have access to the Atlantic ocean. The Northern Fleet alone contains 60% of the Delta, Typhoon and Yankee class SSBNs and nearly 50% of the total tactical submarine force, including Oscar-class cruise missile submarines and all of the new Alfa-class boats. More than 65% of all Soviet surface ships are deployed in the Northern, Baltic and Black Sea Fleets and carry anti-ship cruise missiles. Soviet naval strike aircraft, including Backfire and Badger bombers, two-thirds of which operate from the Baltic, Black Sea and Northern Fleets, must be considered a potential threat to Allied Atlantic forces because of their mobility. See Swarztrauber, *op. cit.*, p. 110 and Adm. Wesley A. McDonald, "Our Atlantic Strategy," *Defense '83*, August 1983, p. 4.

33. Flint, J., "Cheap at Twice the Price," *Forbes*, March 28, 1983.

34. Hanks, R. J., *The Unnoticed Challenge: Soviet Maritime Strategy and the Global Choke Points*, Institute for Foreign Policy Analysis, Tufts University, Boston, 1980, p. 21.

35. *Ibid.*, p. 22. There are reports that the Soviet Union may begin stationing some of their Delta-class submarines in the South Atlantic, perhaps in the ocean area between Brazil and Africa, because of a shortage of sea space in the Northern Norwegian Sea and the Barents Sea. Some form of forward base would be required and, according to Admiral Train, "it is likely we will see such a base established somewhere in West Africa." If such a base were established in West Africa, he claims, it is likely that support ships would be deployed to the area. These might include the Kirov-class, nuclear-powered cruiser, the Udaloy destroyer and perhaps some of their maritime patrol craft. "If they do that, that forward deployed fleet will be squarely astride these vital sealanes through the South Atlantic." See statement of Admiral Harry D. Train, II, Commander-in-Chief, Atlantic, *Hearings on Military Posture and H.R. 5968*, Department of Defense Authorization for Appropriations for Fiscal Year 1983 before the Committee on Armed Services, U.S. House of Representatives, GPO, Washington, D.C., 1982, p. 964.

36. Vego, M., "The Cuban Navy 1959-1982," *Navy International*, May, 1983, p. 1064.

37. *Ibid.*, p. 1068.

38. *Military Posture, op. cit.*, p. 976.

39. See Nitze and Sullivan, *op.cit.*, pp. 75-76, 86-88, 388; Norman Friedman, "The Soviet Fleet in Transition," U.S. Naval Institute *Naval Review 1983*, p. 161; Daniel, *op.cit.* pp. 228-231; McConnell, *op.cit.*, pp. 4-23.

40. Nitze and Sullivan, *op.cit.*, p. 75.

41. See McConnell, *op. cit.*, pp. 23-39; Friedman, *op. cit.*, pp. 156-173; Swarztrauber, *op. cit.*, pp. 113-114; and Bildt, C., "Sweden and the Soviet Submarines," *Survival*, July-August 1983.

42. McConnell, *op. cit.*, p. 32.

43. Friedman, *op. cit.*, p. 161.

44. *Ibid.* The October 1981 "Whiskey on the rocks" incident (in which a Soviet Whiskey-class diesel submarine ran aground in Swedish territorial waters) and dozens of subsequent coordinated Soviet incursions into sensitive Scandinavian coastal waters are a sign of the heightened significance given to the North Atlantic-North European area in Soviet operational planning in recent years. The Submarine Defense Commission investigating these incidents viewed them as "preparation for actual missions to be undertaken in case of war," such as covert mining in areas of importance to NATO, sabotage raids against vital command and control and other military installations, or landing "diversionary forces." Bildt, *op. cit.*, p. 167.

45. Vego, *op. cit.*, p. 1068.

46. *Ibid.*

47. Flint, *op. cit.*, p. 40.

48. McDonald, *op. cit.*, p. 7.

49. Cole, J. A., "Air Power in the Western Hemisphere: A Perspective," *Air University Review*, July-August 1983, p. 8.

50. *Ibid.*

51. "The shortest distance from North America to the Channel is via Strait of Belle Isle, between Newfoundland and Labrador. This route includes about 2,000 miles of open Atlantic—through enemy submarines. From Galveston, Texas, the open sea distance is more than double—nearly 4,500 miles. The route from New York, about 2,800 miles. One would normally expect an army division in Texas to embark at a Gulf Port—certainly the most economical system. But if connecting our limited ASW forces along a 2000-mile sea route, instead of spreading them thinly over a 4,500-mile sea route, could result in the loss of fewer merchant ships to submarines, perhaps the overland-Great Lakes-St. Lawrence Seaway route is an attractive option." Swarztrauber, *op. cit.*, p. 124.

9
FAR FROM HOPELESS:
An Economic Program for Post-War Central America

Richard E. Feinberg and Robert A. Pastor

When all else fails, the United States muses about Marshall Plans. An economic solution to a grave political crisis in Europe, the Marshall Plan further distinguished itself from much of the rest of U.S. foreign policy since World War II by succeeding. We have reached the point of desperation in Central America where people have again begun to dream of Marshall Plans.[1] After five years of deep involvement under two administrations, the situation in Central America continues to deteriorate: political polarization has advanced considerably; leftist guerrillas and rightist death squads in El Salvador have gained strength; the middle class has been harrassed in Nicaragua or exiled; wars in both countries escalate and threaten to spill over into a regional conflagration; and the United States has become militarily involved, albeit indirectly. For the first time since the U.S. withdrew from a quagmire in Nicaragua fifty years ago, the marines have landed in Central America — for extended military "exercises" in Honduras — and are supported by airpower and aircraft carrier battle groups.

A survey of Central American economies provides an equally grim picture: dramatically high unemployment; sharply declining incomes and living standards; falling levels of savings and investment; the flight of capital and human talent; the destruction of vital infrastructure; the sharp contraction of trade; and the evaporation of foreign exchange reserves. Still, there are poorer regions in the world whose economies are losing ground — including most of sub-Saharan Africa — without provoking much concern from the United States. Americans are not debating whether to undertake a Marshall Plan for Central America because of the state of the region's economy. Rather, the principal motivations are strategic and political: the geopolitical implications of the worsening crisis in Central America, and its polarizing effect on American opinion. The U.S. has come to recognize that it cannot afford to fail in Central America, and that the costs of military involvement are high; some feel too high. A Marshall Plan is tempting in times like these.

Other essays in this volume offer proposals to reduce the region's political strife – a necessary but not suffcient condition for the resumption of economic development. This chapter will consider possible responses to the region's short-term, balance-of-payments crises and its longer-term economic problems. How much money will it take to overcome the region's foreign exchange gap? Can a synthesis be found between the import-substitution industrialization strategy of the Central American Common Market constructed during the 1960s, and the newer, more outward-looking thrust of the Caribbean Basin Initiative? In addition to peace, are there other political preconditions to economic development? Most importantly, what role can the United States and other extra-regional states play in stimulating Central American economies? Is the Marshall Plan relevant to Central America, or is it a misplaced historical analogy that serves to divert attention from the Reagan administration's military-political strategy? In answering these questions, we will describe how the Central American economies changed over the last three decades, analyze the causes of the current economic crisis, and explore the possibilities for the future.

THE TRANSFORMATION OF THE CENTRAL AMERICAN POLITICAL ECONOMY

In the three decades since World War II, Central America experienced rapid economic growth and social change. Far from remaining stagnant "banana republics," the six nations of Central America averaged an annual real rate of growth of 5.3% between 1950 and 1978, and the real per capita income doubled. If the population had remained stable, instead of tripling (from 8.3 million to 23 million), real per capita income would have quintupled.[2]

Primarily banana or coffee exporters in 1950, the six nations multiplied their trade by a factor of eighteen by 1980, and trade has been the stimulus for expanding and diversifying their economies. In 1950, a single commodity export from each Central American country generated on the average about 70% of their foreign exchange; that dependence declined to 36% by 1970. Exports now include a range of agricultural products, manufactures, and services. At the same time, physical infrastructure – roads, telephones, electrical energy, port facilities, mass communications – expanded severalfold, touching the most remote communities of Central America and lifting them into the twentieth century.

U.S. aid played a significant role in contributing to this dynamism. 1962 to 1980, the U.S. provided over $2 billion in bilateral economic aid to the six Central American countries and to the U.S. AID regional office for Central America and Panama (ROCAP) (see Table 9.1). In addition, international organizations provided over $4.1 billion, of which the Inter-American Development Bank and the World Bank authorized over 90% (although some of this is still being disbursed). The U.S. is the largest contributor by far to both banks. In some years, these resources were quite significant in comparison to the levels of domestic savings and investment. Since most multilateral and bilateral aid requires a significant portion of local counterpart funds, the total impact of U.S. aid was actually larger than the numbers below suggest. In comparison to official aid flows, U.S. direct private investment in Central America (excluding Panama) was small; the cumulative total in 1981 was only $1.0 billion.[3]

Table 9.1. U.S. and Multilateral Aid to Central America, 1962-1980 (millions of dollars)

	U.S. Bilateral Aid	World Bank	Inter-American Development Bank	Total
Costa Rica	214.8	334.9	422.8	972.5
El Salvador	243.8	179.5	301.7	725.0
Guatemala	307.0	259.3	379.2	945.5
Honduras	301.7	388.8	435.1	1125.6
Nicaragua	308.5	146.0	266.6	721.1
Panama	383.4	299.2	386.1	1068.7
ROCAP	285.0	–	–	285.0
TOTAL	2,044.2	1,607.7	2,191.5	5,843.4

Sources: U.S. AID, *U.S. Overseas Loans and Grants and Assistance from International Organizations, July 1, 1945-September 30, 1980* (Washington, D.C.: Office of Planning and Budgeting, Agency for International Development, 1981).

The impressive growth rates achieved prior to 1978 can largely be attributed to the creation in 1960 of the Central American Common Market (CACM) and to investment in export-oriented agriculture. The common market created a regional free-trade zone in manufactures protected against world competition by a common external tariff.[4] Private industrialists—local and foreign—were stimulated by a broader, more secure market, as well as by generous fiscal and other incentives. This policy of producing locally what previously had been imported (import-substitution industrialization) spurred the growth of light industry. Industrial production rose from 12% of regional output in 1960 to nearly 18% in 1970. Trade among the CACM countries jumped from $32 million in 1960 to over $900 million in 1978, with manufactures accounting for 95% of the total. At the same time, the region's traditional agricultural crops — coffee and bananas — enlarged their share of the world market. Successful farmers also diversified into cotton, sugar, and cattle.

The vigorous economic expansion was accompanied by substantial progress in health and education. Between 1960 and 1977, the number of physicians in Central America increased more than twice as fast as the population and the number of nurses nearly six times as fast. (Put another way, there was one physician for every 2,533 people in Central America in 1977 as contrasted with one for every 5,358 in 1960; 1 nurse for every 1,106 people in 1977 versus one for every 6,294 in 1960.) The adult literacy rate rose from 44% in 1960 to 72% in 1976. The number of secondary school students as a percentage of their age group more than doubled from 12% to 29% from 1960 to 1978.[5] Nevertheless, these statistics conceal considerable variations between and within countries. Costa Rica and Panama showed much more progress in health and education, while urban residents throughout Central America tended to benefit more than those in rural areas.

OLD AND NEW PROBLEMS: FLAWS IN THE DEVELOPMENT STRATEGY

Despite this progress, old problems fermented; because of this progress, new problems emerged. Development strategies did not sufficiently confront the persistent problems of population growth, rapid urbanization, inadequate social services, and labor force expansion nor did they pay sufficient heed to the simmering conflict over land tenure. Economic success also created a new generation of problems related to the costs of an import-substitution industrialization strategy, the failure to distribute more fairly the gains of regional integration, the widening income inequalities, and the neglect of domestic as opposed to export-oriented agriculture.

An analysis of the underlying problems of the region should begin by considering the demographic earthquake which shook Central America after the Second World War. The nations of the region still have not fully comprehended or adjusted to the shock, which has, paradoxically, made development both more possible — and more difficult. In a report on El Salvador published in May 1979, in the midst of violence and revolutionary turmoil, the World Bank correctly focused its attention on what it identified as "the country's most fundamental long-run problem" — rapid population growth.[6]

Primarily because of improvements in health conditions, the birth rate increased after the Second World War and the mortality rate (particularly of infants) declined. The population nearly tripled from 1950 to 1980; today almost half of the population is under the age of 15. Even with optimistic projections and a gradual decline in the birth rate, the population is expected to double again by the end of the century. Moreover, there was sizable migration from the rural to the urban areas. Two-thirds of the labor force was in agriculture in 1950; 50% in the late 1970s. Unemployment increased as underemployed peasants moved to the cities, and, while the birth rate began to decline, the annual growth of the labor force relentlessly increased — from 2.7% in the 1960s, to 3% in the 1970s, to 3.2% in the 1980s. The generation of jobs is perhaps Central America's most fundamental problem, but governments have not given it priority.

As throughout the Third World, Central America's import-substitution strategy had its costs as well as its benefits. The tariff structure distorted the relative prices of capital and labor by allowing the duty-free entry of machinery. The imported machinery was sometimes more capital-intensive than was appropriate, given the region's labor surplus. Moreover, growing up behind high tariff walls and enjoying captive markets, much of the new industry was relatively inefficient and operated at very low capacity utilization rates.[7] Uncompetitive in world markets, the "hot house" industries could not generate the hard-currency exports needed to balance their import needs.

Furthermore, the centrifugal force of nationalism continually tugged at the Central American Common Market (CACM). While the CACM has been judged the most successful integration experiment in the developing world, it did not escape a problem which weakened the others: the CACM failed to develop a mechanism to distribute more equitably the gains of regional integration.[8]

The economically weaker and less industrialized states — Honduras and, to a lesser degree, Nicaragua — complained that their more advanced neighbors were benefiting disproportionately from the reduction in tariff barriers, and were flooding their markets with manufactures.[9] Following the brief "soccer war" between El Salvador and Honduras in 1969, Honduras formally abandoned the Common Market, although a series of bilateral treaties enabled the country to maintain regional trading links.

The growth strategies of protected industrialization and export agriculture also failed to address directly the glaringly unequal distribution of wealth and income in Central America. In the 1960s, many economists tended to define development in terms of increases in the gross national product and tended to neglect the problem of poverty, assuming that the new wealth would "trickle down" or that the poor could eat more from a larger pie. However, as in the case of Brazil and most other developing countries which experienced rapid economic growth, the gap between the poorest and the richest in Central America widened further.

The failure of trickle down and the increasing inequality can be attributed to several factors. Land and capital were already highly concentrated, and their owners had privileged access to credit and to government subsidies.

Agricultural modernization exacerbated the inequitable concentration of land, and that together with the expanding population meant larger numbers of landless peasants. Governments heavily influenced by conservative business and military interests hampered the activities of labor unions and failed to provide adequate social services. Moreover, rapid population growth created an abundant labor supply that depressed wages. The inflation of the 1970s and early 1980s further cut into purchasing power and probably worsened income distribution.[10]

Large numbers of Central Americans did not share the fruits of economic growth. The United Nations Economic Commission for Latin America recently estimated that 42% of the population in the six countries of Central America live in a state of "extreme poverty."[11]

In addition, scarce financial resources went to industry and export agriculture rather than to the smaller landowners who constitute a significant portion of the poor majority. Government-imposed ceilings on the prices of basic foodstuffs also worked against the small farmer. As a result, the production of food for domestic consumption failed to keep pace with population growth and demand. Whereas Central America as a whole was virtually self-sufficient in the basic staples of corn and beans in the 1960s, net imports of both rose to about 4% of consumption in the 1970s. Scarce foreign exchange was increasingly diverted to pay for food imports. In 1980, Central America spent $408 million on food imports just from the United States.[12]

The public sector has been unusually small in Central America, when compared to other developing countries and even to most industrial nations. Governments followed conservative fiscal policies in order to keep inflation low and exchange rates steady. Public expenditures did increase somewhat during the 1970s, as governments slowly began to accept responsibility for the development of human capital and physical infrastructure, and to attempt to meet the demand for basic social services.[13] Yet, in all countries but Costa Rica, and to an extent Panama, the commitment and capabilities of the governmental bureaucracy still fell far short of development needs. Part of the problem was the resistance of the wealthy elites to higher taxation; the levies on property and income generally remained light.

THE CAUSES OF THE CURRENT CRISIS

Rather than the lack of change, the underlying causes of the current crisis are the unevenness and incompleteness of the profound social and economic changes which transformed Central America over the last three decades. But there is nothing inevitable about revolution in Central America. Many of the old and new problems facing the region are common to many developing countries, both those which are managing these problems adequately and those which are failing to address them. The current crisis was precipitated by two factors which are distinct but mutually reinforcing: the inability of the political-military institutions to either accept or adapt to the social and economic changes, and the negative impact of a global recession on small, open, dependent economies.[14]

The expansive years of the 1960s and 1970s generated new social forces not content with the political status quo. The demographic boom produced a population younger, better educated, and more aware of their countries' obsolete dictatorships and of the world's possibilities. In the rural areas, the mechanization of export-oriented agriculture replaced the traditionally passive *campesinos* of the old latifundia system with more politically-conscious salaried laborers who began to organize. Similarly, new industries led ineluctably to the development of an urban labor movement. The political leadership for this new group emerged from the universities and the expanding middle class.

In the early 1970s, these groups made a peaceful bid for political power in Nicaragua, El Salvador, and Guatemala, and in each case they were blocked by the military and the oligarchy and forced underground or into exile. Only in Costa Rica and Panama was social mobility and a peaceful reallocation of political and economic power permitted. Not suprisingly, these are the only countries which have escaped the violence that currently engulfs their neighbors.

Political unrest was given added impetus by the world recession. The economic success of the previous two decades had left Central America more fully integrated into the international economy, and therefore more vulnerable to adverse swings. By the late 1970s, the region relied on international markets to supply it with about one quarter of its goods and services, and to purchase about one quarter of its production. Furthermore, the region has depended upon foreign sources for petroleum and the international banking system to finance its foreign trade.

Central America weathered the first oil shock in 1973-74 because of high prices for its commodity exports. However, coffee prices slumped in 1978, and the next year brought the second oil shock. Then, as the global economy contracted, Central America's overall terms of trade deteriorated sharply. Demand for its products declined and the prices for its main exports (coffee, cotton, bananas, sugar, and beef) fell. By 1982, one unit of the region's exports was able to purchase only 74% of the imports purchased in 1979.

One consequence of greater integration into the international economy is the effect on Central America of interest rate fluctuations in New York and London. Normally, interest rates fall in a recession, but this time they rose. Fearing that the second round of oil price increases and the loose fiscal policy of the Reagan administration would generate inflation, the Federal

Reserve Board clamped down on the money supply, and real interest rates hit historic highs. The unanticipated jump in the cost of money dealt a harsh blow to the debt-laden Third World and to Central America in particular.

Most international bank debt carries interest rates that fluctuate, and Central American debt is no exception. Since Central American governments and private borrowers owe commercial banks about $5 billion, each one percentage point rise in interest rates costs the region some $50 million a year; *ceteris paribus*, the jump in international interest rates from 6% in 1977 to 13% in 1982 thus cost the region an additional $350 million in 1982 alone.

Central American governments sought to offset the adverse movements in the terms of trade and their rising debt service burden by increased external borrowing. For example, Costa Rica found its revenues from coffee falling from a record $319 million in 1977 to $248 million in 1980, while the oil bill jumped from $83 million to $186 million.[15] As a result, the trade deficit rose steadily, peaking at $366 million in 1980, or 27% of imports. Costa Rica financed its growing trade deficits with increasingly dear external borrowings. In 1980, their total external debt surpassed $3 billion, more than two-thirds of it owed to private creditors. As market interest rates rose, the debt service soared. Interest payments jumped from $60 million in 1977 to $290 million in 1981—to an astounding $510 million due in 1982.

The combination of an expanding trade deficit and mounting interest payments widened Costa Rica's current-account deficit to $664 million in 1980. The bottom fell out in 1981, when external lenders simply declined to continue financing such a large deficit. Suddenly frightened by the magnitude of Costa Rica's financial imbalances, foreign lenders sought to reduce their exposure, and many Costa Ricans placed their savings in hard currency abroad. Data on capital flight are unreliable, but it was surely large. With fewer dollars, imports dropped along with domestic consumption and investment. The gross national product fell by a total of 10% in 1981 and 1982.

External factors—declining prices for coffee and other exports, combined with the higher costs of energy and capital—played an important role in Costa Rica's economic decline. At the same time, the government of Costa Rica bears some responsibility, having overspent during the 1976-77 coffee boom and then failing to reduce expenditures sufficiently when the international environment turned darker. Following the same strategy as the other governments in the region, Costa Rica abandoned its traditionally prudent fiscal management, and the public sector deficit rose to over 12% of gross domestic product.

The international banking system reinforced the adverse impact of the global recession on Central America by cutting access to new credits, and in some cases even by reducing routine lines of trade finance. Eventually, the economic and financial squeeze would make it difficult for every Central American country to remain current on debt service, while Nicaragua and Costa Rica had to formally reschedule their relatively large debts. Throughout Central America, per capita gross domestic product fell by nearly 4% in 1981, by 6.5% in 1982, and continued declining in 1983 (see Table 9.2 for country data). Desperate for cash and under pressure from the commercial banks and official donors, all the states of the region except Nicaragua signed standby arrangements with the International Monetary Fund. These agreements generally required sharp reductions in budget deficits, increased prices for government-provided services, higher local interest rates, and lower real wages. In short, the only path left to adjusting to adverse international events was to lower standards of living.

Table 9.2. Economic Growth Rates (percentage)

	1961-70	1971-75	1976-80	1981	1982	1983 (est.)
Costa Rica	6.0	6.1	5.2	-4.6	-6.3	-2.5
El Salvador	5.7	5.5	3.7	-9.5	-5.4	-2.0
Guatemala	5.5	5.6	5.7	0.9	-3.5	-3.2
Honduras	5.2	2.1	6.6	0.1	-1.0	-1.0
Nicaragua	7.0	5.6	-1.3	8.5	-2.0	N/A
Panama	8.0	5.0	3.4	4.3	4.1	-1.0

Sources: Inter-American Development Bank, *Economic and Social Progress in Latin America: 1980-81 Report,* Washington, D.C.; Comisíon Económica para America Latina, *Notas para el estudio económico de America Latina,* 1982, April 1983; and U.S. Agency for International Development.

Either the obsolete political-military institutions or the economic downturn might have been sufficient to precipitate a crisis in the region; together, they virtually guaranteed it, particularly as each reinforced the other in a negative way. The classic preconditions for a revolutionary situation were in place.[16] The economic growth of the previous two decades had raised expectations, which were first disappointed by political intransigence and military repression, then dissipated by the inflation, and finally catalyzed into public unrest by the falling incomes. While inequality alone does not necessarily produce political upheaval, the failure to address the concerns of the poor and the inability of tax-starved governments to meet the rising need for social services added detonating powder to an already unstable mixture.

Once the violence passed a certain threshold, it fed on itself, and made the possibility of economic improvement or political accommodation more difficult. Not surprisingly, the violence has frightened the private sector. Not only has private investment stopped, but disinvestment has begun on a massive scale. Accurate figures on capital flight are not available, but balance-of-payments data suggest that $2.5 to $3 billion in private capital flowed out of the region between 1979 and 1982. Furthermore, as governments spend more for security, they have less for development. Between 1972 and 1980, the share of government expenditures on national defense doubled as a percentage of GDP in all countries except Costa Rica, and the trend undoubtedly continues.[17]

Insurgents in both El Salvador and Nicaragua have increasingly targeted their nation's economic infrastructure with devastating effect. The El Salvadoran government conservatively estimated that, in the twenty months from September 1980 to May 1982, guerrilla actions caused more than $41.5 million in damage, destroying or disabling railways, public buildings, at least 34 bridges and 145 electrical transmission towers, along with 675 buses (nearly one-quarter of the nation's total). The government attributed the closing of 149 businesses, and the resulting loss of 18,213 jobs between 1979 and 1981, to guerrilla actions. A more recent estimate of cumulative damages reached almost $1 billion. As for Nicaragua, a recent estimate by the Nicaraguan Ambassador to the United States was that insurgents had destroyed as much as $130 million worth of property just in 1983.[18]

In this precarious atmosphere, governments concentrate on urgent problems, with little time and less resources for development. Official corruption thrives with the spirit of *"après moi, le déluge."* Only when some semblance of security is restored will economic ministries and private business be able to resume normal work.

THE ROAD TO RECOVERY AND DEVELOPMENT

Just as the origins of the current economic decline are rooted in the three interrelated factors of external economic shock, domestic development failure, and political stagnation, so does a sustained recovery in Central America depend upon improvements in these three determinants. An upswing in the global economy could improve Central America's balance of payments, especially if coupled with more effective and balanced development strategies. And it cannot be emphasized too strongly that security and political legitimacy are required for investment and sustained growth.

First, we will offer a plan for economic recovery and development, which distinguishes between short-term, balance-of-payments problems and longer-term national and regional development possibilities. Then, we will examine the relationship between economic development and political change, and finally offer some ideas on what the United States could contribute.

Reconstruction

Like the rest of the Third World, Central America needs foreign exchange to develop. The exporters of machinery and technology in the industrial countries — as well as in the more advanced developing nations such as Mexico and Brazil — will not generally accept Salvadoran colones or Guatemalan quetzales. Nor will the sellers of oil, grains or arms. Central America can earn the required hard currency by selling its production abroad. But if import requirements exceed export receipts — as is the case today by a wide margin — then only foreign loans or grants can make up the difference. The shortage of hard currency, therefore, is a key constraint on Central American economies.

A global recovery would certainly help. As the demand for primary commodities picks up, the prices of Central America's main exports can improve. The World Bank estimates that, with a modest but sustained global recovery, the price of cotton will rise from $1.78 per kilo during the first half of 1983 to $1.98 in 1985, while beef will go from $2.57 to $2.85 (in constant 1981 dollars, i.e., corrected for inflation).[19] Although the future of the sugar market is very uncertain, the World Bank estimates that sugar prices are likely to rise. The future for coffee, however, seems less bright, since consumer demand appears to be gradually shifting to other beverages. The future price of oil is another important unknown. All things considered, if Central America's terms of trade improve by 10%, the region would earn approximately $500 million more per year.[20]

If global recovery can occur without reigniting inflation, the advantage for Central America might be even greater. Today's high level of real interest rates seems to be related to the expectation that inflation will indeed resume. But if prices remain low, these expectations should gradually dissipate. The result could be a decline in interest rates. Given Central America's debt to private lenders of roughly $5 billion, a decline in market rates of 3% would, *ceterus paribus*, save the region $150 million a year.

This suggests that the United States can have a significant impact on Central American economies by improving the management of its own economy. In this sense, President Reagan was correct when he remarked in September 1981 that the best service his administration could perform for the international economy in general, and the developing nations in particular, was to revive the U.S. economy:

> No American contribution can do more for development than a growing, prosperous U.S. economy. And as the world's largest single market, a prosperous, growing U.S. economy will mean increased trading opportunities for other nations. Lower U.S. inflation and interest rates will translate into increased availability of financial resources at affordable rates.[21]

Instead of this bright future, however, interest rates remained high and the U.S. economy remained in recession throughout 1982. The U.S. economy finally recovered in 1983, but the magnitude and length of the upswing remains in doubt. Many observers are fearful that inflation will begin again, either as the result of chronic $200 billion fiscal deficits, or inadequate supplies of food, energy, and other commodities. However stimulated, inflation is likely to induce the Federal Reserve Board to step on its monetary brakes and thereby squeeze credit, raise interest rates, and choke off growth. Observers also worry that other industrial countries are pursuing overly cautious fiscal and monetary policies. As in 1977-78, if the United States grows much faster than its main industrial trading partners, its trade deficit — already large in part because of an over-valued dollar — will widen further, and U.S. prosperity will be jeopardized. Part of the solution is greater collaboration among the major industrial countries to coordinate their fiscal and monetary policies, so as to produce a balanced and sustainable global recovery.[22] As members of the one-world economy of integrated commodity and capital markets, Central America's economic future will be greatly affected by the ability of the industrialized nations to sustain an economic recovery.

Buoyant export markets will still not provide Central America with sufficient capital to resume healthy growth. By late 1982, the real per capita income in Costa Rica, Guatemala, and Honduras had fallen to the levels attained in 1976, while in El Salvador and Nicaragua, they had dropped to the levels reached in the early 1960s.[23] The exact size of the "financing gap" — the difference between the resources generated through the countries' own efforts and the required foreign exchange — will depend upon several variables, including terms of trade, interest rates, political stability, social reforms (including tax and land reform), the effectiveness of government economic policy, the responsiveness of domestic and foreign private investment and the desired rate of economic growth. Estimates of the size of the financing gap will also vary depending upon one's model of the way key variables in an economy interact.

Given all the uncertainties, estimates of the financing gap inevitably contain a large margin for error. Nevertheless, various projections, including those by AID, the United Nations, and private and official economists in Washington, tend to converge around $2 to $3 billion per year for the five Central American countries (excluding Panama). In a study prepared for the National Bipartisan Commission on Central America chaired by Henry Kissinger, the U.S. Agency for International Development projected external financing needs of $11 billion over five years (1984-88) to assist four Central American countries — AID excluded Nicaragua — to attain a growth rate of 6.5% by 1988. This would allow per capita income to regain 1979 levels by 1990.[24] AID's forecast is based on several optimistic assumptions regarding strong and sustained global growth rates, substantial net private capital inflows, and efficient and high investment rates. The United Nations Economic

Commission for Latin America released "highly provisional estimates" in 1981 that foresaw a somewhat greater need. The UN economists called for $20 billion in net flows over 9 years (at constant 1982 prices), or $2.2 billion per year. [25] The UN estimate, made before the 1982-83 declines, included financing for Nicaragua. In any event, analysts concur that the region will require substantial infusions of foreign exchange during the 1980s if it is to recoup the losses of recent years and regain forward momentum.

National and Regional Development Strategies

Central America has the climate, soils, hydroelectric potential, and technical expertise to develop diversified and dynamic economies. The challenge is to formulate strategies that provide for sufficient exports to sustain an equilibrated balance of payments, while generating employment and rising incomes. The opportunities offered by the Caribbean Basin Initiative and other export markets and the continuing promise of regional integration must be merged in a coherent strategy. The simultaneous exploitation of external and internal markets would allow for diversified, balanced growth. Combined with equitable stabilization policies and with reforms in tax structures, health distribution systems, and land tenure, gains from growth could be widely and fairly distributed among the population.

A new Central American export strategy could combine a drive to maintain markets for agricultural exports, while finding outlets for nontraditional agricultural products and light manufactures. Feasible items include tropical fruits and "winter" vegetables, seafood, forestry products, processed coffee, sugar cane, milk, and cotton-based textiles. Industrial exports might bring together labor-intensive assemblies (the Asian model) and select, larger-scale industries (the Nordic model — Sweden, for example, specialized in forestry products) where the region possesses a comparative advantage. A more diversified export pattern would also reduce the region's vulnerability to swings in commodity prices.

An export drive would require certain policy reforms. Exchange rates could no longer be overvalued. Those industries and farms that are to be internationally competitive must be able to purchase required imports free of heavy tariff burdens. In sectors where foreign competition would be needed to stimulate efficiency among domestic producers, tariff barriers would also have to be gradually lowered. Governments would have to establish adequate mechanisms for credit, marketing, and technical assistance. Among external donors, the International Monetary Fund and the World Bank are the best placed and equipped to provide advice on such "structural adjustment" matters. Their advice, however, should be sensitive to local conditions and place priority on employment creation.

The Central American Common Market has been suffering from the declining economic fortunes of each of its members. Husbanding scarce foreign exchange, governments have raised restrictions on trade from neighboring states. The wars have also made transport more difficult. As a result, intra-regional trade has declined from $1.13 billion in 1980 to $775 million in 1983. For the Common Market to be revived, these new trade restrictions would have to be lifted. At the same time, the problems accumulated during the CACM's two previous decades must be addressed. For industry to be more efficient and labor-absorbing, some tariffs must be selectively reduced and the winds of international competition allowed to enter through gradually widening cracks. To save foreign exchange, new firms should be created that can use raw materials produced in the region, and that can sell at least a portion of their production locally — be it agricultural implements to farmers, construction materials to builders, or clothes and radios to consumers. To achieve a more equal balance among countries, some industries should be reserved for the weaker states — particularly Honduras — and funds set aside for their development. Finally, greater emphasis should be given to agriculture and to basic grain production. An inspiring target could be the reattainment of regional self-sufficiency in basic foodstuffs.

There is no obvious economic reason why the Central American Common Market could not encompass member states with heterogeneous political systems. Democratic Costa Rica has cooperated with its more authoritarian neighbors. Nicaragua today presents the more complicated case of a partially planned economy, but state-run systems — Yugoslavia, Hungary, Algeria, Saudi Arabia — trade extensively with market-oriented economies. Trade has, in fact, continued between Nicaragua and its neighbors, and its decline has been due more to falling incomes than politics. If political uncertainties preclude full Nicaraguan participation in a revitalized CACM in the near term, Nicaragua might accept an interim, associated status, or sign a series of bilateral treaties as Honduras did in the 1970s.[26]

The industrialization of the 1960s and 1970s occurred alongside an unreformed agricultural sector in most countries. The failure to reform land ownership patterns was an important cause of the skewed distribution of income resulting from economic growth. Indeed, unless assets are redistributed, the existence of a labor surplus and weak unions are likely to keep income distribution highly unequal. While obviously controversial, agrarian reform is probably essential not only to achieve more equitable growth, but also to attain long term political stability. Raising rural incomes would have the added benefit of widening the market for industrial producers. In Nicaragua and El Salvador, it is a matter of consolidating agrarian reform programs already initiated. In Honduras, the agrarian reform begun in the early 1970s should be revived. But a major shift in political power and attitudes will be necessary if Guatemala is to redistribute its fertile lands. Only in relatively egalitarian

Costa Rica is agrarian reform not high on the agenda.

An export-oriented strategy can be married to a Common Market, as it has been in Western Europe. The CACM can be thought of as a protected environment for industry which is passing through growing pains but which then ventures into world markets. Some firms can sell to both regional and world markets, perhaps by selling locally at average cost, and penetrating more competitive foreign markets at the lower marginal cost of production. However, as tariff barriers are selectively lowered to increase efficiency, some CACM-oriented firms will either become more competitive or go bankrupt.

The final balance between export-oriented and CACM industry will depend upon several factors, including the dynamism and openness of world markets, the ability of leaders to overcome national jealousies, and the attitudes of external donors.

POLITICAL CHANGE AND ECONOMIC DEVELOPMENT

Before coming to grips with our initial query — whether the United States should contemplate a Marshall Plan for Central America — let us first examine whether Central America needs to alter its political model in order to achieve economic development. Clearly, political stability is a prerequisite for sustained economic growth.[27] Beyond that, it is difficult to demonstrate strict causality between economic development paths and politics. Economic growth has occurred in the presence of a wide assortment of political institutions. While democracy is consistent with growth (the United States, Barbados, Australia), so is rightist authoritarianism (Brazil from 1968-78, South Korea, Taiwan) and socialism (the German Democratic Republic, Hungary, Romania). Conversely, economies have failed under democracy (Uruguay), authoritarianism (Zaire), and socialism (Czechoslovakia).

Democracy certainly has a better chance to survive amidst sustained economic growth. Pressure groups will compromise more readily when each can claim a slice of a growing pie, while conflict can mount when groups are struggling to preserve existing living standards against austerity measures. The fate of Uruguay — once thought of as the "Switzerland" of Latin America — suggests that Costa Rican democracy could be endangered by an extended economic contraction.

Similarly, gross inequalities in income and political participation are likely to raise doubts about a government's fairness and legitimacy. The converse, however, does not hold. As the examples of Taiwan and South Korea suggest, a relatively equitable distribution of income does not guarantee the emergence of democratic political sentiments or institutions.

Overall, it seems that economic growth, equity, and broadened political participation make democracy more likely. Not surprisingly, the two countries in Central America which have escaped political violence—Costa Rica and Panama—have the highest and most equitable standards of living, the best social policies (health, education, welfare), and the freest channels for political and labor union participation.

Political attitudes and participation are also important independent variables. If dominant political values are more authoritarian, or if a nation feels threatened by its neighbors, growth and equity need not lead to liberalization. In Guatemala and El Salvador, and to a lesser degree in Honduras, the old ruling elites of landlords and military—merging or allying with sectors of the business community—retain paternalistic, anti-democratic attitudes. Many of them fear participatory political processes. These attitudes have not, however, been a barrier to economic growth. Their "oligarchical" political behavior does not prevent them from being responsive to price incentives. Some of their farms are highly competitive and integrated into the world market. Thus, their presence is not inconsistent with economic growth—in the short to medium run. The problem is that their authoritarian attitudes have proven to be politically destabilizing, and thereby to eventually compromise sustained economic development. Whereas a lessening of their power—for example, through profound agrarian reform—is almost certainly a precondition for the emergence of democracy, it may also be necessary if another round of political upheaval is to be avoided.

In summary, economic growth can neither guarantee political stability nor democracy. Sustained growth with equity can only make these political objectives more easily attainable. Reforms of socio-economic structures (such as land tenure patterns) may also be necessary to shift power away from anti-democratic groups, and to permit more popular political participation and a more equitable distribution of the fruits of growth. Even then, political institutions, attitudes, and processes that foster change remain essential to ensure peace, progress, and social betterment.

A CARIBBEAN BASIN COMPACT

Recovery and sustainable economic growth in Central America require as a first step changes in the attitudes and policies of the governments in the region. But it is equally clear that these nations cannot solve their economic problems alone. Since the turn of the century, the United States has been the most significant international actor in Central America's affairs. Given this reality, should the U.S. consider a new Marshall Plan? Could Central America make good use of a massive new financial commitment? And if so, how should it be structured?

The original Marshall Plan had several motivations: stabilizing governments under challenge from the left, providing humanitarian assistance to a war-weary population, and strengthening prospective trading partners. The Marshall Plan was in effect only four years. European reconstruction was rapid, and the global economic expansion provided a buoyant environment for continued European growth. The differences between post-war, industrialized Europe and war-torn, agrarian Central America are vast, but that does not mean that the concept of a massive commitment of assistance by the U.S. is irrelevant to the needs of contemporary Central America. On the contrary, there are three crucial similarities between the two cases which make the idea plausible. First, the U.S. has important interests in helping the countries resolve their bilateral and economic problems. Second, Central America has already demonstrated impressive economic progress, and a substantital infusion of aid under the right conditions could help the countries recover and stimulate further development. Third and most important, the Central American Common Market established in 1960 remains the most effective instrument of economic integration in the developing world, and is an excellent point of departure for a large commitment to development.

For a plan to work, however, it needs to take into account the region's unique qualities. All the nations are small, open, and vulnerable to outside influence, whether favorable or malign. A long-term development strategy should aim to promote regional economic integration and political accommodation; it should aim to balance, on the one hand, short-term payments support (Economic Support Fund monies) and long-term development assistance, and on the other hand, to combine trade concessions with aid. Finally, the plan should aim to promote self-sustaining growth with equity, not persistent dependence.

These objectives cannot be achieved with a massive bilateral aid program – a new Alliance for Progress in which the U.S. alone sets the conditions and doles out balance-of-payments support. Whether the conditions which the U.S. demands are human rights or anti-Communism – or more likely both – the approach risks exacerbating political divisions within and between nations, promoting greater dependence of the region on the U.S., and wasting a good deal of money.

Before describing an alternative vision, let us address three specific problems related to a massive aid program: the question of absorptive capacity; the distorting impact of large aid flows; and the problem of dominance. First, unlike Europe, which had a ready supply of skilled manpower, Central America lacks sufficient managers and skilled technicians to absorb large quantities of funds efficiently.

Second, massive capital inflows can have a distorting effect on the recipient economy. Interest rates and other incentives to encourage domestic savings may be depressed. Governments may feel no need to increase taxation and to reform their fiscal structures. The exchange rate may become overvalued, thus discouraging producers from exporting, while imports overwhelm domestic production. In short, the recipient country is in danger of becoming dependent upon an external life-support mechanism.

A third danger of very large aid flows to very small economies is that foreign governments are inclined to dictate rather than listen. The AID director can become more important than the local finance minister. Local nationals may lose the will to take initiatives, while at the same time becoming resentful of foreign manipulation.

The risk of Central American economies and societies being overwhelmed by a massive U.S. aid program is illustrated by Table 9.3, which compares the impact of the original Marshall Plan with a hypothetical aid program for Central America. The first Marshall Plan provided Western Europe with $13.3 billion over a four-year period (1948-52). Let us suppose that the U.S. authorizes a $10 billion aid program for Central America over a five-year period. In terms of the U.S. economy, the first Marshall Plan was much more onerous, accounting for over 1% of GNP, whereas an annual $2 billion program today would equal less than one-tenth of one percent of current GNP. But the impact on Central America would be many times greater than it was on Western Europe. Whereas U.S. aid equaled about 3% of post-War Europe's GNP, an aid program today of $2 billion would equal nearly 10% of Central America's GNP.

Table 9.3. A Comparison of Marshall Plans

	European Recovery Plan	Hypothetical Central American Plan
U.S. aid/U.S. GNP	1.2%	0.07%
U.S. aid/Recipient GNP	2.9%	9.6%

Sources: U.S. Department of Commerce; Inter-American Development Bank; and the European Economic Community.

There are, however, ways to lessen the potentially adverse effects of such a massive injection of foreign capital into Central America. First, multilateral mechanisms can replace irritating bilateralism. Second, carefully crafted and supervised development plans can check tendencies to avoid adopting painful but necessary economic reforms. Third, development strategies can aim to put donors out of business by enhancing the region's ability to generate its own resources and meet its own needs.

A page from the original Marshall Plan can be lifted in developing a mechanism to channel the new aid flows while reducing dependence and promoting integration. While the capital would be American, Secretary of State

George Marshall wanted the recovery program to be a product of united European efforts. In his famous 1947 address outlining his proposal, Marshall called on Europe to pull itself together, with the assistance—but not the direction—of the United States.[28]

Central American governments have already made initial efforts at working together to design plans for economic recovery.[29] Moreover, regional institutions of the Central American Common Market framework have been in existence for two decades. With enhanced manpower and resources, they could coordinate the development of proposals and assist in their implementation through such organizations as the Secretariat of Economic Integration of Central America, the Central American Bank for Economic Integration which finances development programs, and the Central American Monetary Council which coordinates activities among the region's central banks. To the extent that the five Central American states unify their efforts, they increase their bargaining power with external donors and strengthen regional integration institutions and processes.

Multilateralism at the recipient end could be matched by multilateralism at the donor end. The United States could join with other states—including Mexico, Venezuela, Colombia, Canada, Japan, and the Western European countries—as well as with the multilateral agencies to form a donor consortium. (The Inter-American Development Bank has already taken steps in this direction but some potential donors remain reluctant to become more heavily involved in the current Central American situation.) Venezuela and Mexico have already been providing Central America with some $200 million of annual support through their program of subsidized petroleum sales. With many donors facing many recipients, a process would be created that avoided the pitfalls of a purely bilateral arrangement between a single, powerful donor and a very weak, isolated recipient. A similar mechanism, the Caribbean Group for Cooperation and Economic Development, was created in 1978 for the insular Caribbean, and has functioned with great success.

The United States could work with other donors, especially the international development banks, and with the Central American governments to develop a comprehensive plan or plans for the reconstruction and development of the region. The first draft should come from the region itself. The plan submitted by the Central American finance ministers in Brussels in September 1983, requesting $23 billion over 10 years, could serve such a purpose.[30] The plans should be reviewed each year, with a comprehensive reassessment after five years. Once a plan was approved by all parties, both donors and borrowers would have to modify their individual preferences accordingly. A substantial portion of all donor monies would pass through Central American regional institutions, and bilateral programs would also conform to the consensual guidelines. Genuinely participatory and multilateral, such mechanisms would bring conceptualization, purpose, and coordination to the aid effort.

Ideally, the new aid mechanisms for Central America should be linked to the existing Caribbean Group. The Caribbean Basin Initiative set an important precedent in extending trade preferences to both the isthmus and the islands. Although there are substantial cultural and political differences between the two areas, their small, open economies suffer from similar problems. From the U.S. strategic and economic perspectives, it makes sense to develop a coherent economic policy for both regions, recognizing that such a policy needs to be adapted to the uniqueness of each region and nation. Moreover, it will be easier to maintain Congressional interest in both area if the aid packages are related. From the region's perspective, it also makes sense to break down the barriers that have long separated Central America from the Caribbean and both from Venezuela and Mexico. In the long run, the task is to transform what is by nature a geographic unity into a genuine community of nations.

While there is a need to establish an overarching coordinating mechanism, one should be wary about creating new regional institutions. There are probably more regional institutions in Central America and the Caribbean per capita than anywhere else in the world. In the Caribbean alone, there are at least eleven major regional organizations.[31] A study is needed on whether it is possible to consolidate several of these organizations, which ones ought to be enlarged, and which ones pruned.

Economic aid should be supportive of development strategies that can increasingly become either self-financing or attractive to private capital. Given the smallness of the markets of even an integrated Central America, the region's agriculture and industry will depend heavily on access to external markets. Significant if imperfect access to the world's largest single market — the United States — is already envisioned in the Caribbean Basin Initiative. Central America can potentially benefit from a combined, self-reinforcing package of aid and trade. With the return of political stability in Central America and economic recovery in the U.S., the Caribbean Basin Initiative, which provides duty-free entry for many products from Central America and the Caribbean states, could facilitate investment and export growth. However, the United States ought to consider expanding the coverage of the CBI to include key products like footwear, luggage, handbags, and other labor-intensive items. In addition, the U.S. ought to encourage recipient nations to use the CBI in a way which multiplies its benefits to the local economy.[32] Furthermore, the U.S. should consider granting expanded market access to Central American producers as a group for commodities such as sugar, coffee, beef and textiles that are governed by special trading arrangements (such as quotas).

This process of trade liberalization might occur as part of broader, multilateral trade negotiations. If other countries would extend similar trade concessions, multilateralism in aid could be matched by multilateralism in trade. In particular, Mexico, Colombia, and Venezuela could open their markets to the products of their less developed neighbors. At the current time, there is little non-petroleum trade between the middle powers and the nations of Central America and the Caribbean. For their part, the nations of Central America and the Caribbean would be expected to grant some reciprocal trade concessions.

Initially, the region will need official assistance to take full advantage of the potential offered by external markets. Donors can assist in locating specific markets, and in motivating private firms to invest. Foreign investors, in addition to offering capital, technology, and quality control, can provide access to their home and third-country markets. The U.S. Overseas Private Investment Corporation (OPIC) or other guarantee mechanisms, including new multilateral or regional ones, could help reduce risk. External development agencies can also contribute by reconstructing and improving the transportation, communications and energy infrastructures that are prerequisites for productive investment and trade.

Donors can also concentrate on manpower training programs. There is an urgent need to upgrade the skills of labor and management, if they are to be profitably married to new capital. Moreover, many highly qualified Central American technicians have fled the region, but would return if their security could be assured and if they felt they could contribute to the region's development. Many have had considerable experience with the international development banks, and perhaps could provide the necessary local counterpart management to supervise and expedite additional development projects.[33]

The region's development architects should search for a balance between the two strategies of import-substitution and export promotion. For their part, aid agencies can strengthen regionalism in many ways: by providing credit to the Central American Bank for Economic Integration (CABEI) for on-lending; by fostering the collection and dissemination on a regional basis of economic statistics; by assisting agricultural programs with a regionwide focus covering sanitation, seeds, storage, and marketing; and by financing firms that will sell to two or more Central American states. In 1978, CABEI identified development projects then valued at $8.7 billion, for the five Central American nations over the next decade.[34]

Perhaps most importantly, as the original Marshall Plan demonstrated by requiring the various states to work together to design and implement economic recovery programs, external donors can assist farsighted leadership to contain the centrifugal forces of narrow nationalism for the benefit of the whole. By doing so, the donors can both promote economic development and political accommodation.

A well-planned economic development strategy can foster the integration of nations as well as of contending social forces within nations. Aid programs that finance agrarian reform, assist in designing more efficient and progressive tax structures, and that extend health services to rural areas, can enhance the legitimacy of political systems. Moreover, in the event that Central American nations succeed in negotiating mutual security pacts, economic aid can help bind agreements. The United States, collaborating with other nations, can use the aid to ensure that governments live up to diplomatic accords that foster peace between nations. Such aid would serve a double purpose, since if Central America is to concentrate on economic development, it must find peace. The original Marshall Plan, it is worth recalling, was implemented *after* the war.

To avoid waste and disillusionment, this economic compact for the entire Caribbean Basin should not start until the shooting stops; it cannot succeed unless all six nations of Central America participate, and it should not begin unless it also includes (a) all the Caribbean nations (except Cuba) as recipients; (b) all the appropriate international development banks and interested donors; and (c) agreement that the recipients in the region should draw up regional plans for discussion *and approval by all parties* on how the funds should be allocated—how much to regional projects, how much to each country, how much for development projects, and how much for balance-of-payments support.

Unfortunately, the immediate prospect for Central America is more war. Rather than encouraging unity and the resolution of differences between Central American nations, U.S. policy seems aimed at exacerbating differences and dividing Nicaragua from the rest of Central America. Not surprisingly, the AID presentation to the Kissinger Commission omitted Nicaragua as a Central American nation. Such a strategy delays the time when a proposal along the lines of this chapter could begin. At the current time, regional economic growth and integration appear to be at the very bottom of the U.S. agenda. However, the nations of Central America cannot make it alone or apart from one another. If the U.S. were to turn its agenda upside-down, an economic compact for the entire Caribbean Basin becomes possible. An economic plan could itself contribute to making peace if the U.S. were willing to treat Central America as a region. Until it does, or until the shooting stops, talk about Marshall Plans is nothing more than an expensive diversion from a crisis that will continue to worsen.

From 1960 to 1978, Central America made impressive economic progress, and it can do so again with peace, a good economic program, and substantial external assistance. A future for Central America of economic growth with equity is far from hopeless.

NOTES

For their very helpful comments on earlier drafts of this chapter, we would like to thank Lora Berg, John Lewis, Richard Newfarmer, Paul Meo, John Sewell, Jorge Sol, John Weeks and Jody Williams.

1. For a brief survey of the history of the Marshall Plan concept as a diversion from failing policies, and also for a discussion of the Plan's relevance to the Caribbean Basin today, see Robert A. Pastor and Richard E. Feinberg, "Latin America and the Marshall Plan Reflex," *Vital Issues* (Washington, Connecticut: Center for Information on America, forthcoming, 1984).

2. Data in this essay are drawn from publications of the International Monetary Fund, the World Bank, the Inter-American Development Bank, the Organization of American States, the UN Commission on Latin America, and the U.S. Agency for International Development.

3. Department of Commerce, *Survey of Current Business* (Washington, D.C.), August, 1982. See also John F. H. Purcell, "Perceptions and Interests of U.S. Business in Relation to the Political Crisis in Central America," in Richard E. Feinberg (ed.), *Dimensions of the Crisis* (New York: Holmes and Meier, 1982), pp. 103-123.

4. For a good summary and assessment of the common market, see William R. Cline and Enrique Delgado (eds.), *Economic Integration in Central America* (Washington, D.C.: Brookings Institution, 1978). For another excellent analysis of the Central American economy, see Clark Reynolds, "Fissures in the Volcano?: Central American Economic Prospects," in Joseph Grunwald (ed.), *Latin America and World Economy: A Changing International Order*, (Beverly Hills, California: Sage, 1978), pp. 195-222.

5. World Bank, *World Development Report*, 1981, Tables 22 and 23.

6. World Bank, *Economic Memorandum on El Salvador*, Rept. No. 2287-ES, May 7, 1979, p. i. For an analysis of the implications of demographic revolution in the region, see Robert Pastor, "Migration in the Caribbean Basin: The Need for an Approach as Dynamic as the Phenomenon," in Mary Kritz (ed.), *U.S. Immigration and Refugee Policy: Global and Domestic Issues* (Lexington, Mass.: Lexington Books, 1983), pp. 95-112; Inter-American Development Bank, *Report on Demographic Trends and Projections for Central America* (Washington, D.C., July 1977); and Robert W. Fox and Jerrold W. Huguet, *Population and Urban Trends in Central America and Panama* (Washington, D.C.: Inter-American Development Bank, 1977).

7. John Weeks, *The Economies of Central America* (New York: Holmes and Meier), forthcoming.

8. A report written by the Bureau of Intelligence and Research of the Department of State evaluated ten regional economic integration schemes and concluded that the two best — in the report's phrase, the only ones which "have been unambiguously effective in integrating export-import markets" — were the Caribbean Community and the Central American Common Market. Department of State, *Evaluating Regional Schemes for the Promotion of Inter-LDC Trade*, Report No. 1362 (Washington, D.C., April 14, 1980). For an alternative assessment, but one which also gives high marks to the CACM, see Joseph S. Nye, Jr., *Peace in Parts: Integration and Conflict in Regional Organization* (Boston, Mass.: Little, Brown and Company, 1971), chap. 3.

9. William R. Cline and Enrique Delgado, *op. cit.*; Roger Hansen, *Central America: Regional Integration and Economic Development* (Washington, D.C.: National Planning Association, 1967); and Susanne Jonas, "Masterminding the Mini-Market: U.S. Aid to the Central American Common Market," *NACLA Empire Report*, Vol. 7, No. 5, May-June, 1973, pp. 3-21.

10. On income distribution trends, see Clark W. Reynolds, "Fissures in the Volcano?: Central American Economic Prospects," in Joseph Grunwald (ed.), *op. cit.,*; and United Nations Economic Commission for Latin America, *La Crisis en Centroamerica: Origines, Alcances y Consecuencias,* May 27, 1983, mimeograph.

11. United Nations Economic Commission for Latin America, *Central America: Nature of the Present Economic Crisis, the Challenges it Raises and the International Cooperation for Which it Calls,* E/CEPAL/CCE/402/Rev. 1, 26 August 1981, p. 2.

12. U.S. Department of Agriculture, *Agricultural Situation: Western Hemisphere, Review of 1980 and Outlook for 1981,* June 1981, p. 57; "Agricultural Development and the Caribbean Basin," statement of Robert Pastor before Joint Hearings of the Subcommittee on Department Operations, Research, and Foreign Agriculture, House Committee on Agriculture, and the Subcommittee on Inter-American Affairs, House Foreign Affairs Committee, July 20, 1982, pp. 75-106.

13. Gabriel Siri and Luís Raúl Dominguez, "Central American Accommodation to External Disruptions," in William R. Cline and Associates, *World Inflation and the Developing Countries* (Washington, D.C.: Brookings Institution, 1981), pp. 166-207.

14. For a survey of the causes of the Central American crisis and its implications for the United States, see Richard E. Feinberg, "Central America: No Easy Answers," *Foreign Affairs,* Vol. 59, No. 6, Summer 1981; and Robert A. Pastor, "Our Real National Interests in Central America," *The Atlantic Monthly,* Vol. 250, No. 1, Summer 1982.

15. This section on Costa Rica draws from Richard E. Feinberg, "Costa Rica: The End of the Fiesta," in Richard Newfarmer (ed.), *From Gunboats to Diplomacy* (Johns Hopkins University Press, forthcoming).

16. For a classic statement on the origins of revolution, see Crane Brinton, *The Anatomy of Revolution* (Englewood Cliffs, N.J., 1938); for a more recent assessment, see Chalmers Johnson, *Revolutionary Change* (Stanford: Stanford University Press, 1982).

17. Richard Newfarmer, "The Economic Problems of Central America," in Morris Blachman, William Leo Grande and Kenneth Sharpe (eds.), *U.S. Foreign Policy and the Crisis in Central America,* forthcoming.

18. Ricard J. Meislin, "Economic Losses High in Salvador," *New York Times,* December 5, 1982, p. 19. The $1 billion estimate was made by a World Bank economist, according to Joanne Omang, "Experts Fault Any Plan for New Latin Aid," *Washington Post,* December 12, 1983, pp. A1, A23-A24. Nicaraguan Ambassador to the U.S. Antonio Jarquín, address to the University of Maryland, College Park, November 29, 1983.

19. Telephone interviews with the World Bank, Commodities Division, October 11 and 12, 1983.

20. Calculation based on material in *Regional Report for Central America,* prepared jointly by Costa Rica, El Salvador, Guatemala, Honduras, and Nicaragua for presentation to the international financial community, September 1983, unpublished, tables 1.8 and 2.7.

21. Remarks at the 1981 annual meetings of the World Bank and the IMF, press release no. 3, September 29, 1981.

22. See Overseas Development Council, "Global Recovery: The Contribution of the Developing Countries," statement of the Overseas Development Council for the Williamsburg Summit, May 1983.

23. Statement of the spokesman for Central America, Mr. Carlos Manuel Castillo, at the special meeting in Brussels, with the international financial community, September 8, 1983, p. 4. Marlise Simons, "Central American Nations Refuse to Join U.S. Boycott of Nicaragua," *New York Times,* September 26, 1983, p. A10.

24. Agency for International Development, "A Strategy for the Recovery of Central America," presentation of M. Peter McPherson, Administrator, Agency for International Development, to the National Bipartisan Commission on Central America, October 6, 1983.

According to AID, of the total $11 billion in gross public capital inflows, the U.S. would provide half, or $5.7 billion, while other governments and the multilateral development banks would cover the remainder. The U.S. share would be divided between $4.4 billion in balance-of-payments support and $1.3 billion in development or project loans. In addition, AID proposed that the U.S. contribute a further $2 billion during the two years following completion of the five-year plan. For an earlier, alternative estimate, see Francisco Mayorga, "Crecimiento y requerimientos financieros para el desarrollo en Centroamerica," in Donald Castillo Rivas, (ed.), *Centroamerica: Más All de la Crisis* (Mexico City: Sociedad Interamericana de Planificacion, 1983), pp. 225-259. Mayorga found that to sustain an average growth rate of 4.5% to 5% during the 1980s, Central America would require between $31.4 and $41 billion, or roughly $3.6 billion a year in balance-of-payments support.

25. U.N. Economic Commission for Latin America, *Central America, op. cit.*, p. 9.
26. For excellent article outlining a series of steps for a transitional plan for revitalizing the CACM, see Eduardo Lizano, "El Mercado Común Centroamericano en una época de turbulencia," *El Trimestre Económico*, Vol. 50, No. 199, July-September 1983, pp. 1475-1506.
27. Charles Wolf, Jr., "Economic Success, Stability and the 'Old' International Order," *International Security*, Vol. 6, No. 1, Summer 1981, pp. 75-92.
28. *Documents on American Foreign Relations*, Vol. 9, 1947, p. 11.
29. For example, see *Regional Report for Central America, op. cit.*
30. Joanne Omang, *op. cit.*
31. For a description of a number of these organizations and an assessment of the current state of integration in both the Central American Common Market and the Caribbean Community, see Institute for Latin American Integration (INTAL), Inter-American Development Bank, *The Latin American Integration Process in 1979* (Buenos Aires, 1980), pp. 181-252. Also, Caribbean/Central American Action, *Caribbean Databook* (Washington, D.C. 1983), pp. 287-292.
32. For a detailed series of recommendations, see Robert Pastor, "Sinking in the Caribbean Basin," *Foreign Affairs*, Vol. 60, No. 5, Summer 1982, and an updating in Pastor's testimony before the Senate Finance Committee, Hearings on the Caribbean Basin Initiative, April 13, 1983.
33. A similar proposal for the Caribbean is developed in Robert Pastor and Rosemarie Rogers, "The Impact of Migration on Development In the Caribbean: An Analysis and a Proposal," paper delivered at the American Political Science Association Convention, Chicago, September 4, 1983.
34. INTAL, IDB, *The Latin American Integration Process in 1979, op. cit.*, pp. 216-219.

10
FEET PEOPLE

Leonel Gomez

The Reagan administration fears that communist takeovers in El Salvador and neighboring countries will send hundreds of thousands of Central American "feet people" to U.S. shores, creating a tremendous strain on the economy and society in general. At a Mississippi fund-raising dinner last summer, President Reagan warned that a halt to military assistance to Central American nations friendly to the United States could result in "a tidal wave of refugees — and this time they'll be 'feet people' and not boat people — swarming into our country seeking a safe haven from communist repression to our south."[1]

In a July 1983 debate in the House of Representatives, Rep. Mark Siljander (R-Mo.) noted the reasons traditionally given for refugee migration: "We have had millions of refugees who have come to this nation because they are seeking freedom and opportunity." But, he continued, those opportunities no longer exist as "our nation is now under a terrrible burden of unemployment, social and economic readjustment. And it is just an issue of how many people this country can absorb and handle, especially with the major influx of the potential of Central America, anywhere from 7 to 12 million."[2] Rep. Thomas Coleman (R-Mo.) was more specific. He predicted continued Nicaraguan and Cuban influence in Central America, which would produce "7 million to 9 million additional people coming to the United States seeking jobs, seeking public assistance payments of $25 billion to $40 billion additional payments from the taxpayers."[3]

The current debate, however, overlooks two points. First, in the past few years as many as a half a million illegal immigrants have already come from El Salvador alone. According to the U.S. Immigration and Naturalization Service (INS), over 69,000 undocumented Salvadorans were apprehended and deported from 1978 to 1982. INS officials also state that for every undocumented alien apprehended in isolated border stations, four to five enter the country undetected, and the ratio is much higher in urban areas. That means between 50,000 to 90,000 Salvadorans have entered the United States during each of the past four years.[4] Second, few facts are available about illegal immigration to the United States, and what analysis there is does not necessarily support arguments that increased immigration will be detrimental to the U.S. economy or society.

Indeed, a recent article in the *Atlantic Monthly* noted the unreliability of the data available:

> In the mid-1970s [the then-Commissioner of the Immigration and Naturalization Service Leonard Chapman, said] that there might be as many as 12 million foreigners here illegally. Official estimates are now 50-75 percent lower than that, but no one can say with confidence how many illegal aliens are here and how many more are coming.[5]

Unofficial figures released by the Census Bureau last October indicate that the number of undocumented aliens ranges between 3.5 and 6 million people. Of this total, the bureau estimates that 50% to 60% are Mexican nationals.[6]

One analysis finds that the benefits of illegal immigration could well balance the costs to the economy. This 1982 study by the Rand Corporation maintains that "most analysts agree that immigrants will have little effect on the overall national economy."

> For example, immigrants may place added stress on housing and labor markets and require social services. However, most immigrants (even most illegal residents) pay federal income and Social Security taxes, and few illegals are likely to apply for welfare or Social Security benefits. To some extent, immigrants compete with native labor, but the less-skilled entrants from Asia and the Caribbean basin are certainly not competing for high-paying jobs. And in some cases their cheap labor may be all that is keeping some industries from going out of business or moving overseas.[7]

The study also reported that the U.S. military was studying the possibility of recruiting immigrants in order to make up for the expected shortage of enlistment-age U.S. citizens by 1990.[8] The issue of Central American migration, however, is one that will not diappear. The number of Central American refugees coming to this country will undoubtably grow, due to the economic and political realities of the region: the civil war in El Salvador; U.S.-Nicaragua tensions; Nicaragua's involvement in the affairs of neighboring countries; the militarization of Honduras; and the agony of Guatemala.

THE CENTRAL AMERICAN IMMIGRANTS

The records on immigration to the United States from Central America are misleading because they do not count the hundreds of thousands of illegal immigrants who have come to this country in the past four years, nor do they count the small groups of rich Central Americans who reside, with dubious legality, in the United States.[9] Instead, U.S. policymakers have focused their attention on those illegal immigrants who sold all their possessions to pay the steep prices that "coyotes," or illegal transporters, demand to take them into American territory. The presence of these immigrants here is an embarrassment to U.S. foreign policy in Central America. While it is widely acknowledged that their numbers are large, little else is known about them.

To form an idea of whom these people are, one must consider the conditions in El Salvador that compelled them to leave their country. Most of the illegal Salvadoran population likely came from the larger cities; many were factory workers; and a good number probably belonged to the unions affiliated with Frente Democratic Revolucionario (the Revolutionary Democratic Front-FDR), which formed a coalition with the guerrillas of the Farabundo Martí Liberation Front. One infers then, that they are skilled or semi-skilled workers with a certain degree of sophistication, political awareness and commitment.

Since the failure of the land reform program has been one of the topics on El Salvador highlighted in the U.S. press, it is reasonable to ask whether many of the illegal immigrants were *campesinos*, displaced by military and security forces and the large landowners. Although some immigrants are *campesinos*, most of the displaced *campesinos* have probably remained inside El Salvador or have immigrated to neighboring countries — not to the United States. For the majority of people from the countryside the United States is an impossibly long and costly journey — emotionally and financially — a great number of whom have never traveled much beyond their immediate town or village. Even the capital city, San Salvador, is foreign soil to these Salvadorans; the United States is another universe.

Another reason why Salvadoran peasants are loathe to emigrate is that in the countryside, a person who owns or manages land can at least provide himself and his family and a number of others with a meager living. Despite the failures of the land reform program, an extended family and tight *compadrazco* system enables many rural dwellers to share the meager subsistence extracted from the land of a few.[10] More important, perhaps, a person living in certain areas of the countryside, where there is little or no perceived guerrilla activity, has less reason than a city dweller to fear direct repression.

First, *campesinos* have never been allowed by law to unionize, so their organizations, even when called "unions," are actually local cooperatives. Since these peasants are not well organized to exert strong and consistent political pressure on either the economic elite or the military, the *campesinos* are largely ignored by the military and security forces. However, when cooperative leaders have begun to emerge as local leaders, they have been killed.

Second, in areas which guerrillas do not hold, but pass through, the repression by the army and security forces has not been as selective as in urban areas. In three years of fighting, some 5,000 to 6,000 guerrillas have moved in large units freely around the countryside in broad daylight. There are some 500,000 supporters who care for the wounded, hide their ammunition, transport their arms, give them information on the army, and perform a variety of other tasks. The military and its U.S. advisers have not effectively broken this network, partly because they do not have the extensive system of informers to single out perceived guerrilla sympathizers, which exists in most the urban areas. Thus, a *campesino* has less reason to fear individual retribution. (Those who have been singled out in rural areas are priests and nuns, mayors, agrarian reform technicians, and organizers, seen by the military as fomenting discontent and opposition.) Notwithstanding, once an area has been perceived, with or without foundation, as sympathetic to the guerrillas, the military moves in, massacring large numbers of people.

In the cities, however, the situation is quite different. There are thousands of people readily identifiable as guerrilla sympathizers and are considered a serious threat to the traditional economic order. These are the members of the 12 groups of the FDR. Formed in April 1980, the FDR includes several university and professional groups, and 49 industrial labor unions. These individuals are in constant danger because lists of union members in each factory are supplied to the Ministry of Labor, then passed on to the Salvadoran Intelligence Service, and later to the "death squads." The latter have systematically killed some 37,000 since 1980, many of them members of these unions, who did not go underground to fight.[11] These then are the people who have compelling reasons to leave El Salvador: they are easily identifiable and they and their families may be marked for death.

CAUSES OF IMMIGRATION

A general perception in the U.S. is that the main cause of immigration is poverty. In this type of analysis, the only political event that would provoke an influx of millions of "feet people" is a communist takeover of additional countries in the region, beginning with El Salvador. However, according to Dale Frederick Swartz, President of the National Immigration,

Refugee and Citizenship Forum, poverty, unemployment and underdevelopment do not, in themselves, result in immigration, particularly to the U.S.[12] Why then is it widely believed that poverty and unemployment are the primary reasons for migration?

In the case of El Salvador, there are three reasons why migration is considered to be economically motivated. The first is because that is the explanation Salvadorans themselves have given, the other two stem from U.S. perceptions.

At times, dire poverty in El Salvador is cited by Salvadorans who have immigrated illegally to the U.S. as their primary reason for coming. Some have made statements to the American press that they came looking for a way to earn a better living. Americans regard the Salvadoran refugee problem in the same context as past immigration waves. Yet, one must more closely examine the situation in El Salvador, and the conditions of the immigrants in the U.S. before such statements are blithely accepted as fact. An illegal immigrant in the United States lives in constant danger of being deported to El Salvador. He fully realizes that by drawing the attention of the U.S. authorities, if they knew his political beliefs were at odds with U.S. foreign policy in El Salvador, he could face deportation and subsequent death in El Salvador.

With respect to the perceptions of U.S. policymakers, there are two reasons for not viewing the current influx of Salvadoran refugees as politically motivated. First, in acknowledging the political nature of the immigration problem the U.S. government would have to take responsibility for those who come — providing them political asylum, welfare payments to tide them over while they look for jobs, and a niche in American society. That eventuality is precisely the reason policymakers fear an exodus of "feet people" from El Salvador to the United States if leftists take power. In that case, policymakers would be both politically and morally pressured to provide those benefits.

The second reason for not viewing the current influx of Salvadoran refugees as politically motivated is the implications that admission would have for U.S. foreign policy. Recognizing that Salvadorans have left their own country because their lives are in danger would require the U.S. government to revise drastically Central American policy and to concede that its policy is misdirected.

An examination of Salvadoran history provides neither evidence of substantial economically-motivated immigration, nor reason to believe that El Salvador is currently producing economic refugees. El Salvador is the smallest Central American country and, with 5 million inhabitants, it has one of the world's highest population densities — some 600 persons per square mile. Population is increasing rapidly, at a rate (3.7% per year) which will double the current population in 20 years. As can be expected, many

Salvadorans have gone abroad to look for work; most to neighboring countries. Although there are no reliable figures on recent levels of this migration out of El Salvador, Thomas P. Anderson, a leading U.S. scholar on El Salvador, has written that the 1969 war between El Salvador and Honduras forced 130,000 Salvadoran immigrants living in Honduras to return to their country.[13] So, demographic and economic conditions can result in a significant emigration.

Today, the number of Salvadoran immigrants appears many times greater than in the past. An estimated 500,000 Salvadorans have emigrated to the United States, according to figures of the U.S. volunteer organizations. Mexican government officials believe that some 150,000 Salvadorans have lived in their country legally since the beginning of 1982. Refugee officials in Costa Rica estimate that of the 20,000 to 25,000 refugees who have been given legal status in Costa Rica, 15,000 to 20,000 are Salvadorans.[14] In addition, some 300,000 Salvadorans are counted as displaced persons within their own country.

Even more than the increase in numbers, the fact that Salvadorans are traveling further from their homeland is an indication that conditions have changed. According to Swartz, most of the Salvadoran immigration to the United States has come during the past three years—that is, under the Reagan administration—and the flow is four to five times greater than in previous periods.[15] This unprecedented mobility, both in numbers and distance, must have other causes than population and economic conditions in El Salvador and opportunities in the United States. After all, if Salvadorans, living in what some have called "America's backyard," had found the United States an attractive place to live, many more would have immigrated years ago. Today Salvadorans do not, for the most part, migrate to Honduras or Guatemala, because they can expect to find the same kind of repression that they were seeking to flee in El Salvador. Most refugees avoid Nicaragua, fearing that an escalation of attacks by anti-Sandinista insurgents or a possible intervention by other Central American armies backed by the United States would place them in a combat zone.

The causes for the recent massive migration from El Salvador to the U.S. began in the 1970s as popular pressures against the military government mounted. In the capital, thousands of citizens took to the streets, demanding reform. Marches were organized by centrist organizations and organizations which later became part of the FMLN/FDR. Expectations were high for a few weeks after the reformist coup of October 1979, but plummeted again after the many "countercoups" in its wake.

Since 1980, terror in El Salvador has escalated, demonstrating that political and economic repression are entwined. The evidence of this dual repression remains the same as in the past—mutilated human corpses, mostly those of people demanding economic reform and social justice, left in public view as a warning and a reminder to others of who is in control. The key word is control, economic and political, not democracy.

Thus, it is incorrect to look at El Salvador and conclude, as the Reagan administration does, that people's main reasons for leaving El Salvador are economic or due to guerrilla violence. When factories close because of strikes, when bridges are blown up, when crops are burned, the consequences are economic—but the underlying cause is political.

Contrary to administration claims, U.S. money is not being used to advance justice or to create institutions to serve the public good. Instead, millions of U.S. tax dollars are at stake for the military and economic leaders that the U.S. is spending to "educate" and "enlighten" the power brokers in El Salvador. To cite Senator Christopher Dodd (D-Conn.): "this money is just going down a rathole."[16]

It is also incorrect to take the viewpoint of some of those opposed to the Reagan administration's politics who argue that the sole reason for the exodus from El Salvador is right-wing repression. The left also bears responsibility. The left's violent political culture lead to such actions as the murder of leftist poet Roqué Dalton after he was accused of being a spy for the U.S. Central Intelligence Agency, and of Comandante Ana María, second in command of one of Salvador's four guerrilla groups. These acts alienate many who are sympathetic to the left's causes. Finally, its insistence that its ideology is the only truth makes it difficult for the left to form a broader coalition with those who take a more pragmatic rather than a strictly ideological stance. Such intransigence only heightens the country's disastrous political polarization and prolongs the violence.

While the true popular support of the FMLN/FDR coalition is difficult to measure, given a choice only between the left and the right, most Salvadorans would chose the left, due to its less violent and corrupt history. Still, they wonder how the left would evolve if it came to power—particularly because the left does not have the national unity that the Sandinistas in Nicargua had when Somoza was ousted. Hence it is also difficult to predict whether after a revolutionary triumph in El Salvador, more people would want to leave. But, if the left took power, that mere fact does not necessarily lead to greater immigration—four years of the leftist Sandinista regime in Nicaragua has produced far fewer immigrants than those now fleeing El Salvador. However, given Salvadoran centrists' lack of trust of toward the left, and given the divisions within the left itself, a left-wing government in El Salvador might be more repressive and less flexible than that in Nicaragua. If so, emigration from El Salvador could continue to be high.

A left-wing victory, however, is unlikely. Neither the current U.S. administration nor any succeeding Republican or Democratic administration is likely to permit the FMLN/FDR to take power in El Salvador.

The solution from the standpoint of the welfare of Central American countries—a solution which in the long run would reduce reasons for migration—would be negotiated settlements to the conflicts in Central America, particularly in El Salvador and Nicaragua. Regional negotiations must take place between the United States and Cuba, the Salvadoran government and the FMLN/FDR, the Nicaraguan government and at least one group of armed dissidents (namely the force led by Eden Pastora), and between Honduras and Nicaragua. If not, there is no hope for reconciliation and peace in Central America, let alone democracy or economic growth.

The number of immigrants to the United States and the length of their stay will depend on the political situation in Central America as a whole. In the past three years, Salvadoran reality has become the sum of two factors: reality as El Salvador's five million inhabitants live it and understand it and Salvadoran reality "made in the U.S.A." As long as the situation there is defined by the Reagan administration as the center of an East-West conflict, Central Americans are likely to continue to come to and stay in the United States. There is little incentive to remain close to home, in a region perhaps destined to be the site of the next U.S. war.

EFFECTS

Listening to the current debate on "feet people" and refugees, one can imagine the North American Indians as they witnessed the first Europeans arrive on the their shores. The Indians may have wondered not only why the immigrants had come but, more important to them, what effect the newcomers and the others that followed would have. In later years, American citizens have feared the effects of each new wave of immigrants on their lifestyle. From 1821 to 1979, the U.S. became the home to 49,107,353 documented immigrants. Today as in the past, the fears of the natives often shape immigration legislation, and the treatment of new arrivals.

The dynamics of recent immigration from Central America are different from the traditional waves of immigration to the U.S.—different both because the U.S. role in the world has shifted and because the United States itself has changed. The American economy is tighter than during previous waves of immigration but the structure of the economy has been modified in ways that more easily accept new immigrants. The political structure has been broadened to include more groups, allowing Central American immigrants to gain a say on national politics in a less time than most previous groups of immigrants.

The continued influx of Central American refugees and these changes in U.S. society affect the domestic situation in the U.S. and U.S. foreign policy, with potential repercussions in Central America.[17]

First, Central American immigrants have begun to arrive in great numbers just as the national political stage is being set — in particular during a presidential election year. Hispanic-American groups in the United States are increasingly influential on the national level. Naturally these new arrivals will work with such groups (rather than wait until the second or third generation, as most other immigrant groups have done) in order to make their views known. There are a variety of Hispanic organizations, some dominated by Mexican-Americans, some by Cuban-Americans. The Mexican-American national organizations generally oppose the Reagan administration's policy in Central America; the Cuban-American national organizations are largely supportive. If Salvadorans continue to immigrate illegally to the United States as an escape from right-wing repression, they will more than likely join other Mexican-American groups lobbying for social welfare benefits for the poor, for generous immigration quotas and legislation, and a foreign policy which views Central and Latin America less in East-West terms than in light of the need for social and economic development.

These immigrants will eventually have to be taken into account by American politicians who are now courting the Hispanic vote. At the very least the new Hispanic consitutency will make the problems of Central and Latin America more visible in the coming years.

There may be long-term economic and social effects too. If, as some say, the U.S. economy cannot absorb many more unskilled or low-skilled workers, the competition for jobs will re-create traditional tensions between the native-born population and the new immigrants. However, for those arguing that the United States can utilize the labor now provided by immigrants, the forecast would be different.

By some accounts, these immigrants will move into jobs that Americans do not take. Many of the Salvadoran immigrants, who apparently settle in major urban areas, have been members of unions and are politically aware. Traditionally one of the first places that immigrants have had an impact in the United States has been at the workplace through unions. These new immigrants may well help to catalyze a revival of unionization in the United States. There is also the potential unionization of illegal immigrants, who — under judicial interpretations now under review by the Supreme Court — may have rights including a minimum wage on the same basis as documented workers. No doubt big business generally is in favor of fines for hiring illegal immigrants under immigration legislation now before the U.S. Congress.

More significant perhaps is that the horror of the struggle in Central America may come home to the United States through terrorism. The frustrations and desperation of many people likely to become refugees will eventually explode as occured in August 1983 when, according to the *Washington Post*, the FMLN took credit for one bomb which caused "minor damage to the outside of a building housing a computer operation at the Washington

(D.C.) Navy Yard."[18] Terrorism could come from guerrillas after a U.S. intervention. Or violence could come from former Salvadoran soldiers, trained in the United States or by U.S. troops in El Salvador and Honduras, who return to their village after serving in the army. Dismayed by the worsening corruption and unable to earn a living, these soldiers could join the guerrillas or alternatively migrate to the United States. Here, they are unlikely to find the welcome that they would feel due to men who have fought a war for "democracy." These alienated people would have the most obvious motives for the type of frustration and blind rage against the United States that would provide the impetus for terrorist attacks. But surely there will be many others. The anger of some Cuban-Americans has found an outlet in the terrorist activities of Omega 7; a left-wing counterpart to that group could, at some point, develop.

The effects of massive immigration from El Salvador on El Salvador itself must also be mentioned, particularly as these effects may be factors in the success or failure of U.S. policy there. U.S. policy toward El Salvador is said to be encouraging reforms behind a "military shield." Yet the continued immigration is draining the population of people with the skills and knowledge to carry out those reforms and to modernize the economy. True, these immigrants are sending money back to El Salvador, but their remittances do not begin to equal the amount of money—$1 billion, according to an estimate of a former Salvadoran government official—that is leaving the country because of the war.[19]

Perhaps more than any other immigrant group, the new Central American "feet people" are walking into an open society. In the United States these immigrants have an opportunity to acquire new political skills and blend new political and economic expectations with their own traditions. Over the long run, such expectations only fuel demands for change back home. Thus, while U.S. foreign policy may be a conservative force in Central America for the present—to the degree that it continues to encourage immigration from El Salvador—it may well prove a radicalizing one in the future. The most disturbing phenomenon for U.S. policymakers to cope with may begin when the "feet people" return to their homes.

NOTES

1. L. Cannon, "A Latin Axis Could Take Central America, Reagan Says," *The Washington Post*, June 21, 1983, p. A1.
2. Congressional Record—House, July 28, 1983, p. H5840.
3. *Ibid.* Rep. Bob Livington (R-La.) stated that if "Central America turned into a string of anti-American Marxist dictatorships, we would have to spend billions to take care of Americans losing their jobs due to the loss of all the foreign trade we now have in Central America. We would have to spend billions to beef up our national defenses in the South, billions to defend our shores and sea lanes with our own soldiers and their blood, we would lose thousands of soldiers."

4. Data from the U.S. Immigration and Naturalization Service (INS), November 1983.

5. James Fallows, "Immigration: How It's Affecting Us," *The Atlantic Monthly*, November 1983, p. 46.

6. J. Vialet, "Immigration Issues and Legislation in the 98th Congress," Issue Brief No. IB83087, The Library of Congress, Congressional Research Service, October 14, 1984, p. 5.

7. W. Bute, K. F. McCarthy, R. A. Morrison, and M. E. Vaiana, "Demographic Challanges in America's Future," The Rand Corporation, May 1982, p. 26.

8. *Ibid.*, pp. 34-35.

9. The latter group is very small. It is comprised of wealthy Central Americans who enter and reenter the United States on multiple entry tourist visas valid for successive six-month stays in the country over a period of five years. They live in various parts of the country between trips to their homelands or elsewhere every six months. By doing this, they avoid paying U.S. income taxes, despite their de facto residence in the country. (In the case of those from El Salvador, these wealthy "tourists" reportedly have taken one billion dollars out of the country.)

10. Compadrazco: The reciprocal relationship or the social institution of such relations existing between the godparents and the godchild and its parents in the Spanish-speaking world.

11. Anthony Lewis, "Abroad at Home: On the Side," *New York Times*, December 5, 1983, p. A19.

12. An interview with Dale Frederick Swartz, President of the National Immigration, Refugee, and Citizenship Forum.

13. Thomas Anderson, *The War of the Dispossessed: Honduras and El Salvador, 1969*, University of Nebraska Press, 1981, p. 141.

14. Statistics are from interviews with Mexican government officials and Costa Rican refugee officials in April 1983.

15. *Op. cit.*, Swartz, interview.

16. The result is a system that gives millions of dollars of profit for those few that rule. The ones that control the economy are assured of a cheap labor force, and the ones that control the government are assured that their "above the law" status provides them access to multimillion dollar deals. When the Reagan Administration announces that there have been changes in the high command of the Salvadoran army, all that it means is that the chain of command is working as usual, promoting officers from lieutenant to captain to major to colonel, and then some to millionaire and to Miami.

17. Dale Swartz suggested the analysis of the possible domestic and political implications of Central American migrations.

18. Joseph E. Bouchard, Sandra Gregg, Alfred E. Lewis, Eric Pianin, and Margaret Shapiro, "FBI Lists Bombing Suspects," *Washington Post*, November 9, 1983, A6.

19. Confidential interview with ex-government ministers of El Salvador.

THE POLICY PROCESS

11

REAGAN'S CENTRAL AMERICAN POLICY:
An Isthmus Restored

Viron Vaky

I

Central America is a major foreign policy issue for the administration because of its national security dimension. Were it not for the challenge to U.S. security interests posed by Soviet/Cuban fishing in the region's troubled waters, the administration (and the nation) would be considerably more relaxed about Central America, and would, in all likelihood, extend less attention and lower priority to its problems.

The difficulty is that the security dimension interacts with a larger dimension — serious local problems and strains resulting from inequitable political and social systems, and a long, bitter history of injustice, poverty, brutality, and repression. The agony of the policy task has been how to properly relate and deal with these two discontinuous and often contradictory dimensions.

The interplay of these two sets of factors renders any single-factor conceptualization — as either a straightforward East-West struggle or just a question of development and reform — simplistic and inaccurate. A whole series of considerations and motivations regarding equity, socio-economic reform, human rights, and self-determination are involved which have no intrinsic connection with the global balance of power. Yet, these local complexities cannot be addressed without reference to global power questions, nor can security concerns be met without reference to equity or to the indigenous roots of current violence and turmoil.

The two dimensions differ in time-frames as well. As essential as development and reform programs are for long-term stability, they are not options

233

for dealing with immediate insurgency problems. Nonetheless, preoccupation with such immediate insurgency problems can lead to actions and situations which foreclose options, prejudice long-term prospects for democracy and self-sustaining stability, and sow seeds of future local conflict.

The policy task is further complicated by two sets of background factors. The first stems from the difficulties of delineating and reconciling strategy responsibilities among agencies and individuals, the checks and balances of executive/congressional relationships, and the nature of domestic politics. All importantly affect the steadiness and continuity of policy. There is a growing tendency for each new administration, of whatever party, to regard continuity as a liability, and to seek vigorously to separate itself from its predecessors. As a result, an administration oftentimes defines its initial policies as much in terms of this objective as in terms of the intrinsic foreign policy requirements.

A second set of background factors concerns the effect of ethnocentricity, i.e., the way historic experience, traditions, values, norms and cultural habits determine how Americans perceive and act toward the outside world. The result is a curious set of dualities in the American character, as well as a compulsion to universalize and project into foreign policy our essentially unique historic experience.[1] This tendency has a great deal to do with how Americans conceive of such things as negotiations, the role of force in international relations, how to deal with enemies (or friends), how to handle the tension between Americans' simultaneous instinct for the use of force and compulsion for seeking harmony and consensus. Thus, a significant part of our troubles in Central America (and in foreign policy generally) is rooted in the peculiar habits, fears and illusions intrinsic to the American experience and style.

Meanwhile, the circumstances "on the ground" in Central America, have steadily deteriorated in a constricting, downward spiral, with increasingly fewer available "good" options or alternatives left. This has been due partly to lost opportunities for timely reform and change (stretching back over several years and several administrations); partly to the self-fulfilling nature of various assumptions and premises; and partly to the self-ratcheting escalation/counter-escalation intrinisic in the confrontational way all the actors have dealt with the issues. The spreading effects of "proxy" strategies have led to increasing turmoil and growing polarization, and to what one observer has called "the second Spanish Civil War."[2]

II

How has the Reagan administration dealt with these complexities? What are its basic concepts, premises and assumptions regarding Central America, and what are their implications and probable consequences?

It is not hard to be at best confused and at worst alarmed over the thrust and likely outcome of the administration's policies in the region. The shrillness of the rhetoric has waxed and waned. Terms such as "vital interest" and "security threat" have been freely used without precision, almost as code words. There have been mixed signals from different officials, and a more than usual fragmentation in the policy process.[3] Some of the explanations and defenses of policy have been either disingenuous or cynical. An unusually ideologically-minded administration has intensified the philosophic and strategy debate within the bureaucracy, and, consequently, made internal policy consensus difficult. Some options are foreclosed, several are pursued at the same time, and the impression that U.S. actions are all tactics and no strategy is hard to shake.

From the outset, the Reagan administration conceptualized the Central American situation as essentially a Cold War problem — its task to redress the superpower balance and contain, even reverse, Cuban/Soviet "expansionism" in the isthmus. This categorization of the Central American crisis as an East-West conflict was the result of the Reagan administration's conviction that Carter's "liberal" human rights policies had destabilized the region; that the situation the administration encountered on taking office reflected a loss of control in America's "backyard" and a deterioration of U.S. power which could be reversed by the exercise of will; that the region's violence was essentially fueled by Cuba and the USSR; and that Soviet/Cuban influence and expansionism would continue unless contained "on the ground."[4]

The initial rhetoric was simple, straightforward and belligerent. Conceptually, the administration focused on El Salvador as the central issue, and defined it as the "battleground" in which the line against communist aggression had to be drawn. While critics raised the analogy of Vietnam, the administration saw the analogy as Greece in 1945-48. Threats of "going to the source" were made. Questions of political and social reform were tabled; human rights became a secondary priority; fighting "terrorism" and the Marxist-Leninist threat were first.[5]

As the domestic, political compulsion to distinguish itself from the Carter administration faded with time, the Reagan administration's awareness of Central America's multi-dimensional realities grew. It ran smack into the problems of right-wing death squads, murders of U.S. nuns and labor leaders, U.S. public criticism and skepticism, and congressional insistence on keeping the "indigenous dimension" and local complexities as central considerations. These pressures forced the administration to modify its rhetoric and reformulate its "goals," and gave rise to internal debates about policy and strategy.

Gradually, the rhetorical formulation of policy moved from a single security issue to the four objectives outlined by President Reagan in his speech to the Joint Session of Congress, April 27, 1983: (a) supporting democracy, reform and freedom; (b) supporting economic development; (c) confronting the military challenge from Cuba and Nicaragua with support for the security of threatened nations; and (d) supporting "dialogue and negotiations."[6]

This formulation is psychologically comforting. It simply declares that all the multiple interests and values at stake are goals; it has something in it for everyone. It is in fact, a classic example of what decision theorists have described as the way policymakers deal with "value complexity" and "value conflict."[7] They usually try to avoid painful choices among competing sub-interests in one or both of two ways. One is to stage or schedule satisfaction of these values/interests by a series of separate actions or policies over a period of time and in different time-frames. Thus, some policies are put forward as initial measures, with the other values or goals neglected (or damaged) by the first series, being promoted "later."[8]

A second psychological process is to ignore or downplay competing or contradictory interests in a decisional problem — what is generally referred to in the various psychological theories of cognitive consistency and dissonance. In effect, one avoids the need for trade-offs by rationalizing problems and information in such a way as to believe that contradictory actions actually reinforce each other,[9] e.g., that professionalizing military institutions in these countries makes them apolitical and strengthens democratic processes. Sometimes this rationalization is done deliberately, but most of the time unconsciously. "Consistency-striving" is also stimulated by the political constraints under which policymakers operate. Choice may entail such severe political costs that one unconsciously (or consciously) avoids the necessity of choice.

While the four goals of administration policy represent an ideal formulation satisfying multiple interests, they are also "non-operational" goals. They provide neither operational guidance as to how to achieve the objectives nor criteria by which to compare alternative options. How does one relate and prioritize these different goals? Does not implementation of some render satisfaction of the other interests more difficult?

One might, for example, usefully consider the question of whether U.S. assistance to help the Salvadoran military defeat the guerrillas might not also create a triumphal military that is politically ambitious and determined to defend its institutional interests — which history suggests would be the case. Might America win the war and lose the politics in El Salvador? Or one might ponder the question of what the consequences of the heavy U.S. political presence and military activity in Honduras are for that nation's delicate and fragile internal balance. Have U.S. measures, logically designed for military and security ends, impeded or aided the prospects for a self-sustaining democracy in Honduras?

Behind all the policy fits and starts and tactical debates lies a persistent bedrock premise: the Central American situation is first and foremost a Soviet/Cuban security threat. The president's rhetoric, for example, has never changed much; he has consistently defined the issue as one of Soviet/Cuban aggression in our hemisphere.[10] Between the two thrusts of Central America's reality—the security and the indigenous dimensions—the former clearly takes precedence. For some down the bureaucratic chain of decision-making, the local conditions—concerns and anxieties about human rights, reform and political settlement or a negotiated end to conflict—are viewed cynically as distractions or traps which can divert the United States from its basic need to defeat the communists and thus as concerns to be co-opted, deflected and lulled.

Moreover, over the past three years, the specific target of the administration's concerns and fears has shifted from the critical battleground of El Salvador, to Nicaragua, as the critical source of long-term communist infection. In essence, the central policy debate within the administration now centers on the questions: Can we co-exist with the Sandinista regime? Is the Sandinista regime in its present configuration compatible with peace and security in Central America? The current ascendant view in the administration is "no," but there is no consensus as to what one then does. The high downside cost of the measures that would logically follow forces the process back around the mulberry bush to the original questions. There begins anew the groping for some formulation or tactic to meet multiple objectives, as well as the waiting for some circumstance or condition which might change the calculus.

III

The complex implications of this ambiguity can be seen if one examines more closely the basic operational premises underpinning the administration's approach to the definition of U.S. security interests and the concept of negotiations.

A. Security Interests

The president and major administration foreign policy figures have stated repeatedly and sweepingly that Central America is vital to our national security: "The national security of all the Americas is at stake in Central America. . . . We have a vital interest, a moral duty and a solemn responsibility."[11]

Literally, a *vital* interest is one upon which the nation's survival depends. To use the term has traditionally been a portentous step; it means that the nation will use military force. Over the years, however, this and previous administrations have used the term much less precisely and for many collateral reasons. As one observer has noted, American presidents have declared almost every part of the world to be "vital" except Africa and the Antarctic.[12] "Vital" is now a "buzz word" to gain public and congressional backing without having to provide supporting analysis.

The administration's affirmation that Central America is vital to U.S. security is defended basically on three grounds: (1) credibility; (2) dominoes; and (3) protecting America's rear.

Credibility

The credibility argument states, in effect, that Central America is America's "backyard" and immediate sphere of influence; that superpowers are supposed to control things in their spheres of influence; therefore "defections," such as Nicaragua, will be "seen" as a loss of power and a sign of weakness, discouraging American friends and encouraging adversaries.[13] As President Reagan described it:

> If Central America were to fall, what would the consequence be for our position in Asia, Europe, and for alliances such as NATO? If the United States cannot respond to a threat near our own borders, why should Europeans or Asians believe that we are seriously concerned about threats to them? If the Soviets can assume that nothing short of an actual attack on the United States will provoke an American response, which ally, which friend will trust us then?. . . . If we cannot defend ourselves there [in Central America], we cannot expect to prevail elsewhere. Our credibility would collapse, our alliances would crumble. . . . [14]

The credibility argument rests essentially on *subjective* judgments. It states, in effect, that what matters is how things are *viewed* by others. The *perception* by others of U.S. "resolve" or "will" or "power" is the important point. As one writer has commented: "Washington maintains credibility when relevant others think it means business. Since Washington anticipates how these audiences will react, the correct formula for credibility becomes: 'We have it when we think they think we mean business.'"[15]

It is not that a credibility argument never has substance, but it depends so fundamentally on subjective judgments that it is easy to be wrong. Furthermore, the credibility argument's preoccupation with global images diverts attention from local realities, and fosters simplistic approaches to complex situations. Its concentration on "power," moreover, may foreclose effective diplomatic options. The argument easily leads to a conclusion that the mere *existence* of a Marxist regime in Central America damages U.S. "credibility"

whether or not it is linked to Soviet power; that non-alignment is to be opposed because it detracts from America's ability to control "our" region; we
must prevail—compromise is "no win."

Dominoes

The second major explanation as to why Central America is vital is the
domino theory.[16] Administration officials have repeatedly affirmed that,
unless contained, Marxism-Leninism (read Soviet/Cuban power) will move
inexorably south into South America and north to Mexico, eventually
threatening the United States itself. The domino analogy—like credibility—
has dominated American foreign policy thinking since the end of World War
II. It reached its zenith with reference to Vietnam.[17]

The flaw in the domino argument is that it is presented as if it functioned
automatically. What happens in one country obviously influences what happens in another, but how much, in what form and with what result depends
upon circumstances. The process is not automatic, especially with regard to
countries with very different histories, conditions, strengths and weaknesses.
The "ripple effect" within the confines of the relatively similar nations of
Central America is one thing; its extension to Mexico, Colombia, Venezuela,
and the United States is something else.

"The rhetorical leap from domino to domino," in Theodore Draper's
phrase, is perilous because—like the invocation of "vital interest"—it is frequently substituted for thought. One needs to examine carefully, for example, how El Salvador and Nicaragua could target Mexico and the United
States—or how Cuba and the Soviet Union would target them *from* El
Salvador and Nicaragua.

Strategic Rear

The third major explanation of our security interest in Central America
is that it constitutes America's "strategic rear." The argument is that, up to
now, the United States had a fairly secure Central America which allowed
it to concentrate on world hot spots. Soviet/Cuban influence in the isthmus,
however, threatens America's "strategic rear," and unless the region is
cleansed, the United States will have to devote military and other resources
to contain the beachhead. This response, in turn, will mean a diversion of
resources and attention from the rest of the world, restricting our global
posture. The United States therefore needs to restore a stable, predictable,
supportive, and "low cost" environment of the kind that characterized past
relationships. This argument has been articulated most explicitly by Under-
Secretary of Defense, Fred Iklé:

We should seek to prevent the partition of Central America, a division of this region into two spheres, one linked to the Soviet bloc and one linked to the United States. Such a partition would inexorably lead to a hostile confrontation of large military forces, a confrontation that could last for decades. . . . Nicaragua—if it continued on its present course—would be the bridgehead and arsenal for insurgency for Central America. And once the Sandinistas have acquired the military strength that they have long been planning for, they might well use that strength for direct attacks on their neighbors to help speed up the "revolution without frontiers" that they promised us. At that time, the only way to help protect the democracies might be for the United States to place forward deployed forces in these countries, as in Korea or West Germany. Clearly, we must prevent such a partition of Central America.[18]

What is implicit in this argument is the assumed requirement for hegemony, i.e., for the United States to be the dominant and uncontested external influence in the region. Anything not explicitly supportive or aligned with U.S. interests is a potential danger. Indeed, some administration officials privately argue that the threat is not simply confined to the establishment of Soviet/Cuban military bases. Even conventional forms of relations with the USSR or Cuba are threatening because they may have intelligence functions or, worse, they may provide the platform for future aggression. For others, the vision is neo-Metternichean—a leftist regime with no specific alignment with the Soviets is threatening because of possible future receptivity to Soviet support, because of the domino effect on neighbors' stability, and because the appearance of a non-aligned or Marxist regime in our backyard is a loss to U.S. prestige. The implication of these arguments, moreover, is that a negotiated political settlement will not do if it perpetuates a "leftist" foothold in the region.

Two additional security arguments are frequently made: (a) protecting U.S. sea lanes and (b) avoiding a flood of refugees. These are, however, more in the nature of "kitchen sink" arguments, i.e., they are adduced to rally every possible justification for courses of action already chosen for other reasons. While sea lanes *are* important, it is hard to see how any political or insurgency development in Central America (short of a Soviet/Cuban base) would threaten these communication lines any more than they already are. And while war and violence may result in refugees, migration can also be stimulated by such things as wage differentials and local unemployment. Indeed, demographers have long noted that economic and social development may actually stimulate migration to higher wage areas by improving the skills and ability to move of the migrants.

The administration's formulation of the credibility, dominoes and "secure rear" arguments derives from its belief in a prior set of broader interrelated premises about national security and the Soviet challenge. These may be said to be the following: (a) The greatest threat to the survival of the United States lies in Soviet expansion; (b) the Soviets desire world domination as their goal, and they will inexorably expand unless contained by the United States; (c) their expansionism is in a dangerous phase at present because of the growth in Soviet military strength; (d) the Soviets, through and with the Cubans, are on the move in Latin America; (e) Cuba and the Soviets effectively control the Sandinista regime and will exploit Nicaragua as a base for the further export of subversion and armed intervention in the isthmus; (f) if the the Cuban/Soviet-aided insurgencies seize power elsewhere, the targeted countries will, in the words of former Assistant Secretary of State Thomas Enders, become "totalitarian regimes so linked to the Soviet Union that they become factors in the military balance."[19]

This framework is not novel. Since 1945 the concept of the global balance has been the major arbiter of policy choice. But while concepts of national purpose and overall national interest have remained essentially constant, premises about how best to advance them have varied widely. Premises about the nature and use of power; about the international setting; about Soviet (and Chinese) motivations, capabilities and intentions have been constantly reformulated over the years to reflect obviously changing realities. The history of American foreign policy since World War II, in fact, can be written in terms of the debates over what the balance of power concept meant in any given situation, and over such questions as just how unrequited or unrequitable the Soviet (or Chinese) appetite for expansion really is; whether every leftist regime in the Third World is an automatic addition to the Russian side of the scale and a deduction from ours; and the feasibility of a seamless global web of commitments and actions to contain communism.[20]

The point here is that the Reagan administration's security premises are cast in a Manichaean absoluteness straight out of the 1950s. Seyom Brown's trenchant assessment of the administration's overall foreign policy is especially relevant, and specifically germane to the administration's policy stance on Central America:

> In short, the Reagan foreign policy was to be oriented around a Grand Strategy for containing the Soviet Union, premised on a starkly bipolar view of geopolitics, placing great reliance on the military components of power. . . . The tests of the soundness of a basic foreign policy however, are not so much in its internal self-consistency and its appeal to true believers. Rather, its validity is determined by its consistency with the facts of domestic and international life, and the ability of the programs and actions it spawns to service the security and well-being of the people of the United States. Measured against these criteria of realism and efficacy, the Reagan Grand Strategy ran into trouble from the start, and was faced in one policy area after another

with the need to sacrifice ideological consistency and support from true believers in order not to be foolishly and even dangerously insensitive to the complexities of the contemporary world.[21]

B. Negotiations

The administration's concept of "negotiation" has been shaped in part by the ethnocentric way in which Americans generally think about negotiations with adversaries. The United States is a nation unaccustomed in its internal historic experience to living with fundamental conflicts of ends. Americans are intolerant of such basic differences. Fundamental conflicts of ends are to be eliminated, not lived with or managed; concord and harmony are our norms.

Americans therefore tend to think of adversaries in demonic terms since hostility is by definition abnormal.[22] Consider, for example, how Americans reflexively view negotiating with enemies — they cannot be trusted; they are not sincere; negotiations are a trap; reaching agreement with someone who holds different principles means somehow that our own principles are thereby corrupted.[23]

U.S. domestic experience with negotiation tends to be pragmatic. Americans are accustomed to negotiating differing demands within a framework of fundamental consensus on ends and principles which are taken for granted. We therefore tend to assume that negotiating with the Russians or other foreign adversaries should somehow be like an AFL/CIO union negotiating with a major manufacturer, and we are distressed when it is not. Hence, our customary reflex is to demand agreement on fundamental differences as *preconditions* to a negotiating process, rather than viewing such differences as the *objects* of negotiation and compromise. Conditions for negotiation thus frequently are defined in ways which make them seem like terms of capitulation.[24]

As far as Central America is concerned, the administration has repeatedly affirmed that support for "dialogue and negotiations"[25] is a basic goal of U.S. policy toward the region. Yet, contradictory signals from various officials, the zero-sum implications of security assumptions and the way terms for negotiations in El Salvador and Nicaragua are defined all raise the level of confusion and doubt about what the administration really means or intends.

This uncertainty is particularly significant because of a burgeoning of various multilateral proposals for a Central American political settlement arising out of a generalized fear of where unrelieved violence and tension might lead — the Franco-Mexican communiqué of August 1981; the six-point Honduran Peace Plan of March 23, 1982; the October 1982 San José Declaration signed by the Central American "democracies," Jamaica and the Dominican Republic; and a joint Venezuelan-Mexican initiative of October 1982. All of these proposals have been subsumed and superseded by the "Contadora Process" — now the centerpiece of regional efforts to bring peace to the isthmus.

This effort was launched by the foreign ministers of Mexico, Venezuela, Colombia, and Panama at a meeting on Contadora Island in January 1983. A long series of consultations and meetings has taken place since, and the Central American countries have been drawn into the process. In July 1983 the presidents of the Contadora nations issued a 10-point declaration at Cancún, and in October they produced a 21-point "Document of Objectives" subscribed to by the Contadora countries and all the Central American nations, including Nicaragua. At this writing, officials of the Contadora powers and the Central American nations are engaged in an effort to translate these principles into legal instruments and a regional treaty.

The position and focus of the Contadora nations are still evolving. While concentrating initially — and still centrally — on the establishment of peace in the isthmus, the Contadora group has increasingly dealt with the roots of fear and hostility between Nicaragua and its neighbors; with the need for development and improving the quality of life; and with the importance of internal reconciliation within these countries to the region's security and peace.

The Contadora nations undertook their initiative fearing that a regional war would erupt unless tensions were rapidly defused. The Contadora foreign ministers and chiefs of state have repeated this concern at every juncture with increasing urgency. An unspoken, correlative motive, has been their fear of possible U.S. intervention. This fear reflects both the historic Latin American opposition to U.S. hegemony and "interventionism," as well as their concern that U.S. involvement would draw the region into the vortex of superpower conflict. While sharing U.S. concern about further Marxist penetration of the region, the Contadora nations nevertheless feel that a confrontational approach is self-defeating. However essential U.S. support and participation are in negotiated arrangements, the group realizes that the United States is too much of a protagonist in the region's turmoil to be a credible mediator. The Contadora effort was thus deliberately structured and presented as one independent of the United States. Its international credibility rests on its being perceived as an independent effort and an alternative to proposals being pushed by the United States, such as those of the San José group.[26] The Contadora countries have been careful to preserve this "independence" and their own freedom of action. The independent character of the process is both an attraction and a concern to the administration.

The administration's response to the Contadora process has been ambivalent and passive. Although it has given lip-service to the process, the administration has stood on the side lines, critically appraising the "action" as if the burden of proof rests entirely with the Contadora group. Privately, administration figures raise their skepticism regarding the ability of the Contadora countries to "get their act together." Officials question the differing motives and interests of these countries, and they express doubts about their "realism" and understanding of the Soviet threat. More importantly, they wonder if the Contadora goals are really compatible with U.S. interests.

In addition, the administration follows courses of action that — intentionally or not — cross wires with the Contadora effort. The unilateral Stone diplomatic mission — whose purpose and mandate are far from clear[27] — is at least a distraction for the countries involved and, at most, a conflicting strategy. And U.S. support for the covert paramilitary activity (the *contras*) in Nicaragua has been criticized by some Contadora officials as undermining their efforts.

This reaction to the Contadora process reflects a traditional American attitude toward multilateral diplomacy. Americans do not like to lose "control." While we have always stressed cooperation and consultation, the fact is, as Stanley Hoffmann has noted, "We invite other nations to work with us in carrying out our schemes, and we refuse either to endorse proposals that might entangle us in policies we would be unable to determine, or to allow them to share in the determination of our policies."[28]

In part our reaction also reflects a lack of internal consensus as to the wisdom of any negotiating strategy at all. Pentagon spokesmen have made no secret of their disdain for what they called "the lure of negotiations."[29] And a National Security Council document leaked to the press in April 1983 described one of the policy objectives as "co-opting cut-and-run negotiation strategies by demonstrating a reasonable but firm approach to negotiations and compromise *on our terms*" [emphasis added]. The same document recommended that the United States "step up efforts to co-opt the negotiations issue to avoid congressionally mandated negotiations, which would work against our interests."[30] Under-Secretary of Defense Iklé's September 1983 speech gave no indication of any willingness to consider a political settlement as a solution to Central America's problem. He stated with regard to El Salvador: "We can no more negotiate an acceptable political solution with these people than the social democrats in revolutionary Russia could have talked Lenin into giving up totalitarian Bolshevism."[31]

In the ascendant administration view, any political settlement which would confirm the Sandinistas in power (or permit Salvadoran Marxists to survive) would perpetuate a Soviet/Cuban foothold in the region. This view is based on a conception of the Sandinistas — and leftist insurgents generally — as wholly implacable and probably irredeemable; as "threats" to be deterred, confronted and contained. Concessions to these forces simply weaken *our* position. Negotiations are to be understood only as the continuation of confrontation by other means.

There are two problems with this view. One is that it can be self-fulfilling. An unwillingness to negotiate becomes the justification for one's adversary taking a similar stand. Conflict feeds itself. Second, if one assumes no tolerable modus vivendi is possible or acceptable, then there is no alternative to a "military solution." But the obvious costs of an option calling for force to cleanse the isthmus sends administration policy makers back to search for other "political" alternatives.

In this internal debate between conflict and compromise, the administration has been unwilling or unable to break the cycle of conflict, or to test seriously and sincerely whether a tolerable political compromise can be reached. It is almost like the blind man in the old Chinese folktale who dangles from a bridge with his feet a few inches above a dry river bed. Passers-by tell him to just let go and he will be alright, but out of uncertainty he tenaciously hangs on.

IV

How does the administration's dilemma play out concretely in the cases of El Salvador and Nicaragua?

A. El Salvador

The situation in El Salvador is more one of fragmentation than polarization. Within the broad institutional cohesion of the military, for example, officers express a range of views and differences. Democratic parties and the clerics are divided; businessmen and professionals represent a varied range. The opposition is divided despite a surface unity and organization. Elements of the traditional oligarchy continually use their old military channels to stop reform measures and to restore traditional power patterns.[32]

These elements function in a climate of pathological violence, amid economic and political deterioration. The Salvadoran government and military have been either unwilling or unable to control right-wing death squads and vigilantism. Political institutions remain frail. Adverse economic trends for the country's main exports, infrastructural dislocation, capital flight and disinvestment have all contributed to a dramatic deterioration in the economy since 1979. The vast majority of the population—peasants and workers—remains inert and unable to affect events.

The picture usually painted by the administration's rhetoric of a democracy taking root and growing in strength behind a military shield[33] is far too rosy. The civil war continues, and the insurgents are far from controlled. Official pessimism alternates with optimism, and with each downward turn of the cycle, proposals are heard for more U.S. aid to keep the "momentum."[34]

The situation in El Salvador can move in one of two directions: the zero-sum road of continued conflict until somebody eventually prevails, or a "political road" of negotiated settlement reincorporating opposing elements into a new consensus and political process. The administration, however, flatly opposes any settlement involving "power sharing," an interim coalition government and/or a restructuring of the security forces.

What the administration means by "political solution" is an agreement in which the insurgents lay down their arms and participate in the electoral process being structured by the present government. Such a concept is, however, a non-starter. Even the non-Marxist elements of the opposition will not deprive themselves of their defense against forces they mortally fear, and against which they went into armed resistance in the first place. Moreover, assurances that the government and military can provide security for the opposition in a political campaign are not credible in view of the authorities' inability to stop or control current right-wing assassinations and terrorism.[35]

Few of the major Salvadoran participants now appear flexible enough to reach a workable compromise. Although parts of the opposition are surely desirous of a settlement, some hardcore FMLN elements want to seize power, and their negotiating demands are no less intractable than those of the government. The military concern is that negotiation or reconciliation must at some point focus on the nature and role of the military. Fears of purges and institutional destruction lead to concerns about self-preservation and opposition to negotiations. Reconciliation between opposing forces will not be generated spontaneously. Without U.S. support and guarantees no externally mediated or catalyzed process will work either.

The administration concludes that the insurgents must be eliminated, either by military defeat or by their surrender. As expressed by Under-Secretary of Defense Iklé:

> We do not seek a military defeat for our friends. We do not seek a military stalemate. We seek victory for the forces of democracy. And that victory [means] defeating militarily those organized forces of violence that refuse to accept the democratic will of the people.[36]

Internal strategy debates proceed along two lines. One side urges a military victory; in this view a political settlement is undesirable. Protracted insurgency means the government's growing incapacity to govern. Therefore, U.S. efforts must enable the Salvadoran military to win quickly. Critics of this view argue that it would almost surely weaken the embryonic efforts at social/economic reforms, if only by lowering their priority. The more the fighting continues, the more its urgency will squeeze and polarize the center. Human rights violations would doubtless increase. The dominant role accorded to the military would surely lead to a retention of the political power the military now enjoys – to the detriment of civilian, pluralist government.

As Theodore Moran points out elsewhere in this volume, such a strategy would also be very expensive. It would invite further U.S. involvement and Americanization of the conflict, since there is a point of diminishing returns in adding more arms and sophisticated equipment unless American trainers, advisers and operations are also brought in. And the temptation to become so involved to "protect the investment" could become irresistible.

The second tactical concept is a military effort simultaneously reinforced by efforts to strengthen economic and political development, and to improve justice and human rights. By fortifying the official side and improving its image, the opposition will supposedly either break up or wither away. Such a concept, however, is more psychologically comforting than realistic. First, the military dimension will inevitably receive priority over other efforts. Second, political and economic development is not an engineering problem susceptible to management simply by resource inputs. What is at issue is not merely the amelioration of existing inequities and injustices, but the underlying power patterns which those inequities reflect. If the Salvadoran military, for example, decides to support a given reform measure, such as land reform, but remains the repository of political power, the underlying situation is not changed. How will the Salvadoran peasant, labor union member or small entrepreneur advance and protect their respective interests in the future if these interests cannot be effectively expressed in an open, participatory political process? The problem is not unlike the American experience with civil rights in the Deep South in this country. Only when local power patterns were changed by the pressure of the federal government could blacks be secure in their status and assured of their rights on a permanent basis. It is, in short, the touching of local power patterns that renders political development and social reform so explosive.

The United States is clumsily positioned to effect such delicate societal changes in another culture, and its record is not encouraging in this regard. What usually happens is that the United States insists on "showing them how it is done," and on insuring "efficient" use of its resources. America also suffers from ethnocentric conceptions about social and political processes, and from its tendency to project national experience onto other situations. For example, Americans tend to believe that elections automatically establish democracy, because in their experience they are the means by which political power is allocated. In El Salvador, where power is normally allocated in other ways, elections have not had that function. The March 1982 elections, for example, while a dramatic civic act, paradoxically complicated the democratization process. The results fragmented civilian authority, legitimized the radical right, and shattered the political center. Occurring in the midst of a virtual civil war, this election enabled the minister of defense to consolidate political power further in the military's hands. There is no doubt that the military holds power in El Salvador today, not the civilian president.

In the present circumstances, the March 1984 elections may produce similar results.

Most important of all, however, is that no effort to nurture democracy or clothe the Salvadoran government with respect and authority can succeed as long as the security forces themselves aid and abet terror against their own people. Unless the Salvadoran military puts an end to death squads, little hope can be accorded to the political democratization process. U.S. policy on this point is neither credible nor effective. Exhortations and warnings by the American ambassador and visiting VIPs have had little effect because the perpetrators have believed (rightly so far) that they can ignore them with impunity. Moreover, U.S. sincerity is suspect in the face of Washington's mixed signals, such as the President's pocket veto of legislation linking aid to human rights performance.[37]

Even more revealing for the Salvadoran rightists is the administration's refusal to take any steps against Salvadoran exiles in the United States suspected of paying for and partly directing death squad activities, even though this situation is known and sources within the bureaucracy have pressed for action.[38] Unless the administration somehow conditions military and democratic aid on human rights performance, it has no leverage. Yet up to now it has hesitated to do so for fear that such a condition would hamper the all-important war effort.

In these circumstances, the prospects are that the situation will continue along its present course — with continued conflict and bloodshed; increasing American involvement in El Salvador's national life, and growing temptation to become more deeply involved in the military conflict, either directly with advisers and special personnel or through CONDECA proxies.

B. Nicaragua

The administration views the Sandinista regime as the most serious threat to U.S. security interests. Operationally, the administration sees essentially three policy tasks. The first is to stop Nicaraguan meddling in its neighbors' affairs. The second is to purge the isthmus of Soviet/Cuban influence, and to sanitize Nicaragua's relations with those countries. The third is to prevent the Sandinista regime from consolidating itself as a Leninist regime.

The internal debates over what to do about these operational goals has, from the beginning, weaved between two poles. One is the administration's profound distrust of the Sandinista regime, and its conviction that, in its present configuration, the Sandinista government is incompatible with security and stability in the region. These points have been made most clearly and pithily by President Reagan himself. In a July 1983 press conference, the president responded to a question as to whether he believed a settlement in Central America was possible if the Sandinistas remained in power: "I think it'd be extremely difficult, because I think they're being subverted or they're being directed by outside forces.[39] In a news conference on November 3, 1983, the president responded to a question about Nicaraguan leaders by saying, "I haven't believed anything they've been saying since they got in charge, and you shouldn't either."[40]

The implication of these conceptions is inescapable — the Sandinistas have to go. However, the logical implications of *that* conclusion, in turn, establish the opposing pole; viz., the politically high costs of exorcising the Sandinistas from the region by military force. The result is that the bureaucracy is forced to seek ways and means of working between these limits.

There are some who believe that the efforts in August 1981 to negotiate an understanding with Nicaragua produced the potential for a compromise, but that they failed due to U.S. intransigence and excessive demands, and equal intransigence and diplomatic ineptness on the part of the Sandinistas.[41] The United States indicated that it was seeking at the time a relatively straightforward deal — withdrawal of support for elements seeking the Sandinistas' overthrow in return for withdrawal of Sandinista support for Salvadoran guerrillas. Whatever the reason for the failure of this formula, the administration has since upped the ante. Its current formulation is that a negotiated agreement must contain not only a Sandinista commitment not to export revolution, but a commitment to change its own internal nature and its relations with Cuba — negotiate "power sharing" with the *contras,* call free elections, reduce the size of the Sandinista army and the presence of Cuban advisors.

Since July 1983, the Sandinista regime has made a series of conciliatory gestures which clearly signal that it wants to reach an accommodation with the United States and its neighbors. On October 20, Nicaragua presented drafts of four treaties to the Contadora countries, to the Central American nations and to the United States. The drafts dealt with security and non-aggression commitments; however they carefully avoided the question of internal political systems. In early December, they presented further proposals on disarmament to Contadora officials. Meanwhile, the Sandinista regime also initiated some unilateral gestures — partly relaxing censorship of the newspaper, *La Prensa,* releasing some Miskito Indian political prisoners, and sending home a small number of Cuban teachers and technicians (but not military advisers). It has also announced limited amnesty for anti-Sandinistas to return and participate in national life and elections to be held in 1985.[42]

The administration initially reacted frostily to these gestures. "High officials" questioned whether they were really substantive and meaningful, or just tactical maneuvers to relieve pressure. Interior Minister, Tomás Borge, was refused a visa on the grounds that he was on a "propaganda" mission. No response was made to the receipt of treaty drafts, other than to refer Nicaragua to the Contadora countries. Some rhetorical bows have been made,

made, but basically, the administration has not to this date tested or explored the Nicaraguan gambit. It has simply asked for more.[43]

Two operational problems with regard to a possible "negotiation track" are worth noting. One has to do with trust. Administration officials state flatly that no agreement or treaty can be accepted on the basis of trust; it will have to be "self-implementable." The subsequent demands for verification tend to take such absolute forms as to be beyond feasibility, and to raise suspicions as to their deliberate use to argue against negotiations. The demand for verification is beginning to play the same role and constitute the same obstacle as it does in the nuclear arms control negotiations.

A second aspect is the administration's reluctance to separate objectives according to those suitable for negotiations and those better handled by diplomacy and political strategies. The question of exporting subversion or disarmament, for example, lends itself relatively easily to management by treaty commitment. However, the objective of reconstituting the nature of the Nicaraguan regime is not one that naturally lends itself to negotiation; that is likely to be achieved successfully by diplomatic and political strategies and pressures over time. The administration has shown no willingness to contemplate a long period of political strategy, or even a protracted period of negotiations. Many within the administration maintain that if the internal situation in Nicaragua is not reversed within a year or two, the Sandinistas will have consolidated an irreversible Leninist state.

The administration has not, in short, accorded to the "negotiating track" the full determination which its successful implementation would require, despite its rhetorical commitment to the idea.

Indeed, a good possibility is that — by lukewarm support or by deliberately excessive demands — it may damn the strategy with faint praise, and lay the groundwork for a claim that negotiations will not work or that the Sandinistas do not really want to "negotiate."

The primary thrust of administration tactics has, instead, been one of sanctions and pressure. This includes the display of U.S. military might, the halting of aid and the abolition of the sugar quota, the development of U.S. bases and training centers in neighboring countries, the organization and sustaining of covert paramilitary activity — the *contras* — and the resurrection of the Central American Defense Council (CONDECA).

The use of pressure to force compromise is a traditional and effective tactic. But such use makes sense only if it is a precise part of a precise negotiating strategy. What is unclear is how the administration would convert pressure into negotiating coin. Each Nicaraguan concession is simply met with another demand rather than a corresponding conciliation. It is tempting to argue that if U.S. pressure forced the recent conciliatory gestures, why not just keep it up until the Sandinistas cry "uncle"? Yet it is an axiom of diplomatic strategy that one needs to leave an adversary an exit. Cornering an opponent like the Sandinista *comandantes* will not create capitulation, but irrational desperation.

The major vehicle for U.S. pressure has been the U.S. organization and support of the *contras*. Begun in November 1981, as a small, 500-man, Latin American commando force, it has gradually expanded to close to a 12,000-man army.[44] Although it was originally intended as a commando campaign against "Cuban infrastructure," the administration's public explanation was that the objective was the interdiction of clandestine arms traffic, an explanation (or objective) that may well have been forced on the CIA by Congress.[45] This explanation was never very widely credited, and the policy is now more often justified as pressure to exact concessions. Although administration officials insistently deny that overthrowing the Sandinista government is the U.S. purpose, they readily concede it *is* the objective of the *contras* themselves.

In all probability, the administration fell into the "covert action" gambit the way previous administrations have. Unwilling to incur the costs and disadvantages of overt pursuit of a specific goal, and unwilling to abandon the goal, it is tempting to turn to the CIA and covert action as an easy way out. Covert action, after all, seems attractive — it can be mounted without specific legislative approval, bureaucratic consensus, or public explanation. Such actions are relatively less expensive than similar overt activities, and one can later disclaim any knowledge or responsibility if they do not work. History, unfortunately, suggests that covert paramilitary activity does not have a notable record of success.[46]

In Nicaragua's case the use of covert force has some fatal flaws. First, elements enlisted by the CIA have their own agenda and it is not clear how well they can be controlled. Second, it is extremely unlikely that the *contras* can overthrow the Sandinista regime at the present level of support,[47] if anyone had such a hope. That goal would require a much more overt and massive intervention of U.S. leadership, personnel and equipment. Third, the purpose of "covertness" activity is to enable a government to plausibly disavow responsibility for actions which could be embarassing or damaging. But in this case, the administration is both identified with the *contra* activity and admits it, and so reaps the worst of all worlds. Fourth, covert action of this kind *does* violate treaty obligations (the OAS Charter), and justification of this kind of action under self-defense rubrics of the OAS and UN charters or under normally accepted canons of international law is untenable. There are thus, negative costs to the image of the United States and its claim to high principle.

The use of covert paramilitary activity to carry out any of the various objectives mentioned at one time or another — interdiction of arms traffic, exacting concessions, forcing the Sandinistas to throw in the towel — is a little like performing an appendectomy through the mouth. It is inefficient, hard to do, and it creates all kinds of serious adverse side effects.

Finally, cognizance needs to be taken of the general climate of tension existing throughout the isthmus. Officials visiting the area have been impressed by the anti-Sandinista sentiments of other Central Americans. This sentiment is frequently cited to support the notion that coexistence with the present Sandinista regime is not possible. However, the intractability and felt insecurity of the other Central American countries may also be a function of U.S. policy and goals. The concerns and anxieties of these countries could be lessened by U.S. guarantees or support, and they are not in themselves immutable bars to a reasonable modus vivendi.

The administration has, in sum, projected a confusing picture of ambiguous and cross-cutting tactics with regard to Nicaragua, arousing uncertainty as to its real intentions, purposes and goals. Relations with Nicaragua, indeed, are a classic case of mutual suspicion and recrimination. The two sides are "like one man in front of a mirror with each belligerent move reflected back and prompting a further escalation."[48]

V

To recapitulate, one might conclude the following regarding the administration's Central American policy:

- The Administration approaches Central America from the top, i.e., from the perspective of the cold war. Its policies and tactics are, in effect, designed for extra-regional ends, with an eye on Moscow and Havana, even though they have local content, impact and cost.

- The administration's premises—about the global setting and about Soviet motivations, and its resulting assumptions about the nature of Central American insurgency and Sandinista intentions—define the terms of the internal debates over tactics and operational goals. These premises are responsible, in large part, for the options the administration "sees" and is willing to consider, and the options it does not "see" or rules out.

- The administration's definition of security interests, and what it believes they require, lead to the uncontested assumption that the United States has to exercise dominant power and influence in its "backyard" (hegemony, albeit benign, however rationalized or euphemistically labeled). The administration is also disposed to an undifferentiated and broad definition of security, with a blurred distinction between what the national security *requires* and what would be *convenient* or *preferred*.

- The ideological intensity of the administration's Manichaean conceptualization of relations with the Soviet Union affects its specific perception of Central America. The prevailing view is that not only would Soviet/Cuban military bases constitute a security threat, but *any* Soviet/Cuban relationship with Nicaragua, or any other country in the area, would threaten America's backyard. Many are also alarmed about the rise to power of indigenous "radical" or "leftist" elements because of assumed inevitable objective and subjective convergence with Soviet/Cuban power.

- All these perceptions and premises predispose the administration to view Central America as a zero-sum game, and they point the administration *away* from a strategy of negotiation. Despite the rhetorical affirmation of support for "dialogue and negotiation," the administration has not accepted the concept of negotiation as an accommodation or establishment of a modus vivendi. Negotiations are to be understood as the continuation of confrontation by other means. The goal is still to cleanse the isthmus and restore it to its previous "safe and friendly" relationship.

Within these parameters, different administration actors push varying tactics and agendas, many of them internally inconsistent with each other. The way the administration handles these differing agendas is simply to allow them to compete with each other, to make ad hoc pragmatic decisions as it goes along, and to allow the accumulation of these to define policy direction. It is a policymaking style that plays poker instead of chess.

As 1984 begins, events in Central America appear to be approaching a new threshold. In the words of one Central American diplomat: "Everything is possible right now; the range of war and peace."[49]

Unless the administration redefines its concept of negotiations and its assumptions, the probabilities are that it will simply continue to act as it is doing — but more so. In that event, tensions will continue to mount and the prospects of spreading conflict will grow. The administration will likely increase support of the *contras'* campaign in Nicaragua and the military effort in El Salvador, and build up the U.S. military presence and assistance in Honduras. The administration will then "play it by ear" to see if its actions, or some change of circumstances, will alter the calculus. It will watch, in short, to see how the cards fall.

Central America is a classic Greek tragedy, with the actors on all sides functioning single-mindedly, in terms of their own beliefs, premises, conceptions and perceptions — "fulfilling their nature." The situation, thus, promises to unleash further tests of will, more conflict, bloodshed, and further tragedy. And there is no deus ex machina in sight.

Or is that the group with the Contadora suntan?

NOTES

1. For a stimulating analysis of the "American style" and foreign policy, see Stanley Hoffmann, *Gulliver's Troubles, or the Setting of American Foreign Policy,* published for the Council on Foreign Relations, McGraw-Hill Book Company, 1968. See "Part II, America's Style," pp. 87-213.

2. *The Economist* (October 29-November 4, 1983), "The Second Spanish Civil War," pp. 33-34.

3. See essays by I.M. Destler and Barry Rubin in this volume. For an interesting view by a columnist see Joseph Kraft, "A Scorecard on the Infighting," *Washington Post,* November 13, 1983, p. C7.

4. See especially, "A New Inter-American Policy for the Eighties," Council for Inter-American Security, Inc., 1980. This report was prepared by The "Committee of Santa Fe" composed of L. Francis Bouchey, David Jordan, Roger Fontaine, Gordon Summer and Lewis Tambs. The latter three now hold positions in the administration. That report stated "Containment of the Soviet Union is not enough. Detente is dead . . . for World War III is almost over . . . Latin America and Southern Asia are the scenes of strife of the third phase of World War III." (p. 1) "President Jimmy Carter's Ibero-American policies . . . are the culmination of this accommodation process whereby Latin America is excluded from U.S. strategic concerns and independent Latin American regimes are abandoned to extracontinental attacks by the international Communist movement." (p. 6). "The Committee of Santa Fe contends that U.S. foreign policy is in disarray; that the norms of conflict and social change adopted by the Carter administration are those of the Soviet Union; that the area in contention is the sovereign territory of U.S. allies and Third World trading partners; that the sphere of the Soviet Union and its surrogates is expanding; and that the annual balance sheet of gains and losses favors the USSR."(p. 9). For a more sophisticated but similar view see Jeane Kirkpatrick, "Dictatorships and Double Standards," *Commentary,* November 1979, pp. 34-45, and "U.S. Security & Latin America," *Commentary,* January 1981, pp. 29-40.

5. Early in his tenure, Secretary of State Alexander Haig, specifically placed terrorism above human rights as a priority problem: "International terrorism will take the place of human rights in our concern because it is the ultimate of abuse of human rights." (Secretary Haig's press conference, January 29, 1981, *New York Times,* January 29, 1981, p. 25.) In remarks to the Conservative Political Action Conference in March 1981, UN Ambassador, Jeane Kirkpatrick said, "We know that revolutions in our times are not caused by social injustice. Revolutions are caused by revolutionaries and revolutionaries are people. They are not social forces." (as quoted in Roy Gutman and Susan Page, "Central America: The Making of U.S. Policy," *Newsday,* July 31, p. 26.) This is the first of an excellent three-part analysis of Central American policy. In the same article, see reference to the National Security Adviser, Richard Allen, telling Napoleon Duarte, that he "wasn't much impressed with land reform" (p. 26).

6. Address before a joint session of Congress on April 27, 1983. *Department of State Bulletin,* June 1983, p. 1.

7. See Alexander L. George, *Presidential Decisionmaking in Foreign Policy,* Boulder: Westview Press, 1980. pp. 26-34; and John D. Steinbruner, *The Cybernetic Theory of Decision,* Princeton University Press, 1974, chap. 4, "Cognitive Processes," pp. 88-139.

8. Just before his inauguration in January 1981, President Reagan said in an an interview: "You do not try to fight a civil war and institute reforms at the same time. Get rid of the war. Then go forward with the reforms." *Time,* January 5, 1981, p. 31.

9. See Robert Jervis, *Perception and Misperception in International Politics,* Princeton University Press, 1976, chap. 4, "Cognitive Consistency and the Interaction between Theory and Data," esp. pp. 128-142.

10. Shortly after assuming office, President Reagan said: "The Soviets are, you might say, trying to do the same thing in El Salvador that they did in Afghanistan, but by using proxy troops through Cuba. . . . " (excerpts from Reagan interview, *New York Times,* March 4, 1981, p 5.) In a speech on July 18, 1983, before the International Longshoreman's Association, he said: "There is a war in Central America that is being fueled by the Soviets and the Cubans. . . . This is the first real Communist aggression on the American mainland."

(Department of State, *Current Policy,* No. 499.) In a speech to the OAS on February 24, 1982, the President warned against Cuban and Soviet efforts "to establish Cuban-style Marxist-Leninist dictatorships" throughout the region. (Department of State, *Current Policy,* No 370.)

11. Address to joint session of Congress, *op. cit.,* April 27, 1983.
12. Leslie Gelb, "When is a Foreign Interest Vital?" *New York Times,* August 8, 1983, p A14.
13. For a trenchant dissection of the credibility argument and Central American policy see Eldon Kenworthy, "Why the United States is in Central America," *Bulletin of the Atomic Scientists,* October 1983, pp. 14-20.
14. Address to joint session of Congress, *op. cit.,* April 27, 1983.
15. Kenworthy, *op. cit.*
16. For a stimulating analysis of the domino argument see Theodore Draper, "Falling Dominoes," *New York Review of Books,* October 27, 1983.
17. President Johnson described an extreme formulation, saying it was better to fight in Vietnam than Honolulu. Richard Nixon was equally graphic, stating in 1965 that Vietnam's fate was that of all southeast Asia; if it fell the region from Burma to Indonesia would fall; the Pacific would become a "red sea" and Chinese Communist aggression in Australia would be only four or five years away. (quoted in Draper, *op. cit.,* p. 14.)
18. Speech by Fred C. Iklé, Undersecretary of Defense for Policy, to the Baltimore Council on Foreign Affairs, September 12, 1983. Text as contained in Department of Defense Press Release, No. 450-83, September 12, 1983. Iklé repeated them in a speech to the Dallas World Affairs Council on November 16, 1983: "If we accept a protracted stalemate now, we will have a heavy price to pay. . . . In a few years hence, we would in effect have a second 'North Korea' in the middle of Central America."
19. Testimony to the Senate Foreign Relations Committee from Assistant Secretary of State for Inter-American Affairs, Thomas Enders, February 1, 1982.
20. For an insightful analysis of operational premises underpinning U.S. policy in the postwar period see Seyom Brown, *The Faces of Power: Constancy and Change in United States Foreign Policy from Truman to Reagan,* rev. ed., New York: Columbia University Press, 1983. I have drawn heavily on Brown's scheme of analysis here.
21. *Ibid.,* p. 570.
22. Hoffman, *op. cit.,* pp. 181-184.
23. See, for example, comment by columnist George Will: " . . . eagerness for negotiations makes the United States susceptible to what the Sandinistas are doing. They are using rhetoric about negotiations the way the Soviet Union uses arms control negotiations: to buy time and sow irresolution in the U.S. policymaking. . . ." *Washington Post,* July 31, 1983 "Teaching Latin America to Elect Good Men."
24. A passage in Stanley Hoffmann's book, *Gulliver's Troubles, op. cit.,* published fifteen years ago is uncannily applicable to Central America today: "The assumption of the normalcy of consensus has often led American statesman to offer friendship to foes of the United States on condition that they recognize the universal validity of America's principles. We do not think we are asking a humilating concession of them: once they have 'mended their ways,' they will become partners in the task of ordering the world and will see that their interests are better served thereby than by their currently hostile policies. So we suggest the possibilities of fruitful contacts and even cooperative schemes, which we would be ready to initiate if only they behave properly" (p. 131).
25. The phrase is from the president's speech to the joint session of Congress, *op. cit.*
26. See the texts of the State Department statement of October 5, 1982, and the Final Act of the Meeting of Foreign Ministers of Countries Interested in the Promotion of Democracy in Central America and the Caribbean, October 4, 1982. *Department of State Bulletin,* December 1982, pp. 69-72.

27. Designation of a special envoy to "lend support to the efforts of regional governments to bring peace" to the area was announced by President Reagan in his April speech to the joint session of Congress.
28. Hoffmann, *op. cit.*, p. 199.
29. See the last article in the *Newsday* series by Gutman and Page, *op. cit.* See especially sidebar story, "Pentagon, State Department Promote Separate Policies," *Newsday,* August 2, p. 13.
30. Excerpts from NSC document "U.S. Policy in Central America and Cuba through FY 1984, Summary Paper" as published in *New York Times,* 7 April 1983, p. A16.
31. Iklé's speech to Baltimore Council on Foreign Affairs, *op. cit.*
32. See James LeMoyne, "U.S. May Ban Salvador Exiles in Hired Deaths," *New York Times,* November 19, 1983, p. 1.
33. In his speech to the joint session of Congress, President Reagan stated: "I can tell you tonight, democracy is beginning to take root in El Salvador . . . the Government of El Salvador has been keeping its promise . . . the democratic political parties and factions in El Salvador are coming together around the common goal of seeking a political solution to their country's problems."
34. Under-Secretary of Defense Fred Iklé was reported to have urged increased military assistance to El Salvador following a visit to that country in early November 1983.
35. In a private conversation with the writer on October 21, 1983, Guillermo Ungo commented that the Salvadoran Government refused to meet with the opposition in San Salvador on the grounds that if they could not meet to talk with the goverment, how could the government claim to offer security for an electoral campaign. See Robert Leiken's chapter in this volume for detailed analysis of guerrilla views.
36. Iklé's speech to the Baltimore Council on Foreign Affairs, *op. cit.*
37. In defending his decision, the President said that the congressional restrictions actually increased human rights violations because left and right extremists could end U.S. aid by increasing human rights violations. He also speculated that the left may have been responsible for some of the deaths attributed to the right, and that the Marxists carefully avoided attacking rightists.
38. LeMoyne, *op. cit.*
39. Transcripts of the president's news conferences as published in *New York Times*, July 19, 1983, p. A6.
40. Transcript of the president's news conference as published in *New York Times*, November 4, 1983, p. A16.
41. For a journalist's analysis, see "A Fumbled Chance for Accord," second in three-part series by Gutman and Page, *Newsday, op. cit.* August 1, 1983, p. 4.
42. Steven Kinzer, December 5, 1983, *New York Times,* p. A1.
43. According to press reports, Secretary of State Shultz observed to reporters at a breakfast December 1, 1983 that while some of the things the Sandinistas said were "good to hear," there is the "question of whether there is a reality behind the words." Twice during that breakfast, according to press reports, the Secretary was described as "pointedly declining" to say whether the Administration was prepared to accept the continuation of the Sandinista government, observing: "It's not an attractive regime to us or to its neighbors." *New York Times,* "Shultz Reacts Favorably," p. A3.
44. A description of the development of the covert program is contained in Don Oberdorfer, "Applying Pressure in Central America," *Washington Post,* November 23, 1983, p. A10. This is the fourth in a five-part series on "Reagan and the World."
45. See speculation by former CIA Director Stansfield Turner, "From an ex-CIA Chief: Stop the 'Covert' Operation in Nicaragua," *Washington Post,* April 24, 1983. p. C1.
46. For a perceptive analysis of covert action with specific reference to Central America by a former CIA official, see Tom Polgar, "Forward or Backward, Our Belly Will Hurt," *Miami Herald,* June 5, 1983. See especially p. 15.

47. The *Washington Post* reported November 25, 1983 that the CIA had concluded "that there are no circumstances under which a force of U.S. backed rebels can achieve a military or political victory over the leftist Sandinista government of Nicaragua." (Patrick Tyler, "U.S. Backed Rebels Can't Win in Nicaragua, CIA Finds," *Washington Post,* November 15, p. A1.)
48. Andrew Schmookler, "Think Tank Round-Up," unpublished manuscript, September 1981. The quote is in reference to cases of conflict in major intractable trouble spots, and is particularly applicable here.
49. Quoted in Joanne Omang, "U.S. Seeks Substances in Signals," *Washington Post,* December 4, 1983, p. A1.

12

AT THE ROOT OF THE PROBLEM:
Conceptual Failures in
U.S.-Central American Relations

Howard J. Wiarda

The facts about the crisis in Central America are sometimes unclear and often open to dispute. Observers disagree about whether El Salvador's civil war stems from internal factors, outside interference, or the precise balance between these two; over whether Nicaragua is still somewhat pluralist or hopelessly Marxist-Leninist; over how our aid effects the area and what type of aid can most appropriately achieve the ends desired. These and other issues form the grist of the U.S. policy debate over Central America.

But an at least equally important set of questions has to do with the concepts we use to interpret the area, the frameworks and models of analysis that we employ. Indeed since our assessments of the facts depend largely on the basis of the models of intrepretation that we use, the conceptual problem could be seen as even more important than, and prior to, the factual ones. This chapter argues that our difficulties in understanding and coming to grips with the Central American imbroglio lie here. We have consistently used the wrong or inappropriate models to comprehend and interpret the area. And if our fundamental interpretations have been wrong, it is small wonder that policy has so often gone astray.

BASIC PROBLEMS

At the root of the problem in U.S.-Latin American relations is our lack of knowledge and understanding of the area—what former Congressman James W. Symington referred to recently as "our fundamental, dogged, appalling ignorance of the Latin mind and culture."[1]

259

This lack of comprehension, combined with more than a little disdain, has long and complex origins. It stems from historic assumptions of Anglo-Saxon and Protestant superiority over Latin and Catholic-Inquisitorial civilizations; the idea that our country has been successful historically and Latin America has not; the notion that we are more "developed" and "modern" than they in a moral, political and psychological sense as well as an economic one; even from, doubtlessly, racial and ethnic prejudice.[2] The European basis of this pervasive prejudice dates at least as far back as Hegel's condescending view that Latin America had "no history," a major indictment especially if one recalls the importance of history to Hegel and the Hegelian notion of historical evolution. Then there are Marx's equally disparaging remarks about the area as being primitive and "Asiatic." Europe and the United States have always assumed that Latin America is unworthy of serious study, that its culture and politics have nothing to contribute, that its development has been negligible. Therefore, Latin America can be safely ignored, until some major crisis — Guatemala in 1954, Cuba in the early 1960s, the Dominican Republic in 1965, Chile in 1973, and Central America now — forces it onto our television screens if not into our consciousness.

But the problem is not just a lack of American understanding, which, incidentally, is mutual. Latin America's lack of comprehension of the United States is at least as great as our lack of understanding of Latin America. The problem, however, runs deeper than that. For not only do we not understand Latin America very well but the sad fact is we do not want to understand it. This attitude was captured in the oft-used quote of *New York Times* columnist James Reston who wrote that "the United States will do anything for Latin America except read about it."[3]

These problems of prejudice, condescension, and sense of superiority are especially acute regarding Central America. We may, grudgingly, admit some cultural worth in the larger South American countries of Argentina, Brazil, Chile, Colombia, or Venezuela; but those "banana republics" of Central America? This area provides the stuff of *New Yorker* cartoons and *opera buffe* stereotypes: comical, mustachioed men on horseback who gallop in and out of the presidential palace with frequent regularity. Central America is viewed as chaotic, disorganized, uninstitutionalized, dysfunctional, and wholly devoid of culture and civilization. Indeed, it is precisely because Central American politics are chronically unstable and devoid of institutions, coupled with the fact these countries lie right on our doorstep, that accounts for the repeated involvement of the United States in the domestic and international affairs of the region.

Our attitudes toward Latin America in general, and toward Central America in particular, have been shaped not just by ephemeral biases and prejudices but by values and premises deeply ingrained in the American psyche. These values and premises reverberate widely in the prevailing political culture and are shared by policy makers, theorists of development, and the general public—albeit at different levels.[4] U.S. assumptions about Third World areas, in this case Central America, grow out of what Harvard historian Louis Hartz called "the liberal tradition in America."[5] The liberal tradition shapes not only the U.S. domestic political debate but U.S. foreign policy attitudes and positions as well. These premises are not always articulated as a formal and manifest theology but they are strongly held nonetheless and crucial in enabling us to understand U.S. attitudes and policy toward Central America. They constitute the intellectual baggage that American officials carry with them in thinking about the Third World.

What are these prevailing attitudes that Hartz has called "liberal"? Essentially they stem from the liberal-Lockean premises of American democracy, which include a powerful predilection for stable, nonradical, constitutional, peaceful, republican-representative, and democratic governance. In Hartz's usage almost all American politicians and academics, as well as the general public, are "liberal": Richard Nixon as well as Hubert Humphrey, John Foster Dulles as well as Dean Acheson, Lyndon Johnson as well as John F. Kennedy, Ronald Reagan as well as Jimmy Carter. While all of these policy-makers may disagree on specific policies and partisan orientations, they share a common national dedication to the liberal-Lockean principles of representative government and a free economy. The question for the purpose of foreign policy analysis is the one posed by Hartz: Can a country born "free" and "liberal," as was the United States, *ever* understand societies and polities where these premises do not apply? Or, as posed by Robert Packenham: What happens when our liberal tradition confronts an obdurate foreign reality whose assumptions are often quite different from its own, as in Central America?[6]

CONCEPTUAL MODELS AND U.S.-LATIN AMERICAN RELATIONS

Since World War II the United States has carried out a variety of major foreign aid programs, aimed initially at Western European restoration and later at the Third World. The Cuban revolution, rising U.S. security concerns, and the new Kennedy administration and its foreign policy orientation combined to make Latin America the principal locus for many of these later assistance efforts. During this same period, the late 1950s-early 1960s, American social scientists began theorizing about the processes of development in Third World nations. For the first time, Latin America commanded a major share of attention.

Neither the foreign policy initiatives nor the social science concepts that undergirded them were free of biases and value judgments. Both policy makers and social scientists, whether explicitly or implicitly, had definite ideas and preconceptions — values reflecting the prevailing ones in the American polity — about what constituted good public policy toward and in the Third World. These values were based on the same liberal-Lockean notions that Hartz had identified as dominant within the American domestic political tradition. As applied to foreign policy and the Third World, they implied an over-riding emphasis on democracy, stability, anti-communism, peaceful and evolutionary political transitions, world community, and pro-Americanism.

It is not our purpose to criticize these values as values. They reflect the prevailing American values and are the preferred personal and political values of the author of this chapter. The question is not these values per se but rather their relevance and appropriateness in Central America.

The prevailing liberal-Lockean tradition had a pervasive influence on our attitudes toward Latin America and on the United States foreign assistance programs. Based predominantly on the American experience the following four assumptions help summarize the approach of U.S. policymakers and social scientists:[7]

1. Change and Development are Easy

The assumption here is that if the vast potential in other lands is tapped, if traditional institutions are overcome, and if the right party or government is installed in office, then development can rapidly advance. Little attention was devoted to the wrenching upheavals — as in Guatemala or El Salvador — that such changes imply, the blood and terror to which they often give rise, the frustrations of development and the possiblities, especially in weak, uninstitutionalized, resource-poor countries like those in Central America, not for inevitable progress but for fragmentation and breakdown.

2. All Good Things Go Together

The U.S. believes social modernization, economic growth, and political development can be pursued in concert. That also grows out of the U.S. experience. The possibility that social modernization and economic growth — as in Nicaragua during the 1950s and 1960s — may be disruptive of stability and political development rather than contributing to them is seldom considered. The Central American experience has demonstrated that these forces may not be complementary, but are often contradictory instead.

3. Stability Must be Maintained; Radicalism and Revolutionary Regimes Must be Opposed

But the idea seemed to be contradicted by the fact that many of the programs we fostered with the best of democratic intentions — agrarian reform, community development, and the like—might themselves be profoundly revolutionary and destabilizing. The U.S. emphasis on evolutionary change, moreover, flew in the face of the obdurate opposition to *any* change in many nations (El Salvador's fourteen families, for instance) and the fact that in many countries only radical and revolutionary challenges to existing systems had the potential for achieving the kind of democratic and developmentalist change the U.S. wanted (for example, the Dominican Republic uprising of 1965 and its aftermath).

4. Distributing Power is More Important than Concentrating It

U.S. policy has tended toward the support of pluralism and the separation of powers. In Central America as elsewhere in the Third World, however, the basic problem is not to distribute power through community development and other programs; power in these societies is already fragmented. What is often required is to create strong central institutions where none have existed before, to concentrate power rather than disperse it in order to carry out effective programs.

In these four liberal-Lockean propositions forming the basis of American policy toward developing nations and in the brief qualifications introduced with regard to each, one can already see the possibilities for conflict, contradiction, and failure. Moreover, a high degree of economic determinism has also been implicit (and sometimes quite explicit) in the American foreign assistance programs. This too was based on the American experience of minimalist government involvement in development so as to allow the dynamic economic forces in the country to proceed on their own.

W. W. Rostow's 1960 book, *The Stages of Economic Growth,* was a major and influential expression of this argument.[8] This volume had a significant impact on the development literature then enjoying a considerable boom and consequently on the U.S. foreign assistance programs. Rostow argued that economic forces were the determining ones in development; that political development (by which he meant democratization) inevitably flowed from economic growth; that change in the Third World would inevitably follow the Western model; that such changes could be fostered through U.S. economic aid; and that these changes were beneficent, universal, and unilinear, leading to polities closely resembling that of the United States. The problem in Rostow's formulation was both a rather crude economic determinism and a mechanistic parochialism that assumed that Third World development would be a mirror image of the Western experience.

Another expression of the prevailing American view could be found in the work of Seymour M. Lipset[9] and Karl W. Deutsch[10] on the relations between economic growth, social mobilization, and political development. They similarly focused on the economic and social prerequisites of democracy (economic development, literacy, and per capita radio and television) and suggested that democracy and pluralism were the inevitable result of socio-economic modernization. Their error, which was even more pronounced in their readers and proponents (including policymakers) than in the original formulations of these authors, was to mistake correlation for causation, to assume that since most democracies in the world were often the most economically developed, the latter was the *cause* of the former. It followed then that political democracy and development (in most of the literature the terms were used synonymously) would be a product of economic development, and that democracy and political development would proceed inevitably from the motor force of economic growth. In these ways scholars such as Rostow, Lipset, and Deutsch came to be known as "Dr. Yes" spokesmen for the U.S. foreign assistance programs designed in the early 1960s. As U.S. envoy George McGhee has recently written about this period, "We considered education and economic development the key to the solution of all problems. Democracy was accepted without question as everyone's final goal."[11]

The Rostow-Lipset-Deutsch view was quite congenial to U.S. foreign aid administrators and economists—and not just because Rostow, himself an economist, was the chief White House foreign policy advisor in the early-to-mid-1960s and thus in a position to put his ideas into practice. This view also corresponded closely to the technocratic and generally apolitical preferences of officials of the newly-created Agency for International Development, again largely dominated by economists. They preferred, for professional as well as career reasons, to concentrate on the seemingly easy task of economic aid and to avoid as far as possible the vexing, messy, difficult political variables that always seemed to "get in the way." Economists and aid officials seem almost to prefer to relegate what are in fact difficult political issues and choices (issues of democracy, human rights, civilian versus military rule, corruption and repression, representative government) to the subcategory of "dependent variables" because they are too indeterminate for their taste, and because they tend to interfere with the neat econometric models on which the profession would prefer to make its predictions.

From these major assumptions, biases, and predilections, all strongly ingrained in American political culture, flowed a number of sub-assumptions and specific policy initiatives. An analysis of each of these would require more space than is available here, but a brief review of some of them is required because these assumptions are essential ingredients in the U.S. foreign assistance programs.

1. The Emphasis on Economic Development

Simply put, the rationale of U.S. economic assistance programs in the last quarter century has been that if only we can pour in sufficient economic aid, political stability and democracy, as well as anti-communism, will inevitably result. The difficulties with this proposition are many. For example, Costa Rica developed as a democracy before any U.S. aid was proffered, not as a result of any U.S. assistance. The country that received the most aid per capita of any Latin American country in the early 1960s—the Dominican Republic—exploded in revolution in 1965 that precipitated a U.S. military occupation involving 22,000 troops and presaged our then-accelerating and eventually even more disastrous involvement in Vietnam. The country that received more aid per capita than any other in the late 1960s—Chile—nonetheless elected a Marxist president in 1970 whose radical tendencies and administrative inefficiencies helped lead to a bloody coup in 1973, as well as one of the most repressive regimes in the modern history of the hemisphere.

It would be hard to argue that economic development in Nicaragua led to much of either democracy or stability; rather Nicaraguan economic growth tended principally to strengthen the Somoza dictatorship—until other events overwhelmed Somoza and led to the Sandinistas' victory. One would have to stretch one's definition a great deal to call that a stable or a democratic regime. One would be equally hard-pressed to argue that U.S.-backed economic growth anywhere else in Central America—El Salvador, Guatemala, or Honduras—has led inevitably, unilinearly, or even by fits and starts, to democracy, stability, or moderate, progressive, pro-American regimes. One need not necessarily be biased toward economists to recognize from the Central American experience that something is clearly wrong with much social science and foreign policy development theory that posits a direct and positive relationship between economic development and either democracy or stability.[12]

2. The Role of the Middle Class

Much of our development assistance has been based on the prevailing American social science notion that a large middle class is a bastion of stability, progress, democracy, and anti-communism, as it has been in the United States and Western Europe. Much of our assistance to Central America over the past two decades has been aimed at building up this class. The assumption here is that the middle class in Central America will behave like its North American counterpart, with moderation, pragmatism, and responsibility.

There is no doubt, of course, that the middle class has grown in numbers in Central America, but the expected social and political concomitants of that growth have not been forthcoming. The evidence we have seems to indicate that the Central American middle class is not happily democratic and middle-of-the-road but tends to ape the behavior of the traditional oligarchies, is exceedingly conscious of its newly-won place and position in the society and tends to disdain the lower classes, often supports military takeovers to prevent the lower classes from gaining a share of power, is not necessarily progressive and modernizing but often reactionary, and that instead of being a force for stability it has helped precipitate fragmentation and instability.[13] The Central American middle class tends to support extremist rather than centrist solutions, and in this sense may be rather like its German equivalent historically. The Central American middle class has not become a moderate and progressive influence or a bulwark of democracy, nor is there much evidence even that the trends are inevitably in that direction. Another of the main assumptions of the U.S. assistance programs in the past twenty years, therefore, has been shown to be without much real foundation in terms of actual behavior as compared with theoretical assumptions.

3. Trade Union Development

Another prevalent assumption of U.S. assistance programs is that through our economic aid we could help create a moderate, progressive, democratic, and anti-communist trade unionism in Central America and elsewhere. Once again the model is the generally nonpolitical, non-ideological trade unionism of the United States. Here one can also see the persistent preference for technocratic solutions that eschew any connection with partisan politics of even, one might say, the real nuts and bolts issues (such as poverty, underdevelopment, immense social gaps, political action-oriented labor organizations, class strife) of Central American life is also apparent. A moderate nonpolitical trade unionism, it is argued, would help support moderate democracies and serve as a further bastion against right wing coups on the one hand or communist seizures of power on the other.

In fact, the growth of trade unionism in Central America rather than promoting stability has frequently helped precipitate coups on the part of the armed forces who tend to see the labor unions as potential rivals to their own institutional dominance. Obviously this is not to suggest that we oppose trade unionism in Central America but that we be aware of the possible contradictory implications of U.S. strategies.

In some cases the unions, including at times those supported by the United States, have urged or helped the military to stage coups against more radical elements. A nonpolitical, non-ideological trade unionism has not emerged as a result of U.S. economic support. One could argue in fact that the opposite has occurred — perhaps inevitably given Central America's history of ideological and intensely *political* trade unionism as compared with the generally nonpolitical trade unionism of the United States.[14] A nonpolitical but anti-communist trade unionism is also a contradiction in terms, and to our consternation the U.S. has not always been able to have it both ways in Central America.

Admittedly, scholars have reached different conclusions regarding the U.S. effort to translate its brand of trade unionism to Central America. Further, there is evidence that in recent years the efforts of U.S. labor and its international arm, the American Institute for Free Labor Development (AIFLD), have changed in major ways. But enough has been said to indicate that the U.S. model of trade unionism and collective bargaining has not always worked well or as intended in Central America, it has sometimes worked at cross purposes with other aspects of U.S. policy, and scant evidence exists that the Central American unions will follow the U.S. example anytime soon *or* serve as complementary bastions of stability, democracy, and anti-communism.

4. The Military as Professional and Apolitical

U.S. military assistance programs, in accordance with the economic and other assistance programs noted earlier, have been oriented over the past thirty years (even earlier if one goes back to the Marine occupations of the first third of this century) toward creating in Central America armed forces that are (1) professionalized, (2) apolitical, (3) civic action-oriented, (4) democratic, and (5) anti-communist. There have been many problems with this effort. To begin with, the second and fifth items on the list are often incompatible: a military, like a labor federation, cannot be both apolitical and anti-communist at one and the same time. The first and fourth items may be equally incompatible, for the greater professionalization of the Central American military has led not to less but to more usurpations of power and to longer periods of military rule.[15] The new training that the armed forces have received in development economics, modern management, and national security doctrine has led them to conclude—with considerable reason—that they can run their countries better than the civilians.

Nor have the efforts aimed at involving the Central American militaries in civic action programs worked well, since those tasks involve the officers getting their hands dirty, leaving the amenities of the capital city for the discomforts of the provinces, involving them in programs directed toward the public weal rather than toward their own private enrichment, and in general violating long established cultural norms concerning appropriate behavior for the proud military institution. Many of the same reservations apply to U.S. efforts to get the military in El Salvador to carry the fight to the guerrillas, to cease violating their own people's human rights and to give up their historical practice of supplementing their meager salaries by strong-arm methods and illegal business ventures. Not only have these efforts not proven successful, there is little evidence that the American assistance programs are sufficiently responsive to the society and culture they are dealing with to offer needed alternative incentives.

One could easily expand this discussion of U.S. aid programs to cover agrarian reform, community development, family planning, bureaucratic modernization, tax reform, and a host of others. What is striking about these programs is the degree to which all of them are based upon the American (and secondarily the Western European) experience and model of development. They are all predicated on the notion of an inevitable, unilinear evolution toward a stable, bourgeois, happy, liberal-Lockean, democratic, and middle-of-the-road society and polity that, perhaps not surprisingly, looks just like our own. Whether any of the main facets of that strategy have any prospects of working (let alone succeeding) in Central America, where the societal norms and behavioral expectations are quite different from those of the United States, is another story entirely.

The following section will examine how these assumptions and expectations have worked out in specific U.S. aid programs.

HOW THE WRONG MODELS OFTEN LEAD US ASTRAY

In reviewing the history of the U.S. assistance programs in Central America since World War II, one is struck by how consistent — and how consistently misapplied — they have been. From the Truman administration to the present the assumptions have consistently been the liberal-Lockean ones discussed earlier. Each new administration has had certain nuances and changes of emphases, but the basic assumptions have been the same. If only we could pour in sufficient funds and American know-how, we could modernize these economies, create a stable middle class, professionalize the armed forces, build democracy, create apolitical trade unions, guarantee stability, secure anti-communist regimes, and all the rest — all at once. These programs have been breathtaking in their sweep and characteristically American in their optimism and ethnocentrism. The current crisis, fragmentation, and breakdown in Central America, however, would seem to be the best evidence that the theory and assumptions are in need of thorough reexamination.[16]

The Truman Doctrine

While the message of the 1947 Truman Doctrine was aimed at the Soviet Union, its economic assistance provisions were intended for the benefit of Greece and Turkey. Its rationale was not purely humanitarian but rather the U.S. national interest: the prevention of possible destabilization and communist takeovers. In Greece, the U.S. sponsored elections with the hope that the democratic centrist parties would prevail, stability would be ensured, and a progressive development plan would be carried out. The economic development plans were aimed at producing political order and reducing the appeals of communism.

The efforts to prevent a Communist victory were successful in the short term, but the rest of the program was less so. The program was sweeping and grandiose involving economic aid, military assistance, and democratic political development. Like other American assistance programs to come, it assumed that change and development were easy, that all they required were American capital and expertise. Since all good things go together, political democracy would result from economic growth, because the Turks and the Greeks, presumably, shared the same values as well. The long-term result, however, provides grounds for considerable skepticism that U.S. efforts could engineer democracy or secure stability in Greece and Turkey, provide for a pro-American regime, and guarantee that those countries would develop inevitably in the American mold if sufficient economic aid were forthcoming.[17]

The Marshall Plan

The Marshall Plan had much the same rationale and was part of the same larger strategy as the Truman Doctrine. Political development was contingent on economic assistance. Although the instruments of policy were almost exclusively economic, the goals were political, strategic and assumed to flow from economic assistance: stability, democracy, pro-Americanism, anti-communism, and the establishment of centrist regimes and movements.

The distinctive feature of the Marshall Plan was that its main goals were achieved, within the specified four-year time period and considerably below the dollar amount appropriated by Congress. But when essentially the same plans and programs were tried out later in the Third World and Central America in particular, they did not work. The difference was that Western Europe had the indigenous institutions, parties, and leadership to carry out a major redevelopment program. The real need in Europe was for temporary economic assistance, and when the U.S. made that assistance available democracy and stability were quickly achieved. As Packenham argues, perhaps nowhere else were the conditions so propitious for the "economic development ergo political development" approach. Those same conditions had not been present in Greece and Turkey, and they would not be present in Asia, Africa, or Latin America.

Point Four

The Point Four Program announced by President Truman in his 1949 inaugural address represented an effort to transfer the assumptions of the Marshall Plan to the underdeveloped world. Again the notion was that economic aid and American technical assistance would bring freedom, democracy, pro-Americanism, stability, international understanding, anti-communism, and the end of war. The list of objectives was thus expanded but the same assumptions underlay the program.

Point Four failed to achieve the goals desired not because using American knowledge and assistance was wrong but because of an exaggerated notion of what could thereby be accomplished politically. The program failed to appraise realistically the difficulty of achieving change and development in the emerging nations and of assessing accurately the relationship between economic and political development. Rather than leading to stability and democracy, economic development we now know has the potential to undermine both. These misperceptions were part of the same effort outlined earlier to export liberal-Lockean presumptions and institutions to societies where they did not fit or fit only partially. They illustrate again the American proclivity for assuming that the U.S. developmental experience, or that of Western Europe under the Marshall Plan, has the same relevance in the Third World and in quite different cultural areas.[18]

The Alliance for Progress

The economic achievements of John F. Kennedy's Alliance for Progress were considerable. The pace of change throughout Central America accelerated in the 1960s and on into the early 1970s, per capita income was raised considerably, new industries grew up, the Central American Common Market was launched, and several of the economies of the area "took off." Economic growth in turn stimulated greater social modernization, the building of roads and housing, improved education, advanced sanitation and health care, and the development of agriculture.

The political goals of the Alliance, however, which were the main reasons the program had been launched, were not achieved. As we have seen, the Central American middle class has not developed into a stronghold of democracy and stability. The armed forces have not become both more professionalized and subservient to civilian authority. The trade unions have not become more moderate and apolitical. Economic development did not produce political development. The elites have not evidenced a greater sense of noblesse oblige or responsibility. Indeed, if the basic goals of U.S. policy were—and remain—to secure moderate, stable, pro-American regimes throughout the area, the present situation of conflict, guerrilla insurgency, and civil war must surely make one question the degree of success. Thus, while the economic and social achievements of the Alliance were considerable, its assumptions concerning fundamental political development have proved wrong.

Several reasons may be suggested for the failure of the political agenda of the Alliance. First, the program and its possibilities were exaggerated and oversold; the ambitious goals set forth were both unachievable and, in several areas, internally contradictory. Second, the Alliance was based on economic determinist assumptions derived from the then-current Rostow-Lipsetonian development literature that, we have already seen, was logically flawed and ignored crucial political and cultural differences. Third, the model of a happy, liberal, middle class, yeoman-farmer (hence the motivation for agrarian reform), socially-just, pluralistic, and democratic society and polity were all derived from the United States and had little to do with Central America. Fourth, the institution relied upon to implement the program, the Central American Common Market (CACM), was based too heavily on the European/Marshall Plan concept. The Common Market worked well in Western Europe because the two principal economies involved, the French and German, were closely complementary. But the Central American economies were competitive rather than complementary and hence the Common Market produced only limited success. Political rivalries also tore the CACM apart. Fifth, Central America is a classic case of how U.S. aid policies and modernization helped break down existing traditional institutions (family and kinship groups, patronage networks, clan groups, and patron-client patterns) without creating anything viable to replace them, thus, helping precipitate the instability that now plagues U.S. policy in the area.

Carter's Campaign for Human Rights

As a result of the Carter administration's emphasis on human rights, some political prisoners in Central America were released from jail. Torture was probably used less than previously as an instrument of policy, and some lives were saved. These are certainly not small accomplishments.

On the other hand, the campaign was carried out in a naive missionary style reminiscent of Woodrow Wilson. U.S. criteria for human rights were the only standards used, and the program all too often ethnocentrically reflected the U.S. civil rights movement of the 1960s. It was applied haphazardly, inconsistently, and not always impartially. By its sometimes gross and indiscriminating condemnations of whole countries or whole governments, the policy produced numerous backlashes. It turned otherwise friendly governments against us and often united their peoples nationalistically behind an unacceptable regime only because we had attacked it. Like so many of the overblown and oversold programs we have chronicled, in the final analysis its successes and accomplishments were rather modest compared to the effort expended and the costs incurred.[19]

Project Democracy

Project Democracy (passed by Congress in the form of the Democracy Endowment in November, 1983) is really two different programs, or more accurately, two different conceptions of the same program. One group of its adherents favors a grandiose plan to bring democracy to Central America — political parties like our own, honest and competitive elections, pluralistic interest groups, the full gamut of representative institutions, and the social programs of an advanced industrial society. This group apparently believes both that the United States can export its institutions to other nations *and* that Central America wishes to recast itself entirely in the institutional arrangements of the United States. The second group has a much more modest agenda, involving stepped-up cultural exchanges, a limited amount of assistance to appropriate Central American groups, and some restrained nudges by the United States, where appropriate, in favor of democracy and human rights.

The first approach seems altogether unrealistic.[20] First, one would need to be convinced the U.S. is really committed to democracy in Central America and is not using this merely as a smokescreen for strategic concerns. Second, the notion that by applying U.S. aid the United States can entirely reorient societies and cultures cast in quite different molds from our own is preposterous. Not only is this impossible but the Central Americans do not want it. While Central Americans prefer democratic, representative institutions, they are doubtful whether these work very well in their own fractured situation. They much prefer representative democratic institutions in accord with their own history and traditions (often cast in populist and quasi-corporatist forms and implying ad hoc and mixed formulas) rather than those imported from abroad. There are even doubts as to the capacity of the United States to assist the Latin Americans in *their own* aspirations and struggles for democracy, a strategy that may produce some results in the bigger and better countries of South America but has very limited possibilities for success in the personalistic and less-institutionalized societies of Central America.

Clearly, the more modest agenda is the preferable and more appropriate one. Even that option, though, faces major difficulties. In the first place, the idea remains powerful in the State Department, the Agency for International Development, the Department of Defense and elsewhere and that we know best for Central America and that, given the area's own apparent incapacities, we can solve those countries' problems for them. Ethnocentrism is still alive and well within the United States government and can easily overwhelm even the best-designed of U.S. assistance programs involving real input by the Central Americans themselves.

In the second place, the temptation to support a stronger pro-democracy option, even if the possibilities for success in Central America are modest, is almost irresistible within the United States government. The Congress, the press, the intellectuals, the bureaucracy and major U.S. interest groups are all in favor of such an option. In addition, a strong pro-democracy program abroad enables an administration to stand for the "right and good things," to present a unified, coherent, and publicly acceptable program to the voters, and to take away some major arguments from its opposition. These are all nearly insurmountable reasons for pursuing a stronger stance in favor of democracy than may be realistic or called for. But note all these impulses toward a stronger pro-democracy position have their roots in U.S. domestic policies. They may or may not have a strong basis in the realities of Central America, where numerous opinion surveys reveal considerable ambivalence about democracy and the precise form it should take. This lack of comprehension about the realities of the area is in fact the chief cause of so many failures in the litany of policies pursued by the U.S. in Central America.

A Marshall Plan for Central America

The author of this paper strongly supports a major program of social and economic assistance to Central America, as suggested by the National Bipartisan (Kissinger) Commission on Central America. But exaggerated expectations must be cautioned against, for they cannot be fulfilled and hence may lead to even greater dissatisfaction throughout the area. In addition, there remain major problems with the Marshall Plan idea that need to be resolved. First, it remains quite a vague proposal; none of its specifics has so far been spelled out. Second, it is a long-term proposition on which there is likely to be considerable agreement, but in the meantime the difficult and immediate security and political issues of the region on which there is far more discord will still need to be addressed. A third problem is that the Congress may well not go along with a new, large-scale foreign assistance program. Or it may gut the program in much the same way it gutted the earlier Caribbean Basin Initiative in many of its key provisions, especially those close to Latin American hearts such as duty-free treatment for Caribbean Basin products. Furthermore, the American public is strongly opposed to more foreign aid. Such a program will be especially difficult to pass in an election year if it means that U.S. jobs will be sacrificed for the sake of greater access to our markets for Central American products.

Most of all, however, one fears that the lessons of the past have not been learned. The Marshall Plan idea is being spoken of in some quarters as almost a panacea for Central America's ills. While we can certainly assist, nudge, and cajole, the fact remains that we cannot solve Central America's problems for the region. In addition, any such Marshall Plan for Central America, we hope, would not be based on the same unwarranted assumptions of the Alliance for Progress, such as the faith in the middle class as a stable and progressive force. Finally, the U.S. needs to recognize the basic differences between the nations of Western Europe following World War II and those of Central America today, and the reasons that a Marshall Plan could succeed so well in the former and prove far more problematic in the latter. Once again, the heart of the problem seems to lie in the conceptual frameworks that we use and their relevance and appropriateness in the Central American context.

ELEMENTS OF A CENTRAL AMERICAN MODEL OF DEVELOPMENT

We have been quite critical of past U.S. policies in Central America; the question now remains as to the basis upon which sounder policies can be grounded.

In general terms, policy toward Central America requires grounding on a more realistic, prudent, consistent, pragmatic basis than in the past.[21] This would involve four overall strategies: taking Central America seriously for the first time; having appropriate modesty regarding what we can reasonably expect to accomplish in Central America; understanding Central America in terms of its own institutional standards and practices; and casting aside the pervasive ethnocentrism that, we have seen, has been so strongly present in all the U.S. initiatives toward Central America, going back to the immediate post-World War II period and even much earlier. Theses attitudes are reminiscent of a celebrated case in the nineteenth century, when a wayward U.S. envoy, not knowing much about the area, thought he could best travel to Central America by way of Buenos Aires and, having finally arrived in Central America, did not know where he was and could find "no government" to whom to present his credentials.

Taking Central America seriously for the first time means that the U.S. treats the region not as merely a collection of banana republics, that we not be condescending and patronizing, that we understand and come to grips with its own political dynamics rather than imposing our preferred solution upon it, that we appreciate that Central American society and politics can be as complex and systematic as our own, that we work through the existing institutions and systems of the area rather than trying to substitute others that cannot and will not work, and that we look upon the region's developmental goals with sympathy and understanding. For example, we need to deal with *Latin America's* definitions of development, its aspirations which may be at variance from our own, and its emphasis on economic growth as compared with our preoccupation with security.

Having appropriate modesty regarding what we can reasonably expect to accomplish in Central America means that we eschew grand but unrealistic designs, that we comprehend realistically the social and cultural forces holding back change as well as those forces producing it in the area, that we avoid raising expectations so high that they cannot possibly be fulfilled and therefore give rise both to strong disappointments and to even greater pressures for sweeping revolution, and that we avoid casting aside viable and workable (in that context) traditional institutions.

Understanding Central America in terms of its own institutional practices and avoiding ethnocentrism are really the opposite sides of the same coin. The author has written at length on these themes,[22] and need not repeat all those materials here. Some elements of the case for a non-ethnocentric theory of development need to be presented, however, to show how a more realistic, empathetic, and workable policy can be fashioned.

For example, in focusing on the Central American middle class, we need to know how and why that middle class is different from its Western equivalents and why it does not seem to provide a bulwark for democracy and stability in Central America as it has in Western Europe and the United States. We must similarly come to understand the politicized nature of trade unionism in Central America and its differences from the apolitical collective bargaining model of the United States. We are also woefully ill-equipped to comprehend elite political behavior in Central America, the nature of extended family relationships that often serve as substitutes for political parties, the nature of clan rivalries and competition, and the dynamics of elite power circulations. Some of these elements will be essential in constructing an indigenous Central American model of society and its change processes.

The U.S. needs to understand, further, how greater assistance to and increased professionalization of the armed forces in Central America may lead to greater military involvement in politics rather than less. We do not adequately comprehend the social status consideration within the Central American officers corps, the motives for seeking an officership, or what constitutes acceptable officer behavior. We are therefore unable to provide an adequate incentive system for the officers when we want them to pursue a vigorous anti-guerrilla strategy.

Nor does the U.S. understand the tentative, as distinct from definitive, mandate that elections carry, or their function as devices to ratify an existing regime rather than as means to allow genuine choice. We fail to appreciate the role of the army as virtually a fourth governmental branch in Central America — and all this implies. The U.S. knows little about state-society relations in the area, which are quite different from American-style interest group relations; and Americans have little understanding of the essentially corporate nature of these relations as distinct from the freewheeling pluralist form they take in the United States.

Even the political terms we use have quite different meanings. Such basic concepts as "democracy," "representation," "rights," "separation of powers," and "popular sovereignty" all mean something quite different in Central America from what they mean in the United States. There is little evidence that such differences are understood by U.S. policy makers or by the leaders of either of the two political parties. Or, when they are understood, that they are understood empathetically. Rather, the inclination is to dismiss the Central American meaning of these terms as a sign of inferiority or "underdevelopment" and to substitute our own presumably superior notions and interpretations of them. Not only do Americans often fail to understand Central America in terms of its own institutional arrangements, but when we do, we seek to replace them with a presumably more "developed" kind that consistently bear a striking resemblance to our own institutional preferences. Policies based on that sort of thinking have not worked in the past and they are unlikely to achieve better results in the future.

CONCLUSION

American policy toward Central America has not registered many clear successes. There is much current discussion of the reasons for the many failures and the National Bipartisan Commission on Central America was created in large part to suggest new approaches distinct from the perceived failures of policy in the past.

It has been suggested here that the key reason for our poverty of policy in Central America derives from the poverty of the theories undergirding them. Consistently, in both Democratic and Republican administrations, we have applied the wrong or inappropriate models in Central America, including models of economic development, models of military behavior, models of political change, and models of class or group interaction. These models were based almost exclusively on the Western experience and had little to do with the realities, history, and internal dynamics of Central America. The models used were not only overly rigid, ethnocentric and naive, but they had the additional negative effect of undermining many existing and transitional institutions and thus have contributed further to the very instability our policies have consistently sought to prevent.

The opportunity exits now to begin to break with the past formulas. Hints of such possibilities exist in the younger generation of Foreign Service officers, among Latin American specialists, and in the hearings before and papers presented to the Kissinger Commission.[23] At the same time strong resistance to such changes exists in Congress, the foreign policy bureaucracies, several powerful interest groups and lobbies, and public opinion. However, unless we begin to treat Central America seriously, on its own terms, in its own institutional context, empathetically, and without the condescension and ethnocentrism of the past, the new and worthwhile policy proposals recently put forward, such as Project Democracy, a Marshall Plan for Central America, and other suggestions offered in the reports of the Atlantic Council and the Kissinger Commission,[24] have almost no possibility of achieving success.

NOTES

1. James W. Symington, "Learn Latin America's Culture," *New York Times* (September 23, 1983), p. A27.
2. See, for example, David M. Potter, *People of Plenty: Economic Abundance and the American Character* (Chicago: University of Chicago Press, 1954); Daniel J. Boorstin, *The Genius of American Politics* (Chicago: University of Chicago Press, 1953); Charles Gibson (ed.), *The Black Legend: Anti-Spanish Attitudes in the Old World and the New* (New York: Knopf, 1971); and Reginald Horsman, *Race and Manifest Destiny: The Origins of American Racial Anglo-Saxonism* (Cambridge: Harvard University Press, 1981).
3. These prejudices and biases are treated more extensively in Howard J. Wiarda, *In Search of Policy: The United States and Latin America* (Washington, D.C.: American Enterprise Institute for Public Policy Research, 1984).
4. Donald J. Devine, *The Political Culture of the United States* (Boston: Little, Brown, 1972).
5. Louis Hartz, *The Liberal Tradition in America: An Interpretation of American Political Thought Since the Revolution* (New York: Harcourt, Brace and World, 1955).
6. Robert Packenham, *Liberal America and the Third World: Political Development Ideas in Foreign Aid and Social Science* (Princeton: Princeton University Press, 1973). See also Edward C. Banfield, *American Foreign Aid Doctrines* (Washington, D.C.: American Enterprise Institute for Public Policy Reseach, 1963).
7. The discussion follows that of Packenham, *Liberal America, op. cit.,* p. 20; but see also Samuel P. Huntington, *Political Order in Changing Societies* (New Haven: Yale University Press, 1968).
8. W. W. Rostow, *The Stages of Economic Growth: A Non-Communist Manifesto* (Cambridge: Cambridge University Press, 1960).
9. Seymour M. Lipset, "Some Social Requisites of Democracy: Economic Development and Political Legitimacy," *American Political Science Review,* 53 (March 1959), pp. 69-105.
10. Karl W. Deutsch, "Social Mobilization and Political Development," *American Political Science Review,* 55 (September 1961) pp. 493-514.
11. George McGhee, *Envoy to the Middle World: Adventures in Diplomacy* (New York: Harper and Row, 1983).
12. The theme of the disjuncture between economic growth and political development has been forcefully argued by Huntington, *Political Order, op. cit.*
13. The controversy over the role of the middle sectors in Latin America has generated a good deal of discussion. The classic statement of the "salvation through the middle class" scenario is John J. Johnson, *Political Change in Latin America: The Emergence of the Middle Sectors* (Stanford, CA: Stanford University Press, 1958). For a valuable exchange of views see the discussion between Robert J. Alexander, James Petras, and Victor Alba in *New Politics* (Winter 1962) and (Winter 1965).
14. The literature includes Robert J. Alexander, *Organized Labor in Latin America* (New York: Free Press, 1965); Victor Alba, *Politics and the Labor Movement in Latin America* (Stanford, CA: Stanford University Press, 1968); and Howard J. Wiarda, "The Corporative Origins of the Iberian and Latin American Labor Relations Systems," *Studies in Comparative International Development* 13 (Spring 1978) pp. 3-37.
15. See Alfred Stepan, *The Military in Politics: Changing Patterns in Brazil* (Princeton: Princeton University Press, 1971).
16. The argument here and in the following five paragraphs derives from Packenham, *Liberal America, op. cit.*
17. The best analysis is William Hardy McNeill, *Greece: American Aid in Action, 1947-1956* (New York: Twentieth Century Fund, 1957). In reviewing the literature on the Greek civil war, 1947-1949, and the American response to it, one is struck by the remarkable parallels with El Salvador in the early 1980s.

18. One could argue that the problem is not so much or not only the exporting of liberal-Lockean presumptions and institutions to Third World societies where "they did not fit," but a failure to understand how they evolved in our own history. Economic development, for example, on some occasions "undermined stability and democracy" in 18th and 19th century Europe and America as well as in the Third World. That was the fate of the ancient regime throughout what was called the "Age of the Democratic Revolution"; see Robert R. Palmer, *The Age of Democratic Revolution: A Political History of Europe and America, 1760-1800* (Princeton: Princeton University Press, 1969).

19. A careful and balanced assessment is Larman C. Wilson, "Human Rights in United States Foreign Policy: The Rhetoric and the Practice," in Donald C. Piper and Ronald C. Tercheck (eds.), *Interaction: Foreign Policy and Public Policy* (Washington, D.C.: American Enterprise Institute for Public Policy Research, 1983), pp. 178-208.

20. For a longer—and stronger—critique see Howard J. Wiarda, "Can Democracy be Exported? The Quest for Democracy in United States Latin American Policy," paper prepared for the Inter-American dialogue on U.S.-Latin American Relations in the 1980s, sponsored by the Woodrow Wilson International Center for Scholars, Washington, D.C., March 1983, and forthcoming in a volume edited by Kevin Middlebrook and Carlos Rico.

21. The ideas have been set forth at greater length in Wiarda, *In Search of Policy, op. cit.*

22. See especially: H. J. Wiarda, *Critical Elections and Critical Coups: State, Society, and the Military in the Processes of Latin American Development* (Athens, Ohio: Center for International Studies, Ohio University, 1979); *The Continuing Struggle for Democracy in Latin America* (Boulder, CO: Westview Press, 1980); *Latin American Politics and Development* (Boston: Houghton-Mifflin, 1979 [with Harvey F. Kline]); *Corporatism and National Development in Latin America* (Boulder, CO: Westview Press, 1981); *Politics and Social Change in Latin America: The Distinct Tradition* (Amherst: University of Massachusetts Press, rev. 2nd ed., 1982).

23. The author's presentation before the commission summarized many of these findings; see H. J. Wiarda, "United States Policy in Central America: Toward a New Relationship," Statement presented to the National Bipartisan Commission on Central America, United States Department of State, Washington, D.C., September 28-29, 1983.

24. The Atlantic Council's recommendations were contained in a Policy Paper prepared by its study group on "Western Interests and U.S. Policy Options in the Caribbean Basin"; see also the background papers prepared for the Council by David Scott Palmer, Sidney Weintraub, Jack Child, and Howard J. Wiarda, forthcoming in a volume to be published under Council auspices. The Kissinger Commission report was issued in early 1984.

13

AT SEA IN CENTRAL AMERICA:
Can We Negotiate Our Way to Shore?

Tom J. Farer

Negotiations can serve either to promote compromise or to confirm defeat. This deep ambiguity allows President Ronald Reagan to claim without mendacity that, no less than the critics of his policies in Central America, he favors negotiations. For clearly he is prepared at any time to negotiate the surrender of the Sandinista Government and the Salvadoran opposition. These ends being non-negotiable, at the moment, the President must pursue them through other means.

The administration's compulsion to batter chosen opponents into submission is a sad spectacle because it augurs further suffering for the people of Central America, already mutilated by a terrible history in which the United States has played a conspicuous part. This compulsion is also paradoxical. Normally, self-interest is the force that drives the leaders of one state to impose agony on the people of another. In this instance, any rational definition of self-interest dictates a policy of compromise. A second paradox springs from the President's claim to be animated not merely by a parochial conception of national interest, but also by concern for the men, women and children of Nicaragua, El Salvador and the other countries being sucked into the vortex of regional war. When enumerating his objectives, President Reagan speaks of human rights and democracy in the same breath that invokes threats to U.S. security. Yet, the only possible means of reconciling the humane with the strategic is through the very compromises this administration now seems to eschew — compromises that its own policies may have made possible.

There lies the final and most bitter paradox, that of a president, blinded by ideology, who will not reap what he helped sow. Three years ago the left in El Salvador envisioned an absolute military victory. In that triumphal spirit it rejected negotiations. Now the left pursues them. Three years ago the Sandinista *comandantes* apparently envisioned Nicaragua as the asylum, command point and entrepôt of an isthmus-wide revolution. Now they seem eager to negotiate pacts of mutual tolerance with their neighbors. Both the Sandinistas and the Salvadoran left appear, therefore, to have arrived at a point of convergence with U.S. objectives announced by President Carter and at least nominally adopted by his successor. However, as revolutionary forces have reduced their appetite, ours apparently has grown.

NICARAGUA

The Reagan administration originally justified military aid to opponents of the Sandinista regime, the so-called *contras,* as a means to cut off the arms supply to the Salvadoran guerrillas. In this connection the administration urged the notion of symmetry. Such aid would help the enemies of the Managua government as long as that government helped the enemies of our "friends" in San Salvador. But now, having dined on the first course of its campaign to make Managua more pliable, and having found the eating good, the Administration apparently wants the Sandinistas to serve up something more than an enforceable commitment to neutrality. And that something is themselves.

In April 1983, then-Assistant Secretary of State Thomas Enders told the Senate Foreign Relations Committee:

> Central American democrats . . . are particularly clear on the need for democratization [in the region]. Only in this way could they be confident they will not have to face sometime in the future an aggressive neighbor unconstrained by the limits democracy imposes.[1]

Three months later a senior U.S. diplomat based in Central America informed Christopher Dickey of *The Washington Post* that issues other than the questions of aid to the insurgents in El Salvador probably could not be negotiated successfully with the Sandinistas until they changed their approach to government. He added:

> It is now considered that the only way they can be trusted to keep an agreement is to have the type of government which would force them to do so or make it a public issue.[2]

The administration dispelled any lingering doubts about its objectives when it brushed aside the package of proposals presented by the Nicaraguan government on October 20, 1983.[3] Unlike proposals of a more general character, which Managua had made in 1982, the most recent package included detailed provisions designed to assuage Washington's anxieties concerning aid to possible revolutionary movements and Soviet or Cuban use of military facilities in Nicaragua. Pursuant to the proposed treaty with the United States, Nicaragua would pledge that "it will not permit [its territory] to be utilized to affect or to threaten the security of the United States or to attack any other state."[4] Nicaraguan Foreign Minister Miguel d'Escoto said the agreements required his country to dismantle any command and control facilities on Nicaraguan soil that might exist for use by Salvadoran guerrilla groups to coordinate the movement of their forces inside El Salvador and to arrange for supply shipments.[5] More significant than these verbal commitments is the Nicaraguan government's declared willingness to allow on-site observation as a means of policing compliance. To be sure, the draft treaty in this package directed specifically to the conflict in El Salvador treats the regime and its opponents as equals and even-handedly prohibits aid to both.[6]

If, as some observers believe, the Salvadoran security forces would disintegrate without constant infusions of U.S. aid (even if the guerrillas were also cut off from external suppliers), the treaty in its present form is unsatisfactory. But it would be an odd diplomacy indeed if a country initiated negotiations by conceding all its opposite number's demands. So the inclusion of reciprocal restraints in what the Nicaraguan government simply calls a basis for negotiations does not satisfactorily explain their back-of-the hand reception in Washington, particularly in light of the administration's formal insistence on the significance of external aid to the guerrillas.

The administration's refusal either to accept the proposals as a basis for negotiation or to table any alternative negotiating package, reenforces the impression that Washington seeks to alter the Nicaraguan regime itself rather than its external policies.

On their face, demands for the democratization of Nicaraguan politics are not equivalent to proposals for a unilateral-suicide pact. The statements quoted above could be interpreted as envisioning continued Sandinista preeminence coincident with an institutionalized and secure opposition. One feels, nevertheless, that to the extent the Reagan administration has anything very specific in mind, it must be more than that. If the United States is demanding democratization merely to secure monitors of Sandinist compliance with a no-export-of-revolution agreement, the demand seems gratuitous. It seems gratuitous, first, because the administration's indictment of Nicaraguan aid to the Salvadoran rebels rests on its claimed capability to monitor Managua's behavior. Second, although the opposition is harrassed and censored, the country remains so porous that there is little that happens there which is not quickly and widely known both within and beyond its frontiers.

If a secure political opposition cannot heighten the already high risk of exposure — should the Sandinistas violate a non-intervention commitment — surely something more than exposure is at stake. Must the opposition have a permanent veto on the government's foreign policy in order to mitigate Washington's distrust? That would be a curious constitutional provision, one with little or no parallel in the known world. Even if such a provision existed on paper, would it deter a regime willing to risk exposure and consequent retaliation from the United States? As a practical matter, the only consistently effective domestic political restraint is the threat of electoral defeat. So Washington's linkage of democratization and non-intervention logically implies an opposition that, by means of exposure, can hope to win an election and replace the Sandinista government.

Sandinista acceptance of a competitive political system would not be suicidal. The *comandantes* still appear to enjoy support particularly among younger Nicaraguans. A government wholly reliant on the terror its security forces could impose would not distribute arms broadly among the civil population, as the government in Managua has done. This support has survived conflict with the Catholic Church, economic privation, and betrayal of the original commitment to non-alignment in international affairs. In opening the political system the Sandinistas would concomitantly reduce their electoral liabilities, because the decision to open would be taken as part of a larger decision to pursue reconciliation with the democratic opposition. To achieve reconciliation, the government in Managua would have to make peace with the Catholic Church, lift restrictions on press and speech, give amnesty to political prisoners, and offer attractive concessions to the Miskito and other minorities.

These steps, plus the removal of U.S. economic sanctions, could create the climate of confidence essential to reverse the outflow of capital and managerial talent, and might thus fuel economic growth. Once unencumbered by conflict with the church and a shrinking economy, the *comandantes* — with their far-flung organization, populist program, newspaper, and residual mystique as military leaders of the national revolution — would represent a powerful electoral force, if they remained united. The Sandinistas' potential ability to win an electoral competition makes the U.S. demand for democratization something less, at least in form, than insistence that the *comandantes* self-destruct.

With the Reagan administration dangling the seductive image of an emergent social democracy in Nicaragua, moderates and liberals have found it difficult to unite in opposition to the president's actual policies. Americans who cheered the Nicaraguan revolution have felt betrayed by the subsequent course of events, rather as if they were personally responsible for the overthrow of Anastasio Somoza. President Reagan has played on that feeling, even claiming ignorantly that the Sandinistas had violated a kind of legal commitment to the installation of multi-party democracy.

The truth, of course, is that the United States contributed to the revolution only by doing nothing decisive to block it. A faction within the Carter administration did urge positive steps to force Somoza out; but it lost every battle. With characteristic amnesia, many Americans have forgotten the Carter administration's determined effort, initiated at the first sign of the Somoza's weakness, to assemble an anti-Sandinista coalition, including the civilian apparatus of the Somoza regime with a sanitized National Guard as its chopping edge. That effort could only have produced war without end to defend *Somocismo* without Somoza.

Whether wise or foolish, moral or squalid, the Carter administration's actual behavior during Somoza's last year can hardly be squared with the proposition that, in consideration of U.S. aid in defanging Somoza, the Sandinistas assumed an obligation to institutionalize democracy.

Of course the United States *should* have deployed its political and economic resources to accelerate Nicaragua's transformation. If it had, several tens of thousands of people now dead would be alive. Today Nicaragua would probably be governed by a coalition, including the Sandinistas, committed to non-alignment in foreign affairs and, domestically, to reform within a capitalist framework.[7]

I rake over the past only because its coals still burn among us.

Naturally, Americans committed to the promotion of democratic values everywhere in the hemisphere should complain over authoritarian rule in Nicaragua. We would therefore be right to support the administration's policies if there were still a credible basis for believing that, at reasonable cost to our national interest and the people of Nicaragua, these policies were likely to promote a democratic outcome. Today, such a belief must rest on faith alone.

Had the promotion of human rights been its main concern, the administration's strategy — organizing a military force to challenge the Sandinista government and threatening direct military intervention — would from the outset have seemed a wild gamble. For such a strategy could succeed only if the *comandantes* responded to the military challenge by offering their opponents a non-violent route to power. Yet, historical experience suggests that military threats create an environment peculiarly inclement for political participation or any other kind of human right. As administration ideologues have been quick to point out when defending the delinquencies of right-wing regimes, subversion aggravates the endemic paranoia of authoritarian regimes, leading them to impose a tighter grip on society. Whatever capacity they once had for distinguishing dissent from treason rapidly atrophies. By driving moderates underground where they join the violent opposition, the crackdown further polarizes society, eroding conditions necessary for a politics of accommodation.

Nicaragua's government is conditioned by history and ideology to view the United States as an irreconcilably hostile power regardless of who occupies the Oval Office. Its occupation by a leader of the American right naturally strengthens the belief that the United States will attempt to liquidate any government of the left in the Western Hemisphere, even an elected one. Opposition movements tied politically and militarily to the United States will be seen as means to U.S. ends and, hence, irreconcilable. Thus, concessions are not only useless, but dangerous. Concessions imply recognition of opponents as a substantial political force, a legitimate claimant to rights of participation in the national political order. Once endowed with such legitimacy, a movement is better positioned to invite intervention on its behalf, since intervention by invitation of a substantial, indigenous actor is less quickly characterized as aggression. The strategic dilemma, then, is that the added leverage any opposition group acquires against the Nicaraguan regime by virtue of U.S. support is offset by the tendency of that support to convince the regime of the disutility of compromise.

Although moved by quite different ends, the administration's policy of concentrating support on (indeed largely creating) the Honduran-based opposition group, the Democratic National Front (FDN), with its conspicuous ties to the Somoza order, has somewhat eased this dilemma in that it gives the progressive opposition grouped around Edén Pastora and Alfonso Robelo leverage without the taint of the American connection. As a strategem for promoting democracy in Nicaragua, it seems inspired. The Sandinista government's prudent response would have been to seek reconciliation with Pastora's group, the Democratic Revolutionary Alliance (ARDE) and the establishment of a Popular Front Government.

Among its many virtues, power-sharing in Managua would turn the edge of the U.S. argument for symmetry in dealing with El Salvador and Nicaragua. I once concluded a private talk with Tomás Borge and Daniel Ortega with the warning: "Remember, you have an opportunity to make a unique contribution to fascism in Latin America. To guarantee its ascendancy, to doom hope for reform, all you have to do is force this national revolution into an authoritarian mold." The obverse also remains true: the successful emergence in Nicaragua of a political order as committed to freedom as it is to reform would shake the very foundations of neighboring authoritarian states. In this historical moment, the force of example is greater than the example of force. Believing as they do in the efficacy of raw power, President Reagan and his aides probably are constitutionally disabled from envisioning the ripple effect of a democracy in Nicaragua. Unfortunately, the Sandinistas seem to suffer equally from lack of imagination.

By not being consciously pursued, the strategy has had its best possible test. The Sandinistas know that Washington has not been seeking to induce reconciliation with ARDE and a consequent social democracy in Nicaragua. They believe that Reagan seeks not to reform but rather to destroy their regime. They take his threats seriously, and are prepared therefore to make concessions; but not concessions concerning the distribution of government offices that would amount to an immediate sharing of power. The United States has now done almost everything but invade. It has failed to pry open the regime. One can conclude that military pressure will not bring democracy to Nicaragua.

The democratic promise of present policy being slight, the United States should try one less costly, in the currency both of human rights and national interests and which, coincidentally, is more likely to succeed.

A first objection to current policy is that it kills people and promises to kill many more. Although the *contras* seem unable to pose a serious challenge to the Sandinistas, they have managed to kill hundreds of supporters and employees of the government and doubtless have suffered substantial casualties of their own. We are not doing the killing ourselves. But without U.S. financial support and training, and without the hope of an ultimate ride to victory on the back of a U.S. invasion force, and without the U.S. guarantee of Honduras's security which in turn produces a Honduran sanctuary, the *contras* would soon be reduced to the level of a nuisance.

A second objection is the effect of current policy on the democratic prospects elsewhere in Central America, particularly Honduras. In the course of turning that country into an American base for operations against the Sandinistas, the United States has succeeded in polarizing Honduran politics and strengthening the hand of the most authoritarian elements in the armed forces. A society comparatively free of extreme human rights violence is increasingly marked by goon-squad operations on the right and incipient recourse to armed subversion on the left. U.S. pressure on the armed forces and the civilian right helped to extract the commitment to electoral politics that is now unraveling. The United States will not restore that pressure as long as Honduras is a useful tool for harrassing Nicaragua.

A third objection is the policy's capacity to distract both the Congress and the Executive branch from intrinsically more important issues.[8]

A fourth risk is ingniting and then sucking the United States into a regional war. The Honduran armed forces, made cocky by U.S. backing and eager to take on Nicaragua, might arrange some extreme provocation — for example, crossing the border on the pretext of a prior Nicaraguan incursion, then invoking U.S. guarantees. Or Honduran and *contra* troops, possibly reenforced by Guatemalan and Salvadoran units, might drive into Nicaragua, set up a provisional government, secure recognition from the conspiring regimes and then, when threatened with destruction by Nicaraguan armed forces, launch an appeal our right-wing president might find hard to resist.

A fifth objection is the policy's power to reenforce the image of the United States, so current among the educated youth of Latin America, as the implacable foe of social change, an image which helped shape the mentality of the young men and women who now govern Nicaragua. An administration which seeks pleasant relations with every right-wing thug in the hemisphere is simply unconvincing when it claims to be struggling for democracy in Central America.

A final objection to continuation of the present policy is the availability of an alternative more likely to produce the desired result. The Sandinistas have established nothing like totalitarian control over Nicaragua, not because of U.S. opposition but rather because of the nature of Nicaraguan society and, possibly, of their own movement.

The great mass of the population is Catholic and socially conservative. As an opponent of Somoza during the national rising, the church avoided any taint from the old order. On the contrary, the church enjoys the prestige of participation in the liberation struggle. Within the Sandinista movement itself, Catholics, including priests, play a substantial role. They may be hostile to the hierarchy; they may believe in a socialized economy, but it is highly unlikely they would support an attack on the church as such. Whatever their ideology and ambitions, the *comandantes* have no hope of eliminating this powerful institutional expression of pluralistic values.

Geographic position is an additional obstacle to the perpetuation of rigid, authoritarian rule. Nicaragua, like all of the Caribbean basin, is inevitably subject to the magnetic force of American culture, as it is doomed to dependence on American markets. The country has neither the size nor the resources nor the trained cadres to run an autarchic economic system. Furthermore, the Soviet Union has indicated plainly that it is not prepared to assume responsibility for yet another welfare case. This factor in itself distinguishes the Cuban precedent. By withdrawing the military threat, Washington would itself establish a second decisive distinction. Then unlike Castro, the Sandinistas could not portray themselves as nationalist heroes facing down the regional goliath. In this respect current U.S. policy plays into Sandinista hands, creating a drama in which they can star.

The country's cultural and institutional heritage, together with its geographic position and economic necessities, will exert continuing and ultimately effective pressures for a plural political order, *even if the United States is passive*. Ending the U.S. military threat to the Sandinista regime does not, however, entail passivity. We could continue to deploy economic sanctions and incentives. The Sandinistas need access to American capital and markets, as well as private sector confidence in order to deliver promised economic and social progress. A conservative president is peculiarly well-positioned to extract from Congress the kind and quantity of economic carrots capable of influencing political developments in Nicaragua. Economic cooperation conditioned neither on Nicaragua's openness to U.S. investors nor on Chicago School economics, but rather on its respect for human rights, including the right to participate in government, will augment the internal forces advocating democratic reform. If not tied to conservative theology, U.S. efforts are more likely to attract reinforcing action from democratic governments in Europe and Latin America.

Such a policy does not promise immediate results and cannot guarantee success. For the American right, it will never have the charm of military force with its false promises of decisive consequences. American forces thinly covered by the *contra* fig leaf could, if committed in large numbers, successfully invade Nicaragua and occupy its major cities. They could not, in the foreseeable future, pacify either the urban *barrios* or the countryside. Instead, the United States would incur costs out of proportion even to the most demented conception of the national interest and extract an unspeakable toll on human rights. The Sandinistas clearly have a substantial social base. In case of invasion, nationalists, including present opponents of the regime, would join in defending the country.[9] Faced with determined resistance the United States would use its vast fire power. Those Nicaraguans who collaborated in the resulting holocaust would thus be unable to construct democracy on the blood-soaked ruins. Yet, this opinion continues to lurk in the background of contemporary policy.

Though it has not succeeded in producing democracy in Nicaragua, administration policy has apparently convinced the Nicaraguan government of the need to allay U.S. security concerns. Now is the time to negotiate the sort of compromise settlement former Assistant Secretary of State Thomas Enders apparently offered the Sandinistas almost two years ago, before our appetite grew.[10] Managua would agree to neutralize itself: no military relations with Cuba or the Soviet Union; no assistance to Central American rebels; no army out of proportion in size to or quality of weapons greater than its neighbors. By agreeing to respect Nicaragua's neutral status the United States would offer no further support for the ARDE and FDN,[11] it would withdraw troops from and terminate military aid to Honduras, and encourage Honduran participation in the neutralization negotiations. This agreement is roughly what Contadora states (Panama, Mexico, Colombia, Venezuela) have attempted to achieve. Negotiations would be carried out under their auspices and would include all the Central American states and the United States. In light of Cuba's declared sympathy for the Contadora framework, and the utility of obtaining its formal commitment to the terms of any settlement, Cuba should be invited to participate.[12]

Since, at the urging of the Contadora group, democratization has already been accepted by all the Central American states as one of the bases for a settlement, it should be an issue in the negotiations. As things stand now, a precise enumeration of steps for converting that principle into practice probably cannot be obtained. However, the principle itself should be incorporated in the ultimate substantive agreements, as a latent benchmark of legitimacy. In addition, the United States should insist that leaders of the armed opposition, other than those guilty of collaboration with the Somoza regime, participate in the negotiating process. As de facto representatives of important sectors in Nicaraguan society, their inclusion is essential both to peace and to the opening of Nicaraguan politics. Moreover, the United States should attach to the agreements a declaration that it has become a party to them on the assumption (a) that as the military threat to Managua diminishes, the human rights situation in that country documented by reports of the Inter-American Commission on Human Rights will correspondingly improve, and (b) that the Managua government remains committed to national elections in 1985. Furthermore, the United States should insist that the agreements include a commitment from Managua for amnesty for *all* members of the opposition not accused of crimes during the Somoza period and willing to renounce the use of force. Finally, all parties to the agreements would agree to strengthen existing protections and guarantees for human rights in their respective countries, including the right to free expression of political views.

EL SALVADOR

The political and psychological pressures on Nicaragua to negotiate a specific program for opening its politics would be far greater if the United States were correspondingly prepared to press the virtues of political accommodation on its Salvadoran clients. The United States has, however, ample other reasons for doing that.

Yet, despite its theoretical preference for non-lethal politics, despite its inability to build clients into a winning force, despite the resultant drain on the energy and cohesion of the U.S. decision-making community and despite the subtle but real damage to its image among West Europeans, the administration continues to pursue a military solution. No one can honestly doubt the proposition that the only thing President Reagan wishes to negotiate in El Salvador is the surrender of the left.

With the rumored exception of a brief hesitation during Enders watch, the administration has been fiercely consistent and almost frank. Before assuming office, a future architect of the administration's Central American policies, Jeane Kirkpatrick, responding to a question about how the conflict could end, snapped: "They could give up."[13] Three years later, Under Secretary of Defense Fred Iklé echoed Mrs. Kirkpatrick when he announced:

> We do not seek a military defeat of our friends. We do not seek a military stalemate. We seek victory for the forces of democracy. And that victory has two components [one of which is] defeating militarily those organized forces of violence that refuse to accept the democratic will of the people.[14]

In the same spirit Richard Stone, President Reagan's Central American negotiator, has continuously emphasized that the only negotiable issue is how the left's participation in the elections run by the present government could be facilitated.[15]

Participation in elections conducted under the tender auspices of the Salvadoran Armed Forces is tantamount to surrender not only for those opposition members who aspire to total power, but also for those, like Guillermo Ungo and Rubén Zamora, with unimpeachable democratic credentials. One normally thinks of elections as deciding who shall govern — that is, who shall make all basic policy decisions and control the state's monopoly of legitimate violence. In El Salvador, however, any foreseeable election could bear the weight of that meaning only if one or both of the following conditions were previously satisfied: either (a) the Salvadoran armed forces must have been transformed into an institution actually subject to civilian control or (b) its pre- and post-election behavior must be guaranteed by a superior external force. In the absence of either condition, the election is unlikely to reflect a reasonably informed and uncoerced popular choice. And, even in the remarkable event that the election was not corrupted, it would nevertheless fail in its nominal purpose of determining who shall rule.

"The civilians are not yet the ones that control the situation here," Rey Prendes, leader of the centrist Christian Democrats' caucus in the Consitituent Assembly has said. "The Army still has tremendous power in this country, political power, and in the end the Army makes the decision."[16] Since this has been true for at least half a century, what reason is there to believe it will be less true after another election? To be sure, if the right were to win, its policies would so closely coincide with those of the armed forces' senior officers, purged since 1979 of their more enlightened elements, that the question of who rules probably would not arise. But in the event of victory by a center-left coalition, the question would be unavoidable, and I know no one who believes that it would be resolved in favor of the new government.

The very certainty that the armed forces as presently constituted would not tolerate a government to the left of center (many observers believe that even the prospect of a Christian Democratic, centrist government would precipitate a coup) would taint the election itself. The armed forces and their paramilitary auxiliaries may not be able to identify the preferences of individual voters, but electoral tabulations will reveal the voting tendencies of villages and neighborhoods. In a country with a grand tradition of collective punishment for challenging the preferences of oligarchs and officers, only the very brave and very foolish would vote for parties certain to lose even if they won.

The Reagan administration has insisted that the left's demand for power-sharing in advance of elections constitutes a rejection of democratic processes. The FDR/FMLN's offer for "peace talks among all interested parties," delivered by Foreign Minister Castañeda of Mexico to the then Secretary of State Alexander Haig on March 6, 1982, envisioned negotiation of "a transitional government" to be followed "within six months" by a ratification plebiscite; and thereafter by municipal and then general elections.[17] The administration claims that power-sharing would somehow violate the purity of Salvadoran democracy. Since the left was effectively excluded from the last election, since that election was conducted by the armed forces in conditions of civil war and since, in any event, power remains with the armed forces, El Salvador is not presently a democracy and therefore the claim is spurious.[18] As long as the sharing is provisional, it no more ravages democratic theory than the decision of a ruling parliamentary coalition to alter its policies or enhance its strength by revising the coalition in favor of hitherto excluded parties. Was British democracy violated when, in the early days of World War II, the Conservative Prime Minister organized a government of national unity by distributing ministries to Labor Party leaders?

Rather than violating democratic values, power-sharing is one of the only two routes to authentic democracy in El Salvador. Perhaps it is the only one. An external, election-supervising force could guarantee both an election relatively coercion-free and a transfer of formal power to the victorious coalition. But suppose a right-of-center coalition won? Since its ends would coincide with those of an unreformed army, it would have every incentive to invite the peace force to depart. If, as a condition of participating in elections, the left has laid down its arms, then that force would represent the only obstacle to restoration of the traditional authoritarian coalition of the civilian and military right. The harsh fact is that in a country so deeply divided over economic and social issues and lacking a tradition of political compromise, pluralism must rest precariously on a balance of power. For the opposition groups to lay down their arms and join the so-called electoral competition is nothing less than surrender. They would lose everything including their lives. But the left will not be the only loser. To the extent the United States seeks democracy, social justice and the promotion of human rights in El Salvador, it will have lost all.

One factor behind the young officers' coup of October 1979 and the brief burst of reformist energy that immediately ensued, was a sense of disgust with the endemic corruption of senior officers. Crasser considerations were also at work — notably the intense fear generated among idealists and thugs alike by the dramatic collapse of another brutal and corrupt military establishment, the Nicaraguan National Guard.

Reform served two central purposes in a shrewd strategy of revolutionary prophylaxis. First, reform reduced the flow of recruits from the embittered peasantry to the guerrillas; second, it repaired relations with the United States, while at worst neutralizing the Latin American governments that had aided the fight against Somoza. Popular opposition alone, after all, had not toppled the Nicaraguan dictator. Through sheer firepower and a monstrous will to employ it, Somoza might have survived if his neighbors, particularly Costa Rica and Panama, had continued their normal policy of strict neutrality rather than aiding the rebels and if the United States had remained at least a psychological prop to the tyrant.

Subsequent events confirm the importance of fear in the mix of factors leading to the 1979 coup. The Carter administration, impressed by post-coup reforms and increasingly anxious about the leftward tilt of Nicaragua's new government, moved quickly to reestablish the traditional supportive relationship between the United States and the Salvadoran military. Almost immediately the momentum of reform slackened. Some officers yielded to the blandishments of a regrouped oligarchy. Others had never ceased to think of a military career as a means of extracting wealth from society. Meanwhile, the "progressives," officers with a more exalted conception of their profession or less sure that U.S. support was effectively unconditional, lost influence and position. By the time Ronald Reagan arrived bent on tightening Washington's embrace and beating off congressional efforts to make aid conditional, the Salvadoran armed forces were again suffused with the tolerance of corruption in the name of institutional unity.

If a powerful opposition is the only available instrument for levering reform out of the military, it follows that by pursuing "victory," the United States surrenders shaping a new order in El Salvador which could survive without continually trashing human rights.

The administration has refused to acknowledge this dilemma, much less suggest how it proposes to escape it. This denial of reality in part reflects the place of democracy and reform in the hierarchy of administration values. The president's policies clearly suggest that while democracy is something it would be nice to have, the effort to promote it must be subordinated to the defense of friendly regimes. Given that priority, one might still ask: Why not try to achieve both democracy and, if not a friendly regime at least a neutral one, particulary if by doing so you may reduce the risk of failure or, in order to avoid failure, an investment disproportionate to U.S. interests? The short answer, according to a *New York Times* report based on interviews with leading actors in the administration, is that "Senior administration officials simply do not believe that civil wars are settled by negotiations."[19] History, the *New York Times* correspondent adds, bears out their skepticism. A wiser man would have noted that history will bear any conclusion one is determined to assemble from its vast, randomly assorted shards. To make their case, administration officials cite Nicaragua as an example of the perfidy and competence of Marxists in undermining power-sharing agreements — an example which allegedly reduces U.S. options to "gutting it out" or "cutting and running." But all Nicaragua in fact confirms is that agreements unsupported by an effective network of sanctions and incentives are unlikely to restrain anyone. Curiously, almost no one cites cases, such as the first post-War Gaullist governments in France, where Marxist parties failed to convert power-sharing into dominant power.

The top leadership of the Salvadoran guerrilla groups will inevitably have an instrumental view of democracy and of any settlement agreement. This view, however, is not peculiar to radicals. When a democratic process is seen to threaten important interests, persons who feel threatened suddenly discover values more important than the process and the constitution that institutionalizes it. Neither the United Nations Charter nor the Charter of the Organization of American States (OAS), with their unequivocal prohibitions of intervention, restrained an impeccable conservative, Henry Kissinger, from conspiring with fascists seeking to prevent Salvador Allende's coalition from assuming power in Chile.[20] Under the right circumstances, then, quite varied sorts of people are able to place substantive ends above democratic means.

There is, nevertheless, a conspicuous difference between persons with a powerful commitment to democracy, and persons who, given their choice, prefer authoritarian politics. A preference for authoritarian politics can stem from the cold calculation that, in a particular historical setting, it is more likely to produce leaders and policies compatible with your interests. An inbred oligarchy controlling most of the nation's wealth does not expect to sustain control through fair electoral competition. So it goes knocking on the barracks door to exchange gratuities for protection. (Or, as in the Soviet Union, it equates criticism of the system of privileges with psychosis.) Alternatively, the preference can spring from a theological passion for realizing in society a particular set of values. One of democracy's essential features is a tolerance even of behavior powerful constituencies deem abominable. The preference is also found among those who regard democracy as an illusion concealing the reality of minority control.

While neither the officers and oligarchs of El Salvador nor its guerrilla leaders have a democratic vocation, the latter are more apt to find democracy consistent with their values and interests. Why? Because social mobilization over the past two decades has heightened political consciousness among peasants and workers. Free of coercion they are likely to give the parties of the left a mandate to continue and deepen the reforms initiated after the 1979 coup. Marxism in Latin America emerges from specific social conditions not simply as a fire in the minds of ideologues. It has claimed adherents by providing an explanation of and a diagram for altering social hierarchies inherited from the precapitalist era and rigidly defended often with extreme violence and frequently concealed behind democratic forms. That being the case, the demonstrated ability to establish a more egalitarian society through democratic means could profoundly affect the outlook of the guerrilla left.

Transition via power-sharing to democracy in El Salvador need not, however, rely on the possibility of such an epiphany. In the Nicaraguan case, the disintegration of the National Guard eliminated the internal balance of power and it was not replaced by external guarantees. Unlike the Nicaraguan case, power-sharing in El Salvador would rest on an internal balance of power between army and guerrillas guaranteed by foreign forces. Furthermore, the conditions for transforming an armed truce into a plural political order are more favorable than those that existed in Nicaragua at the end of the Somoza era. Salvador has a larger middle class, better organized peasants and workers, a more developed party structure, and political leaders on both sides of the present divide with an unimpeachable commitment to democracy. El Salvador also has a history of collaboration, symbolized by the fact that Napoleón Duarte, the dominant Christian Democrat, and Guillermo Ungo, leader of the political wing of the opposition, were running mates in the 1972 presidential elections in a coalition with the Communist Party. Cynics accuse American liberals of searching mindlessly for a political middle in countries where there are only extremes. Such hopeless countries exist. It just so happens that El Salvador is not one of them.

The fundamental dilemma for U.S. policy remains: How to reform a system of power which seems responsive only to the threat of its destruction, when we begin by guaranteeing its survival? To exit from this dilemma we must change and condition the guarantee. We must change it because democracy cannot sustain itself alongside a standing army led by a self-perpetuating officer corps hostile to the very idea of civilian control. We can guarantee the physical survival of officers. We can guarantee pensions. And we can guarantee an opportunity to compete for positions in the miniaturized constabulary subject to civilian control that democratic politicians, following the Costa Rican model, would almost surely prefer. But those guarantees must be conditioned on the military institution's support for negotiations with the opposition intended to establish a regime able to manage the transition to democracy. And it must be clear that if the conditions are not satisfied by a stated time, Washington will forthwith suspend all military and economic aid, withdraw its advisors and discourage any other states from continuing to assist the Salvadoran armed forces.

In order to sharpen the alternatives for all interested parties and to rally support among democratic elements inside and outside the country, Washington would initiate this fundamental policy shift toward compromise with a White Paper frankly conceding the impossibility of reconciling existing policy with the ends either of peace or human rights. The White Paper would detail the steps the United States has resolved to take in order to assist democratic forces within the country to unite and assume control of their destiny. Specifically, the statement would recognize that real power remains in the hands of the officer corps and that it has thus far failed to purge itself of criminal elements, to root out right-wing death squads and to reconcile itself to democracy. The U.S. statement would endorse the Franco-Mexican proposition that the FDR/FMLN is a legitimate political force with a substantial social base and draw the necessary conclusion about the opposition's participation in the renewal of the country's political and social institutions. After conceding the legitimate fears of both the government and the opposition, the White Paper would offer military and economic assistance to all groups which demonstrate their commitment to a negotiated settlement. Next it would propose concrete steps for suspending hostilities and beginning negotiations.

In this initial redefinition of policy, the United States would not have to specify all of the means it is prepared to use to protect the negotiating process. It would be useful, however, to state categorically that the United States would regard opponents of negotiations as persons pursuing ends inimical to important U.S. interests, inimical to the democratic values embodied in the Charter of the OAS and inimical to the defense of human rights in El Salvador. Moreover, the United States should be prepared to recognize a transitional regime and, in conjunction with other democratic states, to assist in creating a climate conducive to continued evolution toward an institutionalized democracy. In addition to seeking support among OAS members and European allies, the United States should invite Cuba to assist in bringing about a negotiated settlement. If Havana accepted the invitation in good faith, it would no doubt help deliver the guerrillas to the negotiating table and to press them toward compromise.

Good-faith acceptance would be consistent with Cuban interests. In the first place, a democratic, center-left regime is the best it can hope for in El Salvador now that the United States seems committed against a guerrilla victory. This being apparent even to the Salvadoran left, Cuba's cooperation with the American initiative would not be construed as a betrayal. Moreover, participation would immediately lower the temperature in U.S.-Cuban relations and effectively eliminate the threat of direct, military confrontation. Finally, it might reopen the door, closed at the time of Angola, leading ultimately to the normalization of relations. For one or more of these reasons, in recent months Cuba has signalled its readiness to assist in engineering a negotiated settlement.

CONCLUSION

If the administration announced it was prepared to seek the objectives and take the steps outlined above, the Cubans, the Nicaraguans and the Salvadoran left, including most or all of the guerrilla groups, would enter negotiations conducted under the auspices of the Contadora states. Most of the Salvadoran left would settle for temporary power-sharing followed by elections. And, even if most guerrilla leaders decided to opt for war, the democratic left's participation in government and elections, the demonstration that democracy could be made to work in El Salvador, and the reforms implemented by a center-left government would drain the reservoir of sympathizers and recruits on which the armed left must rely. Without that reservoir, they would soon become little more than a problem for the police.

The United States can negotiate the neutralization of Nicaragua. Accepting neutralization would not mean abandoning Nicaragua to unchecked authoritarian rule. While the United States would agree to end military harrassment, it would continue to treat the country as a pariah, denying the economic assistance and access to American markets necessary to transform Nicaragua into a prosperous polity — until the leadership moved toward objectives announced in the neutralization agreements. And in case of a serious deterioration of human rights, the United States could renew aid to the rebels who would then inevitably reemerge.

America should not underestimate either our material or symbolic assets. A United States ready to lavish aid on a politically plural Nicaragua (even if the Sandinistas rule as a consequence of electoral success) and unencumbered by association with the remnants of the Somoza order, will exert profound influence on the Nicaraguan political system. And if the United States, in the meantime, has succeeded in superintending a settlement of the civil war in El Salvador, and has moved not to coddle but to isolate the leprous regime in Guatemala, the prospects for democracy in Nicaragua will be enhanced.

As it blunders after military solutions without counting the cost to the people of Central America, this administration unintentionally demonstrates the difference between a ruthless and wise diplomacy.

In the debate over this country's Central American policies, the word "symmetry" has done as much or more than any other concept to cloud minds. So it is with some unease that I note, in closing, the essential symmetry of my proposals for dealing with Nicaragua and El Salvaldor.

The symmetry of ends is unmistakable: relatively just, relatively stable, broadly participatory political orders. While there cannot be a perfect symmetry of means, the means I proposed are symmetrical in their most crucial albeit negative feature, namely, this administration's relinquishment of its search for military victory.

I do not, of course, recommend a symmetrial insistence on power-sharing as the ne plus ultra of negotiations. Why? Quite simply because, in El Salvador's case, power-sharing is the only way of halting the slaughter and constructing just and democratic institutions. In the case of Nicaragua, by contrast, an insistence on power-sharing is likely to prolong the killing with little prospect of advancing America's ultimate objective and with considerable risk of making it unobtainable. Moreover, in Nicaragua the objective, including power-sharing, is likely to evolve in the aftermath of a negotiated settlement that deals only glancingly with domestic political arrangements.

The moral and pragmatic reasons for differential treatment with respect to the content of negotiations seem self-evident. But mindful of the confusion the very word *symmetry* appears to sow, perhaps I should more fully recapitulate the differences between these cases, since it is precisely those differences which make the claim for symmetry literally nonsensical. Treating different cases as if they were the same is just as asymmetrical as treating identical cases differently.

Two differences are fundamental. One is character—the history, as well as the institutional and class bases—of the regimes in Managua and San Salvador. A second is the relative autonomy and capacity of the rebels. Since the latter is really a function of the former, in the end the differences are one.

The problem Washington faces in Salvador does not stem from the ideological vagaries or idiosyncratic awfulness of a few, identifiable people. Rather, the problem is inherent in the struggle to wrench power from a self-perpetuating and self-controlled military institution and an oligarchy with precapitalist roots. In supporting the latter coalition, the United States struggles against history. America wages war against the very forces whose triumph will mark another stage in the modernization process and will, ironically, make Salvadoran society more like our own. A vast aid program conceived as a substitute for rather than a concomitant of deep political and social change will only strengthen the forces bidding to crack the society's ancient mold. I refer not primarily to the guerrillas (who are only the cutting edge of change) but to all classes struggling to shape the nation's institutions to their needs.

An oligarchy, clinging not only to its money but to its status as a force above the law, and a parasitic officer corps are utterly incompatible with a relatively modern political and social order. They cannot survive in an authentic participatory political system. They know that. And so to save the stinking hulk of the *ancien régime*, they will fight to the last priest, peasant and reformer. They will fight, that is, as long as the Reagan administration allows them to believe that it won't let them sink.

The Sandinistas, conversely, are a part of the new classes pushing relentlessly against worn out structures of life and thought. In part, because they share many of the objectives of the Nicaraguans—opportunity open to merit; a national rather than a private army; general access to education and medical care; a more even distribution of income and wealth—the armed opposition seems unable to mount a serious threat.

But the Sandinistas' grip on power also owes something to the educative value of experience. Made stupid at first by their ideology, the Sandinistas have gradually and partially adapted to the character of Nicaraguan and international reality.

No doubt some among them still dream of pressing society into a Marxist mold. The Central American wars sustain their dreams. For in the peace the United States and the Latin and European democracies can help create, irreconcilables of the left and right alike will depart from the historical stage into a deserved obscurity.

NOTES

1. "Nicaragua: Threat to Peace in Central America," U.S. Department of State, Bureau of Public Affairs, Current Policy No. 476, April 12, 1983.
2. Dickey, C., "Latins Find U.S. Policy Confusing," *Wasington Post,* July 25, 1983, p. A1.
3. "Juridicial Foundations to Guarantee International Peace and Security of the States of Central America: Official Proposal of Nicaragua Within the Framework of the Contadora Process," Nicaragua Minister of the Exterior, October 15, 1983.
4. Article 6 of "Draft Treaty to Guarantee Mutual Respect, Peace and Security Between the Republic of Nicaragua and the United States of America," *ibid,* p. 9.
5. Tyler, P., "Sandinistas Propose Security Accords to U.S.," *The Washington Post,* October 21, 1983, p. A1.
6. "Draft Accord to Contribute to the Peaceful Solution of the Armed Conflict in the Republic of El Salvador," esp. Articles 1-5, *supra,* note 3, pp. 27-30.
7. See generally Fagen, R., "The End of the Affair," *Foreign Policy,* No. 36, Fall 1979, p. 178.
8. See Ullman, R., "At War with Nicargua," *Foreign Affairs,* Fall 1983.
9. In response to a question at a semi-public forum about what he would do in the event of a U.S. invasion of Nicaragua, Edén Pastora responded: "I would fight alongside my people."
10. "A Secret War for Nicaragua," *Newsweek,* November 8, 1982, p. 42.
11. Since my personal sympathies run to the progressive democrats forced into opposition by the practices and policies of the Sandinsta leadership, I arrived at this prescription with great reluctance.
12. See, *e.g.,* Crossett, B. "Castro Says U.S. Seeks to Deploy Troops Under Guise of Maneuvers," *New York Times,* July 27, 1983, p. A1.
13. *The New York Times,* December 7, 1980, sec. 4, p. 3.
14. "Remarks Prepared for Delivery by the Honorable Fred C. Iklé, Under Secretary of Defense for Policy, to Baltimore Council on Foreign Affairs, September 12, 1983," News Release, Office of Assistant Secretary of Defense for Public Affaris, p. 4.
15. See, *e.g.,* Dickey, C., and McCartney, R., "Little Hope Seen for Salvadoran Peace," *The Washington Post,* September 4, 1983, p. A1.
16. *Ibid.*
17. Loferedo, G. "The Central American Crisis: Mexico's Role in the Search for a Negotiated Settlement," paper prepared for the Latin American Task Force of the Congressional Black Caucus, U.S. House of Representatives, Washington, D.C., March 14, 1982, p. 14. See also "Position of the FDR-FMLN's Political-Diplomatic Commission on Elections and Political Solution," July 22, 1981, and Zamora, R., "Saving Salvador," *New York Times,* January 22, 1982, p. A31.
18. See Farer, T., "Manage the Revolution?" *Foreign Policy,* No. 52, Fall 1983, pp. 96-117.
19. Gelb, L., "U.S. Aides See Need for Big Effort to Avert Rebel Victory in Salvador," *New York Times,* April 22, 1983, p. A1.
20. See Kissinger, H., *White House Years,* Little Brown, 1979, pp. 663-678; *Years of Upheaval,* Little Brown, 1982, pp. 409-13; Sigmund, P., *The Overthrow of Allende and the Politics of Chile, 1964-1976,* U. of Pittsburgh Press, 1977, pp. 113-123.

14
REAGAN ADMINISTRATION POLICYMAKING AND CENTRAL AMERICA

Barry Rubin

Central America, historically of secondary importance to U.S. diplomacy, became a central foreign policy issue during President Ronald Reagan's administration. In forming U.S. policy toward the region, ideological conflicts among political appointees compounded disputes among government agencies. The State Department, emphasizing regional causes of problems, became the stronghold of those open to negotiated political solutions; the National Security Council (NSC) reflected President Reagan's hard-line, global ideology. His personal intervention increased the hard-liner's influence in 1983, but even this temporary victory required two years of effort, the brief tenure of the conservative William Clark as national security adviser, and the formation of personal alliances among similarly-minded people in different agencies.

The Reagan administration faced two types of problems in assembling and carrying through its Central American policy: unifying it and selling it. First it had to overcome divisions in its own ranks. The "realpolitik" group at State and the ideologically conservative Reaganites differed over objectives, timing, strategy, and tactics. Several of the former group's leading figures, including Secretary of State Alexander Haig and Assistant Secretary of State Thomas Enders, were associated with Henry Kissinger, who was suspected by the Republican Party's right wing. Some policy differences were inspired by institutional responsibilities or personal ambitions. For example, moderate White House counselor James Baker worried that a strident Central American policy might damage the president's legislative program in Congress or his reelection prospects. High-ranking military officers balked at direct U.S. armed intervention for fear of "another Vietnam" draining military prestige and resources.

Second, after a policy won internal support, the administration then had to convince Congress, the media, the general public, and foreign allies to support the decisions. The Reaganites believed a highly visible policy would garner mass support forcing Congress to provide necessary funding. The pragmatists feared this would backfire.

SETTING THE STAGE

During President Jimmy Carter's term, the Sandinistas seized power in July 1979. Three months later a reform-minded junta took over in El Salvador. The Carter administration was conciliatory toward Nicaragua and supportive of the junta. Secretary of State Cyrus Vance had said, "By extending our friendship and economic assistance, we enhance the prospects for democracy in Nicaragua. We cannot guarantee that democracy will take hold there. But if we turn our back on Nicaragua, we can almost guarantee that democracy will fail."[1]

The Republican Party's 1980 platform accused Carter of standing by while Soviet-backed Cuba promoted revolution. It deplored the Sandinista takeover of Nicaragua and "Marxist attempts to destabilize El Salvador, Guatemala, and Honduras"; it opposed U.S. aid to Nicaragua and supported "the efforts of the Nicaraguan people to establish a free and independent government."[2] Reaganites marshalled these statements as an endorsement for their position in later conflict within the government. Vernon Walters, later an ambassador-at-large, made a trip to Central America for the Reagan transition team and promised support for conservative military regimes there.

Debate inside the Reagan camp began even before the new administration took office. Extreme conservatives were calling for a tough policy targeted against Cuba. The Council for Inter-American Security issued their Sante Fe Commission report which advocated unremitting support for the Salvadoran military and for the destabilization of Nicaragua. Three of that commission's participants entered the Reagan administration: Lt. General Gordon Sumner became a consultant to the State Department, Roger Fontaine joined the NSC staff, and Lewis Tambs became ambassador to Colombia.[3]

For the Reaganites and Secretary of State Haig, events on the eve of the inaugural enhanced their willingness to put a high priority on the issue. In January 1981 a guerrilla "final offensive" was coming to an unsuccessful end in El Salvador, but the rebels had graphically demonstrated their military capacity. The Salvadoran Army turned over captured guerrilla documents showing that the Soviet bloc supplied arms to the opposition. Developments within Nicaragua also disappointed those in Washington who hoped for a pluralistic and nonaligned regime there.

For the Reaganites, El Salvador's insurgency represented primarily not a civil war to be resolved by internal reforms but a Soviet-Cuban effort to destabilize Central America, with Mexico and the Panama Canal as long-range objectives. The Reaganites saw the conflict not as a secondary issue limited to regional considerations, but as a major test of U.S. global resolve. Nicaragua, the guerrillas' rear area for rest, training, and arms shipments, was itself considered beyond a point of no return on the road to dictatorship and alliance with Cuba. The "pragmatists," and particularly the State Department, saw the crisis as internally generated as well as exploited by the Soviets. Some believed that Nicaragua, under pressure, could become nonaligned, if leftist. Negotiations in El Salvador, conceived as an agreement by civilians in the leftist coalition to join a government-controlled electoral process, could help end the conflict there. These "pragmatists" wanted to support José Napoleon Duarte's reformist moderates, while many hard-liners thought the unbridled rightist forces might be more effective in defeating the Salvadoran insurgency.

This view of Central American conflict as part of a global struggle led to the second difference between the Carter and Reagan adminstrations. The new administration gave Central American problems a much higher priority. President Reagan himself and many of the Reaganites came from California and other western and southwestern states. Latin America loomed larger for them than for the "realpolitik" faction which was more oriented toward Europe. The Reaganites often had close personal contacts with Latin American conservatives, just as liberal Democrats had formed bonds with the area's Christian Democratic and Social Democratic politicians. The battle over the Panama Canal treaties was the first foreign policy test of the newly resurgent right, further sensitizing it to Central American security questions.

Jeane Kirkpatrick, Reagan's UN ambassador, became the President's chief personal adviser on Latin America and the administration's main publicist for its regional policy. Reagan felt her writings articulated his preconceptions. President Carter, she wrote, thought:

> that the cold war was over, that concern with Communism should no longer "overwhelm" other issues, that forceful intervention in the affairs of another nation is impractical and immoral, that we must never again put ourselves on the "wrong side" of history by supporting a foreign autocrat against a "popular movement," and that we must try to make amends for our deeply flawed national character by modesty and restraint in the arenas of power and the councils of the world.

Clearly, the Reagan administration would follow a different course. "The deterioration of the U.S. position in the hemisphere," Kirkpatrick warned, "has already created serious vulnerabilities where none previously existed, and threatens now to confront this country with the unprecedented need to defend itself against a ring of Soviet bases on and around our southern and eastern borders."[4]

HAIG AT THE HELM

When Alexander Haig became secretary of state in January 1981, he immediately opted for a high profile on Central America. The secretary of state was determined to place himself quickly in the leading foreign policy role, but he was aware that the Reaganites thought him too moderate on issues like arms control, the pipeline and NATO. Members of the White House staff closer to him ideologically distrusted his ambition and questioned his loyalty to Reagan's leadership.

By giving Central America top priority in the administration's first weeks, Haig could demonstrate to the Reaganites his anti-Soviet toughness, outmaneuver Secretary of Defense Caspar Weinberger (who was challenging him over NATO and arms control policy), and establish his public credentials as the administration's "vicar" on foreign policy. El Salvador would be made into a symbol of U.S. willpower in opposing Soviet-Cuban aggression. Haig's stridency was fueled by regional developments, such as the recent guerrilla offensive and reports on Nicaragua's use as a training base and arms depot for the Salvadoran insurgents. Nevertheless, Haig's activism ran the risk of stirring up public and congressional opposition by reinforcing the Reagan administration's image as "trigger-happy."

Haig's speeches were supplemented by actions against Nicaragua and Cuba during the administration's first six months in office. Washington quickly suspended wheat sales and economic aid to Nicaragua and opposed its loan requests to the World Bank and Inter-American Development Bank. Haig warned Cuba against involvement in Central America—threatening to "go to the source" of instability there—while presidential counselor Edwin Meese chimed in that the United States "could not rule out any means" of dealing with the war in El Salvador. Diplomatic teams were sent to Europe and Latin America to explain U.S. policy and present documentation of Soviet and Cuban involvement in Central America. State Department internal papers were rewritten to omit warnings about rightist threats to democracy. Haig even speculated that three American nuns killed and raped at a Salvadoran army checkpoint might have been victims of "an exchange of fire" while running a roadblock. Ambassador Kirkpatrick said that the nuns were "political activists on behalf" of the opposition.[5]

The centerpiece of the administration campaign was the State Department "White Paper" of February 23, 1981, using materials captured by the

Salvadoran military to argue that the USSR, Cuba, and Nicaragua were supplying arms and equipment to the Salvadoran guerrillas. The White Paper did not sway public opinion, however, since several critiques which challenged its interpretation on the source documents received wide publicity.[6]

Other State Department appointments were necessary to Reagan's revision of U.S. policy. The Republican Party's extreme right wing hoped to dominate the new administration, demanding one of their number as assistant secretary of state for inter-American affairs. Retired General Sumner was their favored candidate. Conservative Republican Senator Jesse Helms tried to dominate the appointment's process through his aide, John Carbaugh, who headed the transition team on Latin America. Asked about regional policy just after Reagan's inaugural, one high State Department official responded, "Why don't you ask John Carbaugh — he seems to be running things around here."[7]

When Alexander Haig was named Secretary of State, however, he quickly dismissed Carbaugh and nominated Thomas Enders to the post of assistant secretary. Helms reacted by blocking Enders' confirmation for several months and insisted on the hiring of ultraconservatives to deputy assistant secretary positions at State's Inter-American Affairs Bureau (ARA) — preferably Tambs or Sumner. When he did not have his way, Helms prevented Enders from obtaining the normal number of deputy assistant secretaries. Sumner was made a consultant to ARA but Enders relegated him to insignificance.

For Haig's purposes, Enders was a natural choice. Haig took notice of Enders as the deputy chief of mission in Cambodia in 1971, where Enders played an important role in implementing National Security Adviser Henry Kissinger's clandestine military aid program for Cambodia.[8] In the first two years of the Reagan administration, Enders worked well with the prickly Haig and dominated the regional inter-agency committees. Yet Enders' policy views, and jealousy over his accumulation of power, eventually contributed to his downfall.[9]

While limiting Helm's influence, the administration moved to eliminate career people at ARA who disagreed with, or were not trusted to implement, its policy. Carter's last assistant secretary of ARA, William Bowdler, was dismissed within 24 hours of Reagan's inaugural although, as a Foreign Service officer (FSO), he could normally have expected an ambassadorial post. Ambassador to El Salvador Robert White, also a career man, was ousted within 10 days and offered no new assignment.[10] Other ARA personnel, like Deputy Assistant Secretary James Cheek (who conducted the incoming Reagan administration's first Central American policy review) were sent to posts outside the hemisphere. Ambassador Lawrence Pezzullo, who remained in Nicaragua well into 1981, later became diplomat-in-residence at a U.S. university.

Having rejected the policy and personnel he identified with the Carter administration, Haig now had a new team in Washington and in the field. Newly named ambassadors, including Deane Hinton in El Salvador and John Negroponte in Honduras, and the leading officials of ARA in Washington had no regional experience.[11]

The ambassadors removed and the FSOs displaced at ARA or at U.S. embassies in Central America held a variety of opinions, but all were critical of Reagan administration policy. They all advocated putting the main emphasis on negotiations with the Salvadoran opposition and on a policy of diplomatic bargaining with Nicaragua. While the guerrillas in El Salvador could not win the war, they argued, the Salvadoran government could lose it by failing to stengthen its own political base. The Salvadoran regime should put prime emphasis on continued land reform, an end to rightist violence against moderates, and the cooptation of moderate forces from the opposition.[12] Dissenters still in ARA may have leaked information to the media or tried to affect the wording of internal documents, but such efforts had only a marginal effect. Still, the belief that the president's policy was being sabotaged was held by many political appointees outside State and fed their suspicions about the State Department and, thus, of the role played by Enders himself.[13] Despite this hostility, the State Department and Enders largely directed Central American policy from January 1981 until February 1983. During most of that time, there was no other agency capable of challenging them. The president's aides were not primarily interested in foreign policy and the National Security Council (NSC) was either too weak or too preoccupied elsewhere to assert itself.

OTHER ACTORS

At the White House, Chief of Staff James Baker and his deputy, Michael Deaver, were concerned with protecting the president's image, strengthening him politically, and moving his initiatives through Congress. Consequently, during 1981 they preferred that the United States maintain a low profile on Central America lest it interfere with the White House's top priority domestic and economic programs. Just as they were worried about disturbing Capitol Hill over Central America, these White House aides also did not want to inflame the public's fear of military involvement there since such worries might endanger Republican fortunes in the 1982 elections. The third key White House assistant, Presidential Counselor Edwin Meese, responsible for supervising National Security Adviser Richard Allen, was more outspoken. Meese's support for Haig's early public ultimatum on Central America, as well as his poor handling of Allen and the NSC staff, led to later changes in personnel.

During the Reagan administration's first 18 months, the domination of Central America policy by Haig and Enders also went unchallenged by Allen. The new administration entered office determined to downgrade the NSC post which had become so powerful under Henry Kissinger and Zbigniew Brzezinski. The NSC staff was reduced in size and Allen played a much smaller role in policymaking. The position of national security adviser only was revitalized when Allen resigned and was replaced by William Clark in January 1982.

With Haig's support and NSC passivity, Enders was able to dominate the policy process on Central America by chairing interdepartmental committees, controlling access to meetings, and regulating the flow of reports and option papers. As assistant secretaries often do, Enders brought his own friends and allies into the bureau, particularly L. Craig Johnstone, Office Director for Central America Affairs, who had worked with Enders in Cambodia. Luigi Einaudi, head of ARA's Office of Policy Planning and Coordination, who had survived from the Carter era, also played an important role.

Of the NSC staffers on Latin America, Roger Fontaine had little influence, while Al Sapia-Bosch generally cooperated with Enders. In other agencies, however, the beginning of a Reaganite coalition was organized by Undersecretary of Defense for Policy Fred Iklé, Deputy Assistant Secretary of Defense for Inter-American Affairs Nestor Sanchez (a CIA veteran), and the CIA's national intelligence officer for Latin America, Constantine Menges. All of these strongly favored a tough line emphasizing U.S. covert and military activity.

Despite the presence of such activists, the Department of Defense (DOD) and the Central Intelligence Agency (CIA) played important but secondary roles in the early struggle over policymaking. The Joint Chiefs of Staff were not eager for any direct U.S. military role in the region, not even an anti-arms smuggling blockade or increased naval presence in the Caribbean. They placed higher priorities on other parts of the world and were concerned that involvement in an unpopular conflict might endanger approval of their budget requests by Congress. Remembering the Vietnam experience, the armed services did not want to become involved in a war where they would lack public support and be subject to political constraints.

This reluctance surprised the Reaganites. Secretary of Defense Weinberger favored a tougher line but was not ready to push Central America as a top priority. Deputy Secretary Frank Carlucci was even more sympathetic to the armed service's cautious approach. The military's concerns were communicated to the White House. One of the first decisions in the senior interdepartmental group, chaired by Assistant Secretary of State Enders, was to limit the number of U.S. military advisers in El Salvador to 55. Other DOD participants on the interagency group included Lt. Gen. Paul Gorman,

USA, assistant to the chairman of the Joint Chiefs of Staff, and Vice Admiral Thomas Bigley, USN director of plans and policy for the Joint Chiefs of Staff. General Gorman received his fourth star and became the Commander of the U.S. Southern Command (SOUTHCOM) in Panama in August 1983.

On the covert side, CIA Director William Casey lobbied for U.S. aid to the Nicaraguan armed opposition elements and gained support for this effort, but the agency's first task in Central America was to supply intelligence. In the Carter administration's closing days it gathered increasing evidence that Nicaragua was supplying arms to the Salvadoran guerrillas. The CIA had well-established sources in the region, but its reporting was sometimes subject to policymakers' pressure to reach conclusions backing current policy. During the Carter administration, a congressional study noted, CIA reports played down Nicaraguan involvement in El Salvador since the White House had to certify, as a condition for granting aid, that Managua was not subverting its neighbors. In contrast, with Reagan in office, the CIA tended too often to accept Salvadoran government claims and to ignore rightist activities.[14]

State had special, but not insoluble, problems in coping with still another key institution, the Congress. While the legislature was an indirect actor in the policy process, it was a major consideration in gaining necessary funds and public support for administration policy. Yet neither the Senate nor the House of Representatives had the votes or the motivation to affect policy unless alienated to an unusual extent, a situation Enders wanted to avoid. Consequently, while legistative action forced the President to report on progress made in El Salvador over human rights, Congressmen who doubted there was progress could not block continued aid.

Congress also protested U.S. covert assistance to anti-government guerrillas in Nicaragua, but lacked votes in the Senate to cut off funds. Of course, many members of Congress either supported Reagan's policy, were indifferent to Central American issues or feared being held responsible for "losing" El Salvador. Enders, responsible for dealing with the legislators, had leaned toward compromise with them; this coincided with his pragmatic approach to the region. I.M. Destler's chapter provides a thorough description of how Central American issues were approached by the Congress.

THE EMERGING POLICIES

The administration knew that Congress and the voters would strongly object to any deployment of U.S. troops in Central America. Reagan rejected Haig's suggestions for blockading Cuba, while Baker and Deaver worried that even the tough public statements were fostering a crisis that could overshadow their economic programs and stir popular fears that Central America would be "another Vietnam." One White House official told reporters that the "train was going too fast." ARA officials worried that the situation was becoming overheated, ruining chances for negotiation and for maintaining congressional support. Consequently, statements were made in March 1981 to cool the issue. Acting Deputy Assistant Secretary of State John Bushnell warned privately that the mass media was overemphasizing Central America: "This story is running five times as big as it is." His stand was publicly disavowed, since the administration did not want to imply that Central America was unimportant, but for a number of months thereafter Haig and the White House reduced their statements and public emphasis on the problem.[15]

During the rest of 1981, the administration stepped back from the original high-profile policy. Secretly, Reagan approved aid to anti-government Nicaraguan guerrillas at a November 1981 NSC meeting. Publicly, the White House introduced a Caribbean Basin Initiative to provide that region with trade preferences, increased assistance, and incentives for U.S. investment. Much of the administration's effort was directed at winning public and congressional support for El Salvador since administration certification on human rights progress were now due every six months, beginning in January 1982. While Haig repeated warnings to Nicaragua against continued arms shipments to El Salvador, the State Department investigated whether these threats were affecting Managua's activities.

Assistant Secretary Enders went to Nicaragua in August 1981 to offer a bilateral nonaggression pact and a curb on anti-Sandinista military training camps in Florida if Managua stopped its military build-up and the arms shipments to El Salvador. By the end of October, the two sides failed to reach agreement.[16] In March 1982, while refusing to rule out U.S. efforts to overthrow the Sandinistas, the Secretary of State offered financial aid and an end to covert help for anti-Sandinista guerillas, the *contras,* in exchange for an end to Nicaraguan involvement in the Salvadoran war. He also continued to explore contingency plans for U.S. military options — including possible blockades or use of surrogates — and collective action through the Organization of American States.[17] This combination of bargaining and military planning had emerged as a "two-track" strategy during Enders' August 1981 trip to Nicaragua. The United States would use military threats and economic pressure to gain Nicaraguan concessions.

The Reaganites did not oppose this strategy in 1981-82 since they supported moves against Nicaragua, but they were more skeptical about diplomatic initiatives. They estimated that the Nicaraguan government, with Cuba behind it, would stand firm and that negotiations would fail. They thought only a much-expanded U.S. effort would defeat the Salvadoran guerrillas and force Nicaragua's back against the wall. To gain a freer hand for such actions, they favored a strong public campaign, as well as increased covert operations. Disturbing reports that the Salvadoran government was not doing well in the war increased their impatience. Indeed, the government's credibility was so low that even a March 1982 State Department press conference, showing aerial photographs of the Sandinistas' displacement of Indians and construction of new military installations, had scant effect. State Department officials viewed the policy's unpopularity as a response to excessive militancy, while the Reaganites complained of media bias and the lack of a serious campaign to mobilize support.

By mid-1982, however, Jeane Kirkpatrick, Clark and other hard-liners grew increasingly impatient, taking the line that defeat in El Salvador would be due to a lack of congressional support.

CHANGING OF THE GUARD

In El Salvador, the large turnout for March 1982 elections echoed favorably in the United States and convinced the Reaganites that a better U.S. climate existed for increasing support to that regime. The administration feared that the best opportunity to force a change in Nicaraguan policy or to subvert the Sandinistas might soon be past. Contributing to these conclusions were the failure to reach agreement with Nicaragua, its military build-up, and reports of the Sandinista's domestic unpopularity. "The hours are growing rather short" to prevent Managua from becoming another Havana, Haig warned in November 1981.[18]

After William Clark replaced Richard Allen as national security adviser in January 1982, the increasing clashes between Haig and the White House staff led to the secretary of state's resignation in June 1982. His successor, George Shultz, had less interest in Central America. In the short run, Enders' autonomy was increased, but Haig's departure exposed the assistant secretary to Clark's opposition. Haig's removal, Clark's gathering authority, and Shultz's willingness to yield ground facilitated the Reaganites' efforts to take control of Central American policy.[19]

From his exploratory visit to Nicaragua in August 1981 until January 1983, Enders continued efforts to combine the waging of war in El Salvador with new diplomatic initiatives toward Nicaragua, but Reaganite opposition to the latter "track" became stronger and stronger as the months passed. The hard-liners placed more hope than did the State Department on the success of U.S.-backed anti-Sandinista guerrillas operating across the Honduran border. This covert CIA operation was mandated by the NSC with Casey's enthusiastic support and was ostensibly designed to interdict the arms flow from Nicaragua to El Salvador; it also gave the United States an additional card to trade for Managua's agreement to cease its intervention. The

Reaganites also came to think the anti-Sandinista forces might be able to overthrow the Nicaraguan regime.[20]

Embassy dispatches provided ammunition for both factions. Ambassador Hinton's reports that the Salvadoran war was going badly helped convince Enders of the need for diplomatic efforts. Hinton himself made speeches criticizing the disruptive extremism of Salvadoran rightists, whose death squads threatened to destroy the country "every bit as much as the guerrillas." Clark, through the White House, ordered him to cease such statements. Yet Hinton's pessimism was used by Clark and Kirkpatrick to convince the President that Enders' policy was not working.[21]

Bureaucratic friction provided the last element undermining Enders at the end of 1982 and the beginning of 1983. White House aides saw Enders, as they had seen Haig, loyal more to the State Department and the foreign service than to the Reagan administration's objectives. There was an element of guilt by association in the assistant secretary's dilemma. Some appointees accused the State Department of having an "obsession with perfecting the government of El Salvador" rather than prosecuting the battle against the Salvadoran guerrillas and Nicaragua. To mollify Congress, Enders made verbal concessions and public criticisms of the Salvadoran regime. Such pragmatism further fed the White House's suspicion that the State Department was determined to limit the struggle. Finally, Enders' arrogance and his domination of paperwork and meetings raised jurisdictional jealousies.

Clark already felt that Enders was poorly implementing the President's orders. Kirkpatrick wanted the administration to go on the offensive in the battle for public opinion, arguing that appeasing Congress only increased its obstructionism. Baker's mistrust of the State Department moved Enders' key White House ally at least temporarily into Clark's camp on this issue. The scene was also set by the major guerrilla offensives of October 1982 and January 1983 which, Hinton reported, the Salvadoran government was hard-pressed to deflect. This development apparently encouraged Enders to work harder on his diplomatic option of the two-track policy and led to a visit to Spain's socialist Prime Minister Felipe González who had tried to ease Central American tensions. Clark, not informed of the trip in advance, considered it an attempt to arrange talks behind his back.

All these events gave the Reaganites a chance to displace Enders and push for a more aggressive strategy. Clark convinced the President to institute a high-level review of U.S. policy in January 1983 and to dispatch Kirkpatrick on a 10-day trip to El Salvador, Honduras, Costa Rica, and Venezuela, beginning on February 3. Kirkpatrick returned with the conclusion that the Salvadoran government and army were demoralized by uncertainty over future U.S. military supplies and support. She argued that her interviews in the other countries showed they also wanted a firmer U.S. policy, blaming this loss of confidence on congressional criticism and State Department talk about negotiations.[22]

To remedy these preceived shortcomings, Kirkpatrick proposed emergency increases in assistance spending and she urged the president to discourage congressional criticism and to buoy the Salvadoran regime by announcing that the United States would not back down. CIA director Casey argued for expanding the operations of U.S.-supported Nicaraguan guerrillas by claiming that the Sandinistas might be overthrown by the end of 1983. Reagan accepted the recommendations and requested $60 million in supplemental aid from Congress. He also appointed conservative former Senator Richard Stone (D-Fla.) as special envoy for Central American negotiations, further eroding Enders' authority.

One reason for Reagan's intervention was the NSC staff's leak of Enders' two-track memorandum into the press on February 10.[23] The president was displeased to be confronted publicly with a State Department position at variance with his views. Reagan finally moved in February 1983 to support the proposals of Clark, Kirkpatrick, and their allies; two years of leadership by State and Enders on Central American policy was ended.[24]

REAGANITES TAKE CHARGE

A series of dramatic measures followed, making Central America again the administration's top foreign policy priority.[25] Robert McFarlane, Clark's deputy, was put in charge of a special working group on El Salvador and Nicaragua. On March 10, 1983, Reagan declared that the defense of the Caribbean and Central America against Marxism-Leninism was vital for U.S. national security. The public campaign was launched by the president's powerful, and nationally-televised, April 27 speech to a joint session of Congress. If El Salvador was taken over by pro-Soviet forces, Reagan hinted, Congress would be responsible because it failed to provide enough aid. Politicians, aware of precedents for being blamed with the "loss" of a country to communism, dampened their dissent.[26]

The President made similar speeches in the conservative and electorally important South. In San Antonio and Houston, Texas, the administration hoped Chicano voters might become supportive. These were followed by speeches in Miami and Orlando, Florida which have strongly anti-communist Cuban populations, and Jackson, Mississippi. The White House, NSC, State, and the U.S. Information Agency (USIA) developed an active public diplomacy program, including courses to prepare government officials to speak on Central America. The White House had its own operation under Presidential Assistant Faith Whittlesay, who held regular Wednesday meetings with domestic conservative groups to rally their support. At one such gathering in June 1983, they planned to counter a Washington march protesting U.S. involvement in Central America. Otto Reich, the Cuban-born deputy director of the Agency for International Development, was named State Department coordinator for public diplomacy on Central America. USIA worked on the presentation of Washington's policy abroad, particularly in Western Europe, where polls showed great concern over the issue.

Enders' reassignment as ambassador to Spain and Ambassador Hinton's recall in June 1983 confirmed the power shift. Some insult was added as well, when an administration official claimed Hinton was "burned out." But the ambassador's statements showed neither exhaustion nor a change of heart on the two-track approach. Policy had never been intended, said Hinton, to "win" the war but to end it. A U.S. military commitment for victory, he added, would be "so massive that it's not even worth discussing."[27]

Clark planned to keep control of Central America issues himself, and thus preferred to replace Enders with someone ideologically compatible with the Reaganites. The White House seriously considered Ambassador Negroponte in Honduras (a career officer considered enthusiastic about Reagan's approach) for the assistant secretary position and U.S. Ambassador to Guyana Thomas Gerald (a retired admiral) for Hinton's position in El Salvador. A White House staff member voiced the cruder aspect of that institution's anti-FSO feeling by saying, "You don't handle Central American politics with tea and crumpets on the diplomatic circuit." Angry FSOs responded with criticism of "foreign policy amateurs" who ignored expert opinion and on-the-spot evaluations by U.S. embassies.[28]

Undersecretary of State for Political Affairs Lawrence Eagleburger convinced Secretary of State Shultz that State should not surrender too much authority over these appointments. Ambassador to Brazil H. Langhorne Motley, a political appointee close to Clark but also well-known to Congress as a former lobbyist, became the new assistant secretary. The fact that Motley had become the eighth assistant secretary of state for Latin America in nine years did not bode well for that position's job security. State managed to save the ambassadorship to El Salvador for a moderate career FSO, Ambassador to Nigeria Thomas Pickering.[29]

Despite Shultz's victory on the El Salvador ambassadorship, he had lost practical control over the course of U.S. policy in the region. Shultz was far less bureaucratically aggressive than Haig and was concentrating on other issues, but he also carefully avoided challenging White House authority. "The whole secret of this administration," one official explained, "is that the president is not to be humiliated. Whoever does that is dead. George Shultz never does it."[30]

THE POLICY GETS TOGETHER

The Reaganites had now consolidated control over Central American policy. National Security Adviser Clark stood at the apex. The Defense

Department handled U.S. military efforts and training, with Deputy Assistant Secretary Sanchez serving as liaison to Clark. The CIA ran covert operations against Nicaragua from neighboring Honduras, with U.S. Ambassador Negroponte directing action on the scene. Ambassador Jeane Kirkpatrick monitored State Department performance and was the main public advocate of administration policy, while Ambassador Stone was in charge of any actual negotiations. Constantine Menges, who had long argued that Mexico was the ultimate target of Soviet-Cuban efforts in Central America, came from the CIA to the NSC staff. Fontaine and Sapia-Bosch both left.

Ostensibly, the post-Enders policy continued to employ a range of means and goals including economic development, construction of democratic institutions, a broader Salvadoran electoral process, Stone's diplomatic visits to the region, and U.S. support for the regional Contadora group's efforts on Central American negotiations. At the same time, the Reaganites argued that victory was possible in El Salvador and Nicaragua if Congress and the U.S. public would only provide the necessary support. The administration's increased military pressure on Nicaragua was most evident in President Reagan's July 12 agreement to stage Big Pine II, a U.S. military exercise involving 4000 troops and 19 ships in Honduras and the Caribbean, which the Joint Chiefs of Staff had been planning since May at Clark's behest.

On July 18 President Reagan named former Secretary of State Henry Kissinger to head a bipartisan commission to suggest options for Central American policy. Similar bodies, which combined individuals from inside and outside the government had successfully formulated proposals on Social Security and strategic arms policy. The administration hoped the Kissinger commission would decrease congressional criticism and provide a bipartisan framework for future strategy along essentially the same lines it had been pursuing. The months necessary for the commission's research would buy time for entrenching the post-Enders policy.

Immediate political gains from forming the commission were, however, undermined the following day when plans for the Big Pine II maneuvers leaked into the press. U.S. ambassadors, Central American governments, and Secretary Shultz had not yet been told of the final decision. Shultz was outraged and protested directly to Reagan against Clark's failure to keep him informed. The administration was seriously embarrassed and congressional opinion, once again concerned about the possibility of direct U.S. military involvement, became intensely critical.[31]

The legislative opposition and support for the Boland-Zablocki amendment to cut off U.S. aid to Nicaraguan *contras* was reinforced by uncertainty as to administration objectives in Nicaragua. Was the goal to overthrow the Sandinista government or simply to intimidate it into stopping arms shipments to the Salvadoran guerrillas? Kirkpatrick denied that the administration was seeking to overthrow the Managua government. "We have minimal and maximal goals in Nicaragua," she said. "And I truly believe that they are not identical with the *contras.*"[32]

Skeptical of such assurances, the House of Representatives voted in July to end covert aid to the Nicaraguan guerrillas. A similar measure was again passed in October 1983. Without Senate support, these decisions were not binding, but they showed that the administration had not stilled congressional dissent.

On one level, Clark continued Haig's approach of encouraging the Salvadoran government and trying to initmidate Nicaragua and Cuba. As one DOD official put it: "We're playing a little cat-and-mouse game with them, putting a little squeeze on, making them wonder what's going to happen next. Ultimately, the idea is to convince them that allowing the Salvadoran guerrillas to use Nicaragua as their headquarters for revolution is not a good idea if they want to keep their own damn revolution."[33] Neverthless, the administration had gone beyond that approach, which characterized U.S. policy up to February 1983. The best public definition of the new objectives was provided by Undersecretary of Defense Iklé in a September 1983 speech cleared by Clark. "We must prevent consolidation of a Sandinista regime in Nicaragua that would become an arsenal for insurgency," said Iklé. The House of Representatives' opposition to the covert U.S. operation was creating "a sanctuary" for the rebels, who would never settle for a fair democratic process. Consequently, he concluded, "We do not seek a military defeat for our friends. We do not seek a military stalemate. We seek victory for the forces of democracy."[34]

Both Reaganites and "pragmatists" had agreed on a policy of intimidating the Nicaraguans into negotiating. The Reaganites, of course, put the emphasis on the intimidation aspect, while the State Department was more interested in negotiations. The Reaganites had been more interested in affecting the internal situation in Nicaragua, while the State Department had limited its concerns more strictly to Managua's involvement in El Salvador and with the Soviet bloc. The State Department emphasized curbing the ultra-right's activity and seeking government reforms in El Salvador; the Reaganites thought that efforts to bring social change and strengthen centrist forces might divide the leadership and damage the war effort there.

RETROSPECTIVE:
CONTINUING DISPUTES OVER POLICY

The Central American policy process shows that the president's control of foreign policy is potentially constrained by several factors. The chief executive must decide what he wants, whether his subordinates are doing it, whose advice he should listen to, and who should be given authority to implement decisions. When the President intervenes decisively he will get his way. Given the choice between the approach represented by his old friend Clark and his new friend Kirkpatrick and the distant ARA bureau, whose ideological views and loyalty he suspected, Reagan's decision could not be in doubt.

Still, just when the Reaganites' victory over the "pragmatists" seemed final, Reagan agreed to make Clark Secretary of the Interior in October 1983, removing the key man who had ensured the Reagan alliance's success. Clark's successor, Robert McFarlane, had far less personal leverage with the president and McFarlane himself seemed a compromise between Ambassador Kirkpatrick, the Reaganites' candidate, and Baker, who was supported by the "pragmatists" on the White House staff. Both Baker and Secretary of State Shultz had helped wear down Clark through their critique of his Middle East and arms control policies. The State Department now hoped its position would be stregthened by having McFarlane, a seemingly less formidable rival, as national security adviser.

From the outset, the Reagan administration was faced with a war in El Salvador and a leftist government in Nicaragua which was aiding the Salvadoran rebels. Given the administration's reading of U.S. interests, it never seriously contemplated not intervening in El Salvador and accepting a revolution there. Since a compromise with the Salvadoran opposition was seen as inevitably producing a Marxist-dominated government, this option was also rejected. Consequently, the U.S. government backed the Salvadoran regime in fighting the conflict. In this context, the internal U.S. debate could only revolve around whether to encourage a moderate, reform-oriented regime that might muster broader support or a tough rightist government that could supposedly better prosecute the war. Thus, the sole solution was military victory over the insurgents, or what amounted to the opposition's surrender. Either way, the fighting was likely to continue indefinitely.

There was a wider range of options and governmental debate about Nicaragua. Some officials at the State Department felt that negotiations might dissuade Nicaragua from a policy of spreading revolution. Washington could coexist with Managua if it changed its foreign policy. The Reaganites rejected this idea both because they considered Nicaragua an intrinsically unacceptable extension of Soviet-Cuban influence in the hemisphere and because they doubted that any Sandinista government would abandon its revolutionary goals. Consequently, the Reaganites concluded that only the fall of the Sandinista regime would remove the threat to El Salvador and to the region as a whole.

Regardless of their views on the ultimate outcome of U.S. pressure on Nicaragua, all administration factions agreed that intimidation was needed to discourage Nicaragua from involvement in El Salvador. The Reaganites, however, were willing to countenance much higher levels of escalation against

Managua, as their policy after February 1983 demonstrated. The October 1983 invasion of Grenada underlined a willingness to use force in the region and posed an obvious parallel for Nicaragua. Yet it was difficult to assess the actual objective of their strategy; economic, political, and military pressures aimed at securing a change in Nicaraguan policy could not easily be distinguished from those aimed at bringing down the government. This ambiguity was intentional, at least originally. Reaganites thought that Managua's doubt about this distinction would be more likely to produce concessions from Nicaragua.

Internal administration critics argued, in contrast, that the presence of threats without incentives would only toughen Nicaragua's stand, pushing it more clearly into the Soviet bloc and convincing it that a fight to the finish was its only choice. The Reagan administration could offer only unending war in El Salvador and an escalation of intimidation of Nicaragua. There were serious questions about whether the administration was interested in good-faith negotiations with Nicaragua after Enders' departure, while the situation in El Salvador seemed to follow a worrisome, and not unfamiliar pattern, requiring larger and larger amounts of U.S. aid and involvement.

In terms of the administration's policy process—and more general trends in U.S. foreign policymaking—the themes are clear. Ideology and factionalization generated major internal battles over Central American policy. These factors augmented mistrust between political appointees and the foreign service and built on existing institutional competition. Ideological struggles and accelerating personnel shifts made it more difficult to build a consensus, even within the executive branch itself, for directing U.S. foreign policy. Intelligence information and reporting from the field became tools in such battles rather than means for adjusting policy to reality. The Reaganite coalition succeeded by assembling an alliance of powerful officials able to obtain presidential support, but its "victories" will continue to be challenged by external events and internal disputes.

NOTES

1. *Washington Post*, September 28, 1979.
2. 1980 Republican National Convention Platform, reprinted from the *Congressional Record*, July 31, 1980.
3. The Council for Inter-American Security, "A New Inter-American Policy for the Eighties," Washington, D.C., 1980. This is often referred to as the Santa Fe Report. It is interesting to compare it to the report of a study group headed by Ambassador Sol Linowitz produced just before the Carter administration took office. Fontaine, formerly with the Center for Strategic and International Studies and with the AmerEnterprise Institute, also served as Reagan's Latin American adviser during the presidential campaign but had relatively little influence in office. Other articles in this vein include Pedro Sanjuan, "Why Don't We Have a Latin American Policy?" and Roger Fontaine, Cleto Di Giovanni, Jr., and

Alexander Kruger, "Castro's Specter," *The Washington Quarterly*, Autumn 1980. For a summary of the assumptions underlying the Reagan administration's approach, see Viron Vaky's chapter in this volume.

4. Jeane Kirkpatrick, "U.S. Security and Latin America," *Commentary*, January 1981, p. 29. See also her article, "Dictatorships and Double Standards," *Commentary*, November 1979 and Nestor Sanchez, "The Communist Threat," *Foreign Policy*, Fall 1983.

5. Stephanie Harrington, "Salvadoran Runaround," *The New Republic* December 12, 1981; E. Walsh, "U.S. Economic Aid to Nicaragua is Suspended but May be Resumed," *Washington Post*, April 2, 1981, p. A2; J. Vasquez, "El Salvador Takes World's Spotlight: Becomes Symbol in Struggle of the Superpowers," and O. Johnston and R. Toth, "El Salvador Takes World's Spotlight: Reagan Embarks on Daring Gamble to Show Resolve," *Los Angeles Times*, March 8, 1981, p. 1.

6. U.S. Department of State, "Communist Interference in El Salvador: Documents Demonstrating Communist Support of the Salvadoran Insurgency," Washington: February 23, 1981.

7. Stephen Kinzer, "From Capitol Hill, two voices on Latin American policy," *Boston Globe*, April 9, 1981, p. 2. A Latin American trip by former CIA deputy director Vernon Walters on behalf of the Reagan transition team also signaled the change in U.S. policy.

8. On Ender's role in Indochina, see William Shawcross, *Sideshow*, NY, 1979, and Henry Kissinger, *Years of Upheaval*, NY, 1982.

9. Phil Keisling, "The Tallest Gun in Foggy Bottom, "*Washington Monthly*, November 1982; interviews.

10. DeYoung, K. "Envoy Reported Removed From Salvadoran Post, "*Washington Post*, February 2, 1981, p. Al; J. Goshko, "Ousted Ambassador's Testimony Disavowed," *Washington Post*, February 27, 1981, p. A26; K. DeYoung, "El Salvador: A Symbol of World Crisis, Part 1,", *Washington Post*, March 8, 1981, p. Al; "Ex-Envoy to ES Says Views Caused Ouster," March 12, 1981; Carla Anne Robbins," A State Department Purge," *New York Times*, November 3, 1981 p. A19; "U.S. has Replaced Nearly All its Specialists on Central America, " *Boston Globe*, November 23, 1981, p. 8; J. de Onis, "Haig Said to Remove Ambassador To Salvador in Signal of New Policy," *New York Times*, February 2, 1981, p. Al. White's quick firing was partly due to his outspoken dissent on Salvadoran policy. He refused a Pentagon-inspired request from the chief of the U.S. military aid group to sign a cable requesting 75 U.S. military advisers and White also publicly criticized the Salvadoran authorities' investigation of the killing of three American nuns by government security forces. White also warned that the violence of the far right was driving moderates into alliance with the left. "The improvement of the socio-economic conditions in this country is the only long-term solution to the grave problems it faced," White said shortly before his removal. He believed that the left could not win the war but the government could lose it by failing to make political reforms. "What Latin American needs desperately," explained White, "is a non-Communist model for revolution. . . . "

11. The mistrust between the career Latin Americanists and the political appointees is demonstrated by two exaggerated, bitter anecdotes told during interviews. An FSO claimed, "It isn't embarrassing that the secretary of state doesn't know anything about Central America, and it is only modestly embarrassing that the assistant secretary doesn't know very much, but it is very bad when the deputy assistant secretaries and even office directors know so little." The story told among Reagan appointees is that a career officer commented at one meeting, "Let's face it, we have our bastards in El Salvador and the Cubans have theirs and there isn't much difference between the two." On the U.S. ambassadors in Central America, see Christopher Dickey, "The Proconsuls," *Rolling Stone*, August 18, 1983.

12. Several mid-level officials in different agencies produced a position paper before Reagan took office proposing the United States push for negotiations rather than become involved on the side of the Salvadoran government. This was never considered by the administration. The text is published as "Dissent Paper on El Salvador and Central America," Washington, D.C.: November 16, 1980, by the U.S. Committee in Solidarity with the People.

13. In contrast to the political appointees' confidence, career FSOs were much more doubtful about Washington's ability to dominate the situation. One aide to Carter-era Deputy Secretary of State Warren Christopher commented, "We're behaving as though we push buttons in Washington and the Salvadorans jump. It's a fantasy, a self-delusion." Quoted in Richard Feinberg, *The Intemperate Zone*, NY, 1983, p. 14. The most important leak by ARA liberals wa of the forthcoming "Big Pine II" military exercise.

14. U.S. Congress, Permanent Select Committee on Intelligence, "U.S. Intelligence Performance on Central America: Achievements and Selected Instances of Concern," September 22, 1982.

15. Interviews; J. Miller, "High Official Now Plays Down El Salvador," *New York Times*, March 13, 1981, p. A3; H. Smith, "Discordant Voices: a Rash of Opposing Statements Bring Reagan Foreign Policies Into Question," *New York Times*, March 20, 1981, p. A2; C. Dickey, "Salvadoran War Gives Way To Terrorism," *Washington Post*, March 1, 1981, p. A1; K. DeYoung, "Sleuth of the Salvador Papers," *Washington Post*, March 14, 1981, p. A1; C. Dickey, "Guerrillas Take Aim at Economy," *Washington Post*, March 14, 1981, p. A1.

16. Interviews; J. Onis, "House Committee Votes to Restrict Reagan on Arms Aid for Salvador," *New York Times*, July 17, 1981, p. A1; B. Crossette, "Groups Trying to Sway L.A. Policy," *New York Times*, November 18, 1981, p. A24; B. Gwertzman, "Latin Policy: A New Plan," *New York Times*, December 6, 1981, p. A1; *Washington Post*, November 15, 1981; S. Kinzer, "A Washington Shoot-Out Over Nicaragua," *Boston Globe*, September 26, 1981, p. 44.

17. Interviews; L. Gelb, "Haig is Said to Press for Military Options for Salvador Action," *New York Times*, November 5, 1981, p. A1; B. Crossette, "Haig Asserts the Nicaraguans Display Interest in Closer Ties," *New York Times*, December 3, 1981, p. A1; R. Halloran, "Nicaragua Arms Called Peril to Area," *New York Times*, December 3, 1981, p. A12; B. Crossette, "Haig Presses O.A.S. to Join in Halting a Latin Arms Race," *New York Times*, December 5, 1981, p. 1; B. Gwertzman, "U.S. Seeking Right to Use Air Bases in the Caribbean," *New York Times*, March 4, 1982, p. A1.

18. Interviews; L. Gelb, "Haig is Said to Press for Military Options for Salvadoran Action," *New York Times*, November 5, 1981, p. A1; B. Gwertzman, "Haig Warns Time is Growing Short on Nicaragua," *New York Times*, November 23, 1981, p. A15; M. Getler and D. Oberdorfer, "Pressure to 'Do Something' Grows," *Washington Post*, November 22, 1981, p. A1; C. Dickey, "U.S. Nearing Decision on Nicaragua", *Washington Post*, November 22, 1981, p. A1; D. Oberdorfer, "U.S., In Secret Dialogue, Sought Rapprochment with Nicaragua", *Washington Post*, December 10, 1981, p. Al; S. Kinzer, "Debate Flares in U.S. Over Central America," *Boston Globe*, November 22, 1981, p. 1; Enders testimony to Senate Foreign Relations Committee, December 14, 1981; U.S. Department of State, Current Policy No. 352. An April 1982 NSC working paper, "U.S. Policy in Central America and Cuba Through Fiscal Year 1984, Summary Paper," was apparently purposely leaked to the press to stress the administration's "moderate" goals: creating "stable, democratic states" while "not allowing the proliferation of Cuba-model states which would provide platforms for subversion, compromise vital sea lanes and pose a direct military threat at or near our borders." The paper also portrayed U.S. efforts as relatively successful in the region, but stymied by U.S. public and congressional opinion that "jeopardizes our ability to stay the course." For the published text, see L. Gelb, "State Dept. Aides Said to Question Role in Nicaragua," *New York Times*, April 7, 1983, p. A1.

19. Shultz's first State Department press briefing on Central America, June 26, 1982, maintained that "the trend of events in Central America is now running in our favor." It was optimistic about the Salvadoran military, the effect of elections there, the success of arms interdiction, and the degree of cooperation from other Latin American states. This assessment ran contrary to the more worried view that would emerge elsewhere in the administration.

20. Interviews; P. Taubman, "C.I.A. is Making Special Target of Latin Region," *New York Times*, December 4, 1982, p. A1.

21. R. Meislin, "Salvador Prelate Says Vote Reflects Yearning for Peace," *New York Times*, April 5, 1982, p. A1; B. Weinraub, "U.S. Envoy to Salvador is Ordered to Stop Criticizing Rights Abuses," *New York Times*, November 9, 1982, p. A1.

22. Interviews; J. Goshko and D. Oberdorfer, "El Salvador Ascends the U.S. Agenda," *Washington Post*, March 6, 1983, p. A1; see also Kirkpatrick's speech, U.S. Mission to the UN No. 28 (83), May 9, 1983.

23. L. Cannon and J. Goshko, "U.S. Weighs Plan for 'Two-Track' Policy on Salvador," *Washington Post*, February 10, 1983, p. A1; L. Chavez, "Salvadorans Tell Mrs. Kirkpatrick They Oppose Talks to End War," *New York Times*, February 11, 1983, p. A6; B. Weinraub, "Rumor and Bickering on U.S. Salvador Policy," *New York Times*, February 11, 1982, p. A7; U.S. embassy personnel in Central America had already been complaining that their reports were being neglected. These events demonstrated an even further downgrading of such analyses. The embassy in Nicaragua, for example, was far more doubtful of the importance of any military build-up there. Interviews; C. Dickey, "U.S. Diplomats in Central America See Gap Between Policy Facts," *Washington Post*, March 8, 1983, p. A21; J. Gaines, "Washington's Views on Nicaragua 'Out of All Touch,' U.S. Diplomat Says," *Boston Globe*, April 20, 1983, p. 14.

24. Interviews; Morton Kondracke, "Interoffice Interference," *New Republic*, May 23, 1983 and "Enders' End," *New Republic*, June 27, 1983; L. Gelb, "U.S. Denies It Opposes Salvadoran Talks," *New York Times*, March 23, 1983, p. A14.

25. L. Gelb, "U.S. Aides See Need for Big Effort to Avert Rebel Victory In Salvador," *New York Times*, April 22, 1983, p. A1; P. Taubman, "C.I.A. is Reported to Predict Ouster of the Sandinistas," *New York Times*, April 7, 1983, p. A1.

26. Interviews.

27. B. Weinraub, "Friction Reported Over Latin Policy," *New York Times*, March 10, 1983, p. A9; J. Omang, "U.S. Envoys Air Views on El Salvador," *Washington Post*, June 28, 1983, p. A12.

28. Stephen Rosenfled, "The Tea-and-Crumpets Putdown," *Washington Post*, June 3, 1983, p. A21; See also C. Dickey, "U.S. Diplomats Criticize Political Interference," *Washington Post*, June 12, 1983, p. A1; For Schultz's statement, see State Department, Public Affairs No. 199, June 2, 1983.

29. Motley's background is in J. Diehl, "Enders' Successor: High-Profile, Controversial Envoy to Brazil," *Washington Post*, June 11, 1983, p. A19. In Spain, Enders succeeded Ambassador Terence Todman, Jimmy Carter's first assistant secretary for Latin America, who had been sent there after criticizing that administration's human rights policy.

30. Cited in Morton Kondracke, "Nowhere Man," *New Republic*, March 16, 1983, p. 17.

31. L. Cannon, "Aides Propound Scenarios for Central America," *Washington Post*, July 31, 1983, p. A1. Further details of Congressional actions at this time may be found in I.M. Destler's chapter.

32. C. Dickey, "Latins Find U.S. Policy Confusing," *Washington Post*, July 25, 1983, p. A1.

33. L. Chavez, "Salvador Killers Step Up Activities," *New York Times*, September 12, 1983, p. A1.

34. Speech delivered on September 12, 1983 to the Baltimore Council on Foreign Affairs.

15
THE ELUSIVE CONSENSUS:
Congress and Central America

I. M. Destler

From 1981 until early 1983, the Reagan administration and its congressional critics were stalemated over United States' policy toward Central America. Congress trimmed military aid funds and forced shifts in the tone of administration rhetoric, in particular toward greater emphasis on negotiations and human rights. But legislators failed to alter either the basic East-West, confrontational thrust of administration policy, or its predilection for military and paramilitary instruments. The Reagan regime, in turn, persisted in its priorities but had to eschew overt U.S. military threats and live with limited resources.

Early in its third year, the administration sought to break out of this bind. Alarmed by the apparent deterioration of the situation in El Salvador, the National Security Council took policy control from the State Department; the President got personally involved for the first time; the approach toward the Congress shifted. Whereas in 1981 and 1982 the game had been to bargain with Hill moderates — even liberals — to maintain the minimum necessary flexibility and resources to sustain unpopular regional policies, now the administration was upping the ante, challenging the critics, defining the issue as either supporting added funds or taking responsibility for losing the region to Communism.

This approach achieved gains: somewhat more money for the Salvadoran military and valuable endorsement of certain administration policies by strategically-placed moderate Democrats like House Majority Leader Jim Wright. But the issue of Nicaragua proved more divisive. Alarmed by the growing threat of regional war, and the sudden revelation of large-scale joint military maneuvers with Honduras, the House of Representatives passed, by a 33-vote margin, a July measure to terminate aid to the *contras* in Nicaragua. It repeated this action three months later.

As of November, the domestically popular Grenada invasion had generated a political swing in the President's favor. And in its rush to adjournment, Congress gave the administration more aid funds and greater policy leeway. But this did not seem to signal any durable transformation of the politics of Central America policy within the United States. For Grenada could not alter the deeper forces that have rendered domestic support of Reagan's Central America policies so shaky. If broader consensus is the goal, a less ambitious approach to the region might have better prospects of achieving it.

THE CARTER PROLOGUE

Ronald Reagan's political bind was not without its irony. His predecessor had also begun his term determined to institute far-reaching changes in the American approach to the region. But by 1980 Carter was moving to a substantially harder line. Hopes for a limited rapprochement with Cuba had proved unavailing; the campaign to ratify and implement the Panama Canal treaties was arduous and politically draining. Withdrawal of U.S. support for the oppressive Somoza regime in Nicaragua contributed to the success of the Sandinista-led revolution in 1979. But when Carter sought to woo Managua's radical new leaders, and to slow their leftward movement, his proposed program of emergency aid was delayed for ten months and riddled with Congressional restrictions. Prominent among them was a requirement that the President certify that the new regime was not "aiding, abetting, or supporting acts of violence or terrorism in other countries."

Conservatives, particularly in the House of Representatives, found Central America an attractive political issue. So much did they place Democrats on the defensive that, after eking out a five-vote margin for the Nicaragua bill, House leaders were unable to pass the normally routine motion to send it to conference with the Senate, where the restrictions might well have been modified. So the senior chamber, and the administration, had to accept a bill that Senator Edward Zorinsky (D-Neb.) labelled a "legislative wreck" in order to get any action at all.

By Inauguration Day 1981, Carter had approved military aid to the junta ruling El Salvador which, despite its reformist origins, had been unable to control the activities of right-wing "death squads," including the December murder of four American Catholic missionary women. The 1980 election provided the new president a strong mandate for toughness in foreign policy, as popular support for increased military spending became overwhelming. The election also brought unexpected Republican control of the Senate (a 12-seat shift) and 33 more Republicans, largely conservative, to the House. It seemed likely, therefore, that the new administration would have substantial running room as it pressed hard-line policies in a region of traditional United States dominance. The Panama ratification experience had suggested that engaged activism on such issues was skewed toward the right. And as if to signal that priority, arch-conservative Jesse Helms (R-N.C.), whose seniority on the Senate Foreign Relations Committee gave him a choice of subcommittees, elected to chair Western Hemisphere Affairs.

Yet if this was how the situation looked in January, by March it was the hard-liners who were retreating.

THE DISAPPEARING MANDATE

The new Secretary of State, Alexander Haig, promptly declared that Central America was the place to "draw the line" against Soviet-Cuban influence, and perhaps even "go to the [Cuban] source." Ambassador to El Salvador Robert White, the most visible of several moderate-to-liberal career officers distrusted by Reagan aides, was promptly and visibly removed. Others were transferred to assignments outside the region. The State Department prepared a White Paper which sought to document Soviet-Cuban-Nicaraguan participation in arming the Salvadoran guerrillas. Assistant Secretary-designate Lawrence Eagleburger was sent to Europe, armed with this White Paper, to line up NATO support for aggressive U.S. efforts to halt this arms flow. Ambassador at Large Vernon Walters undertook a similar mission to Latin America. Haig himself gave the region, with which he had no strong previous identification, more visible attention than he gave any other — in order, some critics thought, to gain credibility with the hard right and thus leeway for moderation on the NATO issues he cared most about. Since a rebel offensive in El Salvador failed egregiously just before Reagan's inauguration, the Secretary may have sniffed an opportunity for a dramatic, low-cost policy success — a lot of visible pressure, followed by evident improvement in the region, and the administration could claim that its toughness was bearing immediate fruit!

But whatever the hopes, the reality was a mini-disaster for the Reagan White House. Haig's dramatic acts and declarations brought headlines and television cameras. At first the administration encouraged this coverage, only to find public communications to the White House running 10-1 *against* the new approach. The President and his top advisers were determined to give priority to *economic policy*, to exploit their momentum and win enactment of budget and tax cuts. The last thing they wanted was a diverting, politically-draining foreign policy flap. Nor was one welcome in the Pentagon; neither military nor civilian leaders wanted their defense spending boom aborted by public alarms about war.

So the State Department was ordered to cool it; by March 12, the Acting Assistant Secretary for Inter-American Affairs was telling reporters that they were giving El Salvador about five times as much attention as it merited.

Liberals and moderates in Congress, many of them worried about the new approach, were emboldened by this evidence of administration ambivalence. They suddenly had a foreign policy issue on which they could take the offensive. So when, later that month, the administration sought approval from the House Appropriations Subcommittee on Foreign Operations of its request to "shift" $5 million in military aid funds to El Salvador, it had to bring in the chairman and ranking Republican of the full Appropriations Committee to eke out an 8-7 margin. And the latter, Silvio Conte (R-Mass.), explained that his support was in part because "this is the first foreign policy issues this administration has had out of the box."[1]

Why was the public and Congressional reaction so swift and sharp? Most important, perhaps, was the still active "Vietnam syndrome." The same poll data that showed support for defense and generalized toughness revealed strong popular opposition to actual military engagement. As public opinion analyst William Schneider puts it,

> The electorate wanted boldness and self-assertion from the nation's leaders, but not risk or sacrifice. People favored a military buildup but no new foreign policy crusades.[2]

Backing was especially hard to find for involvement in morally complex and operationally-messy civil wars in obscure countries. Reagan's personal vulnerability on this issue exacerbated things. The fear that he might recklessly get Americans into war had been a major minus for him in 1980. The fear was muted but not eliminated by an election strategy that stressed moderation and reassurance. The White House saw the danger that a high-profile, militant approach to Central America would reawaken this dormant fear and bring back "Reagan the warmonger."

But other American political forces were important also. One was the growing concern and engagement of the churches, particularly Roman Catholics, linked to reformist Central American priests and bishops. Progressive clergy in the region had challenged the church's long-standing alliance with the ruling elites, establishing "Christian Base Communities" to pursue social and economic justice for the poor. Church people in the United States took up their cause, aligned with the broader human rights lobby and strengthened by sympathetic press reporting. Revolution might not be very appealing to North Americans, but land redistribution had a broader political market, and opposition to suppression of rights and political murders a broader one still.

Finally, there were changes within the Congress which counterbalanced the shift of the overall membership in the conservative direction. The Senate may have swung sharply to the right, but the new members of the Foreign Relations Committee were foreign policy liberals (Christopher Dodd

[D-Conn.], Alan Cranston [D-Cal.], Charles McC. Mathias [R-Md.]) or moderates (Nancy Kassenbaum [R-Kan.], Larry Pressler [R.-S.D.], Rudy Boschwitz [R-Minn.]). So this atypically liberal committee, with its moderate chairman, Charles Percy (R-Ill.), not one to dominate his colleagues, would be passing on administration policies. Helms was isolated as a hard-line conservative, and among the other Republicans only Majority Leader Howard Baker (R-Tenn.) and Richard Lugar (R-Ind.) were reliable administration supporters.[3]

The shift at House Foreign Affairs was more visible and dramatic. In 1980, its Subcommittee on Inter-American Affairs had been chaired by the moderate, and not overly active, Gus Yatron (D-Pa.). In 1981, committee Democrats, seeking activist leadership to challenge the new administration, replaced the veteran Yatron with a liberal sophomore, Michael Barnes (D-Md.). The Barnes subcommittee was balanced in party and ideology, and the new chairman was a pragmatist without much prior exposure to the region. But his activism gave critics a focal point, an alternative power center to schedule hearings and publicize dissenting views.

Finally, the Foreign Operations Subcommittee of House Appropriations continued to offer an impediment to administration proposals. It had the power of first review for actual aid appropriations, and a de facto veto power over "reprogramming," shifting of funds from one aid account to another. Its moderate, idiosyncratic chairman, Clarence Long (D-Md.), was reinforced in his skepticism about military aid by six very liberal Democrats. Thus, administration majorities on the thirteen-man subcommittee were hard to find. So when the administration showed (intentionally) its toughness and (inadvertently) its political vulnerability, there were strategically placed critics ready to resist. They were genuinely alarmed about the possibility of direct U.S. involvement in war, and about the likelihood that a heavily military American approach would reinforce the hard right within the region. They were worried about alienating neighbors in the region, as well as European allies. They also saw political opportunity. They had preponderant public support, particularly on the matter (keeping out of war) where the President was most vulnerable; they had clear evidence that the White House wanted to finesse the issue, at least for 1981. So though Congress was deeply divided on Central America — as it was during the Carter administration — most of the noise, and most of the action, now came from the liberal and moderate critics.[4]

THE TWO-YEAR STALEMATE

There was no way to overwhelm this resistance, especially with the White House opting out of the battle. Nor could it be ignored, for Congress controlled the aid budget — it set total amounts and allocations and conditions. Presidents had authority, in emergency situations, to circumvent these controls, but use of this authority was not without risk and political cost. So administration Central America policy makers had to pursue a strategy of compromise, settling for three quarters of a loaf when necessary, accepting, in form at least, Congressional preconditions.

The point man in this strategy of limited accomodation was State's Assistant Secretary for Inter-American Affairs, Thomas Enders. He was one of several pragmatic foreign service conservatives whom Haig had chosen for key departmental positions. A formidable bureaucrat, Enders had been an aggressive and controversial economic assistant secretary under Henry Kissinger. His only hemispheric experience had been his subsequent service as U.S. Ambassador to Canada. Like those of several others, his nomination was initially opposed and delayed by Senator Helms, who found him insufficiently supportive of Reagan. In this campaign, the North Carolinian would demonstrate both his isolation and his capacity to cause trouble, but Enders came through only lightly scathed. He was confirmed by a Senate voice vote on June 19, and was in fact working at his new job well before then.

Enders needed Congressional backing; he also needed to limit Central America controversy. So he pursued, out of necessity, a low-profile approach, working with administration allies like Deane Hinton, another conservative foreign service officer who was the new U.S. Ambassador to El Salvador. They kept the issues off the front pages, most of the time. They worked with Congressional moderates as best they could. Both sides saw the exercise not so much as an alliance as an exercise in damage limitation. The congressional critics had no particular confidence in Enders' policy purposes; they knew he was dealing with them only because they possessed relevant power. Nor was he following the strategy some suggested — accepting congressional constraints and turning them to regional advantage, by threatening to cut off our allies on the right unless they curbed their abuses and accepted domestic reform and international negotiations.[5] But Enders managed to get from Congress most of what the administration wanted through two hard years. The main issues during this period were human rights; the magnitude, form, and distribution of aid to El Salvador; and what to do about Nicaragua. Also prominent — though hard for Congress to influence — was the question of Salvadoran and regional negotiations, which critics felt the administration should be pushing much harder that it was.

Concerning human rights, the primary Salvadoran issue was the ongoing murder campaign carried on by elusive right-wing "death squads." The Congressional vehicle for addressing this practice was a new requirement that the president certify that things were improving. In April 1981, as the House Foreign Affairs Committee drafted the foreign aid authorization bill for fiscal year 1982, New York Democrats Stephen J. Solarz and Jonathan B. Bingham won adoption of an amendment requiring the President to determine, before actually providing military aid, that the government of El Salvador was "achieving substantial control" over its armed forces in order to end "indiscriminate torture and murder." The President had to also certify that that government was "implementing essential economic and political reforms, including the land reform program," holding free elections, and demonstrating a willingness to negotiate a political settlement of the conflict. Ironically, this requirement followed the form of the restriction House conservatives had placed on Nicaragua aid a year earlier. Senate Foreign Relations added a similar amendment to its draft aid bill two weeks later.

When the bill reached the Senate floor in September, the Reagan administration sought to neutralize this provision by transforming the certification requirement into a general statement of U.S. policy goals. It failed, as a Lugar-Helms amendment to this effect lost 47-51. Chairman Percy and a majority of Foreign Relations Republicans voted against the administration, after getting a change limiting the number of certifications to one every six months, over the next two years. And with marginal differences resolved in conference, the new requirements became law with the aid bill in December 1981.

In Salvador, "certification" had a modest positive effect, adding leverage to government and embassy efforts to constrain the hard right. It focused international attention, which gave heart to humane forces within the country and pause to extremists. In Washington, certification expressed the prevailing political balance; critics could insist that the administration articulate their values and give some energy to their pursuit, but they could not impose them from Capitol Hill. They could not make them the *main* administration priorities. (Originally Solarz, Bingham and Dodd had proposed that Congress be empowered to veto a Presidential certification, but they lacked the votes to get this through committee.)

Certification was a means to several Congressional policy goals, including land reform, negotations, and free elections. Indeed, when participation was unexpectedly heavy in the balloting of March 1982, the administration would lean heavily on this success to justify continued aid notwithstanding limited gains in other areas. But the primary focus was on the ongoing killings, and the unwillingness or inability of the Salvadoran government to bring their perpetrators to justice.

On this basic human rights issue, certification ended up spawning an elaborate, and rather unseemly, political ritual. Shortly before each deadline—in late January and July of 1982 and 1983—the administration would increase the pressure on the Salvadoran government for positive results to report to Congress. At the same time, representatives of private groups flew down to Salvador to gather material for the counter reports they would issue at the same time. Inevitably, the administration would conclude that while serious abuses regrettably continued, the situation was improving so aid could and should go forward. Just as predictably, the private groups would flood congressional hearings to testify otherwise, and members of Congress — who knew the President was going to certify because the alternative was to abandon his policy — would rise to denounce his action with words like "fraud, pure and simple."

In a larger sense, the whole procedure was a fraud. Congress was dumping on the President's lap a responsibility it was too divided or afraid to assume, all the while leaving its members free to cry out when he did what they knew he would do. The President, in turn, violated the spirit and probably the letter of the law. His administration did not take up the option of denying certification and then blaming Congress for a rigid law and its consequences. Nor did it, in 1982, make a serious effort to get the law changed. One reason, of course, was that its Congressional allies were anything but enthusiastic. Lugar, for example, was "hard to find" for administration Central America policymakers that year, apparently wishing to limit his involvement in an unpopular cause in a year he was up for reelection.

Certification was, of course, a precondition for military aid, and the amount of such aid was the second major issue of executive-legislative contention. The authorizing bills cut administration requests regularly, but the the bottom line was congressional power over appropriations. The administration could circumvent this power at times, and it did, in fact, employ the President's emergency drawdown authority (Section 506[a]) to make available $25 million for Salvadoran military aid in fiscal year 1981 and $55 million in 1982. But overuse of this authority invited Congress to take it away. By 1983, warned by congressional allies as well as adversaries, the administration had stopped reaching into this particular pocket.

In the early 1980s foreign assistance was, if anything, less popular than ever, and its small cadre of congressional advocates were deeply divided between those who pressed security and those who stressed development. Only once in the Reagan period — December 1981 — did they and the administration get together, enabling Congress to enact a regular, comprehensive aid money bill. Otherwise, the aid program operated through continuing resolutions (catch-all statutes which authorized and funded programs not otherwise provided for). Additional money could come from supplemental appropriations enacted later in the year, and reprogramming of funds previously allocated to other countries.

This convoluted funding process tended, on balance, to increase the leverage of the appropriations subcommittees. They had to cooperate in the indirect strategies of getting money, especially since appeal to the full House or Senate was likely to prove counterproductive. The Senate subcommittee, chaired by freshman Robert Kasten (R-Wisc.), was generally cooperative. Clarence Long's House subcommittee, traditionally the more powerful, was not. And that subcommittee was split straight down the middle, with the chairman himself holding the swing vote. So one of the more important mini-dramas of Central American aid politics was the effort of Enders and Hinton to woo the idiosyncratic chairman. By early 1983, with a mix of timely military briefings and meetings with the new Salvadoran President, Alvaro Magaña, these efforts seemed to be bearing fruit, as Long's subcommittee acquiesced in some reprogramming of military funds to El Salvador. Until then, the going was hard. Despite support on the Senate side, the House refused to go along with including any military money for Salvador in the supplemental money bill enacted in September 1982. Insofar as other aid money for Salvador was concerned, Congress generally went along with the administration's requests.

The other primary congressional issue was Nicaragua, against whose regime the administration was conducting a growing, and increasingly visible, "covert" action campaign in support of anti-Sandinista military forces. Internationally, this reflected the view of many in the administration that the very existence of the Sandinista government was a serious, perhaps intolerable, threat to U.S. interests in the region. Domestically, covert action was consistent with the low-profile approach, for one logical response to unwanted controversy was to try to conduct policy underground.

Members of Congress had, beginning in 1974, insisted on being consulted about such intelligence operations. In 1980, new legislation centralized oversight responsibility in the recently created Senate and House intelligence committees, calling upon the executive to keep them "fully and currently informed of intelligence activities."[6] The Reagan administration was more grudging in its compliance than its predecessor had been, and legislators were, in turn, more skeptical about how "fully" they were in fact being briefed. In Nicaragua, the official rationale of CIA involvement and funding was to curb arms traffic to the Salvadoran rebels. But that was obviously not the objective of the Nicaraguan *contras* whose lives were on the line—they wanted to overthrow the Sandinistas. And so, it seemed on the Hill, did at least some policymakers in the administration.

As concern grew in the House intelligence committee, Chairman Edward Boland (D-Mass.) sought to limit the *U.S.* goal by attaching to the intelligence authorization bill for fiscal 1983 a classified condition, a prohibition on any provision of "military equipment, military training or advice, or other support for military activities, for the purpose of overthrowing the government of Nicaragua or provoking a military exchange between Nicaragua and Honduras." After a *Newsweek* cover story in November 1982 spotlighted the deepening U.S. involvement, the Boland amendment went public, attached by a unanimous vote to a defense money bill, after being substituted for a proposal by Representative Tom Harkin (D-Iowa) to outlaw all aid to the *contras*. In the Senate, Dodd tried a somewhat different approach, proposing language more sweeping in import than Boland's (if less binding in impact). This was a declaration that funds ought not be used "in support of irregular military forces or paramilitary groups operating in Central America," whatever their purpose. Dodd lost, 38-56, and the Boland language was approved in conference, and became law for fiscal 1983.

On two geographically peripheral countries, congressmen had a certain impact in 1981 and 1982. They succeeded in averting military aid to the repressive regime in Guatemala. And they insistently called to administration attention the economic crisis which threatened democracy in Costa Rica, with Barnes and Dodd both pressing for expanded aid well before the executive branch acknowledged the need. In addition, responding to Reagan's Caribbean Basin Initiative aimed at encouraging broader regional development, Congress appropriated the requested aid funds in 1982 and and would grant very limited trade concessions in 1983.

But congressional critics had a harder time pressing what a number of them considered crucial: peace negotiations, both within El Salvador and across the region. This issue was particularly hard for legislators to get hold of in any operational sense, although the more serious could talk to the various parties and seek to uncover negotiating options they sensed the administration was neglecting. At the rhetorical level, it was always possible to argue, as many did, that the need was for a political or economic rather than a military solution, or that the goal should be a negotiated settlement rather than military victory. But by seeming to discount the obvious importance of the military factor, this line risked looking as one-sided as the administration's. It was easy to endorse the principle of peace talks in certification requirements, or in broad resolutions like one passed by the House in March 1982, by a 396-3 vote, calling for "unconditional discussions between the major political factions in El Salvador." Moreover, the administration could respond to calls for new initiatives by co-opting the liberals' language, or by token responses, as when Long's call for an independent regional negotiator was met by the designation of conservative former Democratic Senator Richard Stone.

As 1982 drew to a close, executive-congressional politics seemed relatively stable. The administration was feeling a funding squeeze but finding ways to live with it. Congressmen had no choice but to accept, and seek to limit, policies they lacked the power — and in some cases the will — to change. But the pattern was suddenly broken in early 1983. One cause was the growing importance of the anti-Sandinista campaign, the issue on which compromise was most difficult. The second, and more important, was the assumption of policy control by a White House concerned about how the war was going in El Salvador, and its use of that control to press a more assertive, confrontational policy at home as well as abroad. This increased the political risks for everybody — for the President, but also for those who continued to challenge his policies.

REAGAN RAISES THE STAKES

Approval of the Boland amendment in December was followed by increasingly overt *contra* activity, deepening doubts as to whether the effective goal of U.S. support could be anything but overthrow of the Managua regime. The ground for compromise evaporated. Boland now moved to withdraw the leeway he had previously favored, and his House intelligence committee voted, along party lines, to report out a bill on May 3, 1983, cutting off all funds "supporting, directly or indirectly, military or paramilitary operations in Nicaragua." The House Foreign Affairs Committee, after a particularly bitter, secret partisan debate and the breakdown of a compromise initiative by Lee Hamilton (D-Ind.), endorsed the bill 20-14, with only one Republican in favor and two Democrats opposed. The bill proposed to substitute $80 million in overt aid to "friendly" regional governments to block arms shipments to guerrillas.

But the prime contributor to intensification of the debate was the new involvement of the Reagan White House. From the perspective of national security assistant (and Reagan intimate) William Clark, things had not been going well in Salvador. At his encouragement, U. N. Ambassador Jeane Kirkpatrick paid an inspection visit in February. She arrived in a period when the war had been going badly, and returned with a bleak prognosis. Discounting arguments that Congress would resist, Clark urged that the President seek more military aid, and the President responded. He met with congressional leaders at the White House, the first time he had summoned them on that issue. He upped his Salvadoran military aid request for fiscal 1983, which Congress had only partly funded, from $61.3 to $136.3 million, of which $60 million was to be reprogrammed. This reprogramming request went not just to the appropriations subcommittees but, by new arrangement, to Senate Foreign Relations as well. He got $30 million, tied to relatively modest conditions. Shortly thereafter, House Foreign Affairs moved to replace certification with a more constructive process. In compromise language totalling ten draft pages, it called for the Salvadoran government to develop comprehensive "plans" for addressing nine human rights, reform, and negotiating objectives. Brokered by Florida Democrat Dante Fascell, this was approved by 36-1 as an amendment to the proposed foreign aid authorization bill for fiscal 1984. John Felton of *Congressional Quarterly* reported that, if finally enacted, it "would impose on El Salvador the most complicated set of conditions ever required for a recipient of U. S. foreign aid."[7] (In fact, it died, as the full House never acted on that bill.)

This draft language represented a serious effort to develop, on a bipartisan basis, a more constructive way of dealing with the severe Salvadoran internal problems which certification had rather clumsily addressed. And the committee cooperation it manifested was in sharp contrast to the bitter partisan wrangling that would break out over Nicaragua less than a month later. But even as it was underway, Ronald Reagan was pushing his own version of "bipartisan" policy, by which he meant rallying legislators from both parties around his presidential flag. In late April, he took the unusual step of addressing a joint session of Congress. He appropriated the words of liberals and moderates, and deployed them to gain support for El Salvador and antagonism toward Nicaragua. But as he made his brief for what was, essentially, an intensification of existing administration efforts, more fully funded, he took care to spice it with a not very subtle political threat.

> Who among us would wish to bear responsibility for failing to meet our shared obligation? [The President doubted] that a majority in the Congress or the country . . . [would] stand by passively while the people of Central America are delivered to totalitarianism and we ourselves are left vulnerable to new dangers.

Further shoes would drop shortly: the replacement in May and June of conservative pragmatists Enders and Hinton, prime practitioners of the "live with Congress as best you can" strategy; the secret planning of large-scale, prolonged military maneuvers to begin in Honduras that summer. There now seemed at work a new congressional strategy: go for broke, threaten Congress with blame for the failures, and watch legislators run for cover. Under Secretary of Defense Fred Iklé articulated such a strategy in the most unvarnished form in a September 12th speech to the Baltimore Council on Foreign Affairs. "As long as a group in Congress keeps crippling the President's military assistance program, we will have a policy always shy of success." And success was defined quite ambitiously, including a goal hard to distinguish from the one Congress had outlawed: to "prevent consolidation of a Sandinista regime in Nicaragua that would become an arsenal for insurgency."

To judge by the results, the get-tough strategy had some success. Reagan ended up with a good bit less than his total fiscal 1983 military aid request of $136.3 billion for El Salvador, but the $81.3 he extracted was well above the $61.3 he had originally sought. Before Congress adjourned in November 1983, he would get $64.8 million of the $86.3 he had requested for fiscal 1984. Prior to those years, the most the administration had ever gotten Congress to provide was $26 million in 1982. Just as important for the administration, perhaps, was its success in dividing congressional Democrats. Reagan's address to Congress both contributed to and illustrated the split, as House majority leader Wright and certain Democratic senators could not resist signalling their unhappiness with the "Democratic response" delivered by Dodd, even though its language had been the subject of negotiation among all important groups within the party.

To attribute all these results to toughness would be misleading, of course. The administration approach continued to include conciliatory elements, such as the designation of regional envoy Stone in response to pressure from Chairman Long, who had in mind persons of broader regional stature, and the more general administration wooing of the idiosyncratic Marylander — as well as Barnes and Fascell. It was also to include creation of the National Bipartisan Commission on Central America, in July, under the chairmanship of Henry Kissinger.

Nor was toughness always a political asset. In fact, the administration blundered egregiously in late July when it began to implement a secret decision to engage in large-scale, six-month joint military maneuvers with Honduras, labelled "Big Pine II." The story leaked just as the House was preparing to enter secret debate on the Nicaragua covert aid ban, surprising not only the members but (by credible reports) the secretary of state as well. Prior to this development, the vote was expected to be very close, and Clark, Shultz and Kissinger were all working the Hill to defeat it. Now, after a major floor debate it passed by a substantial margin, 228-195, with Wright — who maintained his support for backing El Salvador — leading a reasonably united Democratic majority.

This resolution died without Senate action. But three months later, Chairman Boland proposed to add identical language to a bill the other body could not ignore, the intelligence authorization for fiscal 1984. In the atmosphere following the Soviet shootdown of Korean Airline flight 007, members might well have been inclined to swing the President's way. But it was hard to switch on an issue where they were already on record, so they reaffirmed their opposition, 227-194.

The Senate adopted a more modest restriction of Nicaraguan operations, after its intelligence committee extracted from the administration a rationale more plausible than arms interdiction but short of regime overthrow — getting Nicaragua to stop supporting revolution in its neighbors. It granted $29 million and seemed to promise more later. What Congress finally enacted in the adjournment rush was an appropriation of $24 million, no statutory limit on objectives to replace the original (now-expired) Boland amendment, but no back door funding either. This meant, observers predicted, that the administration would need to seek further funding by June 1984.

Finally, July saw the creation of the Kissinger commission. It was inspired by two earlier political successes: the Greenspan commission which had found a middle ground on the politically volatile Social Security issue, and the Scowcroft commission which had prevented the likely demise of the MX missile and nudged Reagan toward a somewhat more realistic posture on arms control. The hope that Americans might somehow craft a bipartisan approach to Central America was widely shared, and the Greenspan and Scowcroft precedents made a commission the inevitable vehicle. Senator Henry Jackson proposed such a body in June, and Barnes introduced companion legislation in the House. Motives inevitably varied. Some Democratic critics doubtless sought a vehicle for leverage on the administration, as the Scowcroft panel had provided Congressmen like Les Aspin (D-Wisc.) and Albert Gore (D-Tenn.). Others sought political shelter, an excuse to duck, at least for six months, a controversial issue that was now "under study." The White House saw a means of forging a coalition behind its basic approach.

It was the White House that chose the Kissinger Commission's members. Like those of the Scowcroft panel, the ones with weight came from the center and the right. The aim, apparently, was either to isolate pragmatic liberals like Barnes from the sought-after consensus, or to bring them in on the administration's terms. So the most prominent commission Democrats had rather conservative national security orientations: Lane Kirkland of the AFL-CIO, Richard Scammon, and Robert Strauss.

They were chosen with minimal prior consultation. The last thing the White House wanted to do was to bargain with Congress on the composition. Also designated, however, were eight legislators to serve as "counselors" to the commission: Senators Jackson, Bentsen, Mathias, and Pete V. Domenici (R-N. M.) and Representatives Wright, Barnes, Jack Kemp (R-N. Y.) and William S. Broomfield (R-Mich.). Again, the selections were artful, more conservative on balance than the legislators Enders had had to bargain with, but not so much so as to look unreasonable.

Will the commission bring the cherished consensus? The administration did succeed in shifting 1983 congressional action somewhat in its favor while in fact toughening its policies. There was more money for Salvador, albeit with a new condition, proposed by Senator Arlen Specter (R-Pa.), that 30% would be withheld until the accused murderers of the four churchwomen were brought to trial and a verdict reached. But while both houses passed, without dissent, a separate bill extending the certification requirement, the President killed it with a pocket veto after Congress adjourned. On Nicaragua, the administration avoided binding constraints. There was, on the other side, a new statutory prohibition on aid to Guatemala. On balance, the Reagan White House accomplished more with its high-profile strategy than one would have expected.

Reagan's decision to invade Grenada, the first popular thing his administration has done in the broad Caribbean Basin region, seems likely to strengthen him further, at least for a time. Does this mean that he will now have, on Central America, the political running room previously denied him? Probably not, for the enduring sources of policy *dissensus* remain. A better prediction is renewed domestic conflict over Central America in the months to come. The conclusion of this essay will seek to explain why.

CAN GETTING IN DEEPER BRING US TOGETHER?

Consensus has been wanting in recent years on many issues of American foreign policy. But it has proved particularly elusive for Central America. Why has this been the case? What approach to the region, if any, might have better prospects for support across a broad political spectrum?

If we ask simply why Congress has reacted so critically to the Reagan approach to Central America, explanation is not hard to find. One obvious reason is that that approach was, from the start, well to the right on the spectrum of congressional policy preferences. A second is that the responsible committees are to the left of overall congressional sentiment, but not so far left that the administration can roll over them with impunity. A third explanation is the energy and persistence of the human rights lobby, especially the church people. A fourth is the "Vietnam syndrome," the American allergy to involvement in protracted military conflict, particularly in obscure countries where our allies are morally unattractive. A fifth is Ronald Reagan's particular vulnerability to the "warmonger" label, which gave Democrats an early foreign policy issue and made the White House back off from identification with the region for two long years.

An equally lengthy list, differing in its specifics, could be compiled to explain the lack of policy consensus in the four preceding years, under Jimmy Carter. But there is a broader problem, incorporating all such reasons but going beyond them. Just about any approach to Central America, by any administration, is likely to prove unpopular. For none is likely to produce results that Americans want at costs Americans will find acceptable. Any administration that highlights the region, therefore, risks increasing the unpopularity of its policies and their political costs.

We do not wish to "lose" countries to communism, but neither do we want to lose American lives in obscure, intractable civil wars. Right-wing oppressors are politically unattractive, but so are anti-Yankee Marxists. We would like on the Central American isthmus a string of Costa Ricas — stable, democratic, open and moderately reformist in their economic policies, friendly toward the United States. But such regimes are rare. Nor does the mainland contain any Grenadas, places which the United States can hope to transform with a quick coup, to the cheers of their citizenry; places where, as the right used to demand about Vietnam, we have a good chance to win the war and get out. The point is not to endorse the wisdom of the Grenada invasion. This observer does not. It is, rather, that the circumstances that made for our apparent, immediate on-the-ground-success there do not obtain elsewhere. Salvador and Nicaragua are bigger and messier and neither is an island. Each has its deep, dirty, bloody, very personal factional politics, and its anti-democratic traditions.

Because the prospects are so bleak, Central American issues offer a natural advantage for critics, whichever party is in power in Washington, and whatever policy approach it pursues. For nothing is likely to "work" in that administration's lifetime, by the measures of success voters will apply. So congressional supporters will lie low and critics will make hay.

This does not mean that Congress will often overturn a president's policy and impose another. It is not equipped for day-to-day control of key policy instruments — negotiations, military and paramilitary forces, even aid programs. It is weak institutionally, with committees subject to floor challenge, authorizing panels competing with appropriations, substantive specialists in tension with floor leaders. And members will always seek to limit their own political vulnerability. They fear a Ronald Reagan's ability to package the issues on television and blame critics if things go wrong, even as they seek to exploit the president's vulnerability. So though there are some members of Congress who would actually change U.S. policy if they could, most will be content to score points. They will identify themselves with appealing values (negotiations, bringing killers to justice, avoiding Cubas *and* Vietnams) but will take care that responsibility for consequences is left clearly at the opposite end of Pennsylvania Avenue.

Reflecting this pattern, Congress has constrained Reagan's Central America policy in four basic ways. It has trimmed, at the margins, the resources available. It has imposed a substantial tax on the time and energies of administation officials to extract those resources they got. It has forced those officials to give some attention to the values — internal reform, human rights — which the initial Haig approach seemed to ignore. And by both legislation and public advocacy, Congress has increased the cost to the administration of going beyond its stated policies with Nicaragua as the clearest case.

At the end of 1983, the trend is to respond to home and regional pressures by getting deeper into Central America. The Kissinger commission is likely to reinforce this trend, for if there is anything that such groups inevitably recommend, it is increased priority to the problems they were chosen to address. Within this framework, the commission may well put forward a "balanced" approach of more of everything: a large economic aid bone for the moderates, linked to larger military aid and an expanded definition of the stakes for the United States.

Will getting in deeper bring Americans together? It is hard to see how it can do anything but drive us further apart. A more intrusive U.S. engagement in Central America might make sense in regional policy terms, though this observer is very skeptical. But it is almost certainly *not* the route to a durable American consensus. For it means increasing the costs that Americans do not want to pay for outcomes that are nowhere in sight. It means drawing greater attention to the very things that divide us: involvement in controversial, inconclusive activities with unseemly allies. Furthermore, as we raise our definition of the stakes, it becomes harder to avoid what almost everyone still opposes, deployment of U.S. combat troops to Central America.[8]

NOTES

1. *Congressional Quarterly Almanac,* 1981, p. 184.
2. "Conservatism, Not Interventionism: Trends in Foreign Policy Opinion, 1974-1982," in Kenneth A. Oye et al., *Eagle Defiant: United States Foreign Policy in the 1980s,* Boston: Little, Brown, 1983, p. 34.
3. All of these characterizations of Senators and Representatives as liberal, moderate, or conservative are based on the foreign policy indices of the *National Journal/Baron Report* rating system, published in the *Journal* of May 7, 1983. Those with liberal indices for 1981/82 averaging 70 or above are here labelled "liberal," those between 31 and 69 "moderate," and those 30 or below "conservative."
4. For discussion of this broader "reverse pendulum" effect, through which a shift of party and policy in the executive branch triggers a reverse reaction in the Congress, see I. M. Destler and Patricia Cohen, "Congress Swings: Like a Reverse Pendulum, Congress Now Attacks U.S. Central American Policy from the Left," *Foreign Service Journal,* July/August 1982, pp. 19-21 ff.
5. See Robert Pastor, "Winning Through Negotiation: Congress Has the Seed of a Better Idea for El Salvador," *The New Republic,* March 17, 1982, pp. 13-16.
6. Public Law 96-450.
7. *Congressional Quarterly,* June 18, 1983, p. 1230.
8. Suppose we considered a directly opposite approach. Suppose we declared that we had no vital interest in the internal character of Central American regimes, so long as they did not provide bases for Soviet and Cuban military operations. We would retain our preferences for democratic governments against Marxist dictatorships and would use normal policy instruments to advance these preferences. We could work with regional and neighboring countries, such as Mexico and Venezuela, to dampen conflict and promote negotiations. We would aid countries facing overt threats from their neighbors, sometimes even helping them defend against direct military aggression if they sought help. But we would declare that, unlike the Soviet Union, we could live with diversity in the governments of our neighbors, provided that they respected our basic security interests and did not make war on *their* neighbors.

At the same time, we would be prepared to take direct action as John F. Kennedy did in October 1962 against new security threats to the United States. We would "draw the line," but not against revolutions — a high-cost, chancy enterprise. Instead we would draw it against threats much easier to pinpoint, which most Americans would regard as real — Soviet or Cuban bases in countries that do not now possess them.

Such an approach would have *its own* problems of detailed definition and practical operation, though they would pale before those we now face. In the short run, there would be difficult problems of extrication, from our deepening commitment to the anti-Sandinista forces, for example. Nor would a less intrusive approach make Central America policy popular. The right would point to Marxists we were not combatting, the left to outrages we were not preventing. But conducted in the low key that would be appropriate, it could conceivably win the broad public acceptance that more ambitious approaches cannot win. For it would be premised on a common-sense notion consistent with public sentiment: that it is the Russians, not the Sandinistas, who threaten U.S. security. If an administration de-emphasized those intractable internal conflicts in which the mass public is predisposed against involvement, its domestic political adversaries might move on to other issues that they found more rewarding.

ABOUT THE CONTRIBUTORS

Joseph Cirincione, Assistant Editor of this volume, is a staff member of the Central America Project of the Carnegie Endowment for International Peace in Washington, D.C. He recently served as special assistant to the associate director for programs, United States Information Agency on issues of international security affairs, arms control and Central America, and has written several essays on these issues.

Arturo Cruz Sequeira is a former Sandinista official, now a doctoral candidate at Johns Hopkins Unversity School of Advanced International Studies. He writes frequently for the *Christian Science Monitor, The New York Times,* and *The Los Angeles Times.*

I. M. Destler, author of *Presidents, Bureaucrats, and Foreign Policy* and *Making Foreign Economic Policy,* directed Carnegie's project on executive-congressional relations in 1977-83. He is currently a senior fellow at the Institute for International Economics.

Christopher Dickey, who covered El Salvador for *The Washington Post* for four years, currently is the 1983-84 Edward R. Murrow Fellow at the Council on Foreign Relations in New York.

Tom J. Farer, Distinguished Professor at Rutgers University Law School (Camden), has just completed two terms as a member of the Inter-American Commission on Human Rights of the OAS and was the first U.S. citizen to serve as its Chairman (1980-82). His published works include *Warclouds on the Horn of Africa* and *The Inter-American Systems: Are There Functions for its Forms?* Shorter pieces have appeared in such journals as *Foreign Affairs, Foreign Policy,* and *The New York Review of Books.*

Richard E. Feinberg is Vice President of the Overseas Development Council and the author of *The Intemperate Zone: The Third World Challenge to U.S. Foreign Policy.* He has worked in the State and Treasury departments, with the House Banking Committee, and as an adjunct professor at Georgetown University.

Leonel Gomez was Chief Adviser to assassinated President Rodolfo Viera of the Institute of Agrarian Transformation (ISTA) in El Salvador. Since leaving El Salvador in 1981, Sr. Gomez has been active in lecturing and writing, and has been published in numerous journals and periodicals, including *Foreign Policy.*

Leslie C. Hunter is a Latin American analyst working with the Department of the Navy. Formerly she was a researcher in the Soviet-Latin American Project at Georgetown University Center for Strategic and International Studies.

Walter LaFeber is the Marie Underhill Noll Professor of History at Cornell. His publications include *Inevitable Revolutions: The U.S. in Central America* (Norton); *America, Russia, and the Cold War, 1945-1980* (4th ed., Wiley): *The Panama Canal: The Crisis in Historical Perspective* (Oxford); and *The New Empire* (Cornell), which won the Beveridge Prize of the American Historical Association.

Robert S. Leiken is a Senior Associate at the Carnegie Endowment for International Peace and an adjunct Senior Fellow at the Georgetown University Center for Strategic and International Studies (CSIS). He has been Professor of Economic History at Centro de Investigacíon y Docencia Económica (CIDE) and at the National Agricultural Unversity in Mexico. He is the author of *Soviet Strategy in Latin America,* and has published in journals such as *Foreign Policy, The Washington Quarterly,* and *The New Republic.*

Richard Millett is a Professor of History at the Southern Illinois University at Edwardsville, Senior Adviser at Frost and Sullivan, and the 1983-84 President of the Midwest Association for Latin American Studies. He is the author of *Guardians of the Dynasty* (1977), and co-editor of *The Restless Caribbean* (1979).

Theodore H. Moran is Landegger Professor and Director of the Program in International Business Diplomacy at the Georgetown University School of Foreign Service. In 1977-78 he was a member of the policy planning staff at the Department of State with responsibility for political, military, and economic affairs in the Persian Gulf. He has been publishing on the economics and politics of Latin America since 1970. He holds a Ph.D. in government from Harvard.

Robert A. Pastor is currently on the faculty of the School of Public Affairs, University of Maryland, College Park where he is teaching and doing research on U.S. policy toward the Caribbean Basin. He was a guest scholar at The Brookings Institution in 1981-82, and prior to that, he was the senior staff member responsible for Latin American and Caribbean Affairs on the National Security Council from 1977-81. From 1975-76, Dr. Pastor was the Executive Director of the Linowitz Commission on U.S.-Latin American Relations, a private group of distinguished citizens that issued two reports on U.S. policy toward Latin America. He was also a teaching fellow in Government at Harvard University where he received his Ph.D. in Political Science and an M.P.A. from the John F. Kennedy School of Government.

Morris Rothenberg is director of the Advanced International Studies Institute in Bethesda, Maryland (in conjunction with the University of Miami, Coral Gables, Florida). He was formerly director of the Office of Soviet and East European Research with the U.S. Department of State. Mr. Rothenberg is the co-editor of *Soviet World Outlook.*

Barry Rubin is a senior fellow at the Georgetown University Center for Strategic and International Studies and a professorial lecturer at Georgetown University School of Foreign Service. His books include *Secrets of State: The State Department in U.S. Foreign Policy* (Oxford University Press, 1984) and *Paved with Good Intentions: The American Experience in Iran.*

Ambassador Viron Vaky is a retired career Foreign Service officer who formerly served as the assistant secretary of state for inter-American affairs and as Ambassador to Costa Rica, Columbia, and Venezuela. He is currently research professor in diplomacy at the School of Foreign Service, Georgetown University, Washington, D.C.

Howard J. Wiarda is a research scholar and director of the Center for Hemispheric Studies at the American Enterprise Institute for Public Policy Research. He has been a visiting scholar at Harvard University, a visiting professor at MIT, and is professor of political science at the University of Massachusetts in Amherst. He is the author of numerous books and articles on Latin America, Southern Europe, and United States foreign policy.

Adee, Alvey A., 49
Afghanistan, 25, 173, 174
Allen, Richard, 304, 305
Allende, Salvador, 133
Alliance for Progress, 4, 50–51, 52, 53, 59,
  60–62, 270–271, 273
Allies, Central American policy and US, 238,
  288, 311
Álvarez, Gustavo, 12, 87–88
American Institute for Free Labor
  Development, 267
Anaya Montes, Melida, 122
Anderson, Thomas P., 224
Andres Pérez, Carlos, 102, 103
Andropov, Yuri, 25, 134, 139, 141, 142
Angola, 175, 294
Arafat, Yasser, 181
Arbenz, Jacobo, 57–58, 77
Arce, Bayardo, 101, 103, 106, 107, 123, 134,
  140
Arce, Manuel José, 36
ARDE. See Democratic Revolutionary
  Alliance
Ardon, Eric, 126
ARENA. See Nationalist Republican Alliance
Arevalo, Juan José, 57
Armed Forces of Liberation (FAL), 11, 115,
  117, 121
Armed Forces of National Resistance (FARN),
  115–120
Arnson, Cynthia, 118
Association for Honduras (APROH), 12
Australia, 125

BPR. See Revolutionary Popular Bloc
Backyardism, 24–25, 238–239
Baker, Howard, 323
Baker, James, 299, 304, 306, 309, 314
Balance of power concept, 241–242
Baltimore Sun, 56
Barbados, 207
Barnes, Michael, 323, 328, 331, 332
Batista, Fulgencio, 59
Bentsen, Lloyd, 332
Bermudez, Varela Enrique, 84
Big Pine II, 177, 179, 312, 331
Bigley, Thomas, 306
Bingham, Jonathan B., 324, 325
Bishop, Maurice, 9

Boland Amendment, 327–329
Boland, Edward, 327–329, 331
Bolaños Hunter, Miguel, 123
Borge, Tomás, 122, 123, 134, 143, 249, 284
  hardline views of, 100, 101, 103, 106, 107
Boschwitz, Rudy, 323
Bowdler, William, 303
Brazil, 197, 207
Brezhnev, Leonid, 133, 136, 139, 142
Brezhnev Doctrine, 139
Broomfield, William S., 332
Brzezinski, Zbigniew, 305
Bushnell, John, 327
Bustamente, Jorge, 45

CACM. See Central American Common Market
Calero, Adolfo, 84
Cambodia, 303
Canada, 161, 211
Carbaugh, John, 303
Caribbean Basin Initiative, 15, 51, 194–212,
  273, 327, 328
Carlucci, Frank, 305
Carranza, Nicolás, 41
Carroll, Eugene, Jr., 180
Carter administration
  and El Salvador, 64, 291
  and Guatemala, 77, 78
  hardening of policy of, 320–321
  human rights campaign of, 271
  intelligence reports during, 306
  and Nicaragua, 97–98, 282–283, 300
Casey, William, 306, 308, 310
Castañeda, Jorge, 289
Castro, Fidel, 35, 50, 59, 72, 104, 139, 143,
  289
Catholic Church, 7, 115, 282, 286, 322
Cayetano Carpio, Salvador, 12, 13, 115, 116,
  120, 122–123
Central America. See also individual countries
  agrarian reform in, 7, 206–207
  attitudes toward Sandinistas in, 11
  attitudes toward USSR in, 125–126
  background of current crisis in, 197–202
  basic dilemma of American policy in, 333
  benefits of negotiated settlement in, 20–22
  conditions of economic recovery in, 202
  deteriorating economic and political situation
    in, 193, 201, 204, 234

343

changing degrees of emphasis on Central
America, 302, 310, 327
commitment to military solution in El
Salvador, 288–290
and Contadora group, 312
definition of US security interests in Central
America, 237–242
East-West appraoch to Central America of,
160, 174, 202, 205, 209, 226, 235, 237,
279–280, 301–302, 312–313, 319, 321
effects of ideological orientation of, 235,
279–280
and El Salvador, 314
emphasis on military activities in Central
America, 10, 11
focus on Nicaragua, 237
and Guatemala, 78–80
hardliners in, 305, 310–313, 327–328
and Honduras, 54
intelligence reports during, 306
and Nicaragua, 291, 314–315
objectives of, 236, 291
policy differences and rivalries within, 308–
310, 335
and public opinion, 282, 310–311
rethinking Central American issues, 235
summary of approach to Central America,
252–253
views on negotiations of, 242–245, 253,
279, 291
Reagan, Ronald, 174, 203, 279, 284, 291,
331
accepts hardliners' recommendations, 310
approves aid to *contras*, 327
personally involved in Central American
policy, 319
on refugee problem, 219
on Sandinistas, 249
takes domestic political initiative on Central
America, 329–332
vulnerable to "warmonger" label, 322, 333
Red Star, 140
Refugees
attitudes in US toward, 226
causes of, 220, 222–226
countries entered by Salvadoran, 224
economic effects in US of, 220, 226, 227
effect on El Salvador of flow of, 228
number of, 219–220, 224
political impact in US of, 227
preventing flood of, as US goal, 240
and terrorism in US, 227
Reich, Otto, 310
Republican Party, 300, 303
Reston, James, 260
Revolutionary Coordinator of the Masses
(CRM), 117

Revolutionary Democratic Front (FDR), 221,
224, 225, 226
Revolutionary Party of Central American
Workers (PRTC), 115, 117, 121
Revolutionary Popular Bloc (BPR), 116, 117
Revolutionary Workers Movement-Salvador
Cayetano Carpio (MOR), 123
Ríos Montt, Efrain, 7, 78, 79, 88
RN. *See* Armed Forces of National Resistance
Robelo, Alfonso, 85, 284
Rockefeller, Nelson, 50
Romania, 207
Romero, Carlos Humberto, 74
Romero, Oscar, 42, 117
Roosevelt, Theodore, 49
Rostow, W. W., 263, 264
Ruiz, Henry, 101, 107, 133, 134, 136

Salvadoran Communist Party (PCS), 112, 114,
115, 117, 121
Salvadoran Intelligence Service, death squads
and, 222
San José Declaration, 243
San José group, 243, 244
Sanchez, Nestor, 305, 312
Sandinista National Liberation Front (FSLN).
See Sandinistas
Sandinistas. *See also* Nicaragua
Chilean influence among, 101
Cuban influence among, 100, 103–104
desire for strong ties with USSR, 103, 104
development of revolutionary strategy, 100–
102
elements of flexibility among, 106
factional differences among, 100–102, 106–
107
fear of foreign intervention against, 104
military buildup, 104
moderate views within, 95–98
pro-Soviet stance of founders, 100
Reagan administration impact on views of,
106
view of Central America, 104
view of negotiations, 104, 107
view of US, 102–103, 105
world view of, 102–104
Sandino, Augusto César, 56, 64, 72
Sapia-Bosch, A., 305, 312
Scammon, Richard, 334
Scandinavia, 161
Schaufelberger, Albert A., 123
Schneider, William, 322
Sea lanes, Soviet threat to, 184–188, 240
Secretariat of Economic Integration of Central
America, 211
Shultz, George, 308, 311, 312, 314
Siljander, Mark, 219

UNITED STATES OF
AMERICA

G u l f
o f
M e x i c o

MEXICO

BELIZE

HC

GUATEMALA

EL SALVADOR

NICARAGUA

P a c i f i c

COSTA RICA

O c e a n

PAN

GALÁPAGOS
ISLANDS